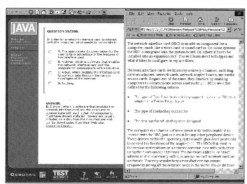

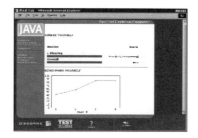

Sun® Certified Programmer

for Java™ 2 Study Guide

Sun® Certified Programmer
for Java™ 2 Study Guide

(Exam 310-025)

Syngress Media, Inc.

Osborne McGraw-Hill

Berkeley New York St. Louis San Francisco Auckland Bogotá Hamburg London Madrid Mexico City
Milan Montreal New Delhi Panama City Paris São Paulo Singapore Sydney Tokyo Toronto

Osborne/McGraw-Hill
2600 Tenth Street
Berkeley, California 94710
U.S.A.

For information on translations or book distributors outside the U.S.A., or to arrange bulk purchase discounts for sales promotions, premiums, or fund-raisers, please contact **Osborne/McGraw-Hill** at the above address.

Sun Certified Programmer for Java 2 Study Guide (Exam 310-025)

234567890 DOC DOC 019876543210

Book P/N 0-07-212370-2   and   CD P/N 0-07-212371-0
  parts of
ISBN 0-07-212372-9

Publisher Brandon A. Nordin	**Project Editor** Lisa Theobald	**Indexer** Valerie Perry
Associate Publisher and Editor-in-Chief Scott Rogers	**Acquisitions Coordinator** Tara Davis	**Computer Designers** Elizabeth Jang Roberta Steele
Acquisitions Editor Gareth Hancock	**Series Editor** Bill Rossi	**Illustrators** Robert Hansen
Associate Acquisitions Editor Timothy Green	**Technical Editor** James W. Archer	Brian Wells Beth Young
Editorial Management Syngress Media, Inc.	**Copy Editor** Lynette Crane	**Series Design** Roberta Steele
	Proofreader Tandra McLaughlin	**Cover Design** Matthew Willis

This book was composed with Corel VENTURA™ Publisher.

From Global Knowledge

At Global Knowledge we strive to support the multiplicity of learning styles required by our students to achieve success as technical professionals. In this book, it is our intention to offer the reader a valuable tool for successful completion of the Java 2 Programmer Certification Exam.

As the world's largest IT training company, Global Knowledge is uniquely positioned to offer these books. The expertise gained each year from providing instructor-led training to hundreds of thousands of students worldwide has been captured in book form to enhance your learning experience. We hope that the quality of these books demonstrates our commitment to your lifelong learning success. Whether you choose to learn through the written word, computer-based training, Web delivery, or instructor-led training, Global Knowledge is committed to providing you the very best in each of those categories. For those of you who know Global Knowledge, or those of you who have just found us for the first time, our goal is to be your lifelong competency partner.

Thank you for the opportunity to serve you. We look forward to serving your needs again in the future.

Warmest regards,

Duncan Anderson
President and Chief Executive Officer, Global Knowledge

The Global Knowledge Advantage

Global Knowledge has a global delivery system for its products and services. The company has 28 subsidiaries, and offers its programs through a total of 60+ locations. No other vendor can provide consistent services across a geographic area this large. Global Knowledge is the largest independent information technology education provider, offering programs on a variety of platforms. This enables our multi-platform and multi-national customers to obtain all of their programs from a single vendor. The company has developed the unique CompetusTM Framework software tool and methodology which can quickly reconfigure courseware to the proficiency level of a student on an interactive basis. Combined with self-paced and on-line programs, this technology can reduce the time required for training by prescribing content in only the deficient skills areas. The company has fully automated every aspect of the education process, from registration and follow-up, to "just-in-time" production of courseware. Global Knowledge, through its Enterprise Services Consultancy, can customize programs and products to suit the needs of an individual customer.

Global Knowledge Classroom Education Programs

The backbone of our delivery options is classroom-based education. Our modern, well-equipped facilities staffed with the finest instructors offer programs in a wide variety of information technology topics, many of which lead to professional certifications.

Custom Learning Solutions

This delivery option has been created for companies and governments that value customized learning solutions. For them, our consultancy-based approach of developing targeted education solutions is most effective at helping them meet specific objectives.

Self-Paced and Multimedia Products

This delivery option offers self-paced program titles in interactive CD-ROM, videotape and audio tape programs. In addition, we offer custom development of interactive multimedia courseware to customers and partners. Call us at 1 (888) 427-4228.

Electronic Delivery of Training

Our network-based training service delivers efficient competency-based, interactive training via the World Wide Web and organizational intranets. This leading-edge delivery option provides a custom learning path and "just-in-time" training for maximum convenience to students.

ARG

American Research Group (ARG), a wholly-owned subsidiary of Global Knowledge, one of the largest worldwide training partners of Cisco Systems, offers a wide range of internetworking, LAN/WAN, Nortel Networks, FORE Systems, IBM, and UNIX courses. ARG offers hands on network training in both instructor-led classes and self-paced PC-based training.

Global Knowledge Courses Available

Network Fundamentals

- Understanding Computer Networks
- Telecommunications Fundamentals I
- Telecommunications Fundamentals II
- Understanding Networking Fundamentals
- Implementing Computer Telephony Integration
- Introduction to Voice Over IP
- Introduction to Wide Area Networking
- Cabling Voice and Data Networks
- Introduction to LAN/WAN protocols
- Virtual Private Networks
- ATM Essentials

Network Security & Management

- Troubleshooting TCP/IP Networks
- Network Management
- Network Troubleshooting
- IP Address Management
- Network Security Administration
- Web Security
- Implementing UNIX Security
- Managing Cisco Network Security
- Windows NT 4.0 Security

IT Professional Skills

- Project Management for IT Professionals
- Advanced Project Management for IT Professionals
- Survival Skills for the New IT Manager
- Making IT Teams Work

LAN/WAN Internetworking

- Frame Relay Internetworking
- Implementing T1/T3 Services
- Understanding Digital Subscriber Line (xDSL)
- Internetworking with Routers and Switches
- Advanced Routing and Switching
- Multi-Layer Switching and Wire-Speed Routing
- Internetworking with TCP/IP
- ATM Internetworking
- OSPF Design and Configuration
- Border Gateway Protocol (BGP) Configuration

Authorized Vendor Training

Cisco Systems

- Introduction to Cisco Router Configuration
- Advanced Cisco Router Configuration
- Installation and Maintenance of Cisco Routers
- Cisco Internetwork Troubleshooting
- Cisco Internetwork Design
- Cisco Routers and LAN Switches
- Catalyst 5000 Series Configuration
- Cisco LAN Switch Configuration
- Managing Cisco Switched Internetworks
- Configuring, Monitoring, and Troubleshooting Dial-Up Services
- Cisco AS5200 Installation and Configuration
- Cisco Campus ATM Solutions

Bay Networks

- Bay Networks Accelerated Router Configuration
- Bay Networks Advanced IP Routing
- Bay Networks Hub Connectivity
- Bay Networks Accelar 1xxx Installation and Basic Configuration
- Bay Networks Centillion Switching

FORE Systems

- FORE ATM Enterprise Core Products
- FORE ATM Enterprise Edge Products
- FORE ATM Theory
- FORE LAN Certification

Operating Systems & Programming

Microsoft

- Introduction to Windows NT
- Microsoft Networking Essentials
- Windows NT 4.0 Workstation
- Windows NT 4.0 Server
- Advanced Windows NT 4.0 Server
- Windows NT Networking with TCP/IP
- Introduction to Microsoft Web Tools
- Windows NT Troubleshooting
- Windows Registry Configuration

UNIX

- UNIX Level I
- UNIX Level II
- Essentials of UNIX and NT Integration

Programming

- Introduction to JavaScript
- Java Programming
- PERL Programming
- Advanced PERL with CGI for the Web

Web Site Management & Development

- Building a Web Site
- Web Site Management and Performance
- Web Development Fundamentals

High Speed Networking

- Essentials of Wide Area Networking
- Integrating ISDN
- Fiber Optic Network Design
- Fiber Optic Network Installation
- Migrating to High Performance Ethernet

DIGITAL UNIX

- UNIX Utilities and Commands
- DIGITAL UNIX v4.0 System Administration
- DIGITAL UNIX v4.0 (TCP/IP) Network Management
- AdvFS, LSM, and RAID Configuration and Management
- DIGITAL UNIX TruCluster Software Configuration and Management
- UNIX Shell Programming Featuring Kornshell
- DIGITAL UNIX v4.0 Security Management
- DIGITAL UNIX v4.0 Performance Management
- DIGITAL UNIX v4.0 Intervals Overview

DIGITAL OpenVMS

- OpenVMS Skills for Users
- OpenVMS System and Network Node Management I
- OpenVMS System and Network Node Management II
- OpenVMS System and Network Node Management III
- OpenVMS System and Network Node Operations
- OpenVMS for Programmers
- OpenVMS System Troubleshooting for Systems Managers
- Configuring and Managing Complex VMScluster Systems
- Utilizing OpenVMS Features from C
- OpenVMS Performance Management
- Managing DEC TCP/IP Services for OpenVMS
- Programming in C

Hardware Courses

- AlphaServer 1000/1000A Installation, Configuration and Maintenance
- AlphaServer 2100 Server Maintenance
- AlphaServer 4100, Troubleshooting Techniques and Problem Solving

About Syngress Media

Syngress Media creates books and software for Information Technology professionals seeking skill enhancement and career advancement. Its products are designed to comply with vendor and industry standard course curricula, and are optimized for certification exam preparation. You can contact Syngress via the Web at www.sygnress.com.

Contributors

Brian Bagnall (Sun® Certified Java™ Programmer and a Sun Certified Developer) works for IBM Global Services in Canada. His current project is designing and programming web-centered office utilities using Java for Portableoffice.com. He would like to say thanks to his father Herb and his wonderful aunt Elaine for their support. Brian can be reached at bbagnall@escape.ca.

Eileen Sauer (Sun Certified Java Programmer, Developer and Architect) is President and CEO of Emprise Computing, Inc. She has more than 13 years of experience doing full software life cycle development, technical training, and mentoring in industries such as brokerage, banking, telecommunications, and insurance. Eileen works with Java, Visual Age, Rational Rose, EJB (Weblogic), Sybase/Oracle, etc., and has a Bachelor's in Math/CS from the University of Notre Dame. Eileen Sauer can be reached at http://www.geocities.com/emprise.

Frank Sauer (MSCS) has been developing object-oriented systems since 1986 using Smalltalk, C++ and Java. His expertise includes object-oriented design and analysis using UML, design and analysis patterns, and distributed object systems. He presently works as an infrastructure modeler for The Technical Resource Connection Inc., a wholly owned subsidiary of Perot Systems Corporation. At TRC, he has been building enterprise distributed object systems using Java, CORBA and, most recently, Enterprise Java Beans (EJB). He has worked on medical information and imaging systems, customer support systems in the financial industry, and supply chain management systems in the food industry. He and his wife Eileen live in Tampa, Florida. When he is not programming in Java, he enjoys classical and new age music, ballroom dancing, and scuba diving.

Jay Foster (BSEE) has been an IT professional since 1989. His expertise includes object-oriented design and modeling, design documentation, software engineering, system testing, and N-tier application development. He presently works for The Technical Resource Connection, Inc., a wholly owned subsidiary of Perot Systems Corporation. Jay has extensive experience in the following technologies: Java Servlets, Enterprise JavaBeans (EJB), Java Server Pages (JSP), Java Database Connectivity (JDBC), Remote Method Invocation (RMI), Java Foundation Classes (JFC), Swing, object-oriented design using the Unified Modeling Language (UML), and CORBA. During the course of his career, Jay has worked on manufacturing process control systems in the automotive and food processing industries, electronic display control systems in the sign industry, and order entry/workflow systems in both the telecommunications and insurance industries. He has been developing object oriented systems in Java for 3 years and is a Sun Certified Java Programmer. Jay is married and currently resides in Tampa, Florida. His hobbies include motorcycles and basketball. Jay can be reached at jfoster@trcinc.com.

Jonathan Meeks (Sun Certified Java Programmer) is a Senior Engineer for DARC Corporation, in Chicago, Illinois, where he works on Enterprise Application Integration adapter technology. He has a wide area of experience, including Oracle RDBMS, XML for e-commerce, and distributed object computing. Mr. Meeks holds a B.A. in Cognitive Science from Northwestern University. He dedicates his work on this book to his wife, Wendy.

Bob Hablutzel has been working in computer technology for much longer than he likes to admit: nearly two decades. In that time, he has worked as an operator, programmer, modeler, analyst, consultant, and architect, and is currently Chief Technology Officer of WebCredit.com. He thanks his wife and his pets for their support and assistance.

Mike Keene (Sun Certified Java Programmer), during his professional career, has acquired a vast amount of experience using the Java 2 Enterprise Edition technologies. Currently, he is working as a consultant for Booz-Allen & Hamilton on a U.S. Customs Service project to locate high-risk vehicles coming into the country. The system is built using Java Server Pages as the front end and utilizing Enterprise Java Beans and the Java Messaging Service in the middle tier with Oracle 8i as the database. He would like to thank his family for giving him the time to produce such an informational and useful book for people.

Rick R. Ratliff (Sun Certified Java Programmer) is the chief software architect for A.B. Watley Group in Allen, Texas. Rick has a Bachelor of Science in Computer Science from Southwest Texas State University and has worked in software development since 1985, specializing in object-oriented technology. He is currently studying for the Sun Certified Java Developer and Java Architect exams, and can be reached at either rick.ratliff@abwg.com or rick@ratliff.org

Tristan Yates (Sun Certified Java Programmer) is an independent Java/Oracle consultant in the Washington, D.C., area. Recent clients have included the Discovery Channel, Qwest, the Library of Congress, and Sallie Mae. He holds certifications in Java, Oracle, and Powerbuilder.

Diego Moriarty (Sun Certified Java Programmer and Developer) started programming as a hobby when he was twelve, and is one of the lucky people who has made a career out of his passion. He has developed software in areas such as telecommunications, e-commerce, banking, internet tools and medicine. He is currently between contracts, traveling around the world and doing some bungy jumping and paragliding.

Chad Tippin has been writing software professionally since 1992 and has been using Java for more than four years. His skills include object-oriented analysis and design, practical application of design patterns and the design of distributed enterprise applications using technologies such as CORBA, RMI, and Enterprise Java Beans (EJB). Chad is a Senior Designer/Developer for The Technical Resource Connection, Inc, a wholly owned subsidiary of Perot Systems Corporation. He currently resides in Tampa, Florida with his wife Tracy and son Ashton. He can be reached at ctippin@trcinc.com.

Series Editor

Bill Rossi (Sun Certified Java Programmer and Developer) is President of Rossi Engineering (http://www.rossi.com), an independent consulting firm specializing in Java and Internet-related projects. He has over a decade of software engineering experience, focusing the last four years on Java development and architecture.

Technical Editor

James W. Archer is a software consultant based in southern New England. With a B.A. from the University of Rhode Island, Jim has more than a decade of experience in object-oriented software design and development. He currently specializes in leveraging client-server, Intranet, and Internet technologies including XML, Java, and Enterprise Java Beans to build extensible, Internet accessible data systems that evolve quickly and easily with the needs of their owners. Jim can be reached at jim@archer.net.

ACKNOWLEDGMENTS

W e would like to thank the following people:

- Richard Kristof of Global Knowledge for championing the series and providing access to some great people and information.

- All the incredibly hard-working folks at Osborne/McGraw-Hill: Brandon Nordin, Scott Rogers, and Gareth Hancock for their help in launching a great series and being solid team players. In addition, Tara Davis, Tim Green, and Lisa Theobald for their help in fine-tuning the book.

CONTENTS AT A GLANCE

xv

CONTENTS

This book's primary objective is to help you prepare for and pass the Sun Certified Java 2 Programmer Exam (310-025). We believe that the only way to do this is to help you increase your knowledge and build your skills. After completing this book, you should feel confident that you have thoroughly reviewed all of the objectives that Sun has established for the exam.

In This Book

This book is organized around the topics covered within the Sun Certified Java 2 Programmer Exam administered at Sylvan Testing Centers. Sun has specific objectives for the Programmer's exam; we've followed their list carefully, so you can be assured you're not missing anything.

In Every Chapter

We've created a set of chapter components that call your attention to important items, reinforce important points, and provide helpful exam-taking hints. Take a look at what you'll find in the chapters:

- Each chapter begins with the **Certification Objectives**—what you need to know in order to pass the section on the exam dealing with the chapter topic. The Certification Objective headings identify the objectives within the chapter, so you'll always know an objective when you see it!

- **Certification Exercises** are interspersed throughout the chapters. These are step-by-step exercises. They help you master skills that are likely to be an area of focus on the exam. Don't just read through the exercises; they are hands-on practice that you should be comfortable completing. Learning by doing is an effective way to increase your competency with the language.

- **From the Classroom** sidebars describe the issues that come up most often in the training classroom setting. These sidebars give you a valuable perspective into certification- and product-related topics. They point out common mistakes and address questions that have arisen from classroom discussions.

- **Q & A** sections lay out specific problems and solutions in a quick-read format.

- The **Certification Summary** is a succinct review of the chapter and a re-statement of salient points regarding the exam.

- The **Two-Minute Drill** at the end of every chapter is a checklist of the main points of the chapter. It can be used for last-minute review.

- The **Self Test** offers questions similar to those found on the certification exam. The answers to these questions, as well as explanations of the answers, can be found in Appendix A. By taking the Self Test after completing each chapter, you'll reinforce what you've learned from that chapter, while becoming familiar with the structure of the exam questions.

Some Pointers

Once you've finished reading this book, set aside some time to do a thorough review. You might want to return to the book several times and make use of all the methods it offers for reviewing the material:

1. *Re-read all the Two-Minute Drills*, or have someone quiz you. You also can use the drills as a way to do a quick cram before the exam.

2. *Review all the Q & A scenarios* for quick problem solving.

3. *Re-take the Self Tests*. Taking the tests right after you've read the chapter is a good idea, because it helps reinforce what you've just learned. However, it's an even better idea to go back later and do all the questions in the book in one sitting. Pretend you're taking the exam. (For this reason, you should mark your answers on a separate piece of paper when you go through the questions the first time.)

4. *Complete the exercises.* Did you do the exercises when you read through each chapter? If not, do them! These exercises are designed to cover exam topics, and there's no better way to get to know this material than by practicing.

5. *Check out the Web site.* Global Knowledge invites you to become an active member of the Access Global Web site. This site is an online mall and an information repository that you'll find invaluable. You can access many types of products to assist you in your preparation for the exams, and you'll be able to participate in forums, on-line discussions, and threaded discussions. No other book brings you unlimited access to such a resource. You'll find more information about this site in Appendix C.

How to Take the Sun Certified Java Programmer Exam

by Bill Rossi
Sun Certified Java Programmer and Developer
Rossi Engineering

This chapter covers the importance of your Java Programmer certification and prepares you for taking the actual examination. It gives you a few pointers on methods of preparing for the exam, including how to study and register, what to expect, and what to do on exam day. The Java certification program was created in late 1996 to address the needs of IT managers trying to find qualified Java professionals. At the time the technology was very new and therefore developers did not have any long-term experience with it. Certification was created as a tool to separate the experts from the rest.

Today, Java has been on the IT scene for several years. It is now possible to distinguish Java professionals by their experience level in addition to certification. Experience, however, does not indicate the same solid understanding of the fundamentals of the language that the certification exams demand. In order to succeed on the Sun Certified Programmer Exam, a candidate must demonstrate a comprehensive understanding of the core language concepts.

Why Certification?

Certification helps identify you as a Java expert. It is a tool that IT managers can use to identify those who have a solid grasp of the core language concepts. This is not to say that there are not good Java professionals that aren't certified, but when taken into consideration with experience, certification can be a powerful tool to the IT manager.

Some people become certified as an aid to compete in the demanding IT marketplace. Some companies use the exam as the final phase of a Java training course. Others take it purely for the challenge. Whatever your reasons for tackling the exam, this book will help you prepare for it.

It would be nice to know some statistics about the exam such as the pass/fail ratio and the number of people certified. Sun however has decided to keep this information confidential. The actual questions on the exam are also kept confidential and are even copyrighted. The questions and materials in this book are therefore based largely upon the experience of those who have previously taken and passed the exam as well as on Sun's publicly stated objectives.

DILBERT® United Features Syndicate / Reprinted by Permission.

Over the years, technology vendors have created their own certification programs because of industry demand. This demand arises when the marketplace needs skilled professionals and an easy way to identify them. Vendors benefit because it promotes people skilled in their product. Professionals benefit because it boosts their career. Employers benefit because it helps them identify qualified people.

Technology changes too often and too quickly to rely on traditional means of certification, such as universities and trade associations. Because of the investment and effort required to keep certification programs current, vendors are the only organizations suited to keep pace with the changes. In general, such vendor certification programs are excellent, with most of them requiring a solid foundation in the essentials, as well as their particular product line.

Corporate America has come to appreciate these vendor certification programs and the value they provide. Employers recognize that certifications, like university degrees, do not guarantee a level of knowledge, experience, or performance; rather, they establish a baseline for comparison. By seeking to hire vendor-certified employees, a company can assure itself that it has also hired a person skilled in the specific products the company uses.

Technical professionals have also begun to realize the value of certification and the impact it can have on their careers. By completing a certification program, professionals gain an endorsement of their skills from a major industry source. This endorsement can boost their current position, and it makes finding the next job even easier. Often, a certification determines whether a first interview is even granted.

Today, a certification may place you ahead of the pack. Tomorrow, it may be a necessity to keep from being left in the dust.

Sun's Certification Program

Currently there are three Java certification exams. They are the *Programmer*, the *Developer*, and the *Architect* exams.

The Programmer Exam

The Programmer exam is designed to test your knowledge of the Java programming language itself. It requires detailed knowledge of language syntax, core concepts, and application programming interfaces (APIs). It does not test any issues related to program design or architecture, and it does not ask why one approach is better than another, but rather it asks whether the given approach works.

The Developer Exam

The Developer exam picks up where the Programmer exam leaves off. Passing the Programmer exam is required before you can start the Developer exam. The Developer exam requires you to develop an actual program and then defend your design decisions. It is designed to test your understanding of why certain approaches are better than others in certain circumstances.

The Architect Exam

The Architect exam operates at an even higher level of abstraction than the Developer exam. It asks whether one technology is better than another at solving a given business problem. The Architect exam has no prerequisites and does not require a detailed understanding of the Java language.

on the
öob

In addition to finding the technical objectives that are being tested for each exam, you will find much more useful information on Sun's Web site at http://www.suned.sun.com/usa/cert_test.html. You will find information on becoming certified, exam-specific information, sample test questions, and the latest news on Sun certification. This is the most important site you will find on your journey to becoming Sun certified.

Sun maintains a Web site for its certification programs at http://suned.sun.com. This Web site will give you instructions on how to register for the exam. It also has the e-mail addresses and phone numbers for the people at Sun who are responsible for the exam.

Don't hesitate to contact Sun if you have questions regarding the exam. They have always been very responsive to questions and appreciate candidate feedback.

Computer-Based Testing

In a perfect world, you would be assessed for your true knowledge of a subject, not simply how you respond to a series of test questions. But life isn't perfect, and it just isn't practical to evaluate everyone's knowledge on a one-to-one basis.

For the majority of its certifications, Sun evaluates candidates using a computer-based testing service operated by Sylvan Prometric. This service is quite popular in the industry, and it is used for a number of vendor certification programs, including Novell's CNE and Microsoft's MCSE. Thanks to Sylvan Prometric's large number of facilities, exams can be administered worldwide, generally in the same town as a prospective candidate.

For the most part, Sylvan Prometric exams work similarly from vendor to vendor. However, there is an important fact to know about Sun's exams: they use the traditional Sylvan Prometric test format, not the newer adaptive format. This gives the candidate an advantage, since the traditional format allows answers to be reviewed and revised during the test.

exam
Watch

Many experienced test takers do not go back and change answers unless they have a good reason to do so. Only change an answer when you feel you may have misread or misinterpreted the question the first time. Nervousness may make you second-guess every answer and talk yourself out of a correct one.

To discourage simple memorization, Sun exams present a different set of questions every time the exam is administered. In the development of the exam, hundreds of questions are compiled and refined using beta testers. From this large collection, a random sampling is drawn for each test.

Each Sun exam has a specific number of questions and test duration. Testing time is typically generous, and the time remaining is always displayed in the corner of the testing screen, along with the number of remaining questions. If time expires during an exam, the test terminates, and incomplete answers are counted as incorrect.

At the end of the exam, your test is immediately graded, and the results are displayed on the screen. Scores for each subject area are also provided, but the system will not indicate which specific questions were missed. A report is automatically printed at the proctor's desk for your files. The test score is electronically transmitted back to Sun.

In the end, this computer-based system of evaluation is reasonably fair. You might feel that one or two questions were poorly worded; this can certainly happen, but you shouldn't worry too much. Ultimately, it's all factored into the required passing score.

exam **Watch**

When you find yourself stumped answering multiple-choice questions, use your scratch paper to write down the two or three answers you consider the strongest, and then underline the answer you feel is most likely correct. Here is an example of what your scratch paper might look like when you've gone through the test once:

21. B or C

33. A or C

This is extremely helpful when you mark the question and continue on. You can then return to the question and immediately pick up your thought process where you left off. Use this technique to avoid having to re-read and re-think questions. You will also need to use your scratch paper during complex, text-based scenario questions to create visual images to better understand the question. This technique is especially helpful if you are a visual learner.

Exam Quality

Because the exam questions are held confidentially by Sun, it may happen that you will come across a question that doesn't seem to have a right answer. Sun does try to quality-check the exam thoroughly, but without an outside review, some badly formulated questions may occur.

Unfortunately, there isn't much you can do about this when you are taking the exam. You can't write the question down and take it with you, so I'd recommend trying to remember the question before you leave and check it out later. If you still believe the question to be in error, contact Sun as soon as possible and try to work out a solution. This at least helps to keep others from having the same problem in the future.

There aren't supposed to be any multiple-choice questions that don't have any right answers. There may be some that have multiple right answers, but they should all have at least one. If you find a question that you think has no correct answers, pick the answer that is the closest to being correct, and contact Sun about the question after the exam.

Question Types

Sun's Java exams pose questions in a variety of formats, most of which are discussed here. As candidates progress toward the more advanced certifications, the difficulty of the exams is intensified, both through the subject matter as well as the question formats.

exam

Watch

To pass these challenging exams, you may want to talk with other test takers to determine what is being tested, and what to expect in terms of difficulty.

True/False

The classic true/false question format is not used in the Sun exams, for the obvious reason that a simple guess has a 50 percent chance of being correct. Instead, true/false questions are posed in multiple-choice format, requiring the candidate to identify the true or false statement from a group of selections.

Multiple Choice

Multiple choice is the primary format for questions in Sun exams. These questions may be posed in a variety of ways.

SELECT THE CORRECT ANSWER. This is the classic multiple-choice question, where the candidate selects a single answer from a list of about four choices. In addition to the question's wording, the choices are presented in a Windows "radio button" format.

SELECT ALL THAT APPLY. The open-ended version is the most difficult multiple-choice format, since the candidate does not know how many answers should be selected. As with the multiple-answer version, all the correct answers must be selected to gain credit for the question. If too many answers are selected, no credit is given. This format presents choices in check box format, but the testing software does not advise the candidates whether they've selected the correct number of answers.

exam
Watch

Make it easy on yourself and find some "braindumps." These are notes about the exam from test takers, which indicate the most difficult concepts tested, what to look out for, and sometimes even what not to bother studying.

Fill in the Blank

Fill-in-the-blank questions are less common in Sun exams. They may be presented in multiple-choice or freeform response format.

Tips on Taking the Exam

There are 59 questions on the exam. You will need to get at least 42 of them correct to pass—just over 71 percent. You are given two hours to complete the exam.

You are allowed to answer questions in any order, and you can go back and check your answers after you've gone through the test. There are no penalties for wrong answers, so it's better to at least attempt an answer than to not give one at all.

A good strategy for taking the exam is to go through once and answer all the questions that come to you quickly. You can then go back and do the others. The code samples provided for some questions may help you with others. For example, if a short-answer question wants the name of the method for taking square roots, another multiple-choice question may contain that information.

Be very careful on the code examples. Check for syntax errors first, count curly braces and parenthesis and make sure there are as many left ones as right ones. Look for capitalization errors and other such syntax problems before trying to figure out what the code does.

Many of the questions on the exam will hinge on subtleties of syntax. You will need to have a thorough knowledge of the Java language in order to succeed.

Tips on Studying for the Exam

First and foremost, give yourself plenty of time to study. Java is a complex programming language, and you can't expect to cram what you need to know into a single study session. It is a field best learned over time, by studying a subject and then applying your knowledge. Build yourself a study schedule and stick to it, but be reasonable about the pressure you put on yourself, especially if you're studying in addition to your regular duties at work.

One easy technique to use in studying for certification exams is the 15-minutes per day effort. Simply study for a minimum of 15 minutes every day. It is a small, but significant commitment. If you have a day where you just can't focus, then give up at 15 minutes. If you have a day where it flows completely for you, study longer. As long as you have more of the "flow days," your chances of succeeding are extremely high.

Another excellent way to study is through case studies. Case studies are articles or interactive discussions that offer real-world examples of how technology is applied to meet a need. These examples can serve to cement your understanding of a technique or technology by seeing it put to use. Interactive discussions offer added value because you can also pose questions of your own. User groups are an excellent source of examples, since the purpose of these groups is to share information and learn from each other's experiences.

Scheduling Your Exam

The Sun exams are scheduled by calling Sylvan Prometric directly at (800) 755-3926. For locations outside the United States, your local number can be found on Sylvan's Web site at http://www.2test.com. Sylvan representatives can schedule your exam, but they don't have information about the certification programs. Questions about certifications should be directed to Sun's training department.

These representatives are familiar enough with the exams to find them by name, but it's best if you have the specific exam number handy when you call. After all, you wouldn't want to be scheduled and charged for the wrong exam (for example, the instructor's version, which is significantly harder).

Exams can be scheduled up to a year in advance, although it's really not necessary. Generally, scheduling a week or two ahead is sufficient to reserve the day and time you prefer. When scheduling, operators will search for testing centers in your area. For convenience, they can also tell which testing centers you've used before.

Sylvan accepts a variety of payment methods, with credit cards being the most convenient. When paying by credit card, you can even take tests the same day you call—provided, of course, that the testing center has room. (Quick scheduling can be handy, especially if you want to re-take an exam immediately.) Sylvan will mail you a receipt and confirmation of your testing date, although this generally arrives after the test has been taken. If you need to cancel or reschedule an exam, remember to call at least one day before your exam, or you'll lose your test fee.

When registering for the exam, you will be asked for your ID number. This number is used to track your exam results back to Sun. It's important that you use the same ID number each time you register, so that Sun can follow your progress. Address information provided when you first register is also used by Sun to ship certificates and other related material. In the United States, your Social Security Number is commonly used as your ID number. However, Sylvan can assign you a unique ID number if you prefer not to use your Social Security Number.

Arriving at the Exam

As with any test, you'll be tempted to cram the night before. Resist that temptation. You should know the material by this point, and if you're too groggy in the morning, you won't remember what you studied anyway. Instead, get a good night's sleep.

Arrive early for your exam; it gives you time to relax and review key facts. Take the opportunity to review your notes. If you get burned out on studying, you can usually start your exam a few minutes early. On the other hand, I don't recommend arriving late. Your test could be cancelled, or you may not be left with enough time to complete the exam.

When you arrive at the testing center, you'll need to sign in with the exam administrator. In order to sign in, you need to provide two forms of identification. Acceptable forms include government-issued IDs (for example, passport or driver's license), credit cards, and company ID badge. One form of ID must include a photograph.

Aside from a brain full of facts, you don't need to bring anything else to the exam. In fact, your brain is about all you're allowed to take into the exam! All the tests are "closed book," meaning you don't get to bring any reference materials with you. You're also not allowed to take any notes out of the exam room. The test administrator will provide you with paper and a pencil. Some testing centers may provide a small marker board instead.

Calculators are not allowed, so be prepared to do any necessary math in your head or on paper. Additional paper is available if you need it.

Leave your pager and telephone in the car, or turn them off. They only add stress to the situation, since they are not allowed in the exam room, and can sometimes still be heard if they ring outside of the room. Purses, books, and other materials must be left with the administrator before entering the exam. While in the exam room, it's important that you don't disturb other candidates; talking is not allowed during the exam.

Once in the testing room, the exam administrator logs onto your exam, and you have to verify that your ID number and the exam number are correct. If this is the first time you've taken a Sun test, you can select a brief tutorial of the exam software. Before the test begins, you will be provided with facts about the exam, including the duration, the number of questions, and the score required for passing. Then the clock starts ticking and the fun begins.

The testing software is Windows-based, but you won't have access to the main desktop or any of the accessories. The exam is presented in full screen, with a single question per screen. Navigation buttons allow you to move forward and backward between questions. In the upper-right corner of the screen, counters show the number of questions and time remaining. Most importantly, there is a 'Mark' checkbox in the upper-left corner of the screen—this will prove to be a critical tool in your testing technique.

Test-Taking Techniques

Without a plan of attack, candidates are overwhelmed by the exam or become side-tracked and run out of time. For the most part, if you are comfortable with the material, the allotted time is more than enough to complete the exam. The trick is to keep the time from slipping away during any one particular problem.

The obvious goal of an exam is to answer the questions effectively, although other aspects of the exam can distract from this goal. Here are some tips for taking the exam more efficiently.

Size Up the Challenge

First, take a quick pass through all the questions in the exam. "Cherry-pick" the easy questions, answering them on the spot. Briefly read each question, noticing the type of question and the subject. As a guideline, try to spend less than 25 percent of your testing time in this pass.

This step lets you assess the scope and complexity of the exam, and it helps you determine how to pace your time. It also gives you an idea of where to find potential answers to some of the questions. Often, the answer to one question is shown in the exhibit of another. Sometimes the wording of one question might lend clues or jog your thoughts for another question.

If you're not entirely confident with your answer to a question, answer it anyway, but check the Mark box to flag it for later review. In the event that you run out of time, at least you've provided a "first guess" answer, rather than leaving it blank.

Second, go back through the entire test, using the insight you gained from the first go-through. For example, if the entire test looks difficult, you'll know better than to spend more than a minute or so on each question. Break down the pacing into small milestones; for example, "I need to answer 10 questions every 15 minutes."

At this stage, it's probably a good idea to skip past the time-consuming questions, marking them for the next pass. Try to finish this phase before you're 50 – 60 percent through the testing time.

Third, go back through all the questions you marked for review, using the Review Marked button in the question review screen. This step includes taking a second look at all the questions you were unsure of in previous passes, as well as tackling the time-consuming ones you deferred until now. Chisel away at this group of questions until you've answered them all.

If you're more comfortable with a previously marked question, unmark it now. Otherwise, leave it marked. Work your way through the time-consuming questions now, especially those requiring manual calculations. Unmark them when you're satisfied with the answer.

By the end of this step, you've answered every question in the test, despite having reservations about some of your answers. If you run out of time in the next step, at least you won't lose points for lack of an answer. You're in great shape if you still have 10 – 20 percent of your time remaining.

Review Your Answers

Now you're cruising! You've answered all the questions, and you're ready to do a quality check. Take yet another pass (yes, one more) through the entire test, briefly re-reading each question and your answer.

Carefully look over the questions again to check for "trick" questions. Be particularly wary of those which include a choice of "Does not compile." Be alert for last-minute clues. You're pretty familiar with nearly every question at this point, and you may find a few clues that you missed before.

The Grand Finale

When you're confident with all your answers, finish the exam by submitting it for grading. After what will seem like the longest 10 seconds of your life, the testing software will respond with your score. This is usually displayed as a bar graph, showing the minimum passing score, your score, and a PASS/FAIL indicator.

If you're curious, you can review the statistics of your score at this time. Answers to specific questions are not presented; rather, questions are lumped into categories, and results are tallied for each category. This detail is also printed on a report that has been automatically printed at the exam administrator's desk.

As you leave the exam, you'll need to leave your scratch paper behind or return it to the administrator. (Some testing centers track the number of sheets you've been given, so be sure to return them all.) In exchange, you'll receive a copy of the test report.

This report will be embossed with the testing center's seal, and you should keep it in a safe place. Normally, the results are automatically transmitted to Sun, but occasionally you might need the paper report to prove that you passed the exam.

In a few days, Sun will send you a package in the mail containing a nice paper certificate, a lapel pin, and artwork for the "steaming coffee cup" logo. You will be given a license to use the logo on your personal stationary and business cards.

Re-Testing

If you don't pass the exam, don't be discouraged. Try to have a good attitude about the experience, and get ready to try again. Consider yourself a little more educated. You know the format of the test a little better, and the report shows which areas you need to strengthen.

If you bounce back quickly, you'll probably remember several of the questions you might have missed. This will help you focus your study efforts in the right area. Serious go-getters will re-schedule the exam for a couple of days after the previous attempt, while the study material is still fresh in their mind.

Ultimately, remember that Sun certifications are valuable because they're hard to get. After all, if anyone could get one, what value would it have? In the end, it takes a good attitude and a lot of studying, but you can do it!

1

Language Fundamentals

This chapter will familiarize you with the Java fundamentals that you need to know to pass the Java 2.0 Programmer exam. Because you are planning on becoming Sun certified, it is probably safe to assume that you know the basics of Java, so this chapter will focus on the details you might not be familiar with, but which are essential for passing the exam.

Source Files

A *source file* is a plain text file containing your Java code. The Java compiler *javac* processes the source file to produce a byte code file, which ends with the suffix *class*.

e x a m
ⓦatch

The exam is concerned with how the Java compiler deals with a source file. For this reason it is a good idea to prepare for the exam using only the Java Development Kit (JDK) 1.2 supplied by Sun, a text editor, and a command line prompt. This may be a little awkward at first for people used to working in an integrated development environment such as IBM's Visual Age for Java. You are roughing it a bit by using only the command line, but perhaps it will give you the same back-to-basics thrill as starting a fire with two sticks.

A Java source file must meet strict requirements, otherwise the Java compiler will generate errors. A plain text file can be compiled using the JDK in the following manner, and will produce no screen output from the compiler if successful:

```
c:\Java Projects>javac Calculate.java
c:\Java Projects>
```

Now, if you look in the Java Projects directory, you will see a file named Calculate.class.

The source file must be saved with the suffix *java*. If you try to compile a source file that does not have the java suffix, the compiler produces an error:

```
c:\Java Projects>javac Calculate.jav
Calculate.jav is an invalid option or argument.
```

Identifiers are names that we assign to classes, methods, and variables. Java is a *case-sensitive* language, which means identifiers must have consistent capitalization throughout. Identifiers can have letters and numbers, but a number may not begin the identifier name. Most symbols are not allowed, but the $ symbol is valid:

```
int 99year; // invalid
int year99; // valid
int hello#; // invalid
int $hello$; // valid
```

File names are also case sensitive. The file itself can contain as many spaces, tabs, and carriage returns as you wish, but they must not break up words within the file. For example, the following file will compile just fine:

```
          public
      class
MyClass { int
month
;}
```

At the very least, a source file must contain... nothing! That's right, the compiler will produce no errors when compiling a blank file. The minimum viable source file, which will produce a class, looks like this:

```
class MyClass {}
```

A source file may only have one public class or interface and an unlimited number of default classes or interfaces defined within it, and the filename must be the same as the public class name. For example, the following file is saved as MyClass.java:

```
// Will not work
public class YourClass {}
```

When we attempt to compile, we get the following error:

```
c:\Java Projects>javac MyClass.java
MyClass.java:1: Public class YourClass must be defined in
a file called "YourClass.java".
```

It is not imperative for the filename to match the name of a class (or interface) in the source file. If there is a public class/interface in the source file, however, then the name of the source file must be the same as the name of the public class. The following file has the filename BobsClass.java, and it will compile fine because there are no public classes:

```
// This works
class YourClass {}
class MyClass {}
class JensClass {}
```

Exercise 1-1 demonstrates how to create a basic source file and compile it. Create a source file containing one public class and two default classes. The classes can be empty, with just curly braces after the class declaration. Save the file with a legal filename and compile it with the standard Sun 2.0 Java compiler.

EXERCISE 1-1

Creating and Compiling a Source File

1. Install Java 2.0 on your computer by following the documentation provided by Sun.
2. Open a text editor and type the class definitions.
3. Save the file with an appropriate filename. Make sure the file ends with .java and not .txt.
4. At a command prompt, type **javac (*filename*).java**
5. If you receive no errors then you have done everything correctly.

CERTIFICATION OBJECTIVE 1.02

Declarations

A *declaration* introduces a class, interface, method, package, or variable into a Java program. A typical example of a source file is as follows:

```
package trades.DataServer;
import java.util.Math;
public class MyClass extends BaseClass implements MyInterface {
     // Code goes in here
}
```

It is not necessary to use each of these declarations, but the order in which you place your declarations in the source file is important. They must appear in the following order:

1. The package declaration (optional)
2. The import function (optional)
3. Any class declarations

Packages

A *package* is an entity that groups classes together. Packages perform the following functions:

- Organize and group classes, normally by function. For example, the java.awt package contains the classes with graphical components.
- Help to specify access restrictions to variables and methods.
- Make it easy to import other programmers' classes into your code, while keeping the code separate from your own.

Placing the package declaration at the top of your source file includes these classes in a package with the name that you specify.

```
package trades.quotes;
```

If no package is explicitly declared, java places your classes into a default package.

The name of the package must reflect the directory structure used to store the classes in your package. The subdirectory begins in any directory indicated by the classpath environment variable. Setting the classpath environment variable is specific to your operating system. The Readme file located in your main JDK directory contains information on how to set this up in UNIX and Windows environments.

Now, with the classpath set, you can start dropping classes belonging to the package trades.quotes into the appropriate subdirectory:

```
c:\MyPackages\trades\quotes\
```

To avoid having different people trying to use the same package name, Sun recommends using the reverse of your internet domain name to package your classes. For example, Sun would keep its classes in the following package:

```
package com.sun.java;
```

Once the classpath is set, any classes in the package can be run from any directory in the system; it is not necessary to be in the same directory as the classes. People commonly have a problem trying to run their class once they include it in a package. For example, if I place a class called Trade in a package called trades.quotes, then try to run it in the normal way, the following error will occur:

```
c:\MyPackages\trades\quotes>java Trade
Exception in thread "main"
java.lang.NoClassDefFoundError: Trade (wrong name:
trades/quotes/Trade)
```

To run this class, you must specify the entire package name after the java command. Again, because the class is in a package and the classpath environment variable has been set, it does not matter where the command prompt is.

```
c:\>java trades.quotes.Trade
```

Exercise 1-2 covers how to create a package and insert classes into the package. You will use the file you created in the previous exercise for this. Try to add this file to a package called com.syngress.

Creating a Package and Inserting Classes

1. Create a directory called Java Packages or any other name you wish. Edit your environment variable classpath to include the directory you just created. For Linux, Solaris, and other UNIX-based systems, do the following:

```
set CLASSPATH = /home/myaccount/JavaPackages
export CLASSPATH
```

Your results may vary based upon which shell you are using, but this syntax should work in most shells. Note the CLASSPATH variable on UNIX systems must be in all capitals, as UNIX environment variables are case sensitive. For Windows users, at a DOS prompt, type the following command (assuming you keep the JDK 1.2 in the following directory). (*Note:* This setting will not be permanent, and it will only apply to the current window.)

```
set classpath = c:\jdk1.2\lib;c:\Java Packages\;
```

2. Create the directory structure com\syngress within the Java Packages directory.
3. Copy your class file to the Syngress directory.
4. Add the package statement to the top of the file:
   ```
   package com.syngress;
   ```
5. Try compiling it. If you did everything properly, it should compile.
6. Try running the class from the command prompt. For example:
   ```
   c:\>java com.syngress.MyClass
   ```

on the Job

Although it is not required for the exam, it is a good idea to become familiar with the java.util package. There are a lot of classes in this package that are frequently used. Among these classes you will find an Arrays class that helps in sorting and searching arrays, a Vector class for storing unsorted data types, and the Random class for generating random numbers. It takes under an hour to familiarize yourself with the classes and methods, and it will end up saving you a lot of time. Nothing is worse than creating a whole new class, then realizing you have just reinvented the wheel.

Classes

Let's briefly review some object-oriented terms. A *class* is a declaration for a potential object. Think of a class as a skeleton or framework that contains methods but no data. Once the class is instantiated it becomes an *object* (sometimes referred to as an instance). The constructor method of a class is invoked when an object is instantiated. The constructor method *initializes*, or assigns values to, all the variables within the class.

It is important to declare your class with the keywords in the proper order. A typical, large class definition looks like this:

```
public abstract class MyClass extends BaseClass implements YourInterface, BobsInterface {}
```

A *modifier* is a keyword in a class, method, or variable declaration that modifies the behavior of the element. An *access modifier* is a modifier that changes the protection of an element (Chapter 2 will explain further). The order of the modifiers and keywords is as follows:

1. public access modifier (optional)
2. final modifier (optional, cannot be used with abstract)
3. abstract modifier (optional, cannot be used with final)
4. class keyword
5. name of the class
6. the class it extends (optional)
7. any interfaces it implements (optional)
8. curly braces {}

It is important to note number two and number three on the list. These cannot be used together when defining a class because the abstract modifier implies the class will be extended, yet the final modifier prevents the class from being extended. This will be further explained in Chapter 2.

Let's briefly review some object-oriented terminology. When we extend a class, we are *subclassing* it and the resulting class is a *subclass* of the class that was extended. This is also referred to as *deriving a class*. Subclasses are also called *derived classes* or *child classes*. The class that was extended is referred to as a *superclass*, a *parent class* or a *base class*. A subclass is *more specific* than the superclass and the superclass is *more general* or *less specific* than the subclass. Because of the way class diagrams are traditionally drawn (with the *least derived* classes at the top and the *more derived* classes moving downward), base classes are at the top of the class hierarchy while more derived classes are at the bottom. Therefore, as we move down the class hierarchy, classes become more specific.

All Java classes must extend a superclass. If you do not specify a class to extend, Java will derive your class from the class Object. Object is the highest-level Java class, and all classes are subclasses of the Object class.

Objects can also refer to themselves by using the keyword *this*. Observe the following code that shows two examples of the keyword this:

```
class Money {
     public double costs;
     public double revenue;
     public double profit;
     public Money (double costs) {
          this.costs = costs;  // Specifying a particular
variable
          profit = Accounting.calculateProfit(this); // Passing
itself to a method
     }
}
```

In the sixth line of the program there are two variables with the same name, *costs*. The instance variable is defined at the top of the code, and the local variable is passed to the Money() constructor method as an argument. To differentiate the two, it is necessary to use the keyword *this*.

Sometimes it is necessary for an object to pass itself to another method, as in line seven of this class. By using *this* it passes a reference of itself to the method calculateProfit().

You can also use this() to invoke a constructor method for a class. The this() method may only be invoked from a constructor method, as in the following example:

```
class ThisSample{
     String screenTitle;
     public ThisSample() {
          this("Main Screen");
     }
     public ThisSample(String title) {
          screenTitle = title;
     }
}
```

Examine line four of the preceding class. It is calling a separate constructor using a string as an argument. It must call the this() method in the first line of a constructor, otherwise it will not compile.

Methods, variables, and inner classes always appear within the curly braces of the class declaration. You might think you could create a class with only one line, for example a variable declaration, and not use the curly braces.

```
class Tiny
     int size;
```

This seems logical, because after an *if* statement if there is only one line, you do not have to create a block of code in curly brackets, so why would you need to with a class? This is not the case; all code belonging to a class must appear in the curly braces. This is just the sort of obscure question they will ask you on the exam.

Inner classes are a type of class and follow most of the same rules as a normal class. The main difference is an inner class is defined within the curly braces of a class or even within a method. The implications of this will be discussed in Chapter 8.

Interfaces

It is really only necessary to know how to define an interface and how to use the Runnable interface. We will go slightly more in depth, however, because it is always better to know more, rather than less, when preparing for the exam.

The Java language designers realized that true multiple inheritance in any language introduces significant technical and theoretical issues, so they came up with an interface to deal with this. Many people starting out with the Java language do not understand why interfaces are used. An *interface* is a nonfunctional class that can contain constants and method declarations but no functional methods. It may seem, logically, if there is no functionality it might as well be a bunch of // statements. Interfaces are used when a class must be treated like more than one type of object.

In actuality, however, it does not inherit method code and is therefore not true multiple inheritance. But what good is extending a class with an interface if you get no function from it? Let's look at an example of something that uses an interface.

Let's imagine you are making a database of furniture objects for a customer. Perhaps you create an abstract class called Furniture that contains a price and a method for returning the total cost.

```
abstract class Furniture {
    private double price;
    public final double TAX = 0.14;
    public double getCost() {
        double cost = price + (price * TAX);
        return cost;
    }
// Additional code goes here
}
```

Next we extend this Furniture class to derive Table, Chair, and Couch subclasses. In this example, we will show only the Chair subclass.

```
class Chair extends Furniture { // Code goes here }
```

The company also specializes in a selection of leather goods, including furniture, and they would like all leather objects to have a method that displays a small square sample of the leather used. We could extend Chair to LeatherChair and Couch to LeatherCouch, but then if we create a method that takes a Leather object and displays the sample of leather, we would have to program separate methods for LeatherCouch and LeatherChair. We would ideally like the following method to take any Leather object and display the sample:

```
void showSample (Leather leatherItem) { // Code goes here }
```

The compiler must be sure any object passed to the method showSample does in fact contain a sample image of the leather. The solution is—and I think you knew I was getting to this—to use an Interface.

```
interface Leather {
    public Image getSample();
}
```

Notice we define a method within the interface, but instead of ending with curly braces we end with a semicolon. The Leather interface ensures any concrete class (one that may be instantiated) that implements this interface will have a method called getSample() that can actually be called. Now, we can create our method to display the sample of leather that only takes objects of type Leather. Let's expand on the Chair class that we previously created.

```
import java.awt.Image;
class Chair extends Furniture implements Leather {
    Image sampleImage;
    public Image getSample() {
        return sampleImage;
    }
// Additional code goes here
}
```

Interfaces are a way for the compiler to ensure that an object being used in a method has all the needed methods. Interfaces can also declare variables, as in the following example:

```
interface ServerCodes {
     public static final int MAXCONNECTIONS = 20;
     public static final int MAXUSERS= 100;
}
```

Interfaces may not, however, declare variables unless they are initialized. This is because variables in interfaces are implicitly public, static, and final (even though the keywords are not used). Examine the following interface:

```
interface Leather {
     Image sampleImage;
     public Image getSample();
}
```

Now if we attempt to compile the preceding example, we will receive the following error:

```
c:\Java Projects\Server>javac Leather.java
Leather.java:2: This final variable must be initialized: Image sampleImage
     Image sampleImage;
1 error
c:\Java Projects\Server>
```

An interface may also extend another interface:

```
interface SubInterface extends BaseInterface {}
```

Notice we do not extend another interface by using the command *implements*. If we try to implement another interface we will get a compiler error.

Java also allows classes to implement more than one interface, as in the following example:

```
class MyClass implements MyInterface, YourInterface {}
```

Implementation of an Interface

The only interface you will need to know for the exam is java.lang.Runnable. The Runnable interface is used to make a threaded class, about which we will go into greater detail in Chapter 9. For now, let's try making a threaded class using the Runnable interface.

```
public class ExponentialGrowth implements Runnable {}
```

If we try to compile the preceding code now, without any of the methods defined in the interface, we will get the following error:

```
c:\Java Projects\Exponential>javac ExponentialGrowth.java
ExponentialGrowth.java:1: class ExponentialGrowth must be declared abstract. It
does not define void run() from interface java.lang.Runnable.
..
```

As we can see, the Java compiler expects us to implement the method run(), defined in the Runnable interface. Let's create a run() method in our class that shows us the value of our money compounding at an interest rate of 10 percent per year.

```
public class ExponentialGrowth implements Runnable {
     public final double INTEREST = 0.10;
     public void run () {
          int dollars = 1;
          int years = 0;
          while (true) {
               System.out.println("$" + dollars + " after " + years + " years");
               dollars *= (1 + INTEREST);
               years += 1;
          }
     }
}
```

Notice there is no need to use an import statement to access the Runnable interface, because it is part of the java.lang package, which is automatically imported. Now, to see our wonderful investment compounding yearly at 10 percent interest, we must create an instance of the class in the main() method.

```
class ShowGrowth {
     public static void main (String [] args) {
```

```
ExponentialGrowth growth = new ExponentialGrowth();
Thread compoundThread = new Thread(growth);
compoundThread.start();
    }
}
```

The code in the main method deserves further examination. The first line in the method creates an instance of the class ExponentialGrowth and assigns it to the variable *growth*. The next line creates a new thread, using the constructor, which takes a Runnable object as the argument. The final line invokes the start() method to begin our thread.

Methods

A *method* gives a class its functionality. A large method declaration can look like this:

```
public static final synchronized double getPrice(int itemCode, Color itemColor)
throws Exception {..}
```

Of course, not all of these keywords must be used. The smallest method declaration, which does absolutely nothing, looks like this:

```
void getPrice() {}
```

Once again, it is important to use the keywords in the proper order:

1. Access modifiers—public, private, protected, or none (default)
2. Special modifiers—abstract, final, native, static, or synchronized (optional)
3. Return type—a type or void
4. Name of method (identifier)
5. Arguments passed to the method within ( ) brackets (none or many)
6. Exceptions thrown (required if the method throws any Exceptions; optional otherwise)
7. Curly braces enclosing the method code (not with abstract or interface methods)

The order of number one and number two is not important. For example, the following method definition is quite valid:

```
synchronized static final public double getSquare (double Number) {..}
```

As with class definitions, abstract and final may not be used in the same method declaration. As noted in number seven, an abstract method or a method defined in an interface must end in a semicolon without curly braces:

```
public abstract void showImage();
```

exam
ⓦatch

Keep in mind how picky the exam will be about the order and combinations of keywords that make up a legal declaration of a method. The exam will test you on every conceivable combination of keywords, and for each example you must know whether or not it is valid.

Main Method and Command-Line Arguments

The main() method is used to start the ball rolling for a Java program. The main() method is declared like any other method, only it contains an array of strings passed from the command line when the class is started.

```
public class MainTest {
    public static void main (String [] args) {
        for (int i = 0;i < args.length;i++) {
            System.out.println("Argument " + i + ": " + args[i]);
        }
    }
}
```

In the preceding example, it is not necessary to name the command-line arguments array *args*, but by convention most programmers go this way. The preceding code will output any command-line arguments, as in the following example:

```
c:\Java Projects\Main>java MainTest Philip K Johnson
Argument 0: Philip
Argument 1: K
Argument 2: Johnson
```

It is important to note that the first argument, *Phillip*, correlates to the index value of 0, and the second argument, *K*, correlates to the index value of 1, and so on.

The code will compile if you create a method named main() without modifying it as static; however, when you try to run the class from the command line it will say no main() method exists.

Constructor Method

When a class is first instantiated, the first method to be invoked is always the *constructor*.

```
class DataServer{
    public String serverName;
    public DataServer () {
        serverName = "Customer Service";
    }
}
```

The constructor is typically responsible for initializing variables. If no constructor method is present for a class, Java uses the default constructor from the superclass. (Remember, if no superclass is specified then the class Object is the superclass by default.)

Constructors are different from normal methods in some important ways:

■ The method name is the same as the class name.

■ The return is implicitly *this* (more on *this* later) and no return type is specified.

■ Constructors can't be inherited as other superclass methods are.

■ The constructor method can't be final, abstract, synchronized, native, or static.

There are times when you will need to manually invoke the constructor of the superclass to initialize first, followed by the constructor of the subclass. This can be accomplished by using the keyword *super().*

```
class DataServer extends Server{
    public String serverName;
    public DataServer (int startCode) {
        super(startCode);
        serverName = "Customer Service";
    }
}
```

FROM THE CLASSROOM

Coding Within the Main Method

Students of the Java language will often run into problems when they try to code within the main method. The compiler starts to say funny things such as, "Can't make a static reference to a non-static variable." This is because the main() method is static, and therefore any methods or variables used by the main() method must also be static. Any methods it tries to use that are not static will cause problems. For example, in the following example, the main() method will try to change the value of a variable defined outside of the main() method:

```
class DataClient {
    int users;
    public static void
main(String [] args) {
        users += 1;
// Non-static variable manipulated
// in static method
    }
}
```

When we try to compile the preceding code, we get the following:

```
c:\Java Projects\Client>javac
DataClient.java
DataClient.java:4: Can't make a
static reference to nonstatic
variable users in class
DataClient.
        users += 1;
1 error
c:\Java Projects\Client>
```

The preferred solution is not to start making everything static (this works but is messy), but rather to create an instance of the class in which the main() method resides. The following code shows a class that makes an instance of itself:

```
class DataClient {
    int users;
    public static void
main(String [] args) {
        DataClient client = new
DataClient();
        client.users += 1;
    }
}
```

—Brian Bagnall,
Sun Certified Programmer for Java

The super() command must be the first line of your constructor method, otherwise the compiler will generate an error. It must also appear in a constructor method; only a constructor may invoke another constructor explicitly. Chapter 2 will discuss constructors in more depth.

Variable Declarations and Identifiers

A *reference variable,* or *variable of reference type,* indicates the location of an object or contains null, meaning it currently refers to no object. It is the location referred to that actually holds the object data. A variable of primitive type, or a primitive variable, is different in that it always holds an actual value itself. A variable declaration is used to assign a variable name to an object or primitive type. The following is an example of a variable declaration at class level and local level:

```
public class Variables {
    public static int users; // Declares an integer named 'users'
    public Variables() {
        int port; // Local variable
    }
}
```

The preceding code sets up a variable of primitive type integer, and assigns memory to store the integer number. Variables may be declared within the curly braces of a class or a method, as the variable *port* is in the example.

The following are the keywords that may be used in declaring a variable:

1. public, private, protected, or none (default)
2. final, static, transient, and volatile (optional)
3. variable type
4. identifier

A *local variable* is a variable declared within a method. These are also known as *automatic variables.* Local variables may only include variable type, identifier, and final. A declaration can also initialize the variable, although for class members this is normally done in the constructor method.

```
public int users = 10; // Declares and initializes an integer
```

Final variables must be initialized only once, because a final variable cannot be changed after it is declared.

Several variables may be declared in the same statement when they are of the same type. This is accomplished by placing a comma after each identifier. For example, we can declare three integers: a, b, and c.

```
int a = 3, b, c = a;
```

Keep in mind that variables cannot be synchronized, abstract, or native. We can declare an object variable. Objects do not have to be initialized, but we will show it being initialized, as in the following example:

```
public Dimension = new Dimension(20,100);
```

The preceding code invokes the constructor method, Dimension(), which initializes an object of type Dimension using the arguments contained in the brackets.

String objects have a special place in the Java language. Strings can be declared in the normal way using *new*, or they can be declared without using a constructor, as in the following example:

```
private String name = "Robert A. Heinlein";
```

CERTIFICATION OBJECTIVE 1.03

Import Statements

All public classes that are in the classpath are accessible to our program, but using an *import* statement allows us to use shorthand in our source code so that we don't have to type a fully qualified name for each class we use. An import statement allows us to individually select classes within a package, or select an entire package of classes that we may use in our code. An import statement appears after any package statement and before any class definitions.

```
import java.util.Dictionary;
```

The preceding code allows us to refer to the class java.util.Dictionary by the abbreviated name Dictionary. We can also import all the classes within a package in one statement.

```
import javax.swing.event.*;
```

You might think it is possible to import every core application programming interface (API) package with the following statement:

```
import java.*;
```

This example will compile, and it will try to import any classes within the directory java. It will not, however, import any of the packages located in subdirectories of java. In the preceding instance, there are no classes located directly in the Java package, therefore nothing will be imported.

It is possible to use a class from a package without using the import statement, but you must specifically drill down through the packages to it.

```
java.util.Date now = new java.util.Date();
```

It is also possible for two classes to belong to different packages but have the same name. In this case it is necessary to discriminate between the two by drilling down with the exact package and class name, as shown earlier, otherwise Java will use the first class it comes upon in the classpath setting.

The java.lang package is imported automatically, making it unnecessary to add an import statement for this particular package.

CERTIFICATION OBJECTIVE 1.04

Java Programming Language Keywords and Identifiers

An identifier is a sequence of upper and lower case letters, digits, the underscore (_) and the dollar sign ($). An identifier must not begin with a digit and may not be a keyword (explained below), true, false or null. *Keywords* are special reserved words in Java. Table 1-1 contains all 47 of the reserved keywords.

These must be memorized for the test. Notice none of the reserved words have capital letters; this is a good first step when weeding out nonkeywords on the exam. You are probably familiar with most of them, but we'll review them anyway. Learning them in their categories makes it easier to memorize them all.

Access Modifiers

The following are access modifiers:

- **private** Makes a method or variable accessible only from within its own class.

abstract	boolean	break	byte	case	catch
char	class	const	continue	default	do
double	else	extends	final	finally	float
for	goto	if	implements	import	instanceof
int	interface	long	native	new	package
private	protected	public	return	short	static
super	switch	synchronized	this	throw	throws
transient	try	void	volatile	while	

TABLE 1-1

Complete List of Java Keywords

- **protected**   Makes a method or variable accessible to classes in the same package or subclasses of the class.

- **public**   Classes outside the package can access the class, methods, or variables.

Class, Method, and Variable Modifiers

The following are class, method, or variable modifiers:

- **abstract**   A method or class that cannot be instantiated, and which may define methods to be overwritten.

- **class**   Keyword used to specify a class.

- **extends**   Used to indicate the superclass that a subclass is extending.

- **final**   Makes it impossible to extend a class, override a method, or reinitialize a variable.

- **implements**   Used to indicate the interfaces that a class will use.

- **interface**   Keyword used to specify an interface.

- **native**   Indicates a method is written in a platform-dependent language, such as C.

- **new**   Used to instantiate an object by allocating storege for the instance and invoking the constructor method.

- **static**   Makes a method or variable belong to an entire class, not just a particular instance of the class (object).

- **synchronized** Indicates that a method can be accessed by only one thread at a time.

- **transient** Indicates which variables are not to have their data written to an ObjectStream.

- **volatile** Indicates the variables may change out unexpectedly.

Control Flow

The following are keywords used to control the flow through a block of code:

- **break** Exits from the block of code in which it resides.

- **case** Executes a block of code, dependent on what the switch tests for.

- **continue** Stops the rest of the code following this statement from executing in a loop and then begins the next iteration of the loop.

- **default** Executes this block of code if none of the switch-case statements match.

- **do** Performs a block of code one time, then, in conjunction with the *while* statement, it performs a test to see if the block should be executed again.

- **else** Executes an alternate block of code if an *if* test is false.

- **for** Used to perform a conditional loop for a block of code.

- **if** Used to evaluate a statement and determine if the result is true or false.

- **instanceof** Determines if an object is an instance of a class or any subclass of the class.

- **return** Returns from a method without executing any code that follows the statement (can optionally return a variable).

- **switch** Indicates the variable to be compared with the case statements.

- **while** Executes a block of code repeatedly while a certain condition is true.

Error Handling

The following are keywords used in error handling:

- **catch**   Declares the block of code used to handle an exception.
- **finally**   Block of code usually following a try-catch statement that is executed no matter what program flow occurs when dealing with an error.
- **throw**   Used to pass an exception up to the method that called this method.
- **throws**   Indicates the method will pass an exception to the method that called it.
- **try**   Block of code that will be tried, but which may cause an exception.

Package Control

The following are keywords used for package control:

- **import**   Statement to import packages or classes into code.
- **package**   Specifies to which package all classes in a source file belong.

Primitives

The following keywords are primitives:

- **boolean**   Boolean literals indicating true or false.
- **byte**   8-bit integer.
- **char**   stores one Unicode character.
- **double**   64-bit floating-point number.
- **float**   32-bit floating-point number.
- **int**   32-bit integer.

- **long**   64-bit integer.
- **short**   16-bit integer.

Variable Keywords

The following keywords are variables:

- **super**   Reference variable referring to the immediate superclass.
- **this**   Reference variable referring to the current instance of an object.
- **void**   Indicates no return type for a method.

Unused Keywords

Two keywords are reserved in Java but are not used. If you try to use one of these reserved keywords, the Java compiler will produce the following:

```
KeywordTest.java:4: 'goto' not supported.
                goto MyLabel;
1 error
```

- **const**   Do not use to declare a constant; use public static final.
- **goto**   Not implemented in the Java language.

You may notice *null, true,* and *false* do not appear anywhere on the list. According to the Java Language Specification these are technically literal values and not keywords. A literal is much the same as a number or any other value. If we try to create an identifier with one of these literal values we will receive errors.

```
class LiteralTest {
    public static void main (String [] args) {
        int true = 100; // this will cause error
    }
}
```

Compiling this code gives us the following error:

```
c:\Java Projects\LiteralTest>javac LiteralTest.java
LiteralTest.java:3: Invalid expression statement.
```

```
                       int true = 100;
  ..
```

In other words, trying to assign a value to *true* is much like saying:

```
int 200 = 100;
```

exam
ⓦatch

The Sun Certified Programmer for Java 2.0 exam is difficult to pass. It is possible for people who are excellent Java programmers with years of experience under their belts to fail the exam because they were not prepared for the level of detail that the exam requires. I can't emphasize how picky the exam can be with details. The difference between right and wrong is sometimes determined by whether or not a single letter is capitalized.

CERTIFICATION OBJECTIVE 1.05

Using a Variable or Array Element That Is Uninitialized and Unassigned

As noted previously, when declaring a variable, Java gives us the option of initializing the variable or leaving it uninitialized. If we then attempt to use the uninitialized variable we will get different behavior. This behavior depends on what type of variable or array we are dealing with (primitives or objects). The behavior also depends on the level at which we are declaring our variable. An *instance variable* is declared at class level, whereas a *local variable* is declared at method level. The Java compiler will produce an error if you try to use a local (automatic) variable without initializing it with a value, as we shall see.

Primitive Type and Object Type Class Members

Class members are variables defined at the class level. These include both instance variables and class (static) variables.

Primitive Type Class Members

In the following example, the integer *year* is defined as a class member because it is within the initial curly braces of the class and not within a method's curly braces.

```
public class BirthDate {
    int year;
    public static void main(String [] args) {
        BirthDate bd = new BirthDate();
        bd.showYear();
    }
    public void showYear() {
        System.out.println("The year is " + year);
    }
}
```

When the program is started, it gives the variable *year* a value of zero. All class level primitives are assigned a default value. Of the eight primitives, the six number primitives are given a value of zero, the boolean primitive is given a value of false, and the char primitive is given the Unicode character of /u0000, which is a blank space by default.

on the **job**

It is a good idea to initialize all your variables, even if you are assigning them with the default value. It makes your code easier to read and it appears more logical to another programmer.

Object Class Members

Objects are a completely different story when they are not initialized (or instantiated). Let's look at the following code:

```
import java.util.Date;
public class BirthDate {
    static Date birthDay;
    public static void main(String [] args) {
        System.out.println("The year is " + birthDay.getYear());
    }
}
```

This code will compile fine. However, when we try to run the BirthDate class, the Java interpreter will produce the following error:

```
c:\Java Projects\BirthDate>java BirthDate
java.lang.NullPointerException
        at BirthDate.main(BirthDate.java:5)
```

The reason we get this error is because the reference variable birthDay does not point to any data. The constructor for the class BirthDate has not been executed, and therefore no object has been instantiated. We can check to see if an object has been instantiated by using the keyword *null*, as the following revised code shows:

```
import java.util.Date;
public class BirthDate {
      static Date birthDay;
      public static void main(String [] args) {
          if (birthDay != null)
              System.out.println("The year is " + birthDay.getYear());
      }
}
```

The preceding code checks to make sure birthDay is not null, and if so, it will attempt to use the getYear() method.

Array Class Members

The third type of entity we will examine is the array. An array is essentially an object. We initialize an array in a different manner from an object or a primitive, but in effect it is doing much the same work as the constructor for an object. Much like an object, it is possible to declare an array without initializing it, but if this is done the array will be unusable.

```
public class BirthDate {
      static int [] year;
      public static void main(String [] args) {
          if(year == null)
              System.out.println("The array year[] is null.");
      }
}
```

When the preceding class is executed we get the following:

```
c:\Java Projects\BirthDate>java BirthDate
The array year[] is null.
```

Much like a normal object, an uninitialized array object equals null. But if we initialize an array, what happens to the objects contained in the array? Objects will equal null if they are not initialized individually with values. If primitives are contained in an array, they will be given their respective default values. For example, in the following code the array year[] will contain 100 integers that all equal zero by default.

```
public class BirthDays {
    static int [] year = new int[100];
    public static void main(String [] args) {
        for(int i=0;i<100;i++)
            System.out.println("year[" + i + "] = " + year[i]);
    }
}
```

If the preceding code is executed, it will produce output that indicates all 100 integers in the array equal zero.

Local (Automatic) Primitives and Objects

Local variables, otherwise knows as automatic variables, are defined within a method.

Local Primitives

In the following year 2000 simulator, the integer year is defined as an automatic variable because it is within the curly braces of a method.

```
public class Y2K {
    public static void main(String [] args) {
        int year = 2000;
        System.out.println("The year is " + year);
    }
}
```

Okay, so it's not much of a simulator. Local variables, including primitives, must be initialized before you attempt to use them (though not necessarily on the same line of code). Java does not supply locals with a default value, therefore you must explicitly initialize them with a value, as in the preceding example. If you try to use an uninitialized primitive in your code, the Java compiler will generate an error:

```
public class Y2K {
    public static void main(String [] args) {
        int year;
        System.out.println("The year is " + year);
    }
}
```

Compiling produces the following output:

```
c:\Java Projects\Y2K>javac Y2K.java
Y2K.java:4: Variable year may not have been initialized.
            System.out.println("The year is " + year);
1 error
```

To correct our code, we must give the integer year a value. In this updated example, we will declare it on a separate line, which is perfectly valid.

```
public class Y2K {
    public static void main(String [] args) {
        int year;
        int day; // Remains uninitialized
        System.out.println("Happy new year!");
        year = 2000;
        System.out.println("Welcome to the year " + year);
    }
}
```

Notice an integer declared in the preceding example called *day* that is not initialized, yet the code compiled and ran fine. It is legal to declare a local variable without initializing it if you do not use the variable, but let's face it, if you declare an integer you are probably going to be using it. It could be important to know this for the exam, however.

Local Objects

Objects also behave differently when declared within a method. As we saw before, you can get away with leaving an object uninitialized if you check to see if it is equal to null before using it. And even if you don't check, the code will still compile. With local objects, however, any attempt to use the uninitialized object will result in a compiler error:

```
import java.util.Date;
public class Y2K {
    public static void main(String [] args) {
        Date date;
        if (date == null)
            System.out.println("date is null");
    }
}
```

Compiling the code results in the following error:

```
c:\Java Projects\Y2K>javac Y2K.java
Y2K.java:5: Variable date may not have been initialized.
        If (date == null)
1 error
```

If you don't wish to instantiate a local object, you can actually initialize it to equal null by using the null keyword:

```
Date date = null;
```

Local Arrays

Likewise, with arrays we must initialize each variable within the array that we intend to use. Generally this is done within a *for* loop, as in the following:

```
public class Century {
    public static void main(String [] args) {
        int [] year = new int[100];
        for (int i=0;i<50;i++)  // Initializing first 50
            year[i] = 1900 + i;
        System.out.println("year[5] = " + year[5]);
    }
}
```

The preceding example compiles and runs just fine. Notice we are only initializing the first 50 integers in the array year[]. Java allows us to use

individual elements of an array that have been initialized with values, even if the other variables in the array have not been initialized.

CERTIFICATION OBJECTIVE 1.06

Ranges of All Primitive Data Types

You will be required to know the range of the various data types for the exam. This could be quite a task because the primitive *long* has a range of -9,223,372,036,854,775,808 to 9,223,372,036,854,775,807. The good news is you will not have to memorize such ridiculous numbers. There is an easier method to calculate the ranges. First, let's review the concepts involved.

All six number types in Java are signed, meaning they can be negative or positive. Table 1-2 shows the number types with their sizes and ranges. The range for float numbers is complicated to determine, but luckily you do not need to know this range for the exam. For a byte, there are 256 possible numbers (or 2^8). Half of these are negative, one is a zero, and half minus one are positive. We use the formula $-2^{(bits-1)}$ to calculate the negative range, and for the positive range we use $2^{(bits-1)} - 1$.

For boolean types there is not a range. Boolean types are either true or false.

TABLE 1-2	Type	Bits	Bytes	Minimum range	Maximum range
Ranges of Primitive Numbers	byte	8	1	-2^7	$2^7 - 1$
	short	16	2	-2^{15}	$2^{15} - 1$
	int	32	4	-2^{31}	$2^{31} - 1$
	long	64	8	-2^{63}	$2^{63} - 1$
	float	32	4	not needed	not needed
	double	64	8	not needed	not needed

Character types contain a single Unicode character. There are only 256 characters in the ASCII set. Because there are more Unicode characters than ASCII characters, it is necessary to use 2 bytes of data to store a Unicode character. Characters run from \u0000 to \uffff, or 0 to 65535 (2^{16}).

Literal Values for Strings

A string literal is a source code representation of a value of a string. For example, the following is an example of a string literal:

```
"Johan Guttenberg"
"Johan" + " Guttenberg"
"Johan" + b // Not a string literal
```

The third example is not a string literal because it contains a variable, which will be computed at run time.

Literal Values for all Primitive Types

A primitive literal is merely a source code representation of the primitive data types.

Integer Literals

There are three ways to represent integer numbers in the Java language: octal (base 8), decimal (base 10), and hexadecimal (base 16).

OCTAL LITERALS Octal integers use the digits 0 to 7. We can indicate that a number is represented in octal form by placing a zero in front of the number, as follows:

```
class Octal {
    public static void main(String [] args) {
        int five = 06; // Equal to decimal 6
        int seven = 07; // Equal to decimal 7
        int eight = 010; // Equal to decimal 8
        int nine = 011; // Equal to decimal 9
        System.out.println("Octal 010 = " + eight);
    }
}
```

Notice when we get past seven and are out of digits to use (we are only allowed the digits 0 to 7 for octal numbers) we revert back to zero, and one is added to the beginning of the number. You can have up to 21 digits in an octal number, not including the leading zero. If we run the preceding program, it displays the following:

```
Octal 010 = 8
```

DECIMAL LITERALS   Decimal integers need no explanation; you have been using them since grade one or earlier and are quite familiar with the system. In the Java language they are represented as is, with no prefix of any kind.

HEXADECIMAL LITERALS   Hexadecimal numbers are constructed using 16 distinct symbols. Because no one has invented single digit symbols for the numbers 10 to 15, it is necessary to use alphabetic characters to represent these digits.

```
0 1 2 3 4 5 6 7 8 9 a b c d e f
```

Java will accept capital or lowercase letters for the extra digits. You are allowed up to 16 digits in a hexadecimal number, not including the prefix *0x* or the optional suffix extension *L*, which will be explained later. In Table 1-3, let's do a little counting in hexadecimal format to make sure the concept is clear:

TABLE 1-3	Decimal	Hexadecimal
	0	0x0
A Practice Exercise for Counting in Hexadecimal Numbers	9	0x9
	10	0xa
	11	0xb
	15	0xf
	16	0x10
	17	0x11

The following hexadecimal numbers are all legal:

```
class LiteralTest {
    public static void main (String [] args) {
        int x = 0x0001;
        int y = 0x7fffffffffffffff;
        int z = 0xDeadCafe;
        System.out.println("x = " + x + " y = " + y + " z = " + z);
    }
}
```

All three integer literals (octal, decimal, and hexadecimal) are defined as *int* by default, but they may also be specified as *long* by placing a suffix of *L* after the number:

```
long l = 110599L;
```

Floating-Point Literals
Floating-point numbers are defined as a number, a decimal symbol, and more numbers representing the fraction.

```
float f = 11301874.9881024;
```

In the preceding example the number 11301874.9881024 is the literal value. The rest (*float f* = and *;*) have nothing to do with the literal value but have been included to show how it looks in Java code.

Floating-point literals are defined as *double* by default, but if you want to specify in your code a number as *float*, you may attach the suffix *F* to the number. You may also optionally attach a *D* to double literals, but it is not necessary because this is the default behavior.

```
float f = 221194.491122F;
double d = 110599.995011D;
```

Boolean Literals
Boolean literals are the source code representation for boolean values. Boolean values can only be defined as either true or false.

```
boolean t = true;
```

Character Literals

Character literals are represented by a single character in single quotes.

```
char a = 'a';
char b = '@';
```

Optionally, we can use a hexadecimal value by using the escape code \u to represent a character:

```
char question = '\uFFFF'; // A question mark
```

You can also use the escape code \" if you wish to represent quotes.

```
char c = '\"'
```

Now that you are familiar with the basic data types and their ranges, you will be able to identify the proper data type to use in a given situation. Here are some possible scenarios and their answers.

QUESTIONS AND ANSWERS

The number of stars in the universe…	long
For a single multiple choice question on a test, with only one answer allowed…	char
For a single multiple choice question on a test, with more than one answer allowed…	char []
The number of dependents in a household…	byte
The amount of money, in dollars and cents, you plan on having at retirement…	float (or double if you are a CEO of a software company)

Arrays

Arrays are objects in Java that store multiple variables of the same type. As objects, they must first be initialized, otherwise they will equal null. Arrays can also store different types of objects if they are derived from the same superclass. Because all objects derive from the class Object, it is possible to create an array that will store many different types of objects by using casting, as will be demonstrated later in this section.

Declaration

Arrays are declared by stating the type, which can be an object or a primitive, followed by square brackets to the left or right of the identifier.

```
int [] key; // Square brackets before name
int key []; // Square brackets after name
```

We can also declare multidimensional arrays, which are in fact arrays of arrays. This can be done in the following manner:

```
String [][][]occupantName;
String [] occupantName [];
```

The first example is a three-dimensional array and the second is a two-dimensional array. Notice in the second example we have one square bracket before the variable name and one after. This is perfectly legal to the compiler.

Initialization

The most common way to initialize (allocate) an array is by using the *new* keyword, followed by the type, then in square brackets the number of elements in the array.

```
Date [] famousYear = new Date [5];
```

An important fact to remember is the constructor for Date is in no way being executed when the keyword new is used here. All of the Date variables within famousYear are not initialized, and therefore equal to null.

Once an array is initialized, the size of the array can't be changed without some extra code. If I try to reinitialize famousYear to an array of five elements instead of ten, the variable famousYear becomes a brand new empty array.

The individual elements in the array can be accessed with an index number. The index number always begins with zero, so for an array of 10 objects the index numbers will run from 0 to 9. Observe the following code:

```
class Counting {
    public static void main (String [] args) {
        int [] number = new int[10];
        for (int i = 0;i<10;i++)
            number[i] = i + 1;
        System.out.println("number[5] = " + number[5]);
    }
}
```

The preceding code fills an array with the numbers 1 to 10. Study it carefully and try to determine what number[5] equals. Let's execute the class to find out what happens:

```
c:\Java Projects\Counting>java Counting
number[5] = 6
```

Java also allows us to initialize the array size and initialize the values in the array in one line, as the following demonstrates:

```
int [] famousYear = {1912, 1941, 1969, 1984, 1999};
```

This creates an array with five elements, all initialized with values. Notice there is a semicolon after the final curly brace. You can also initialize an array of objects in the same way:

```
Button [] button = {new Button("Open"), new Button("Close")};
```

Normally you use a Vector to store a number of unordered and dissimilar objects, but you can also store random objects in an array by using casting. *Casting* is a way to tell the compiler that an object belongs to a specific subclass. To cast, the subclass name is placed in brackets before the object. Because every object we create eventually is derived from the superclass Object, we can create an array of type Object and throw any object into it.

```
import java.awt.Button;
import java.util.GregorianCalendar;
class ArrayTest {
    public static void main (String [] args) {
        Object [] anyObject = new Object[20];
        anyObject[0] = new Button("Close");
        anyObject[1] = new GregorianCalendar();
        Button b = (Button)anyObject[0];  // Casting to get button object
    }
}
```

The preceding code will create an array capable of holding 20 objects. It places a Button and a GregorianCalendar into the array, then assigns the reference variable *b* to the Button we placed into the array by using casting. I would not recommend storing objects in this manner because it can be very error-prone at run time. In the preceding example, if I tried to cast anyObject[1] into a Button, I would get a run time error.

Length

An array object has an integer variable named *length* that we can access to determine the size of an array. This tells us the dimension of the array, not the number of initialized variables within the array.

```
class ArrayTest {
    public static void main (String [] args) {
        Object [][] anyObject = new Object[20][10];
        System.out.println("anyObject.length = " + anyObject.length);
        System.out.println("anyObject[0].length = " + anyObject[0].length);
        System.out.println("anyObject[1].length = " + anyObject[1].length);
    }
}
```

Notice how we reference the main array without using any square brackets. The output from this class indicates the size of anyObject is 20, and the size of each of the 20 arrays is 10.

EXERCISE 1-3

Creating a Program That Outputs Command-Line Arguments

1. Create a program that outputs every command-line argument, then displays the number of arguments.

2. Your completed program should look something like this:

```
public class MainTest {
    public static void main (String [] args) {
        for (int i = 0;i < args.length;i++) {
            System.out.println(args[i]);
        }
        System.out.println("Total words: " + args.length);
    }
}
```

CERTIFICATION SUMMARY

After absorbing the material in this chapter, you should be familiar with some of the nuances of the Java language. Let's briefly review what you should know for the exam.

Source files contain package declarations, import statements, class definitions, and interface definitions. Classes can be public or default, not private or protected. You should be able to define an interface, and the only interface you need to be able to implement is the java.lang.Runnable interface. Also, you must be able to state the correspondence between an array index value and the corresponding command-line argument passed to main().

There will be at least one question dealing with keywords, so be sure you can identify which are keywords and which aren't. Make sure you are familiar with primitives and the ranges of integer primitives. And, although this isn't Java language specific, you must be able to convert between octal, decimal, and hexadecimal literals. You have also learned about arrays, and how to define and initialize them properly.

For the exam, knowing what you can't do with the Java language is just as important as knowing what you can do. Give the sample questions a try. It should be an eye opener for how difficult the exam can be. Don't worry if you get a lot of them wrong. If you find a topic that you are weak in, it would be well worth your time to target those areas for extra study.

TWO-MINUTE DRILL

❑ A source file declares a package, imports packages, and defines classes (in this order).

❑ Packages must be contained in the same directory structure as the package name.

❑ Only one public class can exist in a single source file.

❑ All methods in an interface must be created in a class implementing the interface.

❑ A Runnable thread is started by creating a Thread instance using the Runnable object as an argument, then invoking the start() method of the Thread instance.

❑ Methods can be public, private, protected, or none (default). They may also be abstract, final, native, static, and/or synchronized.

❑ The first argument from a command line passed to main() is index 0 in the array.

❑ There is no return type for a constructor method (not even void).

❑ Local (automatic) variables cannot be public, private, protected, static, final, transient, or volatile.

❑ The '*' symbol can be used to import all classes in a specific package.

❑ Memorize all keywords, and remember: true, false, and null are not keywords.

❑ Primitive class members are initialized with a default value, but not automatic variables.

❑ The range of integer types is from $-2^{(bits-1)}$ to $2^{(bits-1)} - 1$.

❑ You must understand octal, decimal, and hexadecimal numbering systems.

❑ When an array is initialized, objects within the array are not instantiated and therefore equal null. Primitive class variables are given a default value

SELF TEST

The following questions will help you measure your understanding of the material presented in this chapter. Read all of the choices carefully, as there may be more than one correct answer. Choose all correct answers for each question.

1. The following source file is given the name FirstClass.java.

   ```
   import java.*;
   public class FirstClass {}
   public interface Second {}
   abstract class SecondClass {}
   ```

   What error will the compiler likely generate?

   A. Package java not found in import.

   B. Public class FirstClass must be defined in a file called "FirstClass.java".

   C. Public interface Second must be defined in a file called "Second.java".

   D. Class SecondClass may not be defined as abstract.

   E. None. The file will compile fine.

2. You have just entered some Java code into a source file. You now wish to save and compile it. Which of the following will work? (Choose all that apply.)

   A. Save it in a file called MyClass.jav and compile with javac MyClass.jav.

   B. Save it in a file called 1999Work.java and compile with javac 1999Work.java.

   C. Save it in a file called MyClass.java and compile with javac MyClass.

   D. Save it in a file called MyClass.java and compile with javac MyClass.java.

3. Examine the following code:

   ```
   import java.util.Vector;
   public Vector v = new Vector();
   class Test {
       public static void main (String [] args) {
           System.out.println("Good luck");
       }
   }
   ```

   What will happen if we try to compile and run this code?

   A. The code will compile and run fine.

   B. The code will compile fine, but an error will occur when the class is instantiated.

   C. The code won't compile.

4. You have just created a few classes in a source file called Server.java. There is a main class called Server, which begins the program. The top of this file has the line:

   ```
   package com.syngress;
   ```

   The classpath environment setting is properly set so it will look in c:\Java Packages for packages, and there is a subdirectory structure of c:\Java Packages\com\syngress\Server. Which of the following procedures will work?

   A. You place the classes in the directory Server, and type the following:

   ```
   c:\Java Packages\com\syngress\Server>java Server
   ```

   B. You place the classes in the directory syngress, and type the following:

   ```
   c:\Java Packages\com\syngress\Server>java com.syngress.Server
   ```

   C. You place the classes in the directory syngress, and type the following:

   ```
   c:\Java Packages\com\syngress>java Server
   ```

   D. You place the classes in the directory Server, and type the following:

   ```
   c:\>java com.syngress.Server
   ```

   E. None of the above.

5. Which of the following top-level class definitions are legal? (Choose all that apply.)

   A. private class A {}
   B. class B {}
   C. public class C {}
   D. final class Class {}
   E. abstract class E;
   F. final abstract class F {}

6. Which of the following interface declarations are legal?

   A. public interface A {int a();}
   B. public interface B implements A {}
   C. interface C {int a;}
   D. private interface D {}
   E. abstract interface E {}

7. You have just created a class that extends a Runnable interface.

   ```
   public class Century implements Runnable {
       public void run () {
           for (int year = 1900;year < 2000;year++) {
               System.out.println(year);
               try {Thread.sleep(1000);} catch(InterruptedException e) {}
   ```

```
            }
            System.out.println("Happy new millennium!");
        }
    }
    class CountUp {
        public static void main (String [] args) {
            Century ourCentury = new Century();
            // INSERT POINT
        }
    }
```

You now wish to begin the thread from another class. Which is the proper code, placed in the second class at the insert point, to begin the thread?

A. Thread t = new Thread(this);
   t.start();

B. Thread t = new Thread(ourCentury);
   ourCentury.start();

C. Thread t = new Thread(this);
   t.start(ourCentury);

D. Thread t = new Thread(this);
   ourCentury.run();

E. Thread t = new Thread(ourCentury);
   t.start();

8. Which of the following methods will compile properly when inserted into a class? (Choose all that apply.)

A. public static final synchronized getPrice() {}

B. public abstract int getPrice();

C. public static final int getPrice() {}

D. public final static int getPrice(int unit) {}

E. protected volatile int getPrice() {}

F. protected int static getPrice(int unit) {}

9. We would like to create a valid main() method that we can use to start a class from the command line. Which of these candidates will work? (Choose all that apply.)

A. static public void main(String [] args) {}

B. public static int main(String [] args) {}

C. public static void main(String args []) {}

D. public static void main(String [] contract) {}

10. A summer student has just finished creating a class and wants you to review it:

```
class DataServer extends Server{
    public String serverName;
    public DataServer () {
        serverName = "Customer Service";
        super(serverName);
    }
}
```

What do you tell the programmer?

A. The code will compile and run fine.

B. The code will compile fine, but an error will occur when the class is instantiated.

C. The code won't compile because the String serverName must be static.

D. The code won't compile because of something in the DataServer() method.

11. Which of the following variable definitions are legitimate if it is an instance variable? (Choose all that apply.)

A. protected int a;

B. transient int b = 3;

C. public static final int c;

D. volatile int d;

E. private synchronized int d;

12. Which one of these contains only Java keywords?

A. class, Thread, void, long, if, continue

B. goto, instanceof, native, finally, default, throws

C. try, redo, throw, final, volatile, transient

D. true, throws, super, implements, do

E. null, byte, break, switch

13. Study the following class definition carefully:

```
public class Test {
    public int t = 4;
    public static void main (String [] args) {
        new Test().NumberPlay();
    }
    public void NumberPlay() {
        int t = 2;
```

```
                  t = t + 5;
                  this.t = this.t - 2;
                  t = t - this.t;
                  System.out.print(t + " ");
                  System.out.println(this.t);
              }
          }
```

What is the output of this code going to be?

A. 2 5

B. −9 0

C. 0 −9

D. 5 2

E. 7 2

F. 2 7

14. Assuming the array is declared as a class member, which of the following will declare an array of five elements?

A. int [] a = {23, 22, 21, 20, 19}

B. int [] array;

C. int array [] = new int[5];

D. int a [] = new int(5);

15. Examine the following code:

```
public class LocalTest {
     public static void main(String [] args) {
          int i;
          System.out.print("int i = " + i);
          i = 20;
     }
}
```

If you try to compile and run this class, what will happen?

A. It will compile, but will produce an interpreter error when executed.

B. It will compile and output '0' to the screen.

C. It will not compile and will give a compiler error.

D. None of the above.

16. Your manager has given you some insect population data.
    Bees: 48057800
    Ants: 2147483648
    Spiders: 12934853
    Mosquitoes: 35247914580
    You are thinking of using the int data type to store these figures. Determine which of these insect populations could be stored in an int type.

    A. Spiders
    B. Bees, Spiders
    C. Bees, Spiders, Ants
    D. Mosquitoes, Bees, Spiders, and Ants

17. Examine the following code:

    ```
    public class CheckDefault {
        private static boolean test;
        public static void showTest() {
            System.out.println(test);
        }
    }
    ```

    If we invoke the static method showTest(), what will the output be?

    A. true
    B. false
    C. none, the class will not compile

18. Here are two literal numbers: 0x001B and 033. What are these numbers equal to?

    A. 21 and 33
    B. 21 and 27
    C. 27 and 33
    D. 33 and 33
    E. 27 and 27

19. We are given a two-dimensional array named a with the hypothetical dimensions x by y. In this example, x represents the size of the first array, and y represents the size of the second dimension of arrays. The value of x is 10. Which of the following can we use to determine the value of y?

    A. a.length();
    B. a.size();

C. a[0].length;

D. a.length(10);

E. a[].length;

20. Examine the following code:

```
import java.util.Date;
public class Y2K {
    public static void main(String [] args) {
        Date date;
        if (date == null)
            System.out.println("date is null");
    }
}
```

What will happen when we try to compile and run this class?

A. It will compile, but will produce an interpreter error when executed.

B. It will compile and output *date is null* to the screen.

C. It will not compile and will give a compiler error.

D. None of the above.

2

Declarations and Access Control

After wading through the material so far, you should have a good understanding of what kind of knowledge is required for the exam. We touched briefly on declaring classes, methods, and variables and their modifiers in Chapter 1. In this chapter we will go more in depth on how these modifiers affect access control, and their relationships with packages. We will also examine default constructors and legal return types in methods.

Class Modifiers and Access Control

What does it mean to access a class? When we say a class has access to another class, it means it has the ability to do one of three things:

- Create an instance of another class
- Extend a class
- Access methods and variables within the class

In effect, to have access means the class is visible. And, of course, each class determines individually which methods and variables within it may be accessed.

Default Access

A class with default access needs no modifier preceding it in the declaration. Default access allows other classes within the same package to have visibility to this class. Examine the following source file:

```
import certification.SuperClass;
class SubClass extends SuperClass{
    static public void main(String [] args) {
        System.out.println("SubClass.");
    }
}
```

Examine the second source file:

```
package certification;
class SuperClass{
    static public void main(String [] args) {
        System.out.println("SuperClass!");
    }
}
```

As you can see, we have a superclass that resides in a different package from the subclass. The subclass has no package declaration, therefore it is placed into an unnamed default package. The import statement at the top of the SubClass file is attempting to import the SuperClass class. The superclass belongs to the certification package, and it compiles fine. Watch what happens when we try to compile the SubClass file:

```
c:\Java Projects\Package>javac Package.java
Package.java:1: Can't access class
certification.SuperClass. Class or interface must be
public, in same package, or an accessible member class.
import certification.SuperClass;
..
```

This example does not work because the superclass is in a different package from the subclass. There are two ways to make this work. We could leave both classes as default access and add SubClass to the package certification. The other way is to declare SuperClass as public, as we shall see.

Public Access

The *public* keyword placed in front of a class allows all classes from all packages to have access to a class. It is still necessary to import the class with the import statement if it belongs to another package, but otherwise it is completely usable by all other classes.

In the example from the preceding section we may not wish to place the subclass in the same package as the superclass. To make the code work, all we need to do is add the keyword *public* in front of the SuperClass declaration, as follows:

```
package certification;
public class SuperClass{
    static public void main(String [] args) {
```

```
            System.out.println("SuperClass!");
        }
    }
```

This changes the SuperClass class so it will be visible to all classes in all packages. The class can now be instantiated and extended from all other classes.

Final Classes

The *final* keyword restricts a class from being extended by another class. If you try to extend a final class, the Java compiler will give an error. We can modify the SuperClass code by placing the keyword final in the declaration:

```
package certification;
public final class SuperClass{
    static public void main(String [] args) {
        System.out.println("SuperClass!");
    }
}
```

Now, if we try to compile the SubClass code as it appeared earlier, we receive the following:

```
c:\Java Projects\Access>javac SubClass.java
SubClass.java:3: Can't subclass final classes: class
certification.SuperClass class SubClass extends
SuperClass{
1 error
```

As we can see, the compiler will not allow a final class to be extended.

Abstract Classes

An *abstract class* is a type of class that is not allowed to be instantiated. The only reason it exists is to be extended. Abstract classes generally contain methods and variables common to all the subclasses, but the abstract class itself is of a type that will not be used. For example, we can make an abstract class called Furniture and a subclass of Furniture called Chair. Examine the following abstract class:

```
abstract class Furniture {
    private double price;
    public static final double TAX = 0.14;
    public double getCost() {
        double cost = price + (price * TAX);
        return cost;
    }
// Additional code goes here
}
```

The preceding code will compile fine. However, if you try to initialize the class Furniture you will receive a compiler error, as follows:

```
AbstractClass.java:7: class certification.SuperClass is
an abstract class. It can't be instantiated.
            AbstractClass a = new AbstractClass();
1 error
```

You may also create functional methods within an abstract class, or specify certain methods as abstract, which we will see later in this chapter. Abstract classes may not be declared as final, because an abstract class exists only to be extended (the final keyword would prevent the class from being extended).

EXERCISE 2-1

Creating an Abstract Superclass and Subclass

The following exercise will test your knowledge of public, protected, final, and abstract classes. Create an abstract superclass named Fruit and a subclass named Apple. The superclass should belong to a package called *food* and the subclass can belong to the default package. Make the superclass public and give the subclass default protection.

1. Create the superclass as follows:
   ```
   package food;
   public abstract class Fruit{ // any code you want}
   ```

2. Create the subclass in a separate file as follows:
   ```
   import food.Fruit;
   class Apple extends Fruit{ // any code you want}
   ```

3. Create a directory called *food* off the directory in your class-path setting.

4. Attempt to compile the two files.

Method and Variable Access Control

Access control can be a difficult concept to learn because there are a lot of factors and combinations of factors that can make a difference in which members can be accessed. These concepts are essential to know for the certification exam.

Methods and variables are collectively known as *members*. Because method and variable members are protected in exactly the same way, I will explain them in the same section.

There are four types of member access control:

■ Public

■ Private

■ Protected

■ Default

Default protection is achieved by using no access modifier in the member declaration. The default and protected access control types have almost identical behavior, except for one difference that will be mentioned later.

exam
⚠ atch

It is very important to know access control inside and out for the exam. There are at least five questions that will deal specifically with this topic. Each question will test several concepts of access control at the same time, so not knowing one small part of access control could blow an entire question.

What does it mean for a class to have access to members of another class? For now, ignore any differences between methods and variables. If a class has access to another member, it means it is visible to it. When a class has no access to another member, the compiler will behave as though the member you are attempting to reference does not exist (even though it is only hidden).

There are two types of accessing that we must look at. One type is when a method tries to access a method or a variable of a class or object. The following class shows a method trying to access an instance member. As we can see, the method showId() is accessing another method, getId(), from an instance of TimeZone (tz).

```
public class InstanceAccess{
     void showId(TimeZone tz) {
          String id = tz.getId();   // method member of
java.util.TimeZone
          System.out.println("The id is " + id);
     }
}
```

The second type of access that we are concerned with is when a class extends another class. A subclass can access certain members of the superclass, depending on what the protection is on those members.

Table 2-1 shows that different modifiers can control access to a class member based on whether the class belongs to the same package or a different package. The third and fourth columns show whether the subclass can access the member of the superclass. As was explained earlier, if the class itself can't be accessed then no members within it can be accessed either. The information in this table will be discussed in depth later.

TABLE 2-1   Access to Class Members

Access Modifier	Instance in Same Package	Instance in Different Package	Subclass in Same Package	Subclass in Different Package
public	yes	yes	yes	yes
private	no	no	no	no
protected	yes	no	yes	yes
default	yes	no	yes	no

exam
ⓦatch

Often, new students of Java wonder what the effects are of different combinations of class and member access (such as a private class with a public variable). The solution to this is to first look at the access level of the class. If the class itself will not be visible to another class, then none of the members will be either, even if the member is declared public. Once it is confirmed that the class is visible, then it is okay to look at access levels on individual members.

Public Members

When a method or variable member is declared public, it means all other classes, regardless of the package that they belong to, can access the member (assuming the class itself is visible). Examine the following source file:

```
import certification.OtherClass;
class AccessClass {
    static public void main(String [] args) {
        OtherClass o = new OtherClass();
        o.testIt();
    }
}
```

Examine the second file:

```
package certification;
public class OtherClass {
    public void testIt() {
        System.out.println("OtherClass");
    }
}
```

As you can see, these classes are in different packages. However, because the method testIt() is declared public, the first class can invoke the method without any problems.

When a member is declared public, it can also be accessed directly from a subclass as though it belonged to the class itself. Examine the following code:

```
package certification;
public class SuperClass {
    public int x = 9;
}
```

This code declares the integer member *x* as public. Now we can use this member in any subclass, even if it is in a different package.

```
package other;
class SubClass extends SuperClass {
    public void testIt() {
        System.out.println("Variable x is " + x);
    }
}
```

Notice that in the preceding code the variable *x* is used without having to preface it with the keyword super.

exam
ⓦatch

Students of the Java language often wonder how the protection of the class or method doing the accessing affects accessing a member. The answer is simple: the access level of the class or method doing the accessing has no effect on accessing members. In the preceding example, notice that SubClass is given default access. This means it will not be visible to other packages. However, because SuperClass has no need to see SubClass, this does not cause any problems. The access level of a subclass is irrelevant.

Private Members

Private members can't be accessed by any class other than the class in which it is declared. The *private* keyword essentially makes the variable or method invisible to all but itself. Let's make a small change to OtherClass from an earlier example.

```
package certification;
public class OtherClass {
    private void testIt() { // Changed access to private
        System.out.println("OtherClass");
    }
}
```

Line three now declares the method testIt() as private, so no other class may use it. If we try to compile the first source file, we now get the following compiler error:

```
c:\Java Projects\Access>javac AccessClass.java
AccessClass.java:5: No method matching testIt() found in
class certification.OtherClass.
                o.testIt();
1 error
```

As you can see, it is as though the method testIt() does not exist.

Now what about a subclass trying to access a private member? When a member is declared private, it can't be accessed from a subclass.

```
package certification;
public class SuperClass {
    private int x = 9; // Declared private
}
```

The altered code now declares the integer *x* as private. The variable is now off limits to all other subclasses; even those in the same package:

```
package certification; // Same package
class SubClass extends SuperClass {
    public void testIt() {
            System.out.println("Variable x is " + x); //
Won't work
        }
}
```

If we attempt to compile the class SubClass, we will get the following error:

```
c:\Java Projects\certification>javac SubClass.java
SubClass.java:4: Undefined variable: x
            System.out.println("Variable x is " + x);
1 error
```

on the
Job

Java allows variables to be public, but in practice it is often best to keep all variables private except for constants. If variables need to be changed or set, programmers generally use what are known as accessors, or access methods, to modify the variables. The access method is also able to check the new value to ensure that it is legal. All JavaBeans use access methods to change variable values. The concept of combining data and methods together and using access methods to change or read the values of variables is called encapsulation. Chapter 7 will discuss encapsulation in more detail.

Protected and Default Members

Protected members are preceded by the keyword *protected*, but default members have no modifier. Default access is often referred to as *friendly access*, but there is no *friendly* keyword in Java. The protected and default types give almost identical access. A protected member may be accessed only if the class accessing the member belongs to the same package. Examine the following class:

```
import certification.OtherClass;
class AccessClass {
    static public void main(String [] args) {
        OtherClass o = new OtherClass();
        o.testIt();
    }
}
```

Examine the second file:

```
package certification;
public class OtherClass {
    protected void testIt() {
        System.out.println("OtherClass");
    }
}
```

As you can see, the testIt() method in the second file is protected. Also, the first class belongs to a different package from the second class. Will AccessClass be able to use the method testIt()? Let's find out.

```
c:\Java Projects\Access>javac AccessClass.java
AccessClass.java:5: No method matching testIt() found in
class certification.OtherClass.
              o.testIt();
1 error
```

From the results you can see that AccessClass has no visibility to the method testIt() because testIt() is declared with the protected keyword.

Default and protected behavior differs when it comes to subclasses in packages. This difference is rarely used in actual practice, but this does not mean it will be absent from the exam! You will very likely be asked this. Let's now examine the difference between the two.

If the protected keyword is used to define a member, the subclass will be able to access it. It does not matter if the classes are in different packages; it will still be visible. This is in contrast to the default behavior, which will not allow a subclass to access members from the superclass. Let's first look at the protected keyword with superclass members.

```
package certification;
public class SuperClass {
    protected int x = 9; // protected access
}
```

The preceding code now declares the integer *x* as protected. This makes the variable accessible to other classes in the certification package, as well as any subclasses of the SuperClass. Now let's create a subclass and attempt to access the variable *x*.

```
package other; // Different package
import certification;
class SubClass extends SuperClass {
    public void testIt() {
        System.out.println("Variable x is " + x); //
Will work
    }
}
```

The preceding code compiles fine. Now let's take a look at the default behavior of a member with a subclass. We will modify the SuperClass member *x* to make it default.

```
package certification;
public class SuperClass {
    int x = 9; // No access modifier
}
```

Notice we did not place an access modifier in front of the variable *x*. We will now attempt to access it from the SubClass class that we saw earlier. When we compile the SubClass file, we receive the following error:

```
c:\Java Projects\certification>javac SubClass.java
SubClass.java:4: Undefined variable: x
        System.out.println("Variable x is " + x);
1 error
```

The compiler gives the same error when a member is declared as private. This is because SubClass has no visibility to *x* in the superclass. Now what about the default behavior with two classes in the same package?

```
package certification;
public class SuperClass{
    int x = 9;
}
class SubClass extends SuperClass{
    static public void main(String [] args) {
        OtherClass o = new OtherClass();
        o.testIt();
    }
    public void testIt() {
        System.out.println("Variable x is " + x);
    }
}
```

The preceding source file compiles fine, and the class SubClass runs and displays the value of *x*. This proves that default members are visible only to the subclasses that are in the same package.

Methods

For method access, we are referring to the ability of one class to invoke a method from another class. Let's review the other modifiers that apply to methods.

Abstract Methods

An *abstract method* is a method declaration that contains no functional code. The reason for using an abstract method is to ensure that subclasses of this class will include this method. Any class that is not abstract, and therefore capable of being instantiated, must override this method. (Chapter 7 will explore overriding.) A typical abstract method declaration is as follows:

```
public abstract void showSample();
```

Notice that the abstract method ends with a semicolon instead of curly braces. It is illegal to have an abstract method in a class that is not declared abstract. Examine the following illegal class:

```
public class IllegalClass{
    public abstract void doIt();
}
```

The preceding class will produce the following error if you attempt to compile it:

```
c:\Java Projects\abstract>javac IllegalClass.java
IllegalClass.java:1: class IllegalClass must be declared
abstract. It does not define void doIt() from class
IllegalClass.
public class IllegalClass{
1 error
```

You can, however, have an abstract class with no abstract methods. The following example will compile fine:

```
public abstract class LegalClass{ }
```

Final Methods

The final keyword prevents a method from being overridden in a subclass. For this reason, final and abstract may not be used together in a method declaration. A typical final declaration looks like this:

```
class SuperClass{
    public final void showSample() {
        System.out.println("One thing.");
    }
}
```

It is legal to extend SuperClass; however, we will not be allowed to override the method showSample() in our subclass, as the following code attempts to do:

```
class SubClass extends SuperClass{
    public void showSample() {
```

```
            System.out.println("Another thing.");
      }
}
```

Attempting to compile the preceding code gives us the following:

```
c:\Java Projects\final>javac FinalTest.java
FinalTest.java:5: The method void showSample() declared
in class SubClass cannot override the final method of the
same signature declared in class SuperClass. Final
methods cannot be overridden.
      public void showSample() { }
1 error
```

Static Methods

The static keyword declares a method that belongs to a class (as opposed to belonging to an instance). A class method may be accessed directly from a class, without instantiating the class first. Let's look at a class with two methods. One of the methods is static and one is not.

```
class TestStatic {
      public static void greetUser(String name) {
            System.out.println("Good day, " + name);
      }
      public void greetUser2(String name) {
            System.out.println("Good day, " + name);
      }
}
```

The first method is static, and therefore it can be accessed without instantiating the class TestStatic. The second is a normal instance method and can only be invoked on an instance of the class. We also need a class to test this with:

```
public class BookTest {
      public static void main(String [] args) {
            BookTest b = new BookTest();
            b.testMethods();
      }
      public void testMethods() {
            TestStatic.greetUser("Arthur");            // OK
```

```
                    TestStatic.greetUser2("Agatha");          // bad
                    new TestStatic().greetUser(" Arthur "); // OK
                    new TestStatic().greetUser2("Agatha");  // OK
            }
    }
```

If we attempt to compile the second class, we receive the following error:

```
c:\Java Projects\StaticTest>javac BookTest.java
BookTest.java:8: Can't make a static reference to method
void greetUser2(java.lang.String) in class TestStatic.
            TestStatic.greetUser2("Agatha");
    1 error
```

Note that in line nine of the BookTest class, the static method can be called from an instance as well. Line ten shows the greetUser2() method being called from an instance.

Synchronized Methods

The synchronized keyword indicates that a method may be accessed by only one thread at a time. Threads will be discussed more in Chapter 9. A typical statement looks like this:

```
public synchronized int methodName(int id) { }
```

Native Methods

The native keyword indicates that a method is written in a platform-dependent language, such as C. You will not need to know how to use native methods for the exam, other than knowing that *native* is a reserved keyword.

Variables

Variable access refers to the ability of one class to read or alter (if it is not final) a variable in another class.

Instance Variables

Instance variables may be accessed from other methods in the class, or from methods in other classes (depending on the access control).

Instance variables may not be accessed from static methods, however, because a static method could be invoked when no instances of the class exist. Logically, if no instances exist, then the instance variable will also not exist, and it would be impossible to access the instance variable.

Static Variables

A *static variable* exists only once for each instance of the class. If we instantiate the same class ten times as ten different objects and that class contains a static variable, the value of that static variable will be the same in each object and each object can modify that variable. Static variables are also called *class variables*. A static variable, much like a static method, may be accessed from a class directly, even though it has not been instantiated. Examine the following code:

```
class TestServer {
    static int users = 0;
    public void logIn() {
        users += 1;
    }
}
```

This class demonstrates a static variable, *users*. Notice that to modify this static variable, we do not need to use a static method. The variable *users* can be modified in the instance method logIn() without any problems.

Automatic (Method Local) Variables

Automatic variables are variables that are declared within a method and discarded when the method has completed. Automatic variable declarations contain no modifiers (such as public and static), other than the type. Before an automatic variable may be used, it must be initialized with a value.

```
class TestServer {
    public void logIn() {
        int count = 10;
    }
}
```

Typically the variable is initialized in the same line in which the variable is declared, although there can be good reasons for initializing it after some code has run.

An automatic variable may not be referenced anywhere in the code except for within the method in which it is declared. In the preceding code, it would be impossible to refer to the variable *count* anywhere else in the class except within the method logIn().

Final Variables

The final keyword makes it impossible to reinitialize a variable once it has been declared. For primitives, this means the value may not be altered once it is initialized. For objects, the data within the object may be modified, but the reference variable may not be changed. Final variables must be initialized in the same line in which they are declared. Even if the variable is an instance member, it will not take the default value of zero. Examine the following code:

```
class FinalTest{
    final int x; // Will not work
    public void showFinal() {
        System.out.println("Final x = " + x);
    }
}
```

Attempting to compile the preceding code gives us the following:

```
c:\Java Projects\final>javac FinalTest.java
FinalTest.java:2: Blank final variable 'x' may not have
been initialized. It must be assigned a value in an
initializer, or in every constructor.
    final int x;
1 error
```

It is illegal to change the value of a final variable once it is initialized. Let's look at declaring an object variable as final. We will create a class that creates an instance of a date, manipulate data in it, and then try to reinitialize it.

```
import java.util.Date;
 class TestClass {
    final Date d = new Date();
```

```
        public void showSample() {
            d.setYear(2001); // Altering data in instance
        }
    }
```

In line five in the preceding class, the year is modified within the instance. This is perfectly legal, and the class will compile fine because an instance can have its data modified even though it is final. Now let's see what happens when we reinitialize an object.

```
import java.util.Date;
class FinalTest {
    final Date d = new Date();
    public void showSample() {
        d.setYear(2001);
        d = new Date(); // Will not work
    }
}
```

Line seven now tries to reinitialize the variable *d.* If we attempt to compile the preceding class we receive the following error:

```
c:\Java Projects\final>javac FinalTest.java
FinalTest.java:6: Can't assign a value to a final
variable: d
        d = new Date();
1 error
```

As we can see, with final variables, the reference variable may not be changed after it is assigned to an instance.

Transient Variables

The transient keyword indicates which variables are not to have their data written to an ObjectStream. You will not be required to know anything about *transient* for the exam, other than the keyword.

Volatile Variables

The volatile keyword indicates that a variable may change unexpectedly. You will not be required to know anything about *volatile* for the exam, other than the keyword. Please see Chapter 9 for more on using the *volatile* keyword.

Default Constructors

When an object is instantiated, a constructor is always invoked. Java supplies a default no-arguments constructor only if no constructor has been created for the class. If a constructor is created, Java will no longer create a default no-arguments constructor for you.

```
class Constructor {
    public static void main(String [] args) {
        System.out.println("Initializing a new Constructor...");
        Constructor c = new Constructor();
    }
    public Constructor(int i) {
        System.out.println("The Constructor(int i) constructor ran.");
    }
}
```

Notice that in the preceding example we are trying to initialize a constructor with the default Constructor() method. If we try to compile this, the following error occurs:

```
c:\Java Projects\Constructor>javac Constructor.java
Constructor.java:4: No constructor matching Constructor() found in class
Constructor.
            Constructor c = new Constructor();
1 error
```

For now, this is all you need to know about default constructors. Chapter 7 will discuss invoking superclass constructors and overloading constructors.

exam
⑩atch

The only time that a default constructor is supplied for a class is when the programmer has not supplied a constructor. As soon as you supply any constructor with any signature, Java will no longer create a no-arguments default constructor.

EXERCISE 2-2

Creating a Superclass and a Subclass

This exercise will familiarize you with constructor methods. Create a superclass and a subclass. One of the class' constructors will display the word *Hello* and one will display the word *there* to make a coherent greeting

1. Create the superclass as follows:

```
class BaseClass{
    public BaseClass() {
        System.out.print("Hello");
    }
}
```

2. Create the subclass in a separate file, as follows:

```
class SubClass extends BaseClass{
    public SubClass() {
        System.out.print(" there.");
    }
    public static void main(String [] args) {
        SubClass m = new SubClass();
    }
}
```

3. Compile and run the subclass to see if it works.

CERTIFICATION OBJECTIVE 2.04

Legal Return Types

For the exam, you will need to be able to state the legal return types for any method, given the declarations of all related methods in this or parent classes. A *return type* is the variable that a method may return when the method is finished executing. A *declared type* is the type stated in the method declaration. The return type may actually be different from the declared type. A return type is legal if it can be implicitly converted to the declared type. This concept will become clear when we start looking at integer return types. To introduce the concept, we'll start with the boolean primitive.

boolean

If you create a method that returns a type of boolean, the only type of value that can be returned is a boolean. Java will not accept a boolean object, nor an integer value, nor any other type.

char

char is similar to boolean. A method with a return type of char can return only a char value. It is not legal to return a String object containing only one character.

Integer Primitive Types

A method that declares a return type of an integer (int, byte, short, or long) can return only an integer value. Examine the following method:

```
public int getValue() {
        int a = 200;
        return a;
}
```

This is a very simple method that declares the return type as an int type. If we look in the method, we can see it is returning an int variable named *a*. This is all very normal, but we can also return other integer types. Examine the following revised code:

```
public int getValue() {
        byte a = 100;
        return a;
}
```

This method will work just fine in a class. The reason it works is because an int value is larger than a byte; therefore int is able to store a byte value. A short or long type can also store a byte, because they too are larger than a byte.

When a method has a declared type of integer, it can not return a float type (float or double), even if the float has no fraction after the decimal. Examine the following code:

```
public int getValue() {
        float a = 100;
        return a;
}
```

If we insert this method into a class and attempt to compile the code, it will result in the following error:

```
c:\Java Projects\BookTest>javac Return.java
Return.java:4: Incompatible type for return. Explicit
cast needed to convert float to int.
        return a;
1 error
```

Notice that it says an explicit cast may be used. We can actually cast the float into an integer as the following code illustrates:

```
public int getValue() {
        float a = 100;
        return (int)a;
}
```

Casting the variable *a* effectively knocks off any digits after the decimal to give a return type of an int variable.

Table 2-2 shows the integer types that other integer variables can store legally.

exam
ⓦatch

A good way to figure out if an integer return type is legal or not is to think of the number of bits that a primitive can hold. If the bits value of the return type is less than the declared return type, it is legal. Converting a type from one with fewer bits to one with more bits is known as performing a widening conversion, or promoting.

TABLE 2-2

Legal Return Types for Integer Numbers

Declared Type	Legal Return Types
byte	byte
short	byte, short
int	byte, short, int
long	byte, short, int, long

Float Primitive Types

Floating-point return types are slightly more complicated than integer types. A method with a return type of a floating-point number can return integers as well as float types. Examine the following method:

```
public double getValue() {
        long a = 100;
        return a;
}
```

The preceding method declares a return type of double. If we look within the method, however, we see it is actually returning an integer type of long. This works because a double is capable of storing numbers with or without fractions after the decimal. The following table shows the legal return types for floating-point numbers. Notice that a 32-bit float can actually return a 64-bit long. This is because float numbers can be represented exponentially.

Declared type:	Legal return types:
float	byte, short, int, long, float
double	byte, short, int, long, float, double

It is also worth mentioning that a method with a *double* return type can also return a type of *float*. This is because a 64-bit double has enough space to hold a 32-bit float.

```
public double getValue() {
        float a = 8920.12518;
        return a;
}
```

Object Return Types

A method with an object return type can return the same object type, or subclasses of the object. For example, the Component class is a base class for the various AWT components, such as Button, Label, and TextField. We can write a method that declares a return type of Component, as follows:

```
public Component getComponent() {
        Button b = new Button("Close");
        return b;
}
```

As you can see, this method is returning a Button object. You could also create a method that returns any object by using a return type of Object, because every Java class extends the Object class.

String objects operate as any other type of object. You might think that a method with a return type of String could return an array of chars, but in fact it does not. The only objects that a method with a String return type can return are String types, since String cannot be subclassed.

Now that you have a better idea of return types, here are some possible declared types and their possible legal return types.

Declared Type	Possible Legal Return Types
byte	byte is the only one
Object	Absolutely any object, but not a primitive
float	byte, short, int, long, float
Component	Component, Checkbox, Panel, Button, and so on (Refer to the Java Core API specification.)

CERTIFICATION SUMMARY

You now have a good understanding of access control as it relates to classes, methods, and variables. You can also determine which constructor will be invoked for a given class, as well as which return types are legal for a method definition. Let's review what you have learned from this chapter.

Access control is handled differently for classes and members. Classes may only have default or public access. For classes and members, it is important to recognize the package relationships to determine if an entity will be visible. Classes, methods, and variables all have their own modifiers. For the test, be sure that you know which keywords apply to these elements.

There is some overlap, but some keywords (such as synchronized) are for one type of entity only.

The default constructor is the no-arguments constructor that Java creates for you if none is implicitly created by you. Make sure you are comfortable with legal return types for a given method declaration.

TWO-MINUTE DRILL

- ❑ Default class access allows access only to classes in the same package.
- ❑ Public class access opens the class to all other classes.
- ❑ Final classes and methods may not be extended or overridden.
- ❑ Abstract classes may not be instantiated.
- ❑ Public members may be accessed from all other methods.
- ❑ Private members may be accessed only by the class in which the member is declared.
- ❑ Protected members of a class may be accessed only by members of the same package or by subclasses of the class that the member is in. Class members with default, or friendly, access are available only to other members of the same package.
- ❑ Subclasses may access members of the superclass that are public or protected; default and private members can't be accessed.
- ❑ Static methods may not access instance members.
- ❑ If you provide no constructor, Java will supply a no-arguments default constructor.
- ❑ Methods with declared floating-point return types can return any integer type.
- ❑ Methods that return integers can return any type of integer that has the same width (number of bits) or is narrower (has fewer bits) than the declared type.
- ❑ Methods may return subclasses of the declared class type.

SELF TEST

The following questions will help you measure your understanding of the material presented in this chapter. Read all of the choices carefully, as there may be more than one correct answer. Choose all correct answers for each question.

1. A trading firm, Gardener, Ross, and Cunningham, has hired you to improve the code for its systems. They have an object that contains the names of their employees on the trading floor. The company representative, Sally Ross, is interviewing you for some consulting work. She shows you two objects:

```
package payroll;
class EmployeeNames{
    public static String [] names ={"Ian","Paul","Adam","Jansky"};
    public static String [] getNames() {
        return names;
    }
}
```

And the following:

```
package client;
import payroll.EmployeeNames;
class TraderNames extends EmployeeNames{
    public static String [] traders = {"Marty", "Ziggy", "Niko",
"Chris"};
}
```

She would like to know what will happen when these are compiled and instantiated. What do you tell her?

A. The file with class EmployeeNames will not compile.

B. The file with class TraderNames will not compile.

C. The files will both compile, but an error will occur when the class TraderNames is instantiated.

D. The files will compile, and when either class is instantiated, it will work fine.

2. Sally was obviously impressed by your answer and would like you to examine several other prototypes of their objects:

```
package payroll;
final class EmployeeNames{
    public static String [] names = {"Ian","Paul","Adam","Jansky"};
    public static String [] getNames() {
        return names;
```

```
        }
    }
```

And the following:

```
package payroll; // New package
class TraderNames extends EmployeeNames{
    public static String [] Traders = {"Marty", "Ziggy", "Niko",
"Chris"};
    }
```

What do you tell her about the objects this time?

A. The file with class EmployeeNames will not compile.

B. The file with class TraderNames will not compile.

C. The files will both compile, but an error will occur when the class TraderNames is instantiated.

D. The files will compile, and when either class is instantiated, it will work fine.

3. Sally shows you a third prototype for your opinion:

```
package payroll;
class EmployeeNames{
    public static String [] names = {"Ian","Paul","Adam","Jansky"};
    public static String [] getNames() {
        return names;
    }
}
```

And the following:

```
package payroll; // New package
abstract class TraderNames extends EmployeeNames{
    public static String [] Traders = {"Marty", "Ziggy", "Niko",
"Chris"};
    }
```

What will you tell her this time?

A. The file with class EmployeeNames will not compile.

B. The file with class TraderNames will not compile.

C. The files will both compile, but an error will occur when the class TraderNames is instantiated.

D. The files will compile, and when either class is instantiated, it will work fine.

4. Sally pulls a fourth prototype out of her briefcase. You now begin to suspect that this is just a test to see how well you know your stuff.

```
package payroll;
class EmployeeNames{
    private static String [] names = {"Ian","Paul","Adam","Jansky"};
    public static String [] getNames() {
        return names;
    }
}
```

And the following:

```
package payroll; // New package
class TraderNames extends EmployeeNames{
    public static String [] Traders =names;
}
```

What will happen when these classes are compiled and run?

A. The file with class EmployeeNames will not compile.

B. The file with class TraderNames will not compile.

C. The files will both compile, but an error will occur when the class TraderNames is instantiated.

D. The files will compile, and when either class is instantiated, it will work fine.

5. Sally seems very impressed so far, but she wants to be thorough in testing you. She shows you a fifth prototype:

```
package payroll;
public class UserConnection{
    protected final int MAXUSERS = 20;
    public static String getServerName() {
        return "Main Server";
    }
}
```

And the following:

```
package client;
import payroll.UserConnection;
class ServerConnection extends UserConnection{
    public final int MAXCONNECTIONS = MAXUSERS * 10;
}
```

What will happen when these classes are compiled and run?

A. The file with class UserConnection will not compile.

B. The file with class ServerConnection will not compile.

C. The files will both compile, but an error will occur when the class ServerConnection is instantiated.

D. The files will compile, and when either class is instantiated, it will work fine.

6. After your last answer, she throws you a knowing smile and pulls out a sixth piece of Java code:

```
package payroll;
public class UserConnection{
      final int MAXUSERS = 20;
      public static String getServerName() {
            return "Main Server";
      }
}
```

And the following:

```
package client;
import payroll.UserConnection;
class ServerConnection extends UserConnection{
      public final int MAXCONNECTIONS = MAXUSERS * 10;
}
```

What will happen when these classes are compiled and run?

A. The file with class UserConnection will not compile.

B. The file with class ServerConnection will not compile.

C. The files will both compile, but an error will occur when the class ServerConnection is instantiated.

D. The files will compile, and when either class is instantiated, it will work fine.

7. She comments that no applicant has done this well so far, as she pulls out a seventh piece of code for examination.

```
package payroll;
public class UserConnection{
      protected int users = 0;
      public static String getServerName() {
            return "Main Server";
      }
}
```

And the following:

```
package client;
import payroll.UserConnection;
class ServerConnection {
```

```
        UserConnection u = new UserConnection();
        u.users += 1;
    }
```

What will happen when these classes are compiled and run?

A. The file with class UserConnection will not compile.

B. The file with class ServerConnection will not compile.

C. The files will both compile, but an error will occur when the class ServerConnection is instantiated.

D. The files will compile, and when either class is instantiated, it will work fine.

8. Sally nods her head and passes you another. You feel nervous, and wonder how you are doing so far. She promises there are only two more to go.

```
    package server;
    public class ServerNames{
        abstract public static String sendName();
    }
```

What will happen when the class is compiled and run?

A. The file will not compile.

B. The file will compile, but an error will occur when the class ServerNames is instantiated.

C. The file will compile, and when the class is instantiated, it will work fine.

9. Sally hands you the final prototype and leans back in her chair.

```
    package server;
    public class ServerNames{
        protected final int MAXUSERS = 20;
        public final static String sendName() {
            return "Main Server";
        }
    }
```

And the following:

```
    package client;
    import server.ServerNames;
    class Retrieve extends ServerNames{
        public final int MAXCONNECTIONS = MAXUSERS * 10;
        public static String sendName(String s) {
            return s;
        }
    }
```

What will happen when these classes are compiled and run?

A. The file with class ServerNames will not compile.

B. The file with class Retrieve will not compile.

C. The files will both compile, but an error will occur when the class Retrieve is instantiated.

D. The files will compile, and when either class is instantiated, it will work fine.

10. You are creating a small class for a call center. The class will keep track of the number of users who log in.

```
class TestServer {
    static int users = 0;
    public void logIn() {
        users += 1;
    }
}
```

What will happen when this class is compiled and run?

A. The file will not compile.

B. The file will compile, but an error will occur when the class is instantiated.

C. The files will compile, and when either class is instantiated, it will work fine.

11. You try another piece of prototype code to test static members.

```
class TestServer {
    int users = 0;
    static public void logIn() {
        users += 1;
    }
}
```

What will happen when this class is compiled and run?

A. The file will not compile.

B. The file will compile, but an error will occur when the class is instantiated.

C. The files will compile, and when either class is instantiated, it will work fine.

12. Examine the following piece of code:

```
class TestVariable {
    int users = 1;
    public TestVariable() {
        this(2);
```

```
            users += 1;
        }
        public TestVariable(int users) {
            users -= 2;
            this.users += 1;
        }

    }
```

The class is instantiated with the following line of code:

```
    TestVariable t = new TestVariable();
```

What is the value of users after TestVariable has been instantiated?

A. 5

B. 4

C. 3

D. 2

E. 1

F. The class TestVariable will not compile.

13. Examine the following piece of code:

```
    class TestServer {
        public TestServer() {
            int users = 1;
        }
        public void increment() {
            users = users + 1;
        }
        public static void main(String [] args){
            increment();
            System.out.println("Variable users = " + users);
        }
    }
```

What will the output of this class be?

A. Output is 1.

B. Output is 2.

C. The file will compile, but will give an error when run.

D. The file will not compile.

14. Examine the following piece of code:

```
class TestServer {
     static final int users = 20;
     public TestServer() {
          int users = this.users * 10;
     }
     public static void main(String [] args){
          System.out.println("Variable users = " + users);
     }
}
```

What will the output of this class be?

A. Output is 200.

B. Output is 20.

C. The file will compile, but will give an error when run.

D. The file will not compile.

15. Examine the following code:

```
class SuperServer {
     public SuperServer() {
          System.out.print(35);
     }
     public SuperServer(int y) {
          y = y + 2;
          System.out.print(y);
     }
}
class TestServer extends SuperServer{
     public TestServer(int y) {
          y = y * 10;
          System.out.print(y);
     }

     public static void main(String [] args){
          TestServer ts = new TestServer(10);
     }
}
```

What will the output of this class be?

A. 12100

B. 10012

C. 1224

D. 35100

16. Examine the following code:

```
class SuperServer {
    public SuperServer() {
        System.out.print(" all ");
    }
    public SuperServer(int y);
        this();
        System.out.println {" good ");
    }
}
class TestServer extends SuperServer{
    public TestServer(int y) {
        System.out.print(" things ");
    }
    public TestServer() {
        super(10);
        System.out.print(" come ");
    }
    public static void main(String [] args){
        TestServer ts = new TestServer(10);
    }
}
```

What will the output of this class be?

A. good things

B. all things come

C. all things

D. all good things

17. Which of the following methods are legal?

```
class Force
{
    public short Jerec() {
        byte Kyle = 20;
        return Kyle;
    }
    public int Pic() {
        long Gorc = 200;
        return Gorc;
    }
    public Boolean Sariss() {
        boolean Boc = true;
        return Boc;
    }
```

```
        public long Maw() {
            float Yun = 2000F;
            return Yun;
        }
    }
```

A. Jarec

B. Pic

C. Sariss

D. Maw

18. Which of the following methods are legal?

```
    class Music {
        public float airbag() {
            long airbag = 1980;
            return airbag;
        }
        public float paranoidAndroid() {
            double paranoidAndroid = 2056;
            return paranoidAndroid;
        }
        public double subterraneanHomesickAlien() {
            float subterraneanHomesickAlien = 2623.12F;
            return subterraneanHomesickAlien;
        }
        public double letDown() {
            byte letDown = 2000;
            return letDown;
        }
    }
```

A. airbag

B. paranoidAndroid

C. subterraneanHomesickAlien

D. letDown

19. You have created some classes for a supermarket database. The following are some of the classes you have created so far:

```
class Food implements Eatable{}
class Vegetable extends Food {}
class GreenPeas extends Vegetable {}
class Meat extends Food {}
```

You have also programmed a method, as follows:

```
public Vegetable getSomething() {
      // returns something here
}
```

Choose all of the legal lines that could be inserted into the method getSomething().

A. return new Vegetable();

B. return new Food();

C. return new Meat();

D. return new GreenPeas();

20. You have created some classes for a supermarket database. The following are some of the classes you have created so far:

```
class Food{}
class Vegetable extends Food implements Eatable{}
class GreenPeas extends Vegetable {}
class Meat extends Food implements Eatable{}
```

You have also programmed a method as follows:

```
public Eatable getSomething() {
      // returns something here
}
```

Choose all of the legal lines that could be inserted into the method getSomething().

A. return new Vegetable();

B. return new Food();

C. return new Meat();

D. return new GreenPeas();

3

Operators and Assignments

This chapter will thoroughly examine the various operations and comparisons that can be performed on primitives and objects. We will cover the basic mathematical operations that are used on a day-to-day basis, but more importantly we will be reviewing (or more likely introducing) several obscure operations that are guaranteed to be tested on the exam.

CERTIFICATION OBJECTIVE 3.01

Using Operators

Operators produce new values from one or more operands. The result of performing an operator is a *boolean*, a numeric value of type *int* or *long*, or an object of type String.

Assignment Operators

The = sign is used for assigning a value to a variable. When speaking of variable assignments, we must differentiate between objects and primitives.

When assigning an existing instance to a new reference variable, you must keep in mind the two reference variables will point to the same object. Examine the following code:

```
import java.awt.Dimension;
class ReferenceTest {
    public static void main (String [] args) {
        Dimension a = new Dimension(5,10);
        System.out.println("a.height = " + a.height);
        Dimension b = a;
        b.height = 30;
        System.out.println("a.height = " + a.height + "after change to b");
    }
}
```

In the preceding example, a Dimension object, *a*, is declared and initialized with a width of 5 and a height of 10. Next, Dimension *b* is declared as a reference to *a*. Finally, the height property is changed using the *b* reference. Now think for a minute: Is this going to change the height property of *a* as well? Keep in mind that variables for objects are merely pointers to the actual object itself. Let's see what the output will be:

```
c:\Java Projects\Reference>java ReferenceTest
a.height = 10
a.height = 30 after change to b
```

From this output we can conclude that both variables point to the same instance of the class Dimension. When we made a change to *b*, the height property was also changed for *a*.

It is important to differentiate how String objects behave. Examine the following code:

```
class Strings {
    public static void main(String [] args) {
        String x = "Java";
        String y = x;
        System.out.println("y string = " + y);
        x = x + " Bean";
        System.out.println("y string = " + y);
    }
}
```

You might think String *y* would contain the characters *Java Bean* after the variable *x* is changed, because strings are objects. Let's examine the output to find out:

```
C:\Java Projects\BookTest>java String
y string = Java
y string = Java
```

As you can see, even though *y* is a reference variable to the same object that *x* refers to, when we change *x* it does not change *y*. This is because a brand new String object is created every time we use the + operator to concatenate two strings.

In contrast to objects, primitive number assignments are stored as values. Let's look at some code for an explanation of this:

```
class ValueTest {
    public static void main (String [] args) {
        int a = 10;
        System.out.println("a = " + a);
        int b = a;
        b = 30;
        System.out.println("a = " + a + "after change to b");
    }
}
```

This code is very similar to the previous example using objects, except we are using primitive values instead of objects. The output from this program is the following:

```
c:\Java Projects\Reference>java ValueTest
a = 10
a = 10 after change to b
```

Notice this time the value of *a* stayed at 10. This is because primitive types are assigned by value and not by reference.

Comparison Operators

Comparison operators always result in a boolean value. This boolean value is most often used in an *if* statement, but it can also be assigned directly to a boolean primitive:

```
class CompareTest {
    public static void main(String [] args) {
        boolean b = 100 > 99;
        System.out.println("The value of b is " + b);
    }
}
```

Four comparison operators can be used to compare any combination of integers, floating-point numbers, or characters:

- > greater than
- >= greater than or equal to

■ < less than

■ <= less than or equal to

Let's examine some legal comparisons:

```
class GuessAnimal {
    public static void main(String [] args) {
        String animal = "unknown";
        int weight = 700;
        char sex = 'm';
        double colorWaveLength = 1.630;
        if (weight >= 500) animal = "elephant";
        if (colorWaveLength > 1.621) animal = "gray " + animal;
        if (sex <= 'f') animal = "female " + animal;
        System.out.println("The animal is a " + animal);
    }
}
```

In the preceding code we are using a comparison between characters. It is also legal to compare a character primitive with any number, as the code shows (though this isn't great programming style). Running the preceding class will output the following:

```
C:\Java Projects\BookTest>java GuessAnimal
The animal is a gray elephant
```

instanceof Comparison

The *instanceof* comparison operator is available for object variables. The purpose of this operator is to determine whether an object belongs to a given class (or any of the superclasses). This comparison may not be made on primitive types and will result in a compile-time error if it is attempted. Let's examine a typical example of instanceof:

```
import java.awt.*;
class CompareTest {
    public static void main(String [] args) {
        Button b = new Button("Exit");
        boolean compare1 = b instanceof Button;
        boolean compare2 = b instanceof Component;
        System.out.println("Is b a Button? " + compare1);
        System.out.println("Is b a Component? " + compare2);
    }
}
```

This class creates an instance of a Button, and then uses instanceof to see if it is of type Button and Component. Running the preceding program produces the following:

```
C:\Java Projects\CompareTest>java CompareTest
Is b a Button? true
Is b a Component? true
```

There is a very important point about using instanceof. If we attempt to compare an instance to a class and the variable has been declared as a class type that is not in the same object hierarchy, the compiler will produce an error. Examine the following code:

```
import java.awt.*;
class CompareTest {
    public static void main(String [] args) {
        Button b = new Button("Exit");
        boolean compare = b instanceof String;
        System.out.println("Is b a String? " + compare);
    }
}
```

The code simply creates a Button object, then tests to see if it is a String object. The String type is not in the hierarchy of Button, therefore this will not work. If we attempt to compile this code, we receive the following:

```
C:\Java Projects\CompareTest>javac CompareTest.java
BookTest.java:5: Impossible for java.awt.Button to be instance of java.lang.String.
        boolean compare = b instanceof String;
1 error
```

The Java compiler knows it is impossible for Button *b* to be a String because it is explicitly declared as a Button, and String is nowhere in the object hierarchy of Button. One small change to our code will allow this to compile:

```
import java.awt.*;
class CompareTest {
    public static void main(String [] args) {
        Object b = new Button("Exit");
        boolean compare = b instanceof String;
        System.out.println("Is b a String? " + compare);
    }
}
```

We have changed the type of *b* to Object, therefore *b* is not explicitly declared as a Button at compile time. Theoretically, when the program is run, *b* could become a String, a Date, or any other class type. In this case it is initialized on the same line as a Button, but it still could become anything else, so Java allows this to be tested with instanceof.

Equality Operators

Equality can be tested with the operators equals and not equals:

- ■ == equals
- ■ != not equals

Equality operators compare two entities and return a boolean value. There are four types of entities they can test for:

- ■ Numbers
- ■ Characters
- ■ Boolean primitives
- ■ Reference variables

Equality for Primitives

Most programmers are familiar with comparing primitive values. The following code shows some primitives being compared for equality:

```
class ComparePrimitives {
    public static void main(String [] args) {
        System.out.println("character 'a' == 'a'? " + ('a' == 'a'));
        System.out.println("character 'a' == 'b'? " + ('a' == 'b'));
        System.out.println("5 != 6? " + (5 != 6));
        System.out.println("5.0 == 5L? " + (5.0 == 5L));
        System.out.println("true == false? " + (true == false));
    }
}
```

Notice that in line six we are comparing an integer to a float number. This program produces the following output:

```
c:\Java Projects\Equality>java ComparePrimitives
character 'a' == 'a'? true
character 'a' == 'b'? false
5 != 6? true
5.0 == 5L? true
true == false? false
```

As we can see, if a float is compared with an integer and the values are the same, the == operator returns true as expected.

Equality for Reference Variables

A *reference variable* is a name that is used in Java to reference an instance of a class. As was previously stated, two reference variables can point to the same object, as the following code snippet demonstrates:

```
Button a = new Button("Exit");
Button b = a;
```

After running this code, both variable *a* and variable *b* will refer to the same object (a button with the label Exit). Reference variables can be tested to see if they point to the same object by using the == operator. Examine the following code:

```
import java.awt.Button;
class CompareReference {
    public static void main(String [] args) {
        Button a = new Button("Exit");
        Button b = new Button("Exit");
        Button c = a;
        System.out.println("Is reference a == b? " + (a == b));
        System.out.println("Is reference a == c? " + (a == c));
    }
}
```

This code creates three reference variables. The first two, *a* and *b*, are separate Buttons that happen to have the same label. The third reference variable, *c*, is initialized to point to the same instance that *a* refers to. When this program is run, the following output is produced:

```
Is reference a == b? false
Is reference a == c? true
```

As we can see by this result, both *a* and *c* reference the same instance of a Button. Because strings are also objects and not primitives, strings with the same characters may not be equal when we test them using the == operator. This will be discussed in detail later in this chapter.

Arithmetic Operators

Most people are familiar with the basic arithmetic operators. They are the following:

- \+ addition/positive
- – subtraction/negative
- * multiplication
- / division
- % remainder

These can be used in the standard way:

```
class MathTest {
    public static void main (String [] args) {
        int x = 5 * 3;
        int y = x % 4;
        System.out.println("The remainder of 15 % 4 is " + y);
    }
}
```

It is possible to abbreviate each of these operators if the operation is being done to a single variable, as follows:

```
class MathTest {
    public static void main (String [] args) {
        int x = 15;
        x %= 4; // same as x = x % 4;
        System.out.println("The remainder of 15 % 4 is " + x);
    }
}
```

Note that the plus sign and the minus sign can be used as prefixes on numbers to denote a positive or negative value:

```
int y = -20;
```

String concat Operator

The plus sign can also be used to concatenate two strings together, as you have witnessed previously in this book:

```
String animal = "Grey " + "elephant";
```

Increment and Decrement

There are two operations that will increment or decrement a variable by exactly one. They are the following:

- ++ increment

- -- decrement

The operator is placed either before or after a variable to change the value. There is an important difference in the behavior of the operator, depending on whether it is before or after the operand. Examine the following:

```
class MathTest {
    static int users = 0;
    public static void main (String [] args) {
        System.out.println("Users online: " + users++);
        System.out.println("The value of users is " + ++users);
    }
}
```

Notice that in the fourth line of the program the increment operator is after the variable *users*. This is called a *post increment* and will cause the variable *users* to be incremented by one after the value is used in the function. When we run this program, it will output the following:

```
c:\Java Projects\Increment>java MathTest
Users online: 0
The value of users is 2
```

Notice when the variable is written to the screen, at first it says the value is zero. This is because the incremental operator occurs after the line of code executes. The next line increments *users* by one and outputs it to the screen, so the value now equals two.

Shift Operators

The following are shift operators:

- >> right shift
- << left shift
- >>> right shift including negative bit

exam
Watch

*The more obscure the topic, the more likely it will appear on the exam. Operators such as +, -, *, and / will probably not be on the exam because they are commonly used. Shift operators are rarely or never used; therefore they will most definitely be tested.*

The shift operators shift the bits of a number to the right or left, producing a new number. Shift operators are used on integer numbers only. To determine the result of a shift, it is necessary to convert the number into bits. Let's look at an example of a bit shift, without using code yet.

We'll start with a simple example. Let's try using the right-shift operator on the int number 8. First, we must convert this number to a bit representation:

```
0000 0000 0000 0000 0000 0000 0000 1000
```

An *int* is a 32-bit integer, so all 32 bits must be displayed. If we apply a bit shift of one to the right, using the >> operator, the new bit number is:

```
0000 0000 0000 0000 0000 0000 0000 0100
```

We can now convert this back to a decimal number (base 10), to get 4. Now let's examine how to do the exact same thing with code:

```java
class BitShift {
    public static void main(String [] args) {
        int x = 8;
        System.out.println("Before shift x equals " + x);
        x = x >> 1;
        System.out.println("After shift x equals " + x);
    }
}
```

When we compile and run this program we get the following output:

```
c:\Java Projects\BitShift>java BitShift
Before shift x equals 8
After shift x equals 4
```

Shift operations can take place on all integers, regardless of the base they are displayed in (octal, decimal, or hexadecimal). The left shift works in exactly the same way, except all bits are shifted in the opposite direction. The following code uses a hexadecimal number to shift:

```
class BitShift {
    public static void main(String [] args) {
        int x = 0x80000000;
        System.out.println("Before shift x equals " + x);
        x = x << 1;
        System.out.println("After shift x equals " + x);
    }
}
```

To understand the preceding example, it is necessary to convert the hexadecimal number to a bit number. Fortunately it is very easy to convert from hexadecimal to bits. Each hex-digit converts to a four-bit representation, as we can see:

```
8    0    0    0    0    0    0    0
1000 0000 0000 0000 0000 0000 0000 0000
```

In the preceding example, the very leftmost bit represents the sign (positive or negative). When the leftmost bit is 1 the number is negative, and when it is 0 the number is positive. Running our program gives us the following:

```
c:\Java Projects\BitShift>java BitShift
Before shift x equals -2147483648
After shift x equals 0
```

As we can see, shifting the bits one to the left moves the bit right out of the number, giving us all 0 bits.

When there is a negative bit and we shift to the right, the operator shifts the bit to the right but also keeps the negative bit. For example, let's use the hex number 0x8000000 again:

```
1000 0000 0000 0000 0000 0000 0000 0000
```

Now we will shift this, using >>, one to the right:

```
1100 0000 0000 0000 0000 0000 0000 0000
```

As we can see, the bit is shifted to the right but, and this is important, the negative bit remains behind. Let's try some code that shifts it four to the right:

```java
class BitShift {
    public static void main(String [] args) {
        int x = 0x80000000;
        System.out.println("Before shift x equals " + x);
        x = x >> 4;
        System.out.println("After shift x equals " + x);
    }
}
```

In line five of this program, the number will be bit shifted four to the right. Running this program gives us the following output:

```
C:\Java Projects\BookTest>java BitShift
Before shift x equals -2147483648
After shift x equals -134217728
```

The number now equals the following in bit representation:

```
1111 1000 0000 0000 0000 0000 0000 0000
```

Notice that the bits filled in from the left were 1's and not 0's. This is because the left-most bit was a 1. If the left-most bit were a 0, 0's would have been filled in instead.

We can use a special shift operator if we choose to not keep the negative bit. This is the operator >>>. Let's change the code slightly to use this operator:

```java
class BitShift {
    public static void main(String [] args) {
        int x = 0x80000000;
        System.out.println("Before shift x equals " + x);
```

```
            x = x >>> 4;
            System.out.println("After shift x equals " + x);
        }
    }
```

The output for this program is now the following:

```
C:\Java Projects\BookTest>java BitShift
Before shift x equals -2147483648
After shift x equals 134217728
```

As we can see, the new number is positive because the negative bit was not kept. In bit representation, the new number is:

```
0000 1000 0000 0000 0000 0000 0000 0000
```

We can also use the Java shorthand on all of these operators:

- ▪ <<=
- ▪ >>=
- ▪ >>>=

Using Shift Operators

1. Try writing a class that takes an integer of 1, shifts the bit 31 to the left, then 31 to the right.

2. What number does this now represent?

3. What is the bit representation of the new number?

The program should look something like the following:

```
class BitShift {
    public static void main(String [] args) {
        int x = 0x00000001; // or simply 1
        x <<= 31;
        x >>= 31;
        System.out.println("After shift x equals " + x);
    }
}
```

The number should now equal −1. In bits, this number is:

```
1111 1111 1111 1111 1111 1111 1111 1111
```

Bitwise Operators

The bitwise operators compare two bit numbers, using and/or to determine the result on a bit-by-bit basis. There are three bitwise operators:

- & and
- | or
- ^ exclusive or

The & operator compares corresponding bits between two numbers or it can compare two boolean values, treating them as bits. If both bits are 1, then the final bit is also 1. If only one of the bits is 1, then the resulting bit is 0. Once again, for bitwise operations we must convert numbers to bit representations. Let's compare two numbers, 10 and 9, with the & operator:

```
1010 & 1001 = 1000
```

As we can see, only the left-most bit is a 1 in both locations, hence the final number is 1000 in bit representation (or 8 in decimal). Let's see this in some code:

```
class Bitwise {
    public static void main(String [] args) {
        int x = 10 & 9; // 1010 and 1001
        System.out.println("1010 & 1001 = " + x);
    }
}
```

When we run this code, the following output is produced:

```
c:\Java Projects\Bitwise>java Bitwise
1010 & 1001 = 8
```

The | (or) operator is very similar to the & (and) operator, except when we compare corresponding bits, a 1 is the result if either bit is a 1. So, for the numbers 10 and 9, we get the following:

```
1010 | 1001 = 1011
```

In this case, because we have 1's in bit positions 0, 1, and 3 (numbered right to left), those bits are carried forth. It produces the number 11 (in decimal). Let's examine this in some code:

```
class Bitwise {
    public static void main(String [] args) {
        int x = 10 | 9; // 1010 and 1001
        System.out.println("1010 & 1001 = " + x);
    }
}
```

When we run the preceding code, we receive the following:

```
C:\Java Projects\BookTest>java Bitwise
1010 & 1001 = 11
```

The ^ operator is not tested on the exam, but you should be aware of its existence for programming, especially with graphics applications. The ^ operator compares two bits to see if they are different. If they are, the result is a 1. Examine the numbers 10 and 5 in bit representation:

```
1010 ^ 0101 = 1111
```

As we can see, the result is 15 in decimal form. Let's examine 8 and 13 in this example:

```
1000 ^ 1101 = 0101
```

The result is 5 in decimal form.

Logical Operators

There are two logical operators:

- && conditional and
- || conditional or

The && operator is similar to the & operator, except it only evaluates boolean values. The && operator evaluates the left side of the equation first, to see if a false exists. If it does, it does not bother looking at the right side of the equation, because it already knows no matter what the value of the right bit is, the result will be a false.

```
class Logical {
    public static void main(String [] args) {
        boolean b = true & false;
        System.out.println("boolean b = " + b);
    }
}
```

When we run the preceding code, we receive the following:

```
C:\Java Projects\BookTest>java Logical
boolean b = false
```

The || operator is similar to the && operator, except it evaluates the left side to see if a true is present. If it is, it knows the result will be a true, so it does not bother looking at the right side of the equation.

exam
ⓦatch

The || and && operators only work with boolean operands. The exam may try to fool you by using integers with these operators, so be on guard for this.

Bitwise Complement Operator

The ~ operator is the reverse-bits operator. This operator will not be tested on the Java exam, but it is a good idea to be familiar with it. It will change all 1's to 0's and vice versa. Examine the following code:

```
class Bitwise {
    public static void main(String [] args) {
        int x = 5; // 000..0101
        System.out.println("x is initially " + x);
        x = ~x;
        System.out.println("~x is equal to " + x);
    }
}
```

This program is changing every bit into its complement, thus the output from this program is the following:

```
C:\Java Projects\Bitwise>java Bitwise
x is initially 5
~x is equal to -6
```

In bit representation, the conversion looks like this:

```
~0000 0000 0000 0000 0000 0000 0000 0101
```

converts to

```
1111 1111 1111 1111 1111 1111 1111 1010
```

Conditional Operators

Conditional operators are used to evaluate boolean expressions, much like *if* statements, except instead of executing a block of code, a conditional operator will assign a value to a variable. A conditional operator is constructed using the characters ? (question mark) and : (colon).

Let's take a look at a conditional operator in some code:

```
class Salary {
    public static void main(String [] args) {
        int salary = 30000;
        String status = (salary<15000)?"poor":"not poor";
        System.out.println("This salary is classified as " + status);
    }
}
```

A conditional operator starts with a boolean operation, followed by two possible values for the variable. The left value is assigned if the boolean is true, the right if it is false. You can also apply many conditional operators in one statement.

```
class AssignmentOps {
    public static void main(String [] args) {
        int salary = 50000;
        String status = (salary<15000)?"poor":(salary<40000)?"middle
class":(salary<70000)?"upper middle class":"upper class";
        System.out.println("This salary is classified as " + status);
    }
}
```

As we can see, we can stack these operators into one long statement.

Casting

Casting can be used on primitives or instances to specify the type. In general, you can have an implicit cast when a widening conversion is done, but an explicit cast when a narrowing conversion is done. For primitives, narrowing means loss of precision, and for objects it means loss of generality.

Primitive Casting

Integers may be used when a double is required without explicitly casting the integer.

```
double d = 100L;
```

In the preceding statement, a double is being initialized with an integer value of long. No cast is needed in this case because a double can hold every piece of information that an integer can store. If, however, we wish to assign a double value to an integer type, we will run into problems:

```
class Casting {
    public static void main(String [] args) {
        int x = 3957.229;
    }
}
```

If we try to compile the preceding code, the following error is produced:

```
C:\Java Projects\Cast>javac Casting.java
Casting.java:3: Incompatible type for declaration. Explicit cast needed to convert
double to int.
        int x = 3957.229;
1 error
```

In the preceding code, an integer is being assigned a floating-point number. Because an integer is not capable of storing decimal places, an error occurs. To make this work, we will cast the floating-point number into an integer:

```
class Casting {
    public static void main(String [] args) {
        int x = (int)3957.229;
        System.out.println("int x = " + x);
    }
}
```

When we perform a cast on a floating-point number, it causes it to lose all the digits after the decimal. Running the preceding code will produce the following output:

```
c:\Java Projects\Cast>java Casting
int x = 3957
```

We can also cast a larger number type, such as a long, into a smaller number type, such as a byte. Examine the following:

```
class Casting {
    public static void main(String [] args) {
        long l = 56L;
        byte b = (byte)l;
        System.out.println("The byte is " + b);
    }
}
```

The preceding code will compile and run fine. But what happens if the long value is larger than 127? Let's modify the code and find out:

```
class Casting {
    public static void main(String [] args) {
        long l = 130L;
        byte b = (byte)l;
        System.out.println("The byte is " + b);
    }
}
```

The code compiles fine, and when we run it we get the following:

```
c:\Java Projects\Cast>java Casting
The byte is -126
```

Java does not produce a runtime error, as you might expect. It actually starts counting up from −128 when we go over 127.

EXERCISE 3-2

Using Casting

Create a float number type of any value, and assign it to a short using casting.

1. Declare a float variable: float f = 234.56F;

2. Assign the float to a short: short s = (short)f;

Your completed program should look something like this:

```
class Cast {
    public static void main(String [] args) {
        float f = 234.56F;
        short s = (short)f;
    }
}
```

Casting Objects

Objects may also be cast. When an object is cast, the subclass is implicitly stated. For example, the Button class is a subclass of Component. We can create an object of type Component, and assign it to a Button variable. If we want to assign our Component to a Button variable, then we must cast our Component to a Button. The following illegal code will clarify this:

```
import java.awt.*;
class Casting {
    public static void main(String [] args) {
        Component c;
        c = new Button("Close");
        Button b = c; // Does not work
    }
}
```

As we can see in the preceding code, it is trying to assign our Component to a Button variable, *b*. If we attempt to compile this class, we will receive the following error from the compiler:

```
c:\Java Projects\Cast>javac Casting.java
Casting.java:6: Incompatible type for declaration. Explicit cast needed to convert
java.awt.Component to java.awt.Button.
        Button b = c;
1 error
```

This generates an error, as we can see. To correct this, we must cast the variable *c* into a Button:

```
import java.awt.*;
class Casting {
    public static void main(String [] args) {
        Component c;
        c = new Button("Close");
        Button b = (Button)c;
    }
}
```

This brings us to an interesting point. What if we were attempting to cast *c* into a Button, but in fact *c* was a different Component, such as a Label?

```
import java.awt.*;
class Casting {
    public static void main(String [] args) {
        Component c;
        c = new Label("Close");
        Button b = (Button)c;
    }
}
```

This code will actually compile fine. The error is generated at runtime, as the following shows:

```
C:\Java Projects\Cast>java Casting
Exception in thread "main" java.lang.ClassCastException:
java.awt.Label at Casting.main(Casting.java:6)
```

exam
Ⓦatch

For the exam it will be important to note when a runtime error will occur, and when a compile time error will occur.

QUESTIONS AND ANSWERS

Now that you have a better idea of operators and how they function, here are some operators in action and the results.

1 & 3	1
1 | 3	3
5++	6
1 << 2	4
new Button("Lock") instanceof Component	true

Boolean equals() Method

The equals() method is a special method contained in the Object class that compares properties between two objects. The properties that the method tests are determined by the type of object being tested. This is in contrast to the == operator, which tests whether two reference variables are the same, as was described earlier in the chapter.

The equals() method is typically overridden in a subclass. When this method is not overridden, it is identical to the == operator (it compares two reference variables). For the Java exam you will need to know the behavior of String, Boolean, and Object types.

java.lang.String

The String.equals() method compares the characters within a string to determine if they are equal. Let's examine this in some code:

```
class Equals {
    public static void main(String [] args) {
        String ja = "Ja";
        String va = "va";
        String java1 = ja + va;
        String java = "Java";
        System.out.println("java.equals(java1)? " + java.equals(java1));
        System.out.println("java == java1? " + (java == java1));
    }
}
```

The preceding code creates two strings that contain the same string characters. Notice that the program goes to great lengths to create the variable java1 in lines three to five by concatenating two strings together at runtime. The reason for this will be explained later, but for now this shows the difference between equals() and the == operator. When we run this code we receive the following:

```
c:\Java Projects\Equals>java Equals
java.equals(java1)? true
java == java1? false
```

Notice that the equals() method shows the strings as equal, but the == operator does not indicate they are equal. To contrast this with the == operator, it will be beneficial to see how the == operator works (and the == behavior of String objects is necessary for the exam).

The following code tests various string references to see whether they are equal, and, thus, referring to the same object. This may seem to run counter to what you previously thought when comparing two strings. Normally when comparing two strings you use the String method equals(); however, there are instances in which Java references the same String object. I will explain this further in a moment. For now, examine the following code and try to guess which statements are true.

```
class StringLiteral {
    public static void main(String[] args) {
        String java = "Java", va = "va";
        System.out.println(java == "Java");
        System.out.println(Other.java == java);
        System.out.println(java == ("Ja"+"va"));
        System.out.println(java == ("Ja"+va));
    }
}
class Other { static String java = "Java"; }
```

Let's examine the output of this program to see if you were correct.

```
c:\Java Projects\StringLiteral>java StringLiteral
true
true
true
false
```

The first true value demonstrates that the variable *java* equals the literal value of *Java*. The reason for this is because the variable java is calculated as an instance at compile time, as are any variables that are assigned a literal. The Java language will share unique instances of strings if they are calculated at compile time, referencing them to the same object instead of creating unique objects.

The second true value shows us that strings in other classes refer to the same string object. This applies to classes in other packages as well.

The third true is basically a reiteration of the first point. Ja + va is a literal value that is exactly the same as Java, and is assigned at compile time

The false value shows what happens when we compare a string computed at runtime, and not compile time. Because it is computed at runtime, a new string object is created that is brand new and therefore not equal to our other string object. This is the same as comparing two separate, non-static strings that contain the same series of characters.

java.lang.Boolean

The Boolean.equals() method is similar to the String.equals() method. Examine the following code:

```
class Equals {
    public static void main(String [] args) {
        Boolean a = new Boolean(true);
        Boolean b = new Boolean(true);
        System.out.println("a.equals(b)? " +
a.equals(b));
        System.out.println("a == b? " + (a == b));
    }
}
```

The preceding code creates two boolean objects, both with a value of true. When we use the boolean.equals() value, it compares the boolean property, but when we use the == operator it compares reference variables, which of course are not equal because there are two separate objects. The output is as follows:

```
a.equals(b)? true
a == b? false
```

java.lang.Object

As we mentioned earlier, the Object.equals() method is contained in the Object class that compares properties between two objects. The Object.equals() method itself works in the same way that the == operator does when it is not overridden in a subclass; it compares the reference variables. Examine the following code:

```
import java.util.*;
class Equals {
    public static void main(String [] args) {
        Equals a = newEquals();
        Equals b = newEquals();
        Equals c = b;
        System.out.println("a.equals(b)? " + a.equals(b));
        System.out.println("a == b? " + (a == b));
        System.out.println("b.equals(c)? " + b.equals(c));
    }
}
```

The preceding code demonstrates what happens when the equals() method is not overridden in the subclass. The method Equals.equals() compares the reference variables of two objects. When we run the code, we get the following:

```
c:\Java Projects\Equals>java Equals
a.equals(b)? false
a == b? false
b.equals(c)? false
```

As you can see, this is clearly comparing reference variables and not some other property.

CERTIFICATION OBJECTIVE 3.03

Passing Variables into Methods

When passing object arguments to a method, you must keep in mind it is a reference variable that is being passed, and not the actual object itself. A *reference variable* is a name that points to a location in the computer's memory where the object is stored. This leads to two different types of behavior when an object or a primitive is passed to a method. First, let's look at what happens when a primitive is passed to a method:

```
class ReferenceTest {
    public static void main (String [] args) {
        int a = 1;
        ReferenceTest rt = new ReferenceTest();
        System.out.println("Before modify() a = " + a);
        rt.modify(a);
        System.out.println("After modify() a = " + a);
    }
    void modify(int number) {
        number = number + 1;
        System.out.println("number = " + number);
    }
}
```

In this simple program the variable *a* is passed to a method called modify(), which simply increments the variable by 1. The resulting output looks like this:

```
C:\Java Projects\Reference>java ReferenceTest
Before modify() a = 1
number = 2
After modify() a = 1
```

Note that *a* did not change after it was passed to the method. It is as though a copy of *a* is passed to the method. When a primitive is passed to a method, it is *passed by value*. Passing by value means that the numeric value, and not a reference to a variable, is passed to the method.

Now let's see how the preceding performs when we use an object instead of a primitive. For this example we will import the Dimension class from the java.awt package:

```
import java.awt.Dimension;
class ReferenceTest {
    public static void main (String [] args) {
        Dimension d = new Dimension(5,10);
        ReferenceTest rt = new ReferenceTest();
        System.out.println("Before modify() d.height = " + d.height);
        rt.modify(d);
        System.out.println("After modify() d.height = " + d.height);
    }
```

```
void modify(Dimension dim) {
    dim.height = dim.height + 1;
    System.out.println("dim = " + dim.height);
}
}
```

exam
Watch
The exam will show some pretty tricky code examples. Make sure you have practiced looking at enough code to quickly analyze a program. You must be able to understand a program and determine values of variables and output.

When we run this class, we get different behavior than we did by using a primitive.

```
C:\Java Projects\Reference>java ReferenceTest
Before modify() d.height = 10
dim = 11
After modify() d.height = 11
```

Notice when an object is passed to a method, any changes to the object that occur inside the method also occur to the object outside the method. This is because the reference variables *d* and *dim* both point to the same object. Hence, a change made within the method changes the data in the same object. The object was *passed by reference*.

CERTIFICATION SUMMARY

If you have studied this chapter diligently, you should have a firm understanding of all operations that can be used in the Java language. You should also understand the difference between the == operator and the equals() method, and you know how primitives and objects behave when passed to a method. Let's review what you have learned in this chapter.

Most of the operators in this chapter will comprise at least one question on the exam. For example, the bit shift operator will probably be one whole question that will test every aspect of bit shift operators. Common operators such as arithmetic and comparison operators will probably not be explicitly tested because it is assumed you will know this already. Behavior of variables passed into methods will be thoroughly tested, so be prepared!

One more note: The names of all of these operators are included, but it is not necessary for you to know these names for the exam. You only need to be able to recognize the operators and what they do.

TWO-MINUTE DRILL

❑ Instances of objects are accessed using reference variables.

❑ Primitive variables are stored as values.

❑ The instanceof operator can only be used to test objects with class types that are in the same class hierarchy.

❑ The equality operators (== and !=) compare reference variables when used on objects, and values when used on primitives.

❑ The >> operator shifts bits to the right while keeping the sign bit. The >>> operator moves all bits to the right, including the sign bit.

❑ The & and | operator are used for integer or boolean values only.

❑ The && and || operators are used for boolean types only.

❑ Conditional operators evaluate and return a value.

❑ Floating-point numbers may be cast to integer types.

❑ Larger numbers may be cast to smaller types explicitly, and smaller types to larger ones implicitly.

❑ Superclass object references may be cast to subclass types.

❑ The equals() method compares properties in objects when overridden.

❑ Primitive types are passed by value, object types are passed by reference.

SELF TEST

The following questions will help you measure your understanding of the material presented in this chapter. Read all of the choices carefully, as there may be more than one correct answer. Choose all correct answers for each question.

1. Your company hired a contractor to write several classes for a sales software package. Unfortunately, his term has expired and now it is up to you to work out any bugs left in the classes. You examine the first class:

```
import java.util.Date;
class  TimeStamp{
    public static void main (String [] args) {
        Date d = new Date();
        addDay(d); // *
    }
    public static void addDay(Date old) {
        long newTime = old.getTime() + 60*60*24*1000;
        old.setTime(newTime);
    }
}
```

When the object *d* is initialized, it stores the current date and time. The date method setTime() will reset the time to whichever value is passed to it. Approximately what value will the Date object *d* have after the method addDay() is run?

A. Approximately the present time.

B. Something other than the present time.

C. Nothing, this class will not compile.

2. This class was programmed to keep track of inventory using a special numbering system. The convertCode() method creates a unique inventory number:

```
class  Inventory{
    public static void main (String [] args) {
        int code = 237;
        convertCode(code); // *
    }
    public static void convertCode(int inv) {
        inv = inv + 100000;
    }
}
```

What will the variable code equal after the method convertCode() is run?

A. 237

B. 100237

C. Nothing, this class will not compile.

3. The contractor didn't even have time to compile the next piece of code. You have a feeling that there may be something wrong with this:

```
import java.awt.*;
class CompareTest {
    static public void main(String [] args) {
        Component b = new Button("Exit");
        boolean compare = b.instanceof (Button);
    }
}
```

Which lines do you think contain errors?

A. class CompareTest {

B. static public void main(String [] args) {

C. Component b = new Button("Exit");

D. boolean compare = b.instanceof (Button);

E. Nothing is wrong with this class.

4. The contractor has started a Ticker class to post the company stock price.

```
import java.awt.*;
class Ticker extends Component {
    public static void main (String [] args) {
        Ticker t = new Ticker();
        // Insert statement here
    }
}
```

Which of the following statements could legally be inserted into this code? (Choose all that apply.)

A. boolean test = (t instanceof Ticker);

B. boolean test = t.instanceof(Ticker);

C. boolean test = (t instanceof Component);

D. boolean test = t.instanceof(Object);

E. boolean test = (t instanceof String);

5. What will the output be when the following code is compiled and executed?

```
class Equals {
    public static void main(String [] args) {
        int x = 100;
        double y = 100.1;
        boolean b = (x = y);
        System.out.println(b);
    }
}
```

A. True

B. False

C. Nothing, the code will not compile.

D. Nothing, the code will compile but not execute.

6. Which of the following comparisons are legal to use in code? (Choose all that apply.)

A. 'a' == 'b'

B. 12.1 == 12L

C. 'a' == true

D. 'a' == 12

E. 1 == true

7. What will be the output from the following program?

```
import java.awt.Button;
class CompareReference {
    public static void main(String [] args) {
        Button a = new Button("Exit");
        Button b = new Button("Exit");
        Button c = a;
        System.out.println((a == b) + " " + (a == c));
    }
}
```

A. true false

B. true true

C. false true

D. false false

E. Nothing, this will not compile.

8. Which of the following lines of code are illegal? (Choose all that apply.)

   A. x =% 3;

   B. x++;

   C. String animal = "Gray Elephant" – "Gray ";

   D. –y;

   E. String animal = "Gray " + "elephant";

9. The following program was written by the contractor to keep track of the number of times people have logged in. What will be the output of the following program?

```
class Logins {
    static int users = 0;
    public static void main (String [] args) {
        System.out.print(++users);
        System.out.print(users++);
    }
}
```

   A. 01

   B. 02

   C. 12

   D. 11

   E. None of the above.

10. The following program uses bit shifting. What is the output from the following program?

```
class BitShift {
    public static void main(String [] args) {
        int x = 0x80000000;
        System.out.print(x + " and ");
        x = x >> 31;
        System.out.println(x);
    }
}
```

   A. -2147483648 and 1

   B. 0x8000000 and 0xffffffff

   C. –214783648 and -1

   D. –1 and –214783648

   E. None of the above.

11. What is the output from the following bit-shift program?

```
class BitShift {
    public static void main(String [] args) {
        int x = 0x80000000;
        System.out.print(x + " and  ");
        x = x >>> 31;
        System.out.println(x);
    }
}
```

A. -2147483648 and 1

B. 0x8000000 and 0x00000001

C. –214783648 and -1

D. 1 and –214783648

E. None of the above.

12. What is the output from the following program?

```
class Bitwise {
    public static void main(String [] args) {
        int x = 11 & 9;
        System.out.println(x);
    }
}
```

A. 20

B. 9

C. 11

D. 2

13. What is the output from the following program?

```
class Bitwise {
    public static void main(String [] args) {
        int x = 10 | 5;
        System.out.println(x);
    }
}
```

A. 15

B. 0

C. 9

D. 2

14. What will be the result of compiling and running the following code?

```
class AssignmentOps {
    public static void main(String [] args) {
        int x=2;
        String sup = (>15000)?"Pencil":(>=5)?"Eraser":"Pen";
        System.out.println(sup);
    }
}
```

A. Pencil

B. Eraser

C. Pen

D. This code will not compile.

15. Which of the following are legal lines of code? (Choose all that apply.)

A. int w = (int)888.8;

B. byte x = (byte)1000L;

C. long y = (byte)100;

D. byte z = (byte)100L;

16. Examine the following classes:

```
class Hardware {}
class Monitor extends Hardware{}
class HardDrive extends Hardware{
    public void test() {
        Monitor a = new Monitor();
        Hardware b = new Monitor();
        HardDrive c = (HardDrive)a;
        Monitor d = b;
    }
}
```

Which of the preceding lines are illegal? (Choose all that apply.)

A. Monitor a = new Monitor();

B. Hardware b = new Monitor();

C. HardDrive c = (HardDrive)a;

D. Monitor d = b;

17. Examine the following code:

```
class StringLiteral {
    public static void main(String[] args) {
        String java = "Java", va = "va";
        System.out.println(java == "Java");
        System.out.println(java == ("Ja"+"va"));
        System.out.println(java == ("Ja"+va));
        System.out.println(java.equals("Ja"+va));
    }
}
```

What will be the order of booleans produced by this program?

A. true true true true

B. true false false true

C. true true false true

D. true false false false

18. Examine the following code:

```
class Equals {
    public static void main(String [] args) {
        Boolean a = new Boolean(true);
        Boolean b = new Boolean(true);
        System.out.println(a.equals(b));
        System.out.println(a == b);
    }
}
```

What is the order of boolean values produced from this program?

A. true true

B. true false

C. false true

D. false false

19. Examine the following code:

```
class ReferenceTest {
    public static void main (String [] args) {
        int a = 1;
        ReferenceTest rt = new ReferenceTest();
        System.out.print(a);
        rt.modify(a);
        System.out.print(a);
    }
    void modify(int number) {
        number = number + 1;
    }
}
```

What will be the output?

A. 12

B. 10

C. 11

D. Nothing, this class will not compile.

20. Examine the following code:

```
import java.awt.Dimension;
class ReferenceTest {
    public static void main (String [] args) {
        Dimension d = new Dimension(5,5);
        ReferenceTest rt = new ReferenceTest();
        System.out.print(d.height);
        rt.modify(d);
        System.out.println(d.height);
    }
    void modify(Dimension dim) {
        dim.height = dim.height + 1;
    }
}
```

What is the output from this code?

A. 55

B. 56

C. 01

D. 00

E. Nothing, this class will not compile.

4

Flow Control

T he true power of any programming language is to convince the computer to rapidly perform mathematical or relational computations on data to produce vital information to the user. Java is no different in that it also has its own version of these flow control statements. These statement types are *conditional/decision*, *looping*, and *jumping* statements. With these necessary language constructs, the programmer is able to control the logical direction of his or her program.

The *if* statement and the *switch* statement are types of conditional/decision controls that allow your program to perform differently at a proverbial "fork in the road." Java provides three different looping constructs, which allow you to perform the same code over and over again. Java's version of jumping statements are found in *break* and *continue*. With these tools, you are able to produce an extremely powerful program that will be able to handle all logical situations with ease. Let's delve into the usage of all of these constructs and get you on your way to becoming certified.

Writing Code Using if and switch Statements

The if and switch statements are commonly referred to as decision statements. When you use decision statements in your program, you are asking the program to calculate a given expression to determine which course of action is required. Let's examine the if statement first.

exam
ⓦatch

Look at the code examples carefully. On the exam, you will be asked if the code will compile.

The basic format of an if statement is as follows:

```
if (expression)          //expression that returns a boolean result
{
    System.out.println("Inside if statement");
}
```

The expression in parenthesis must evaluate to a boolean true or false result and if a compound expression is used, you must have all the expressions surrounded by the parenthesis. If you are only performing one line of code in the body of the if statement then you do not need to have the brackets encompassing the body of the decision statement. The following code example illustrates this point.

```
if ( x > 3 )
    System.out.println("x is greater than three");
```

There might be a need to perform one block of code if the condition is true and another block of code if the condition is false. To do this, Java provides the keyword *else,* which labels one line of code or a block of code that will be performed if the condition is false. Following are two code examples that are variations of the if statement using the keyword else. The first example shows the use of one condition and the second shows the use of two conditions. You can set up an if...else statement to accept numerous conditions that could be tested.

```
if (hours > 40)
{
    hoursOvertime = (hours - 40) * 1.5;
    amount = (40 + hoursOvertime) * rate;
}
else
{
    amount = hours * rate;
}
```

The second example uses two conditions:

```
if (price < 300)
{
    buyProduct();
}
else if (price < 400)
{
    getApproval();
}
else
{
    dontBuyProduct();
}
```

Another way to simulate the use of multiple if statements is with the *switch* statement. Let's look at the syntax of a switch statement, followed by a comparison between an if statement and a switch statement.

The basic switch statement:

```
switch (integral primitive)
{
    case value1:   {
                    System.out.println("The value is " + value1);
                }
    default:   {
                    System.out.println("It did not match the other case values");
                }
}
```

It is important to note that the only values that the switch can evaluate are the following: byte, short, int, and char. If another primitive date type or an object reference is used, you will not be able to compile the program. The values with the case label also have to be one of these types, and must be constants. The default keyword is used to denote what will happen if none of the case values match the variable that is being used in the expression. You should also know that the variable must be enclosed in a pair of parenthesis or you will not be able to compile the code.

The following code shows a comparison between an if statement and a switch statement:

```
int x = 3;

if ( x == 1 )
{
    System.out.println("x is equal to 1");
}
else if ( x == 2 )
{
    System.out.println("x is equal to 2");
}
else if ( x == 3 )
{
    System.out.println("x is equal to 3");
}
```

```
else
{
     System.out.println("The program doesn't know what x is");
}
```

The preceding statement is the same as:

```
int x = 3;

switch ( x )
{
     case 1:  {
                System.out.println("x is equal to 1");
                break;
              }
     case 2:  {
                System.out.println("x is equal to 2");
                break;
              }
     case 3:  {
                System.out.println("x is equal to 3");
                break;
              }
     default  {
                System.out.println("The program doesn't know what x is");
              }
}
```

You will learn more about why the break command is used here later in this chapter. You should also be aware that the default keyword is not needed in the switch statement. If it is left out and there is no corresponding case value to the expression used, then none of the code of any of the case values will be performed. Also, it is not required that you put brackets around bodies of code in the case statement.

Legal Argument Types for if and switch Statements

If and switch statements can only accept a certain set of argument types. I have briefly mentioned these before, however, it is very important that you understand this to successfully complete the exam. If statements are limited to expressions that yield a boolean result. This is achieved by using one or more of Java's relational operators inside the parenthesis of the statement to compare two or more variables. Also, you can simply use the reserved word *true* as the expression to force execution of the block of code. What you cannot do is use an assignment or a number as the expression. For example, an old C language convention is to use the number 1 to force execution of the conditional. This is not valid Java syntax and will not work. If you are trying to force execution of a conditional, you should use the keyword true. A more complex example of how you can use an object reference in an if statement is shown in the following code to illustrate the point that it is a very useful tool.

```
int age = 18;
String sex = "Male";

if ((age >= 18) && (sex.equals("Male")))
{
     register4SelectiveService();
}
```

The expression in the switch statement can only evaluate to an integral primitive type that can be implicitly cast to an int. These types are byte, short, char, and int. Also, the switch can only check for an equality. This means that the other relational operators like the greater than sign are rendered unusable. The following is an example of what is valid as an expression using an object reference in a switch statement.

```
String s = "xyz";
switch (s.length())
{
     case 1:  System.out.println("length is one");
              break;
     case 2:  System.out.println("length is two");
              break;
     case 3: System.out.println("length is three");
              break;
     default:
}
```

There are also rules that govern the types that can be associated to the case label. The primitive data types byte, short, int, and char can be used as valid expressions to the case label. Also, variable constants of the same types can be used. This allows you to set constant variables equal to other variables that you want tested in a switch statement. The following is an example, however you must be aware that if the final keyword is omitted then the code will not compile.

```
final int one = 1;
final int two = 2;
int x = 1;
switch (x)
{
      case one:  System.out.println("one");
                 break;
      case two:  System.out.println("two");
                 break;
}
```

CERTIFICATION OBJECTIVE 4.02

Writing Code Using Loops (while, do-while, for)

Looping constructs are very important for useful program execution and are required knowledge on the Certification Exam. Java provides three flavors of loops (or iterations) consisting of the *while, do-while,* and *for* loops. The *while* loop is usually used in a situation where the program needs to execute certain Java commands an unspecified number of times while a given condition equates to true. The syntax for a while statement is as follows:

```
int x = 2;
while ( x == 2 )
{
      System.out.println( x );
      x++;
}
```

In this case, as in all loops, the expression must evaluate to a boolean result. Any variables used in the expression of a while loop must be declared before the expression is evaluated. The program's execution cycle will only enter the loop if the condition results in a true value. If the body of the loop is only one line, then the brackets are not needed. Once inside the loop, the program will remain inside until the condition is no longer met and evaluates to false. In the previous example, program control will enter the loop because *x* is equal to two. However, *x* is incremented in the loop, so when the condition is checked again it will evaluate to false and exit the loop.

exam
Ⓦatch

Be prepared to type out one of the looping constructs on the exam. Be precise.

The *do-while* loop is slightly different from the while statement in that the program execution cycle will always perform the commands in the body of a do-while at least once. It does adhere to the rule that you do not need brackets around the body if it is just one line of code. Following is an illustration of the syntax used in a do-while statement to print out an arbitrary phrase:

```
do {
    System.out.println("Inside loop");
} while ( false );
```

The phrase in the System.out.println statement will print out once even though the expression evaluates to false, because this looping construct will always perform what is in the loop at least once. The expression is not checked until after the body is performed. Please note the use of the semicolon at the end of the expression. The same syntax is used in C/C++ for the do-while; however, none of the other Java looping controls use a semicolon in this manner.

The *for* loop is an especially useful flow control statement when you already know how many times you need to execute the statements in the loop's block. There are three main parts to a for statement. They are the declaration and initialization of variables, the expression, and the incrementing or modification of variables. Each of the sections are separated by semicolons. The following are two examples of the for loop. The first one shows the parts of a for loop in a pseudo-code form, and the second shows the actual syntax for the loop.

```
for (/*Initialization expression*/ ; /* Conditional expression */;  /* Iterator expression */)
{
     /* loop body */
}

for (int i = 0; i<10; i++)
{
     System.out.println("i is " + i);
}
```

The for loop is a remarkable tool for developers because it allows you to declare and initialize zero, one, or multiple variables inside the parenthesis after the for keyword. If you declare more than one variable, then it needs to be separated by a comma. This is the first part that gets executed when the program encounters a for loop. The next section that executes is the conditional expression, which must evaluate to a boolean value like the other looping statements. Like other looping constructs, you can have multiple expressions in a for loop but they all must be enclosed in at least one pair of parenthesis. The next step is the execution of the loop's body. Lastly, the iterator expression is executed. It is important to note that none of these sections are required for the code to compile. The following example is perfectly legal:

```
for ( ; ; )
{
  System.out.println("Inside an endless loop");
}
```

In the preceding example, all the parts are left out so it will act like an endless loop. For the exam, it is important to realize that with the absence of the initialization and increment sections, the loop will act in the same manner as a while statement. An example of how you would do this is as follows:

```
int i = 0;

for (;i<10;)
{
    i++;
    //do some other work
}
```

The last thing to note is that all the sections of the for loop are independent of each other. The three expressions in the for statement do not need to operate on the same variables. In fact, the iterator expression does not even need to iterate a variable; it could be a separate Java command. The following is an example of this.

```
int a = 2;
int b = 3;
for (a = 1;  b != 1; System.out.println("iterate"))
{
    b = b - 1;
}
```

CERTIFICATION OBJECTIVE 4.03

Using break and continue

The *break* and *continue* keywords are used in conjunction with Java's looping and conditional features. These two statements are key in allowing a program to maintain normal execution when the need to exit out of a loop arises. The need to exit out might be caused by a problem encountered by the program, a correct value being found in a switch statement, or by program design. For whatever reason they are used, the program will "jump" to a different section of the program.

The break statement causes the program to stop execution of the innermost looping construct or switch statement and start processing the next line of code after the block. As mentioned earlier in the chapter, the break statement is usually used in switch statements as well. When the program encounters the word *break* during the execution of a switch statement, the next command after the switch statement will be performed. If break is omitted, then the program keeps executing the different case blocks until the break command is found or the switch statement ends. Examine the following code.

```
int x = 1;

switch ( x )
{
    case 1:  System.out.println("x is one");
    case 2:  {
                System.out.println("x is two");
                break;
            }
}
```

The code will print out the following:

```
x is one
x is two
```

This combination prints out because the break statement is not found. Another way to set up this logic is shown in the following code. You might find this example to be a little more applicable in a real world environment.

```
int x = someNumberBetweenOneAndTen;

switch ( x )
{
    case 2:
    case 4:
    case 6:
    case 8:
    case 10:  {
                System.out.println("x is an even number");
                break;
            }
    default:  System.out.println("x is an odd number");
}
```

This switch statement will print out the correct phrase, depending on whether the number is between one and ten, and is odd or even.

The continue statement causes the current iteration of the innermost loop to cease and the next iteration of the same loop to start if the condition of the loop is met. In the case of using a continue statement with a for loop, you need to consider the effects that the continue has on the loop iterator. Examine the following code, which is explained in the next paragraph.

```
for (int i = 0; i < 10; i++)
{
    System.out.println("Inside loop");
    continue;
}
```

The question: is this an endless loop? The answer is no. When the continue statement is encountered, *i* will increment before the condition is checked again. One issue to consider is that the continue statement should only be used when the need to check the condition of the loop and possibly re-enter the loop arises. If the condition can't be met if the continue statement is used, then a break statement is much more appropriate for the situation.

Unlabeled Statements

Both the break statement and the continue statement can be unlabeled or labeled. In most cases the use of the two commands is unlabeled, except when necessary to achieve correct program execution. As stated before, when unlabeled, the break statement will exit out of the innermost looping construct and proceed with the next line of code. This will happen even if the break statement is located inside an if statement that is embedded in a loop. An example of this concept is as follows:

```
boolean problem = true;
while (true)
{
    if (problem)
    {
        System.out.println("There was a problem");
        break;
    }
}
//next line of code
```

In this example, even though the break is encompassed by the if statement, the program execution will proceed to the first command after the while loop. The concept you need to gain from this is to realize that the break statement has no effect on the exiting of an if statement. It only applies to loops and switches.

In the previous example, the use of the break statement is unlabeled. The following is an example of a continue statement that is also unlabeled:

```
while (!EOF)
{
    //read a field from a file
    if (there was a problem)
    {
        //move to the next field in the file
        continue;
    }
}
```

In the example, there is a file being read from one field at a time. When an error is encountered it moves to the next field in the file and uses the continue statement to go back into the loop (if it is not at the end of the file) and keeps reading the various fields. If the break command were used instead, the code would stop reading the file once the error occurred and would perform the next line of code.

Labeled Statements

The use of the break statement and the continue statement when they are labeled and when they are unlabeled is completely different and it is important that you understand the difference for the exam. A break statement will exit out of the labeled loop as opposed to the innermost loop if the break keyword is combined with a label. An example of what a label looks like is in the following code:

```
labelName: for (expression)
        {
            . . .
        }
```

The label must adhere to the rules for a valid variable name and should adhere to the Java naming convention. The syntax for the use of a label

FROM THE CLASSROOM

Rules for the break and continue Statements when Combined With Labels

It is important to note that a label does not necessarily need to precede a looping construct. A label can be found almost anywhere in a program; however, there are certain rules that the break and continue statements must adhere to when they are combined with labels. First of all, a continue statement must be found in a loop. This is actually true whether or not it is combined with a label. Also the continue statement's label must refer to a loop. This is not the case for the break statement; The use of a labeled break will work in any situation where a label is defined as encompassing any block of code. The following code shows you in detail how this works.

```
Outer:  if (true)
        {
            if (true)
            {
                System.out.println("Inside second if statement");
                break outer;
            }
            System.out.println("Last statement of first if");
        }
}
```

This code is perfectly legal and will compile. If the continue were used instead of the break, it would not compile. In this case the break statement is not used in a loop or a switch statement, but it will cause the program to exit out of the first if statement. The phrase "Inside second if statement" will be the only thing that prints out of this code example before execution is stopped. You might ask me why this conflicts with what I have said in the rest of this chapter. The answer is, this is very unusual to see, and most people don't use it. Also, it is not on the exam! However, I did want to give you a complete explanation of what will work and what won't. It does add some confusion for people the first time they see and understand what this is about so I will not mention it again in the chapter.

—Michael Keene,
Sun Certified Programmer for Java

name in conjunction with a break statement is the break keyword, then the label name, followed by a semicolon. A more complete example of the use of a labeled break statement is as follows:

```
outer: for (int i=0; i<10; i++)
       {
              for (int j=0; j<5; j++)
              {
                     System.out.println("Hello");
                     break outer;
              }
       }
System.out.println("Good-Bye");
```

In this example the word *Hello* will be printed out one time. Then, the labeled break statement will be executed and the flow will exit out of the loop labeled *outer*. The next line of code will then print out *Good-Bye*. Let's see what will happen if the continue statement is used instead of the break statement. The following code example is the same as the preceding one with the exception of the two keywords being switched. The break is now replaced by the continue.

```
outer: for (int i=0; i<10; i++)
       {
              for (int j=0; j<5; j++)
              {
                     System.out.println("Hello");
                     continue outer;
              }
       }
System.out.println("Good-Bye");
```

In this example, *Hello* will be printed out ten times. After the continue statement is executed, the flow continues with the next iteration of the loop identified with the label. Finally, when the condition in the outer loop evaluates to false, the println statement will execute and *Good-Bye* will be printed.

exam
Watch

The labeled continue statement must be inside the loop that has the same label name.

Now that you have a better idea of flow control techniques, here are some possible scenario questions and their answers.

QUESTIONS AND ANSWERS

What do I need to know for the exam?	This entire chapter is fair game for the exam, but you should pay close attention to the combination of the break and continue statements with the looping constructs. Note: Be prepared for questions on the test that don't have an answer. In this situation you will have to leave the answer blank.
I saw that *goto* is a Java reserved word. Why didn't you explain its use in this chapter?	Java does reserve the word *goto* for possible future use; however, there is not a current implementation of the statement.
If an if-then-else statement can be rewritten as a switch statement, which is faster at run time?	The switch statement tends to be faster because it only evaluates the expression once, whereas the if statement evaluates it every time the execution cycle comes into contact with the expression.

CERTIFICATION SUMMARY

This chapter has covered a lot of information about various ways that you can control the flow of your program using statements in Java. First you learned about if and switch statements. The if statement evaluates one or more expressions to a boolean result. If the result is true, the program will execute the code in the block that is encompassed by the if. If an else statement is used and the expression evaluates to false, then the code following the else will be performed. If the else is not used, then none of the code associated with the if statement will execute.

The switch statement is used to replace multiple if-then-else statements. The switch statement can only evaluate integral primitive types that can be implicitly cast to an int. Those types are byte, short, int, and char. At run time, the Java Virtual Machine will try to find a match between the argument and the switch statement with an argument in a corresponding case statement. If a match is found it will execute the statements in the following brackets until a break statement is found or the end of the switch statement occurs. If there is no match, then the default will execute if it appears.

You have learned about the three looping constructs that Java makes available. Those constructs are the for loop, the while loop, and the do-while loop. In general, the for loop is used when you know how many times you need to go through the loop. The while loop is used when you do not know how many times you want to go through, and the do-while is used when you need to go through at least once. In the for loop and the while loop, the expression will have to evaluate to true to ever get inside the block and will check after every iteration of the loop. The do-while loop does not check the condition until after it has gone through the loop once. The major benefit of the for loop is the ability to initialize one or more variables and increment or decrement those variables in the for loop definition.

The break and continue statements are useful tools when designing your program. Both of the statements can be used in either a labeled or unlabeled fashion. When unlabeled, the break statement will force the program to stop processing the innermost looping construct and start with the line of code following the loop. Using an unlabeled continue command will cause the program to stop execution of the current iteration of the innermost loop and proceed with the next iteration. When the break or continue statement is used in a labeled manner, it will perform the in the same way, with one exception. The statement will not apply to the innermost loop, instead it will apply to the loop with the label. The break statement is used most often in conjunction with the switch statement. When there is a match between the switch expression and the case value, the code following the case value will be performed. To stop the execution of the code, the break statement is needed.

✓ TWO-MINUTE DRILL

- ❑ If statements must have all conditions enclosed by at least one pair of parenthesis.
- ❑ Switch statements can only evaluate the byte, short, int, and char data types.

❑   For loops are the most commonly used looping construct.

❑   All loops and if statements can use the keyword true to automatically enter the loop.

❑   You cannot use a number (old C-style language construct), or anything that does not evaluate to a boolean value, in a condition for an if statement or looping construct.

❑   The three parts of the for loop are the declaration and initialization, the condition, and the iterator.

❑   None of these parts are required for the for statement.

❑   If the condition in a switch statement matches a case value, it will perform all code in the switch following the matching case statement until a break or the end of the switch statement is encountered.

❑   The do-while loop will enter the body of the loop at least once even if the condition is not met.

❑   An unlabeled break statement will cause the current iteration of the innermost looping construct to stop and the next line of code following the loop to be executed.

❑   An unlabeled continue statement will cause the current iteration of the innermost loop to stop, the condition of that loop to be checked, and if the condition is met, will perform the loop again.

❑   If the break statement or the continue statement is labeled, then it will cause similar action to occur on the labeled loop, not the innermost loop.

❑   The default keyword should be used in a switch statement if you want to perform some code and none of the case values match the conditional value.

❑   If a continue statement is used in a for loop, the variable is incremented (if it is supposed to be), then the condition is checked.

❑   If a variable is incremented or evaluated in a for loop, it must be declared before or at the for loop declaration.

SELF TEST

The following questions will help you measure your understanding of the material presented in this chapter. Read all of the choices carefully, as there may be more than one correct answer. Choose all correct answers for each question.

1. Will the following code compile?

```
int I = 1;
long L = 2;
if (I == 1) && (L == 2)
{
      System.out.println("Inside if statement");
}
```

   A. Yes
   B. No

2. Which parts of a for loop are required? (Choose all that apply.)

   A. Initialization
   B. Condition
   C. Increment
   D. None of the above

3. There is one error in the following code. What is it?

```
for (int I = 0; I < 10;)
{
      if ( I = 0 )
            System.out.print("I equals 1");
      I++;
}
```

   A. If *I* is initialized in the for loop, it must be incremented in the for loop.
   B. In Java, there must be brackets after an if statement.
   C. There is something else wrong with the code.
   D. There is nothing wrong with the code.

4. The use of the break statement causes what to happen when it is unlabeled? (Choose all that apply.)

   A. The current iteration of a loop to stop and the next line of code after the loop to start.

   B. The current iteration of a loop to stop and the next iteration to start.

   C. An exit from all loops.

   D. An exit from a switch statement.

5. What are the valid types for the expression in a switch statement? (Choose all that apply.)

   A. int

   B. long

   C. byte

   D. String

6. What will be the value of *I* when it is printed?

```
int I = 0;
outer: while (true) {
    I++;
    inner: for (int j = 0; j < 10; j++) {
        I += j;
        if (j == 3)
            continue inner;

        break outer;
    }
    continue outer;
}
System.out.println("I is " + I);
```

   A. 1

   B. 2

   C. 3

   D. 4

7. You are writing a program that uses a switch statement. You need to have the switch statement do something if there are no matches found for the condition. What Java keyword should you use?

   A. case

   B. default

C. else

D. do

8. Which looping construct are you guaranteed to enter?

    A. while

    B. do-while

    C. for

    D. None of them

9. Will the following code compile?

```
int I = 0;
while ( 1 )
{
        System.out.print("I plus one is " + (I + 1));
}
```

    A. Yes

    B. No

10. What would be the output of the following code block?

```
for (int I = 0; I < 2; I++)
{
        switch (I)
        {
           case 0:  {
                        System.out.println("I is " + I);
                        break;
                     }
           case 1:  {
                        System.out.println("I is " + I);
                        break;
                     }
        }
}
System.out.println("Out of for loop");
```

    A. I is 0
        I is 1
        Out of for loop

    B. I is 0
        Out of for loop

   C. I is 0
       I is 1
       I is 1
       Out of for loop
   D. Out of for loop

11. What happens if a labeled continue statement is used in a for loop? (Choose all that apply.)

   A. The next line of code after the continue keyword is executed.

   B. The current iteration of the loop stops and the next iteration of the innermost loop starts.

   C. The current iteration of the outermost loop stops.

   D. If a variable is incremented in the labeled for loop, it is incremented.

12. Write a labeled while loop. Make the label "outer" and provide a condition to check if a variable age is less than or equal to 21. Do not use any extra spaces that you do not need to use.

13. Will the following code compile?

```
for ( ; ; I++)
{
    int I = 0;
    System.out.println("I is " + I);
}
```

   A. Yes

   B. No

14. Will the following code block compile?

```
for ( ; ; )
{
    System.out.println("Inside the loop");
}
```

   A. Yes

   B. No

15. What will be printed after this loop has executed?

```
do
{
    System.out.println("Inside do-while loop");
    break;
} while (false);
```

A. Nothing; it will not compile.

B. "Inside do-while loop" will print once.

C. Nothing; the condition is false.

D. "Inside do-while loop" will print an infinite number of times.

16. What is wrong with the following piece of code? (Choose all that apply.)

```
for (int x; ; )
{
      x = 5;
      if (x == 5)
            System.out.println("x is equal to " + x);
      break;
}
```

A. The value of *x* must be assigned in the for loop declaration.

B. The if statement needs to have brackets around its body.

C. If *x* is declared in the for statement, then it must be incremented in the for statement.

D. None of the above is correct.

17. What will the output of the program be?

```
for ( int I = 0; I < 2; ++I )
{
      System.out.println("I is " + I);"
}
```

A. I is 1
   I is 2

B. I is 1

C. I is 0
   I is 1

D. I is 0

18. What will be printed from the following code?

```
for (int I = 0; I < 2; I++)
{
      switch (I)
      {
          case 0:  {
                      System.out.println("I is 0");
                      continue;
                  }
```

```
        case 1:  {
                    System.out.println("I is 1");
                    break;
                 }
          }
      }
```

A. I is 0
   I is 1

B. I is 0
   I is 1
   I is 1

C. I is 0

D. Nothing; it will not compile.

19. Will the following code compile, and if so, what will be printed?

```
int I = 1;
do while (I < 1)
        System.out.println("I is " + I);
while (I > 1);
```

A. The code will not compile.

B. I is 1 is printed once.

C. Nothing is printed.

D. I is 1 is printed twice.

20. Will the following code compile, and if so, what will be printed?

```
int I = 0;
label: if (I < 2)
        {
                System.out.println("I is " + I);
                I++;
                continue label;
        }
```

A. It will not compile.

B. I is 1 will be printed.

C. I is 0
   I is 1 will be printed.

D. None of the above.

5

Exception Handling

There is an old maxim in software development that says "80 percent of the work is used 20 percent of the time." Although trite, the maxim makes a good point. The 80 percent referred to is the effort required in checking for and handling errors. In many languages, writing program code that checks for and deals with errors is tedious and bloats the application source into confusing spaghetti. Still, error detection and handling may be the most important ingredient of any robust application. Java arms developers with an elegant mechanism for detecting and handling errors that produces efficient and well-organized error handling code: exception handling.

Exception handling allows developers to easily detect errors without writing special code to test return values. Better, it lets us handle these errors in code that is nicely separated from the code that generated them. It also allows us to handle an entire class of errors with the same code, and lets a method defer the handling of its errors to a previously called method.

We'll discuss each of these concepts and others in detail. Also, we'll look at examples that demonstrate not only how to properly use exception handling but how not to use it as well. Before we begin, let's introduce some terminology. The term *exception* means "exceptional condition" and is an occurrence that alters the normal program flow. Exceptions are caused by a variety of happenings, including hardware failures, resource exhaustion, and good old bugs. When an exceptional event occurs, an exception is said to be *thrown*. The code that is responsible for doing something about the error is called an *exception handler* and it *catches* the exception.

CERTIFICATION OBJECTIVE 5.01

Catching an Exception Using try and catch

Exception handling works by transferring the execution of a program to an exception handler when an error, or exception, occurs. For example, if you call a method that opens a file but the file cannot be opened, execution of that method will stop and code that you wrote to deal with this situation will be run. Therefore, we need a way of telling the compiler where to look for errors and what code to execute when a certain error happens. To do this, we use the *try* and *catch* keywords. Try is used to define a block of code in which errors may occur. This block of code is called a *guarded region* and the try keyword is said to *govern* this region. One or more catch clauses match a specific error (or class of errors—more on that later) to a block of code that handles it. Here is how it looks in pseudo code:

```
 1: try {
 2:    // This is the first line of the "guarded region"
 3:    // that is governed by the try keyword.
 4:    // put code here that might cause some kind of exception
 5:    // We may have many code lines here or just one
 6: }
 7: catch(MyFirstError) {
 8:    // put code here that handles this error
 9:    // This is the next line of the exception handler
10:    // This is the last line of the exception handler
11: }
12: catch(MySecondError) {
13:    // put code here that handles this error
14: }
15:
16: // Some other unguarded code begins here
```

In this pseudo code example, lines 2 through 5 constitute the guarded region that is governed by the try clause. Line 8 is an exception handler for an exception of type MyFirstError. Line 11 is an exception handler for an exception of type MySecondError. Notice that the catch blocks immediately follow the try block. This is a requirement; if you have one or more catch blocks, they must immediately follow the try block. Also, the catch blocks must all follow each other.

Execution starts at line 2. If the program executes all the way to line 5 with no exceptions being thrown, then execution will transfer to line 15 and continue downward. However, if at any time in lines 2 through 5, the governed region inside the try block, an exception is thrown of type MyFirstError, execution will immediately transfer to line 8. Lines 8 through 10 will be executed so that the entire catch block is executed and then execution will transfer to line 15 and continue.

This example demonstrates one of the benefits of using exception handling to remedy errors. Code to handle any particular error that may occur in the governed region needs to be written only once. There may be three different places in our try block that can generate a MyFirstError, but wherever it occurs it will be handled by line 6. We'll discuss the primary benefits of exception handling near the end of this chapter.

finally

Try and catch provide a terrific mechanism for trapping and handling exceptions, but we are left with the problem of how to clean up after ourselves. Because execution transfers out of the try block as soon as an exception is thrown, we can't put our cleanup code at the bottom of the try block and expect it to be executed if an error occurs. Almost as bad an idea is placing our cleanup code in the catch blocks. Exception handlers are a poor place to clean up after the code in the try block because each handler would have to have its own copy of the cleanup code. If, for example, you allocated a network socket or opened a file somewhere in the guarded region, each exception handler would have to close the file or release the socket. This design produces many opportunities to forget to do cleanup and a lot of redundant code. To address this problem, Java offers the *finally* block.

A finally block encloses code that is always executed at some time after the try block, regardless of whether an exception was thrown. Even if there is a return statement in the try block, the finally block executes right after the return statement. This is the right place to close your files, release your network sockets, and perform any other cleanup your code requires. If the try block executes with no exceptions, the finally block is executed immediately after the try block completes. If there was an exception thrown, the finally block executes immediately after the proper catch block completes.

Let's look at another pseudo code example.

```
 1: try {
 2:    // This is the first line of the "guarded region"
 3: }
 4: catch(MyFirstError) {
 5:    // put code here that handles this error
 6: }
 7: catch(MySecondError) {
 8:    // put code here that handles this error
 9: }
10: finally {
11:    // put code here to release any resource we
12:    // allocated in the try clause
13: }
14:
15: // More code here
```

As before, execution starts at the first line of the try block, line 2. If there are no exceptions thrown in the try block, execution transfers to line 11, the first line of the finally block. On the other hand, if a MySecondError exception is thrown while the code in the try block is executing, execution transfers to the first line of that exception handler, line 8 in the catch clause. After all the code in the catch clause is executed, the program moves to line 11, the first line of the finally clause.

Finally clauses are not required. If you don't write one, your code will compile and run just fine. In fact, if you have no resources to clean up after your try block completes then you probably don't need a finally clause. Also, the compiler does not require catch clauses. Sometimes you will run across code that has a try block immediately followed by a finally block. Such code is useful when the exception is going to be passed to the calling method, as explained in the next section. This allows the cleanup code to execute in that case as well.

You must provide either a catch clause or a finally clause. A try clause by itself will result in a compiler error.

exam
Watch

Any catch clauses must immediately follow the try block. Any finally clauses must immediately follow the last catch clause. You may omit either the catch clause or the finally clause, but not both. If you have a try block alone, the code will not compile.

CERTIFICATION OBJECTIVE 5.03

Propagating Uncaught Exceptions

Why aren't catch clauses required? What happens to an exception that's thrown in a try block when there is no catch clause waiting for it? Actually, there is no requirement that you code a catch clause for every possible exception that could be thrown from the corresponding try block. In fact, it's doubtful that you could accomplish such a feat! If a method does not provide a catch clause for a particular exception, that method is said to be "ducking" the exception.

So what happens to a ducked exception? Before we discuss that, we need to briefly introduce the concept of a *call stack*. Most programming languages have the concept of a method stack or call stack. Simply put, the call stack is the chain of methods that your program executes to get to the current method. If your program starts in method main and main calls method a, which calls method b that in turn calls method c, the call stack consists of the following:

```
Main
A
B
C
```

A call stack is said to grow downward. As you can see, the last method called is at the bottom of the stack. If you could print out the state of the stack at any given time, you would produce a *stack trace*. The method at the very bottom of the stack trace would be the method you were currently executing. If we move up the call stack, we are moving from the current method to the previously called method.

Now let's examine what happens to ducked exceptions. Exceptions are like bubbles in an aquarium. They start right where they are thrown, at the bottom of the stack, and if they are not caught by the current method, they float up the call stack to the previous method. If not caught there, they again float up to the previous method, and so on until they are caught or until they reach the top of the call stack. This is called *exception propagation*.

If they reach the top of the call stack, it's like reaching the surface of the water; they burst. And so does your program. Any exception that is never caught will cause your application to stop running. A description, if one is available, of the exception will be displayed and the call stack will be dumped to the screen. This helps you debug your application by telling you what exception was thrown from what method and what the stack looked like at the time.

CERTIFICATION OBJECTIVE 5.04

Defining Exceptions

We have been discussing exceptions as a concept. We know that they are thrown when a problem of some type happens, and we know what effect they have on the flow of our program. Earlier, you learned that an exception is an occurrence that alters the normal program flow. There is another way to describe an exception and that is as an instance of a class derived from class Exception. When an exception is thrown, an object of a particular type is instantiated and handed to the exception handler as an argument to the catch clause. An actual catch clause looks like this:

```
try {
    // some code here
}
catch (ArrayIndexOutOfBoundsException e) {
    e.printStackTrace();
}
```

In this example, *e* is an instance of a class called ArrayIndexOutOfBoundsException. Like any other object, its methods, including those of its superclasses, may be called.

Exception Hierarchy

All exception classes derive from class Exception. Class Exception derives from class Throwable that derives from class Object. Figure 5-1 is a hierarchy chart for the exception classes.

Hierarchy chart for the
exception classes

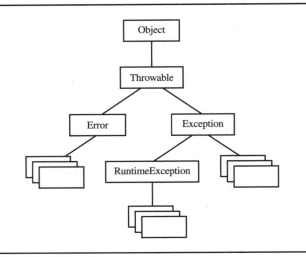

As you can see, two subclasses are derived from Throwable, Exception and
Error. Classes that derive from Error represent unusual situations that are not
caused by program errors or by anything that would normally happen during
program execution. Generally, your application won't be able to recover from
an Error, so you're not required to handle these conditions. If your code does
not handle them, and it usually won't, it will still compile with no trouble.
Although often thought of as exceptional conditions, Errors are technically
not exceptions because they do not derive from class Exception.

on the
job

*There is sometimes confusion in discussions about exceptions because
two different concepts share the name "exception." The concept of an
exceptional condition as an event that requires attention is the first.
The next is an Exception as a type of object. Any class that subclasses
the type Exception is an Exception object. Often, objects of type Error
are referred to as exceptions in the exceptional condition sense even
though they are not Exceptions in the object type sense.*

All of Java's exception types derive from class Exception. In general,
an exception represents something that happens not as a result of a
programming error but rather because some resource is not available or

some other condition required for correct execution is not present. For example, if your application is supposed to communicate with another application or computer that is not answering, this is an exception that is not caused by a bug. Figure 5-1 also shows a subtype of Exception called RuntimeException. These exceptions are a special case because they actually do indicate program errors when they occur. They can also represent rare, difficult to handle exceptional conditions. Runtime exceptions will be discussed in greater detail later in this chapter.

Java provides many exception classes, most of which have quite descriptive names. There are two ways to get information about an exception. The first is from the type of the exception itself. The next is from information that you can get from the exception object. Class Throwable provides its descendants with some methods that are useful in exception handlers. One of these is printStackTrace(). As expected, if you call an exception object's printStackTrace() method, as in the earlier example, a stack trace from where the exception occurred will be printed. This method is overloaded to accept either no arguments, in which case the output is directed to standard error; to accept a printStream object, in which case the output is directed to the printStream; or to accept a printWriter object. We discussed that a call stack grows downward with the most recently called method at the bottom. You will notice that this method prints the most recent method first and continues printing the name of each method as the function works its way up the call stack (this is called *unwinding the stack*) from the bottom. The result is that the stack is printed upside down, with the most recently entered method at the top and the first method called at the bottom.

Other helpful methods include getMessage() and toString(). The getMessage() method retrieves a string that was given to the exception when it was instantiated, if there was one. Otherwise, null is returned. We'll discuss this further when we cover making your own exceptions. The toString() method returns a string composed of the name of this exception's class, followed by a colon and the same string that is returned by the getMessage() method.

Handling an Entire Class Hierarchy of Exceptions

We have discussed that Java's catch keyword allows you to specify a particular type of exception to catch. You can actually catch more than one type of exception in a single catch clause. If the exception class that you specify in the catch clause has no subclasses, then only the specified class of exception object will be caught. However, if the class specified in the catch clause does have subclasses, any exception object that subclasses the specified class will be caught as well.

For example, class IndexOutOfBoundsException has two subclasses, ArrayIndexOutOfBoundsException and StringIndexOutOfBoundsException. You may want to write one exception handler that deals with exceptions produced by either type of boundary error, but you may not be concerned with which exception you actually have. In this case you could write a catch clause like the following:

```
try {
    // Some code here that can throw a boundary exception
}
catch (IndexOutOfBoundsException e) {
    e.printStackTrace();
}
```

If any code in the try block throws either an ArrayOutOfBoundsException exception or a StringIndexOutOfBoundsException exception, the exception will be caught and handled.

This can be a convenience but should be used sparingly. By specifying an exception class' superclass in your catch clause, you are discarding valuable information about the exception. You can find out exactly what exception class you have, but if you're going to do that, you're better off writing a separate catch clause for each exception type of interest.

Additionally, resist the temptation to write one quick, catchall exception handler such as the following:

```
try {
    // some code
}
catch (Exception e) {
    e.printStackTrace();
}
```

This code will catch every exception generated. Of course, no single exception handler can properly handle every exception, and programming in this way defeats the design. Exception handlers that trap a lot of errors at once will probably reduce your program's reliability because it's likely that an exception will be caught that the handler does not know how to deal with.

Exception Matching

If you have an exception hierarchy composed of a base type exception and a number of subtypes, and you are interested in handling only one of the subtypes in a special way but want to handle the rest together, you need only write two catch clauses.

When an exception is thrown, Java will try to find a catch clause for the exception type. If it does not find one, it will search for a handler for a supertype of the exception. If it does not find a catch clause that matches a supertype for the exception, then the exception is propagated up the call stack. This process is called *exception matching*.

Let's look at an example:

```
1: import java.io.*;
2: public class ReadData {
3:    public static void main(String args[]) {
4:       try {
5:          RandomAccessFile raf =
6:             new RandomAccessFile("myfile.txt", "r");
7:          byte b[] = new byte[1000];
8:          raf.readFully(b, 0, 1000);
9:       }
10:      catch(FileNotFoundException e) {
11:         System.err.println("File not found");
12:         System.err.println(e.getMessage());
13:         e.printStackTrace();
14:      }
15:      catch(IOException e) {
```

```
16:                 System.err.println("IO Error");
17:                 System.err.println(e.toString());
18:                 e.printStackTrace();
19:         }
20:     }
21: }
```

This short program attempts to open a file and to read some data from it. Opening and reading files can generate many exceptions, most of which are IOExceptions. For whatever reason, in this program we are interested in knowing what the exact exception is only if it is a FileNotFoundException. Otherwise, we don't care exactly what the problem is.

FileNotFoundException is a subclass of IOException. Therefore, we could handle it in the catch clause that catches all IOExceptions, but then we would have to test the exception to see if it was a FileNotFoundException. Instead, we coded a special exception handler for the FileNotFoundException and a separate exception handler for all other IOExceptions.

Notice that the catch clause for the FileNotFoundException was placed above the handler for the IOException. This is very important. If this is done the opposite way, the program will not compile. The handlers for the most specific exceptions must always be placed above those for more general exceptions.

If this code generates a FileNotFoundException, it will be handled by the catch clause that begins at line 10. If it generates another IOException, perhaps EOFException, which is a subclass of IOException, it will be handled by the catch clause that begins at line 15. If some other exception is generated, such as a runtime exception of some type, neither catch clause will be executed and the exception will be propagated up the call stack.

exam
ⓦatch

Catch clauses that catch subclasses of exception types caught by other catch clauses relating to the same try block must be placed above the others! Be sure that if you catch both a subtype and a supertype of the same exception that the most specific type is caught first. If you don't, your program will not compile. When looking at exam questions, be sure to check that the question followed this rule. If it didn't, the answer is probably that the code won't compile.

CERTIFICATION OBJECTIVE 5.05

Runtime Exceptions and Checked Exceptions

Runtime exceptions are a special case in Java. Because they have a special purpose of signaling events that happen at runtime, usually as the result of a programming error, or bug, they do not have to be caught and typically are not. When they appear and are not caught, they stop your application and print the name of the exception and a stack trace, as discussed earlier. Some of the most common causes of a RuntimeException are the use of a null reference, incorrect array indices, and so on.

Runtime exceptions are referred to as *unchecked exceptions*. All other exceptions, meaning all those that do not derive from java.lang.RuntimeException, are *checked exceptions*. A checked exception must be caught somewhere in your code. If you use a method that throws a checked exception but do not catch the checked exception somewhere, your code will not compile. That's why they are checked exceptions; the compiler checks them to make sure they are handled. Many of the methods supplied in Java's runtime classes throw checked exceptions, so you will often write exception handlers to cope with exceptions generated by methods you didn't write.

exam
Watch

When an object of type Exception or of type Throwable is thrown, it must be caught. These objects are checked exceptions.

Remember, objects of type Error are not exception objects, although they do represent exceptional conditions. When an object of type Error or a subclass of type Error is thrown, it is unchecked. You are not required to catch Error objects or Error subtypes.

exam
Watch

All runtime exceptions derive from class RuntimeException and are unchecked exceptions. If an Exception object does not subclass RuntimeException, it is a checked exception and must be either handled or specified.

on the Job

Because Java has checked exceptions, it is commonly said that Java forces developers to handle errors. This is not true. Yes, Java forces us to write exception handlers for each exception that can occur during normal operation. But it's up to us to make the exception handlers do something useful. A catch clause can contain anything from a semi-colon to a complete solution to the problem. It's the semi-colons that are a problem. Don't make the mistake of believing that just because a program is written in Java, all the potential exceptional conditions are handled correctly.

CERTIFICATION OBJECTIVE 5.06

Exception Specification and the Public Interface

So, how do we know that some method throws an exception that we have to catch? Just as a method must specify what type and how many arguments it accepts and what is returned, the exceptions that a method can throw must be specified. The list of thrown exceptions is part of a method's public interface. The *throws* keyword is used as follows to list the exceptions that a method can throw:

```
void myFunction() throws MyException1, MyException2 {
   // code for the method here
}
```

This method returns void, accepts no arguments, and throws two exceptions of type MyException1 and MyException2.

If you wish, you may specify that an exception is thrown by a method, but then not actually throw it. Also, your method may specify an exception that is thrown by some other method that your method calls. If you do this, you will not need to handle the exception. Instead, it will propagate up and be handled by a method further up the stack. Each method must, however, either handle all checked exceptions by supplying a catch clause or list each unhandled checked exception as a thrown exception. This rule is referred to as Java's *catch or specify requirement*.

Again, there is an exemption to these rules. An object of type RuntimeException or Error, or any of their subclasses, may be thrown from any method without being specified as part of the method's public interface. Also, a handler need not be present. Objects RuntimeException, Error, and their subtypes are unchecked exceptions and unchecked exceptions need not be specified or handled.

Here is an example:

```
public void myMethod1()
    throws EOFException
{
    return myMethod2();
}
public void myMethod2() throws EOFException
{
    // Some code that actually throws the exception goes
here
}
```

Let's look at myMethod1. Because EOFException subclasses IOException and IOException subclasses Exception, it is a checked exception and must be listed as an exception that may be thrown by this method. But where will the exception actually come from? The public interface for method myMethod2 called here specifies that an exception of this type can be thrown. Whether or not that method actually throws the exception itself, or calls another method that throws it, is unimportant to us; we simply know that we have to either catch the exception or specify that we throw it. The method myMethod1 does not catch the exception, so it specifies that it throws it.

Now let's look at another example, myMethod3.

```
public void myMethod3()
{
    // Some code that throws a NullPointerException goes here
}
```

According to the comment, this method can throw a NullPointerException.

Because RuntimeException is the immediate base class of NullPointerException, it is an unchecked exception and need not be specified. We can see that myMethod3 does not specify any exceptions.

Overriding Methods

When you override a method, you may not specify different exception types than the base method did. You may, however, specify that the overridden method throws exception types that are subclasses of those thrown by the base method. Also, the overriding method may throw the same exceptions as the overridden method or no exceptions at all.

Here is an example:

```
1: public class MyBaseClass {
2:     public void myMethod() throws java.io.IOException { }
3: }
4:
5: class OkSubClass0 extends MyBaseClass {
6:     public void myMethod() throws java.io.IOException {}
7: }
8:
9: class OkSubClass1 extends MyBaseClass {
10:     public void myMethod() throws
        java.io.FileNotFoundException {}
11: }
12:
13: class OkSubClass2 extends MyBaseClass {
14:     public void myMethod() {}
15: }
16:
17: class NotOkSubClass extends MyBaseClass {
18:     public void myMethod() throws java.awt.AWTException {}
19: }
```

The code in this example declares a base class, called MyBaseClass, that is subclassed four times. The base class has only one method, myMethod, that specifies that it throws an exception of type IOException.

The first subclass, OkSubClass1, overrides the method correctly because it specifies the same exception type to be thrown. The second subclass also overrides myMethod correctly at line 10 because it specifies that it throws a subclass of IOException, FileNotFoundException. The third subclass, OkSubClass2 also correctly overrides myMethod at line 14, because it specifies no thrown exceptions. A method that overrides another need not throw the same exceptions that the base method throws.

The last subclass, NotOkSubClass, is incorrect at line 18. Here, myMethod attempts to specify an AWTException. AWTException is not a subtype of IOException; therefore, this method will generate a compiler error.

CERTIFICATION OBJECTIVE 5.08

Writing and Throwing Your Own Exceptions

We have seen that the Java language has many exceptions that it can throw, either from its application programming interface (API) methods or from the Java Virtual Machine (JVM) itself when a runtime error occurs. Java developers may also throw exceptions from their own methods. Additionally, you can write your own exception classes.

Throwing an exception is quite easy. You just use the throw keyword with an instance of an exception object to throw, like this:

```
throw new RuntimeException();
```

That's all there is to it. This code instantiates an object of type RuntimeException and then generates an exception by throwing the object. Whenever you create an instance of an exception object, a stack trace is saved in the object and the current method is at the bottom of that trace. If the catch clause that catches this exception prints out the call stack, the method from which this exception was thrown will be at the bottom.

Each exception has two constructors, the default constructor, which accepts no arguments, and one that accepts a string as a parameter. If you instantiate an Exception object with a string in its constructor, this string will be returned when the exception object's getMessage and toString methods are called.

You can throw an exception from any place in a method where you wish to signal an error. One interesting place to throw an exception from is in an exception handler. Throwing an exception from within a catch clause is no different from throwing one from anywhere else. As you would expect, if you instantiate and throw a new exception from a catch clause, the stack trace information will indicate that the exception was thrown from the method that contained the throw keyword, not the location from which the original exception was thrown.

Re-throwing the Same Exception

Just as you can throw a new exception from a catch clause, you can also throw the same exception you just caught. Here is a catch clause that does this:

```
catch(NullPointerException e) {
    e.printStackTrace();
    throw e;
}
```

When the throw executes here, the exception is handed to the next level up to be processed. All additional catch clauses associated with the same try block are ignored. Also, the stack trace information does not change. If the next exception handler to catch this exception prints the stack trace, the output will be identical to that generated by the call to printStackTrace() in the preceding catch clause.

If you prefer to have the stack trace indicate that the catch clause from which the object was re-thrown is the original location of the exception, you can call the fillInStackTrace() method of the exception, as follows:

```
Catch(NullPointerException e) {
    e.printStackTrace();
    Throwable changedE = e.fillInStackTrace();
    throw changedE;
}
```

What's interesting here is that the fillInStackTrace() method returned an object of type Throwable, which is the superclass of Exception. It was that returned object that was actually thrown. The fillInStackTrace method is used primarily to hide the original location where the exception was created. The stack information placed in the exception object when it was created is replaced with the stack trace to the current location when this method is called.

If you do throw an object of type Throwable, your method needs to specify that. Here is an example that generates an IOException, changes its origin, and re-throws it.

```
 1: import java.io.*;
 2: public class Test
 3: {
 4:     public void foo() throws Throwable
 5:     {
 6:         try {
 7:             new FileInputStream("nonexistent-file");
 9:         }
10:         catch (IOException e) {
11:             throw e.fillInStackTrace();
12:         }
13:     }
14: }
```

In line four, method foo specifies that it throws a Throwable. Line 10 catches an IOException. Line 11 modifies the stack trace and throws an object of type Throwable.

Catching a Throwable is just like catching an Exception. Here is a fragment that shows how to catch a Throwable.

```
catch(Throwable t) {
    // Handler code here
}
```

Rather than actually throwing the object returned by fillInStackTrace as a Throwable, it's usually a better idea to cast it down to the Throwable subtype that it was when it was caught. Here is the earlier example again, modified to cast the Throwable to an IOException.

```
 1: import java.io.*;
 2: public class Test
 3: {
 4:     public void foo() throws IOException
 5:     {
 6:         try {
 7:             new FileInputStream("nonexistent-file");
```

```
 9:        }
10:        catch (IOException e) {
11:            throw (IOException) e.fillInStackTrace();
12:        }
13:    }
14: }
```

on the **!**job

If you want to handle an exception in more than one handler, you can re-throw the exception. If you want to hide the details of the exception's true origin from the additional handlers, call the exception's fillInStackTrace method. This will change the stack trace information in the exception so that the bottom of the trace is the current method.

Writing Your Own Exceptions

It's easy to create your own exception classes. All you need to do is to inherit from an existing exception. Here is a complete exception class:

```
class MySpecialException extends Exception {
   public MySpecialException() {}
   public MySpecialException(String s) { super(s); }
}
```

This simple class inherits all the functionality of its base class, Exception, and adds no functionality. If you subclass RuntimeException, Error, or any of their subclasses, you are creating an unchecked exception. Likewise, if you subclass Exception or any Exception subtype other than RuntimeException, you are creating a checked exception.

It is possible to add additional functionality. An exception class is like any other class. However, developers don't generally expect to find extra behaviors in their exception objects. If you're writing a library for other developers, especially one that will be distributed outside your own organization, it's best to not add anything new to exceptions.

Putting It All Together

Here is an example that combines many of the topics we have discussed in this chapter:

```
1: import java.io.*;
2:
3: // This is our own Exception
4: class MyCheckedException extends Exception {
5:     public MyCheckedException() {super();}
6:     public MyCheckedException(String s) {super(s);}
7: }
8:
9: class Catapult
10: {
11:     public static void main(String args[]) {
12:         System.out.println("Starting Catapult");
13:         myMethod1();
14:     }
15:
16:     public static void myMethod1() {
17:         try {
18:             System.out.println("Entering myMethod1()");
19:             myMethod2();
20:             System.out.println("This line never executes");
21:         }
22:         catch(MyCheckedException e) {
23:             System.out.println("Caught MyCheckedException in myMethod1");
24:             System.out.println("Printing stack trace of the Exception's origin:");
25:             e.printStackTrace();
26:         }
27:         finally {
28:             System.out.println("Executing myMethod1() finally clause");
```

```
29:        }
30:    }
31:
32:    public static void myMethod2() throws MyCheckedException {
33:        try {
34:            System.out.println("Entered MyMethod2 and throwing MyCheckedException");
35:            throw new MyCheckedException("Jim's Exception");
36:        }
37:        finally {
38:            System.out.println("Executing myMethod2() finally clause");
39:        }
40:    }
41: }
```

Here is the output this program produces:

```
Starting Catapult
Entering myMethod1()
Entered MyMethod2 and throwing MyCheckedException
Executing myMethod2() finally clause
Caught MyCheckedException in myMethod1
Printing stack trace of the Exception's origin:
MyCheckedException: Jim's Exception
        at Catapult.myMethod2(java1.java:34)
        at Catapult.myMethod1(java1.java:19)
        at Catapult.main(java1.java:13)
Executing myMethod1() finally clause
```

Let's review the source code. At line 4, we write a class called MyCheckedException that subclasses Exception. Therefore, we know that MyCheckedException is a checked exception. We carefully overloaded the constructor for the two standard Exception constructors and called the superclass constructors.

At line 16, we can see that myMethod1 specifies no exceptions, so we know it does not throw any exceptions that we are required to catch in main (that is, checked exceptions). Also, myMethod1 calls myMethod2, which specifies that it throws a MyCheckedException object. Because myMethod1 does not specify any exceptions, it has to catch the exception specified by myMethod2. Therefore, myMethod1 has a catch clause to trap exception MyCheckedException. Also, there is a finally clause at line 27. Obviously, this method does no more than call myMethod2 and catch its exception.

At line 32, we see that myMethod2 does specify that it throws a MyCheckedException. It has a try block and a finally clause, but no catch clause. At line 35, the MyCheckedException is actually thrown.

Execution begins at line 12. After printing that the program has started, the main method calls myMethod1. MyMethod1 prints that it has been entered and calls myMethod2. MyMethod2 announces its presence and immediately throws an exception at line 35. Because myMethod2 has no catch clause for this exception, its finally block at line 38 is executed next.

At this point, execution goes to the catch clause in myMethod1 at line 23. Note that line 20 was not executed. The exception handler announces that it has caught the exception and calls the exception's printStackTrace method, which MyCheckedException inherited from its Throwable subclass. Next, myMethod1's finally clause executes, the method returns, and the program is done.

How Does Exception Handling Improve the Application?

Exception handling actually goes a long way toward helping developers write robust code. There are three primary benefits of exception handling.

Exception Handlers Are Separated from a Method's Primary Logic

In many languages, a method's success or failure is determined by accepting its return code and testing it. After each method call, an if statement tests the return and executes some error code if the method failed. Although this system can work, significant diligence and effort is demanded of you, the developer, to make sure that every potential error is checked for. Even the best developers tend to miss a few return value checks.

When each and every return code is checked, the program may suffer as a result. Checking each method return code right after the method is called tends to add several extra code lines for each method. Worse, they are added right in the middle of your method, adding significant clutter that obfuscates the logic of the method. Usually, you end up with spaghetti code that is very hard to debug and maintain.

By moving all the error handling code into its own special location, the readability and maintainability of the source is increased, which increases the code's reliability.

Similar Errors Can Be Handled Together

Another important benefit provided by Java's exception handling is that it allows us to handle related errors together if we choose to. This is implemented when we place a supertype into a catch clause so that it will handle any subtype exception.

For example, when conducting file operations, we can catch all exceptions of type IOException in a single catch clause. We won't need to test an error code and say if the error is this type or that type or the other type then do this or that or the other thing. We can use one exception handler for all the exception subtypes. If any of the subtypes need to be handled differently, we can easily provide a catch clause for each of them and allow the more generic catch for the supertype to handle the rest.

on the **job** *Although being able to handle entire hierarchies of exceptions is a benefit of the exception handling philosophy, it can be easily abused and result in less reliable code. It's very important to avoid writing exception handlers that are too general. If you try to catch too many errors in one handler, there is a good chance that the solution in your handler won't work right for each subtype and the exception will be handled improperly. Also, don't write general handlers that test the type of the exception to decide how to handle it. If you need to handle subtypes of an exception differently, write a catch clause for each one.*

Exception Propagation

The exception propagation mechanism is another significant benefit provided by exception handling. By allowing the methods that called the method we wrote to handle errors that we report by throwing exceptions, we increase the number of situations in which our code can be used. Very often, we won't know what corrective action to take when an exception is generated, so being able to defer to our caller is a valuable capability.

Imagine that we are writing a class library that we intend to distribute widely. Perhaps one of the methods in our library will do something as simple as connect to another computer across a network. Our method is passed the name of the other computer, but we are unable to connect to it. We don't know why we were trying to connect and we certainly don't know what to do about it. Do we try again? Do we try another address? There is no way to know, and we should avoid making any assumptions about how our library is being used. The only good solution is to report the problem to our user, who in this case is the developer of the application we are running in, and let them decide what to do. So, we throw an exception that reports the problem. We don't need to write any special code to pass a return code back to our caller. We let Java handle that for us.

As good as exception handling is, it's still up to the developer to make proper use of it. Exception handling makes organizing our code and signaling problems easy, but the exception handlers still have to be written. You will find that even the most complex situations can be handled, and after they are, your code is still reusable, readable, and maintainable.

CERTIFICATION SUMMARY

Error handling is one very important requirement for any application. Java provides an elegant mechanism for error handling called exception handling. Exceptions are occurrences in our program that alter the normal program flow. Exception handling allows developers to isolate their error correction code into separate blocks, so that the main line of code does not become cluttered and confusing. Also, similar errors can be handled together and error handling can be deferred to methods that were previously called.

Java's try keyword is used to specify a guarded region, which is a block of code in which errors will be detected. The try clause is said to govern the region. An exception handler is the code that is executed when an exception occurs. The handler is defined by using Java's catch keyword. All catch clauses must immediately follow the related try block. Java also provides the finally keyword. This is used to define a block of code that is always executed, either immediately after a catch clause completes or immediately after the associated try block in the case that no exception was thrown. Use finally blocks to release system resources and to perform any cleanup required by the code in the try block. Finally blocks follow the catch clauses and are not required.

An exception object is an instance of class Exception or one of its subclasses. The catch clause takes, as a parameter, an instance of an object of a type derived from the Exception class. Several useful methods are provided in exception objects. These include toString(), which prints out the name of the exception and any message it contains; getMessage(), which returns any string that the exception object may contain; and printStackTrace (), which displays a listing of the current method and all previously called methods in the order in which they were called. Java requires that each method either catch any exception it can throw or else specify that it throws the exception. The exception specification is part of the method's public interface. To specify what exceptions are thrown, the throws keyword is used in a method definition along with a list of all thrown exceptions.

Runtime exceptions are exceptions that are of type RuntimeException or are derived from that type. These exceptions are not required to be handled or specified, so they are a special case. Again, Errors are of type java.lang.Error or its subclasses, and they also are not required to be handled or specified. Checked exceptions are exception types that are not RuntimeExceptions or Errors. If your code fails to either handle a checked exception or specify that it is thrown, it will not compile.

Your code may throw exceptions using the throws keyword. Additionally, you may create your own exception types by subclassing class Exception or one of its subclasses.

✓ TWO-MINUTE DRILL

❏ An exception, or exceptional condition, is an occurrence during your program execution that alters the normal flow.

❏ An Exception object is an instance of the class Exception or one of its subclasses.

❏ An Error object is an instance of the class Error or one of its subclasses.

❏ A section of code enclosed in braces and started with the keyword try is referred to as a guarded region. The try keyword governs this region. This is the code that will be watched for exceptions.

❏ The catch keyword is used to define an exception handler for a particular type of exception object and its subclasses, if any.

❏ Catch blocks must always immediately follow the try block they pertain to and the other catch clauses for the same try block. Catch blocks are not required.

❏ The appropriate catch clause is executed immediately after an exception is thrown. The remaining code in the try block is not executed.

❏ The finally keyword is used to define a block of code that is always executed after the catch clause or after the try clause if no exceptions occurred. This block is typically used to release resources and to perform any needed cleanup for the try clause. Finally blocks are not required.

❏ Either a catch clause or a finally block must be specified with a try block.

❏ Any method from which an exception can be thrown must either handle this exception by providing a try block or else specify that the exception can be thrown. This rule is referred to as the catch or specify requirement.

❏ Specifying a thrown exception is done by using the throws keyword after a method's parameter list and following it with a list of exception types.

❏ A runtime exception is an instance of the class RuntimeException or any of its subclasses.

❏ Runtime exceptions and Errors are exceptions to the catch or specify requirement. Runtime exceptions may be thrown from any method without being handled or specified.

❏ A checked exception is any exception that is neither a RuntimeException nor an Error. Checked exceptions are subject to the catch or specify requirement. If checked exceptions are neither handled nor specified, the Java compiler will produce an error, and the application will not be compiled.

❏ Exceptions are thrown by instantiating an Exception class and using the throw keyword, like this:

```
throw new RuntimeException("MyException");
```

❏ You can create your own exceptions by subclassing any existing Exception class or any of its subclasses.

❏ An exception can output a stack trace to its origin point through its printStackTrace() method.

❏ Once caught, an exception may be re-thrown. A re-thrown exception will contain the same stack trace information as it did when it was originally thrown. You can modify the stack trace by calling an Exception object's fillInStackTrace method. This method returns an object of type Throwable.

❏ The advantages of exception handling are as follows:

    ❏ Exception handlers are separated nicely from the main body of your methods and may be used any time that the same error occurs.

    ❏ Related types of errors may be handled together.

    ❏ Exceptions can be propagated up the call stack to be handled by a previously called method.

SELF TEST

The following questions will help you measure your understanding of the material presented in this chapter. Read all of the choices carefully, as there may be more than one correct answer. Choose all correct answers for each question.

1. Given the following program:

```
public class MyProgram {
    public void main(){
        try {
            System.out.println("Hello World ");
        }
    }
}
```

   A. The program will compile correctly.
   B. The program will not compile because there is no catch clause.
   C. The program will not compile because there is no catch clause and because there is no finally clause.
   D. The program will not compile because main does not specify any exceptions but there is a try block.

2. Given the following program:

```
public class MyProgram {
    public static void main(String args[]){
        try {
            System.out.print("Hello world ");
        }
        finally {
            System.out.print("Finally executing ");
        }
    }
}
```

   What will the output of this program be?
   A. Nothing. The program will not compile because no exceptions are specified.
   B. Nothing. The program will not compile because no catch clauses are specified.
   C. Hello world
   D. Hello world Finally executing

3. Given the following program:

```
public class MyProgram {

public static void throwit()
    {
       throw new RuntimeException();
    }
    public static void main(String args[]){
       try {
          System.out.println("Hello world ");
          throwit();
          System.out.println("Done with try block ");
       }
       finally {
          System.out.println("Finally executing ");
       }
    }
}
```

Which answer most closely indicates the behavior of the program?

A. The program will not compile.

B. The program will print "Hello world", then will print that a RuntimeException has occurred, then will print "Done with try block," and then it will print "Finally executing."

C. The program will print "Hello world," then will print that a RuntimeException has occurred, and then it will print "Finally executing."

D. The program will print "Hello world," then will print "Finally executing," then it will print that a RuntimeException has occurred.

4. Given that EOFException and FileNotFoundException are both subclasses of IOException, which statement is most true concerning the following code?

```
System.out.println("Start ");
try {
   System.out.println("Hello world");
   throw new FileNotFoundException();
}
System.out.println(" Catch Here ");
catch(EOFException e) {
   System.out.println("End of file exception");
}
catch(FileNotFoundException e) {
   System.out.println("File not found");
}
```

A. The code will not compile.
B. The code will print File Not Found.
C. The code will print End of file exception.
D. The code will print Start Hello world Catch Here File not found.

5. Given that EOFException is a subtype of IOException, what can be said about the following code?

```
try {
    throw new EOFException();
}
catch(IOException e) {
    System.out.println("IO Exception caught ");
}
```

A. The code will not compile.
B. The code will run and print "IO Exception Caught."
C. The thrown exception will be ignored because there is no catch clause for it.
D. The thrown error will propagate up the call stack and the program will terminate.

6. Which methods are available in all Exceptions? (Choose all that apply.)

A. toString
B. retry
C. printStackTrace
D. getMessage

7. Which class is a base class for all Exceptions?

A. String
B. Error
C. Throwable
D. RuntimeException

8. Unhandled checked exceptions:

A. Terminate the application
B. Are ignored at runtime
C. Cause the program to not compile
D. Are handled automatically by the Java VM

9. Unhandled unchecked exceptions:

A. Terminate the application

B. Are ignored

C. Cause the program to not compile

D. Are handled automatically by the Java VM

10. Given that EOFException and FileNotFoundException are subtypes of IOException, what can be said about the following code?

```
try {
    throw new FileNotFoundException();
}
catch(IOException e) {
    System.out.println("IO Exception caught");
}
catch(EOFException e) {
    System.out.println("EOF Exception caught");
}
```

A. The code will not compile.

B. The code will print "IO Exception Caught."

C. The thrown exception will propagate up the call stack.

D. The code will print "EOF Exception caught."

11. Exceptions that are not RuntimeExceptions or Errors:

A. Must be either caught or specified

B. Need not be caught or specified

C. Must not be caught

D. Must not be specified

12. RuntimeExceptions:

A. Must be either caught or specified

B. Need not be caught or specified

C. Must not be caught

D. Must not be specified

13. RuntimeExceptions usually:

A. Cannot be caught

B. Are just like other exceptions

C. Represent program bugs

D. Must be specified

14. Finally clauses:
    A. Are executed only after a try block executes with no exceptions
    B. Are only executed if an exception is thrown but no matching catch clause is found
    C. Are always executed after try and catch blocks
    D. Are only executed if a catch clause is executed in the current method

15. Overridden methods:
    A. May add exceptions from new hierarchies to the method's exception specification
    B. May not add exceptions from new hierarchies to the method's exception specification
    C. May not throw exceptions
    D. May only throw RuntimeExceptions

16. An exception object's getMessage method:
    A. Returns the exact type of the exception object
    B. Prints the name of the method in which the object was instantiated
    C. Returns a string containing an explanation of the exception
    D. Returns the string, if any, that was passed to the constructor of the object

17. An exception object's fillInStackTrace method:
    A. Changes the object's origin point to reflect the location where the object was created.
    B. Prints a stack trace from the object's original origin.
    C. Prints a stack trace from the object's current location.
    D. Returns an object of type Throwable and changes the object's origin point to reflect the current location.

18. The following code fragment:
    ```
    class MySpecialRunException extends RuntimeException {
        public MySpecialRunException() {}
        public MySpecialRunException(String s) { super(s); }
    }
    ```
    A. Will prevent a code module from compiling
    B. Creates a type of checked exception
    C. Creates a type of unchecked exception
    D. Will compile but not run

19. The following code fragment:

```
class MySpecialException extends Exception {
    public MySpecialException() {}
    public MySpecialException(String s) { super(s); }
}
```

A. Will prevent a code module from compiling

B. Creates a type of checked exception

C. Creates a type of unchecked exception

D. Will compile but not run

20. Which of the following is not an advantage of exception handling?

A. Exception handling improves code organization by separating a method's error handling code from the body of the method.

B. Exception handling allows a method to defer the handling of its errors to a previously called method.

C. Exception handling improves an application's performance.

D. Exception handling allows similar errors to be handled by a single handler.

6

Garbage Collection

T his chapter introduces you to garbage collection, the process that Java uses for managing unused memory. Garbage collecting ensures that objects that you allocated dynamically will not be freed before you are done using them, and won't hang around cluttering memory after you are finished with them. It greatly simplifies the design and implementation of your code. Garbage collection is nothing new; it has been utilized in languages such as Lisp and Smalltalk for many years.

Although the Java specification doesn't require it, most implementations of the Java language use a mark-sweep garbage collection system. In this system, objects become eligible for deletion as soon as the last reference to them drops, but they don't actually get deleted until free memory is exhausted. When the system determines that it needs memory, it deletes any object that it can determine is no longer used. This takes the deletion control out of the hands of the programmer—the programmer has no way of telling when an object is going to be deleted. To alert the programmer that an object is about to be deleted, the object's finalizer is called. The finalizer of the object is simply a method of an object that is called just before the object is deleted; the finalizer for an object isn't required and is often omitted.

The Java language provides some built-in routines for controlling garbage collection: the routines System.gc() and System.runFinalization(). These routines are requests to the runtime system, and can be ignored by it. Most implementations will attempt to do something reasonable when you call these methods. System.gc() requests that garbage collection be run. System.runFinalizers() asks that finalizers be executed but that memory not necessarily be freed. We'll discuss the difference. We'll also talk about the new classes in java.lang.ref that can be used for more advanced memory management.

Although garbage collection simplifies the writing of Java code, it is not an excuse to get lazy. You have to understand the trade-offs that garbage collection imposes, and what decisions you have to make so the system works efficiently. After you read this chapter, you'll be able to make those decisions.

Garbage Collection System

When a Java application runs, it uses memory. Memory is one of the most basic computer resources, and tends to be one of the most limited. The action of creating a new object is the biggest use of memory in a Java application. Because it is hard to tell how many objects are going to be created when a program runs, it is hard to tell how much memory a program will need.

Java manages memory in a structure called a *heap*. Every object that Java creates is allocated in the heap, which is created at the beginning of the application and managed automatically by Java. Java attempts to ensure that there is always enough memory in the heap to create a new object. It does this through a process called *garbage collection.*

The basic idea behind a garbage collection system is simple: if memory is allocated, it eventually has to be freed. There is only so much memory on a computer—even today's modern machines with huge amounts of memory have an upper limit. If a program repeatedly allocates memory without freeing it, eventually the system will run out of memory and the program will fail.

The problem with freeing memory is that it can be very hard to determine when memory should be freed. It is always clear when memory is allocated; each and every object can be tracked down to the single new statement that created it. It is not so clear when an object is no longer being used. An object may be in use by many different parts of a program at once; determining which of these parts is the last one to use the object can be impossible to figure out before the program runs.

Consider a class that represents a company with employees. Each of the employees has a reference to the company. There are an unknown number of employees in the system. If all the employees for the company are freed, the company is no longer being used and should be freed. However, the company should not be freed until all the employees have been freed.

Now you have a problem: how do you know when to free the company object? If you free the company object too soon, when there are still employees referring to the company, then those employee objects may fail when they attempt to reference the nonexistent company. If you free the company object too late, when there are no employees referring to the company, then we are using up memory unnecessarily and risk running out of it.

Although the individual programmer could solve this problem, it would have to be solved by every programmer, and for every class. Java relieves the programmer of having to do this by moving the determination of which objects are in use into the Java runtime system. The runtime system can look behind the scenes to figure out which objects are in use, and automatically free those that aren't.

This may sound like a trivial advance in programming languages, but studies have shown that up to 90 percent of all programming errors are related to poorly written memory management. By automatically managing memory, Java automatically removes up to 90 percent of the possible bugs in your programs!

Although garbage collection does a nice job of making sure that objects are freed once they are no longer used, it cannot give you an infinite amount of memory, and it cannot make your program use less memory. If you continuously add objects in a Java program without dropping references to them, the program will still run out of memory. Garbage collection makes sure that well-behaved programs have enough memory; it doesn't ensure that poorly behaved ones have enough.

Classic Garbage Collection

The first part of this chapter deals with classic garbage collection: garbage collection as it was introduced in the first Java releases. In classic garbage collection, the Java Virtual Machine (JVM) has the responsibility for making sure that unused objects are deleted from memory, or *collected*. It does this by looking at what objects are referred to by other objects; an object that is not referred to at all is considered unused and can be collected.

Java manages these objects through *references*. A reference is what is returned from the *new* statement; it allows one object to refer to another. An object can have any number of references pointing to it; once the last of these references is dropped, the object can be collected. Java manages this for you, so you never have to delete an object explicitly. Actually, you can't do this.

exam **Watch** *If you get nothing else from this chapter, understand that for the purposes of the exam, the most important thing to understand is that Java manages memory for you automatically. You don't have to do any memory management for yourself.*

Mark-Sweep

The Java language specification gives implementers a great deal of flexibility in how garbage collection is implemented. The specification describes how the system works from the programmer's point of view, and not from an internal point of view. So long as the programmer interface is the same, the internal implementation can be very different.

Having said that, most Java Virtual Machines implement garbage collection using a variant of the *mark-sweep* algorithm. This algorithm gets its name from the two passes that it takes over memory. It takes the first pass to mark those objects that are no longer used, and a second pass to remove (sweep) those objects from memory.

When discussing a garbage collection algorithm, the term *reachable* is used to describe objects that are in use. The idea is that active objects in memory find a great big interconnected web; any object that is on that web can be reached by traversing from another object that is in use. If no objects refer to an object, then it is unreachable and can be removed from memory.

Mark-sweep starts with the assumption that some objects are always reachable. The main application object, for example, will be in use as long as the program is executing. The main functions of threads, which will be covered in Chapter 9, are always reachable for similar reasons. Objects that are always reachable by definition are considered to be *root* objects, and are used to start traversing the web of objects. If an object can be reached from a root object, then it is in use. If an object can be reached from an object that can be reached from a root object, then it is in use. If an object can be reached from an object that can be...well, you get the idea.

The mark phase of the mark-sweep garbage collection starts with the root objects and looks at all the objects that each root object refers to. If the object is already marked as being in use, then nothing more happens. If not, then the object is marked as in use and all the objects that it refers to are considered. The algorithm repeats until all the objects that can be reached from the root objects have been marked as in use.

When the mark phase completes, the sweep phase starts. The sweep phase looks at each object in memory and sees if it was marked as in use by the mark phase. If it was, the sweep phase clears the in-use flag and does nothing more to the object. If, however, the object was not marked as in use, then the sweep phase knows that that object can be safely freed. The sweep phase then removes that object from memory.

Garbage Collection and Performance

As you can imagine, it can take a lot of time to walk through all the associations in memory. While the garbage collector is walking through these associations, it has to make sure that none of the associations change. As a practical matter, this means that all other processing in the virtual machine stops while the garbage collector runs. This is one of the big disadvantages of garbage collection: the pause while the garbage collector runs.

One way that garbage collectors attempt to alleviate this overhead is by running the garbage collection only when needed. If there is plenty of free memory still available in the system, then there is no need to run a garbage collection. Java runs the garbage collector only when a request for memory allocation comes in that cannot be satisfied by the amount of free memory available on the system. Until then, the unused objects are allowed to remain in memory. They do not affect the performance of the system; they are merely objects that are taking memory that they no longer need.

When Java does attempt to allocate more memory than it has available, then the garbage collector is activated. The garbage collector suspends the normal functioning of the virtual machine and executes a mark-sweep pass. After the garbage collector executes, the JVM attempts again to allocate memory. Hopefully, the mark-sweep pass freed enough memory for the request to be satisfied. If the mark-sweep pass did not free enough memory, then the request fails (and the error java.lang.OutOfMemoryError is thrown).

So the good news is that the JVM delays the running of the garbage collector as long as possible. The bad news is that garbage collection could be run at any time. You don't get prior notice that the garbage collector is about to run. So *any* request for more memory could result in the garbage collector running and making your program wait. This has been one of the big problems with using Java for a real-time system—in a real-time system you have to know when the pauses will be.

This is also the reason that garbage collection systems have the (undeserved) reputation for being slow. The total time that a garbage collection system takes to manage memory is only slightly more than the total time that it takes to manage memory by hand. The difference is that a hand-written memory management scheme will rarely wait until memory is exhausted and then delete a whole bunch of objects at once. It is the action of deleting a whole bunch of objects at once that causes the system to pause. So a garbage collected system might be only slightly slower overall, but may appear to be jerkier—performing a lot of work and then pausing—than a hand-written memory management scheme.

Forcing Garbage Collection

Java provides some routines that can help you control when the garbage collection pauses take place. For example, if you are about to perform some time-sensitive operations, you probably want to make the chances of a garbage collection pause as small as possible. The routines that Java provides are requests, and not demands; the virtual machine will do its best to do what you ask, but may not be able to comply.

The routines that Java provides are members of the Runtime class. The Runtime class is a special class that has a single object (a singleton) for each main program. The Runtime object provides a mechanism for communicating directly with the virtual machine. To get the Runtime instance, you can use the method Runtime.getInstance(), which returns the singleton. Alternatively, for the routines we are going to discuss, you can use the same routines on the System class, which are static methods and do the work of obtaining the singleton for you.

The first method is Runtime.gc() (or System.gc()). This method asks the virtual machine to perform a garbage collection pass. Theoretically, after calling Runtime.gc() you will have as much free memory as possible, and should be able to perform several allocations without having an unexpected garbage collection.

I say theoretically because this routine does not always work that way. First off, the virtual machine you are running under may not have implemented this routine; the language specification allows for this routine to do nothing at all. Also, another thread (again, see Chapter 9) may perform a substantial memory allocation right after you run the garbage collection. You also have no idea how much memory was really freed by performing this garbage collection—it might not have been enough memory for the work that you wanted to do in the first place.

This is not to say that Runtime.gc() is a useless method. It's better than nothing. You just can't rely on Runtime.gc() to free up enough memory so that you don't have to worry about the garbage collector being run.

The routine Runtime.gc() does not take any arguments; it is simply a request to trigger a garbage collection. You may decide to use System.gc() rather than Runtime.gc() (if you call these routines at all) to avoid calling Runtime.getInstance(), but that is a personal choice.

Discovering That an Object Was Collected

Another side effect of not controlling memory management is that you can't predict when an object is going to be deleted. If you controlled the deletion, then you would know when the object is deleted; it would be deleted when you deleted it. Because you don't control the deletion, you don't automatically know when an object is deleted.

In general, this is okay. One of the real reasons that you need to be able to tell when an object is deleted is to make sure that it frees up any resources that it owns. In other words, you have to know when an object is deleted to make sure that memory leaks don't occur; when the object is deleted, you make sure that any dynamic objects owned by that object are also deleted.

In a garbage-collected system, you don't have to worry about this. The garbage collector does this for you. If an object is the last reference to another dynamically allocated object, then both objects will be deleted at the same time. To be precise, neither object will be reachable in the mark phase of the garbage collection, and both will be collected in the sweep phase.

Of course, there are other good reasons for knowing when an object gets collected. You might be keeping a count of live objects; you might be attempting to debug an application; or you just might be curious. Additionally, if the object owns resources that are not a part of the Java garbage collection scheme (such as database connections, resources allocated in Java Native Interface (JNI) code, and so forth) then you still have the responsibility of making sure those resources are cleaned up.

To allow for these contingencies, Java provides a notification mechanism that tells you an object is about to be collected. Every class has a special method, called a *finalizer*, which is called just before an object is collected. The JVM calls the finalizer for you as appropriate; you never call a finalizer directly.

Think of the finalizer as a friendly warning from the virtual machine. Your finalizer should perform two tasks: performing whatever cleanup is appropriate to the object, and calling the superclass finalizer. If you don't have any cleanup to perform for an object, then you're better off not adding a finalizer to the class.

The finalizer method has a special name: *finalize*. It returns void, and takes no arguments. It will always be an override of a superclass method. If nothing else, your class derives from *Object*, which defines the finalize method.

The virtual machine invokes the finalize method as the first step in collecting an object. The virtual machine reserves the right to not immediately collect the memory associated with an object after calling the finalizer. This allows the garbage collector to limit its own execution time. Garbage collectors may decide to run only for so long at once, and may run a set of finalizers and go back later to actually collect the memory. They are free to do this; you can't rely on the internal behavior of the garbage collector.

Objects that have had finalizers run but have not had their memory deallocated are known as *phantoms*. We'll talk more about phantoms in a little bit.

You can ask the garbage collector to run finalizers for you by invoking the *System.runFinalization()* method. This method is a request to the garbage collector to run finalizers for any objects that are currently unreachable, but that have not had finalizers run yet. The garbage collector may or may not decide to actually honor this request, and may or may not decide to deallocate the memory for those objects for which it does run finalizers. Just like the System.gc() method, this is a wrapper around the method Runtime.runFinalization(), and you can use either interchangeably.

Memory Management and Object Lifetimes

It is a common misconception to say that an object will be automatically deleted as soon as the last reference to the object is dropped. This is not exactly true. First, there will be a time lag before the garbage collector runs. Also, the garbage collector has the goal of freeing enough memory to satisfy an outstanding request; it may not decide to collect all the eligible objects at any given pass.

One common technique uses the heuristic that objects generally fall into two camps: short-lived (temporary) objects, and long-lived objects. There are a lot of objects that are created for a single time use and then dropped. If an object isn't immediately eligible for deletion, then it tends not to be eligible for quite a long time. (Remember that computers think about "quite a long time" very differently than you and I do—"quite a long time" for a computer could be [gasp] two seconds!)

Because figuring out which objects are still alive takes a considerable amount of time, some garbage collection implementations stop looking at objects after a while, or more precisely, look at them less frequently. This is known as *promoting* an object. An object that has been promoted might be considered as reachable, by definition, for ten passes of the garbage collector, which reduces the number of objects considered in each pass.

Garbage collectors that use this technique are known as *generational* garbage collectors. Generational garbage collectors make the trade-off of running faster for the cost of leaving garbage lying around longer. With today's large memory machines, this is a very reasonable trade-off to make. However, this means that an unreachable object might not be collected for a while, even if the garbage collector runs.

Of course, the garbage collector has the primary goal of ensuring that there is enough memory available, not that the program runs within any specific timelines. If the garbage collector runs a quick pass and does not get enough memory, it will start over, considering older objects. It will continue running, considering older and older objects, until it either has enough memory to satisfy the request or there are no other possible objects to collect.

QUESTIONS AND ANSWERS

I want to allocate an object and make sure that it never gets deallocated. Can I tell the garbage collector to ignore an object?	No. There isn't a mechanism for marking an object as undeletable. What you probably want to do instead is to create a static member of a class, and store a reference to the object in that. (Remember that static members are considered always to be live objects.)
My program is not performing as well as I would expect. I think the garbage collector is taking too much time. What can I do?	Well, first off, if it really is the garbage collector (and it probably isn't) then you are creating and dropping references to a lot of temporary objects. Try to redesign your program to reuse objects, or require fewer temporary objects.
I am creating an object in a function, and passing it out as the function result. How do I make sure the object isn't deleted before the function returns?	The object won't be deleted until the last reference to the object is dropped. If you return the object as a function return value, then the function return itself is a reference to the object. So returning an object from a function is safe, even if it was created in that function.
How do I drop a reference to an object if that object is referred to in a member of my class?	Set the member to null. Whenever you set a reference to a new object, the old object loses one reference. If that were the last reference, the object becomes eligible for deletion. You can always set a reference to the null object, without having to create a new object.
I want to keep objects around only so long as they don't interfere with memory allocation. Is there any way I can ask Java to warn me if memory is getting low?	Prior to Java 1.2, you would have to check the amount of free memory yourself and guess. Java 1.2 introduced soft references for just this situation. They are discussed in the following section.

Generational garbage collectors may run multiple generations: really short-lived objects, longer-lived objects, even longer-lived objects, and so forth until the root objects are reached. As objects survive several garbage collections in a particular generation, they will be promoted to a higher one. Some implementations will promote objects into the root object set, at which point they will never be collected, even if all references are dropped.

At this point, we've covered most of the basics of garbage collection. When you write Java programs, you will mainly be using what we have already discussed.

Memory Management and References

Up to this point, we have been discussing the original Java memory management model. With Java 2 (the 1.2 JDK release), the original model was augmented with *reference classes*. Reference classes, which derive from the class *Reference*, are used for more sophisticated memory management.

Of course, as so often happens in this field, the term *reference* now has two meanings. In the original memory management model, references are how objects refer to each other. The *new* function returns a reference to an object, and so long as that reference is maintained, the object will not be collected. *Reference* used in this context is somewhat of a generic term; it means "a way that one object refers to, keeps track of, points to, or uses another object."

In the new usage, *Reference* is the name of a class used in advanced memory management. It is *not* the same as a reference, although it is closely related. It helps that the Reference class itself is never instantiated; it is only an abstract superclass for the *WeakReference, SoftReference,* and *PhantomReference* classes. Like some other Java components, these classes are predefined for you; you cannot create your own reference classes.

By default, you work with strong references. When you hear people talking about references (at parties, on the bus), they are usually talking about strong references. This was the classic Java way of doing things, and is what you have unless you go out of your way to use the Reference classes. Strong references are used to prevent objects from being garbage collected;

a strong reference from a reachable object is enough to keep the referred-to object in memory.

When we specifically talk about weak (or soft, or phantom) references, we are talking about an extension to the language added in the Java Development Kit (JDK) 1.2 release. These additions give the programmer a greater amount of control over the lifecycle of an object, and are really an external representation of garbage collector internals. By using these classes, we are giving hints to the garbage collector to give it an idea of how we are using objects in our application.

The different reference types reflect successively less control over the lifecycle of the object. A strong reference tells the garbage collector that the referred-to object cannot go away as long as the referring object is alive. A soft reference tells the garbage collector that the referred-to object can go away, but you'd rather it didn't. A weak reference tells the garbage collector that you don't care if the referred-to object goes away, you just want to know about it. A phantom reference tells the garbage collector that the object can be collected and finalized, but that the memory should not be reused until you release it.

The different reference types seem confusing at first, but they each have a specific use. Once you see examples of how they are used, they become clearer.

Shared Interface

References share a common set of methods, inherited from the abstract Reference class. These methods include the clear(), enqueue(), isEnqueued(), and get() methods. Of these, you will probably use get() a lot, and the others rarely if at all.

The get() method returns the object that the reference refers to, which is known as the *referent* of the reference. Because reference objects are generic, the get() method returns an object of type *Object*, and you have to take it from there. You will generally cast the results of the get() call to whatever class you know is really being referred to. If you are wrong, the normal cast exception mechanism will kick in.

The get() method will return one of two things. It will return the object that you passed in when creating the reference, as long as the object has not been collected yet. It will return *null* after the object is collected, so you can tell that the reference is no longer valid. Phantom references act a little bit differently (they always return *null*). The phantom reference section later in the chapter provides more information.

You will call the other methods very infrequently. They are really for the internal use of the virtual machine. The *clear()* method is called to set the reference to null; once you call clear(), the get() method will always return *null*. The *enqueue()* method adds the reference to the reference queue that the reference is associated with; *isEnqueued()* returns *true* if the reference has been added to the queue. This won't make much sense until we talk about reference queues, and you'll probably never directly call these functions even after we talk about reference queues.

These are the generic methods, but they describe how the reference reacts. Each type of reference (soft, weak, and phantom) imposes a different protocol on the referent object. These are discussed in the following sections.

Soft References—Managing in Memory Caches

Let's start with *soft references*. The Java language specification states that soft references can be used to create memory-sensitive caches. So what exactly is a memory-sensitive cache?

Consider an application that manipulates images. The application functions by applying operations to images; each operation results in a *before* image and an *after* image. The operations on the images are reversible, so you can get the after image from the before image by applying the operation, or get the before image from the after image by applying the reverse of the operation.

Applying the operations to images takes a while; the larger the image, the longer the operation takes. If we want to support an undo feature in the application, we can do this one of two ways. First, we can store the new image and the reversing function. If the user wants to undo the operation then we apply the reversing function to the image. Or, we can store both the before image and the after image, so we can instantly restore the before image.

Storing the before image is great, as we can instantly undo and redo with very little performance penalty. However, images take up a lot of memory, and if we want to support undo for multiple images (or multiple levels of undo), we can quickly eat up huge amounts of memory.

Enter soft references. A soft reference tells the runtime system that we would rather this object not be removed from memory. We don't *require* that the object not be removed from memory, we just would rather that it not be removed from memory. We can store the inactive image (the before image if we have performed an operation, and the after image if we have undone the operation) with a soft reference.

We create the soft reference by creating a new SoftReference object. Assume we have a data member *inactiveImage* of class *SoftReference*:

```
inactiveImage = new SoftReference( activeImage, null );
```

When we create the soft reference, the first argument is the object to which we want to maintain a soft reference. The second is the reference queue that is associated with reference; we will talk more about reference queues in a moment. For now, we use *null* to specify that the reference is not associated with a queue.

Now that we have a soft reference to the object, we can freely run the transformation to create the after image, and store the resulting image as the active image:

```
activeImage = transformation.transform( activeImage );
inUndoState = false;
```

The preceding line of code replaces the active image with the new active image. At this point, we have a strong reference to the new active image (the transformed image) and a soft reference to the old active image (the before image). We do not have any strong references to the before image anymore; we only have a soft reference to the image.

So what happens if the garbage collector runs? Well, we have an object with no strong references to it (the before image), which would normally be eligible for collection. However, we have a soft reference to this object. With the soft reference, we are telling the garbage collector that we would rather it not collect the object unless it has to. Because of this, the garbage collector will take a look at the amount of memory it can free up without touching the softly-referenced object. If it can free enough memory without touching that object, it will leave the object alone.

The softly-referenced object may stick around for quite a while. If you have a lot of memory on your computer, the object could stick around forever (until you drop the soft reference to the object). Of course, if you have a small amount of memory on your computer, the object could go away almost immediately.

The key point here is that the soft reference is *memory sensitive*. The garbage collector will attempt to keep the object in memory as long as possible, but not at the expense of having to go through an out-of-memory exception.

So long as the object is in memory, we can use the soft reference to obtain a strong reference to the object. The SoftReference class has a member get() that can be used to obtain a strong reference to the object that the soft reference manages. The method returns an object of type Object, which you will have to cast to the appropriate type. We can use this in our image application to process the undo command in the following way:

```
SoftReference newInactive = new SoftReference( activeImage, null );
activeImage = (Image) inactiveImage.get();
inactiveImage = newInactive;
inUndoState = true;
```

So what happens if the object does go out of memory? The get() method of the SoftReference class will return *null*; this is our signal that the object was collected. In this case, we would have to perform the reverse transformation of the image; it is not as quick but the user still gets what they expect. The following code checks for this case and performs the reverse transformation if the before image is null:

```
SoftReference newInactive = new SoftReference( activeImage, null );
if (beforeImage.get() == null)
{
   activeImage = transformation.reverseTransform( activeImage );
}
else
{
   activeImage = (Image) inactiveImage.get();
}
inactiveImage = newInactive;
inUndoState = true;
```

Weak References—Watching Someone Else's Objects

In addition to soft references, Java supports *weak references*. Weak references are similar to soft references in that they allow you to refer to an object without forcing the object to remain in memory. Weak references are different from soft references, however, in that they do not request that the garbage collector attempt to keep the object in memory.

Weak references are best used if you are tracking an object that someone else owns. You don't want to keep the object in memory; you just want to know if the object is still in memory. As soon as all the strong references to the object are dropped, the object is eligible for collection regardless of the amount of memory that the garbage collector needs. Unlike soft references, which might stick around for a while even after their strong references drop, weak references go away pretty quickly.

So why would you want to track someone else's objects? After all, you either are using an object in your application, or you aren't; why would you want to keep track of an object you aren't directly using?

Let's say that we wanted to add a menu to a Java application that allowed the user to select any open window and bring it to the front. To do this, we have to make sure that the menu contains the list of all the open windows at any time. As windows are created they have to be added, and as windows are closed they have to be removed.

There are two ways we could implement this; we could modify all the window classes to register themselves with the menu, or we can use weak references. Weak references are easier, as we don't have to make a lot of modifications to the window classes. Better yet, weak references are safer and cleaner. They are safer because the windows are automatically deregistered. They are cleaner because the window classes do not have to have any special knowledge of the window menu.

To understand how the weak references work, think of what would happen if we added a regular strong reference to the window menu for every window that we created. The window menu would get all the windows, to be sure, but the window objects would never be collected. The window menu itself would have a reference to the window object, which would be enough for the window object to not be collected.

Weak references allow the window menu to have a reference to the window, but this reference is not enough to maintain the object in memory. As long as the window remains open, the reference will remain valid. However, and this is the key part, as soon as the window closes, the weak reference to the window becomes invalid. More precisely, the weak reference would not be enough to keep the window in memory, and the window object would be collected. This would cause the weak reference to become null.

The difference between weak and soft references is that weak references disappear more quickly. As soon as all the strong references are dropped for an object, the object is collected and the weak references are set up as null. This happens as soon as the next mark-sweep, and it happens even if the garbage collector doesn't necessarily need the memory. Weak references don't have the hint to the garbage collector that soft references do; the garbage collector makes no special effort to keep weakly-referenced objects in memory.

Now all we have to do is manage the menu so that we can tell when the weak references become null. We can do this by using a *reference queue*, which is another part of the java.lang.ref package.

Reference Queues—Being Told When References Change

In talking about weak and soft references, we discussed how they become null when the object they refer to is collected. This is true, but it isn't the whole story. In addition to going null, the references are optionally added to a *reference queue*. The reference queue gives you a means for determining in bulk which references have changed.

You don't have to add a reference to a queue—all the previous examples didn't. Reference queues simply give you a quick means for determining which of the references you created have changed, without having to test the results of the get() method.

When you create a reference, you can optionally supply a reference queue as the second argument to the reference constructor. If you pass in null, then no queue is associated with the reference. If you do pass in a queue, however, that queue will be associated with the reference until it is destroyed. There isn't an interface for changing the queue associated with a reference—you have to make that decision when you create the reference.

Reference queues give the virtual machine a mechanism for telling you that it has collected an object, or more precisely, that the reference has moved to an invalid state. Take the case of soft references. At some point, the virtual machine will need the memory that the object is occupying (assuming that only soft references remain to that object) and will collect the object. At that point, if the soft reference has a reference queue associated with it, the soft reference is added to the queue. This is called *enqueuing* the object and is performed with a call to the *enqueue()* method. You can then tell that a reference has been invalidated by checking to see if the reference has been added to the queue. Of course, you can also call the get() method to see if the method returns null.

If you do decide to use the reference queues, there are a couple of ways you can do it. You can set up a separate thread (there are those threads again) to constantly watch for references to be added to the queue. You can also check the queue when the user calls one or more of your methods; probably those methods that will use references that may have been queued.

There are three methods to the *ReferenceQueue* class: *poll(), remove(),* and *remove(long timeout)*. The poll() method returns a reference if there is one in the queue, and returns null otherwise. It will never wait for a reference to be added and it does not remove the reference from the queue. The remove() method also returns null if there is no reference in the queue, but will both return the reference and remove it from the queue if there is. The only difference between the two methods is that you can specify a timeout on one of them; the one that does not take a timeout will wait forever until a reference is added to the queue.

There is one final thing to know about reference queues. When weak or soft references are added to a reference queue, they are automatically cleared. In other words, the reference will become null and be added to the queue at essentially the same time. There will never be a reference in a queue that does not return null from the get() method. This only applies to soft and weak references; phantom references are not automatically cleared.

I guess the inevitable had been delayed long enough; it is time to talk about phantom references.

Phantom References—Delaying Memory Collection

You might have noticed that the discussion of phantom references was put off as long as possible. Phantom references provide a means of delaying the reuse of memory occupied by an object, even if the object itself is finalized. A *phantom* object is one that has been finalized, but whose memory has not yet been made available for another object.

Phantom references are a bit different from soft and weak references. First off, phantom references track *memory* rather than *objects*. Secondly, you can never actually get to the object that a phantom reference references. It wouldn't make sense to do so—you aren't watching an object, you are watching the memory that an object occupies. Finally, although reference queues are optional with soft and weak references, phantom references require their use.

There are two reasons why you might want to delay the reuse of memory: performance, and native code. If you have native code that obtains the location of an object and remembers that location, then phantom references provide a means of alerting that code to drop the reference before the memory is reused. Phantom references can also delay the returning of the memory to the heap. If you have very time-dependent code, the slight time savings may be valuable.

When the garbage collector determines that an object is only reachable through phantom references, it will finalize the object and add the reference to the reference queue associated with the reference when it was created. The memory for the object will not actually be collected until you call *clear()* on the reference, so it is your responsibility to poll the queue frequently, remove the references on the queue, and call clear() for those references. Phantom references, unlike soft and weak references, are *not* automatically cleared when they are added to the queue.

The get() method for phantom references is overridden to always return null. This is to prevent you from attempting to reincarnate an already collected object. This is very different from soft and weak references, where the get() method will return the referent object while it is reachable, and null afterwards. You can never retrieve the referent object from a phantom reference.

Relative Reference Strength

Objects are placed into one of several categories, depending upon what kinds of references can be used to get to the object. References are ordered as follows: strong, soft, weak, and phantom. Objects are then known as *strongly reachable, softly reachable, weakly reachable, phantom reachable*, or *unreachable.*

If an object has a strong reference, a soft reference, a weak reference, and a phantom reference all pointing to it, then the object is considered strongly reachable and will not be collected. An object without a strong reference, but with a soft reference, a weak reference, and a phantom reference will be considered softly reachable and will be collected when memory gets low.

An object without strong or soft references, but with weak and phantom references, is considered weakly reachable and will be collected at the next garbage collection cycle. An object without strong, soft, or weak references, but with a phantom reference, is considered phantom reachable and will have been finalized, but the memory for that object will not have been collected.

What about an object without strong, soft, weak, or phantom references? Well, that object is considered unreachable and will already have been collected or will be collected as soon as the next garbage collection cycle is run.

CERTIFICATION SUMMARY

Garbage collection is one of the most popular and powerful features of the Java language, but is also one that requires the least programmer interaction. For most applications, the garbage collection system simply manages memory for you. Garbage collection ensures that objects that are no longer required are automatically removed, while objects that are still in use stay alive. Most importantly, garbage collection determines automatically which objects are in use, relieving the programmer of having to do this.

You don't have to do anything special for basic garbage collection; it is all automatic. When you create an object using *new*, you obtain a reference to the object, which is used to refer to it. When there are no more references to an object, the *finalize()* method is called and the object is collected. There is no need for a delete function, so the language does not provide one.

Although for most applications the basic memory management model is enough, some programs can benefit from more advanced memory management. The Java 1.2 specification adds this advanced memory management in the form of reference objects. There are three flavors of reference objects: soft, weak, and phantom.

Soft references allow an object to stay in memory even if there are no more strong references to it. This allows an object to be cached so long as there is enough free memory. Weak references don't keep an object in memory, but allow you to refer to an object only as long as the object is in memory through other means. This allows you to maintain a reference to an object without forcing that object to stay in memory. Phantom references are the least powerful; they don't control objects at all, but rather the reuse of the memory underlying the object.

Associated with references are reference queues. Reference queues give a mechanism for determining whether an object has changed state. For soft and weak references, reference queues are optional because the get() method will return null when the object changes state. For phantom references, whose get() method always returns null, reference queues are required.

Overall, the Java 1.2 garbage collection mechanism is a powerful addition to the language. The basic functionality is simple to use and adequate for most applications. The language mechanism also supports more powerful interactions with the garbage collector, at a slight price in complexity. Either way, the program can be simpler to understand and more reliable to run because the language itself is involved in the management of memory.

TWO-MINUTE DRILL

- ❑ Java memory management is generally automatic with no programmer interaction.

- ❑ The Java Virtual Machine has the responsibility of finding unused objects and making sure that the memory they occupy is freed.

- ❑ The automatic detection and deletion of unused objects is known as garbage collection.

- ❑ Garbage collection imposes some runtime overhead, but makes code simpler and more understandable.

- ❑ Most Java Virtual Machine implementations use mark-sweep garbage collection, which can delete objects even if they refer to each other cyclically (provided no other live objects refer to them).

- ❑ Java applications can still run out of memory. The amount of memory on your computer and the amount of memory your application needs, not how well that memory is managed, determine whether the application will run out of memory.

- ❑ Java 1.2 introduces soft, weak, and phantom references, as well as reference queues, to provide more control over the memory management of your program.

- ❑ Soft references are used for memory-sensitive caches.

- ❑ Weak references are used to track objects that you don't directly own.

- ❑ Phantom references are used to track the memory that an object occupies.

- ❑ Reference queues provide a mechanism for detecting that a soft, a weak, or a phantom reference has changed state.

SELF TEST

The following questions will help you measure your understanding of the material presented in this chapter. Read all of the choices carefully, as there may be more than one correct answer. Choose all correct answers for each question.

1. What does a Java programmer have to do to release an object that is no longer needed?
   A. Use the delete statement
   B. Call the finalize() method for the object
   C. Call System.gc()
   D. Nothing

2. Can a Java application run out of memory?
   A. Yes, if there are too many soft references
   B. Yes, if there are too many strong references
   C. Yes, if you do not override the finalize() method for an object
   D. No, garbage collection ensures that there will be enough memory

3. When should you directly invoke the garbage collection system?
   A. Before entering a time-critical section of code
   B. Before attempting a large number of allocations
   C. After leaving a method with a large number of temporary objects
   D. Never, garbage collection is automatic

4. Complete the following sentence. Garbage collection...
   A. Is faster than hand-written memory management
   B. Is only available in the Java language
   C. Is more reliable than hand-written memory management
   D. Uses less memory than hand-written memory management

5. Complete the following sentence. Soft references...
   A. Were added in JDK 1.1
   B. Require the use of reference queues
   C. Allow for memory-sensitive caching algorithms
   D. Allow for recovery of previously deleted objects

6. Complete the following sentence. Phantom references...

   A. Are used to manage memory allocated with native code through the JNI interface
   B. Prevent memory from being reused
   C. Allow the recovery of previously deleted objects
   D. Are interchangeable with weak references

7. Complete the following sentence. Using weak references...

   A. Allows an object to be collected when not used
   B. Allows an object to be tracked even after collected
   C. Is required for complex Java programs
   D. Allows for memory-sensitive caches

8. Complete the following sentence. Reference queues...

   A. Are required for soft references
   B. Are required for strong references
   C. Are required for phantom references
   D. Are never required for any reference type

9. Complete the following sentence. The get() method on a Reference object...

   A. Always returns the referent object
   B. Returns the referent object until it is collected, then returns null
   C. Returns the referent object until clear() is called
   D. Returns the referent object only for soft and weak references

10. Complete the following sentence. The clear() method...

   A. Is called automatically when the reference is created
   B. Is called automatically for all references when the reference is enqueued
   C. Is called automatically for soft and weak references only when they are enqueued
   D. Is called automatically for phantom references only when they are enqueued

11. Complete the following sentence. Calling the new statement for an object...

   A. Creates a new soft reference to the object
   B. Creates a new weak reference to the object
   C. Creates a new phantom reference to the object
   D. Creates a new strong reference to the object

12. Prior to Java 1.2, all references were what?

   A. Strong

   B. Weak

   C. Soft

   D. Phantom

13. Complete the following sentence. The Reference class…

   A. Can be subclassed to make your own custom reference types

   B. Has four subclasses: StrongReference, WeakReference, SoftReference, and PhantomReference

   C. Cannot be subclassed by Java programmers

   D. Is used directly to manage memory for an object

14. Complete the following sentence. Calling Runtime.gc()…

   A. Guarantees enough memory for the next memory allocation request

   B. Always frees up some memory, but may not free enough for the next allocation request

   C. May have no effect, based on the virtual machine implementation

   D. Should be performed before every memory allocation request

15. Complete the following sentence. The Java Virtual Machine specification…

   A. Requires mark-sweep garbage collection

   B. Requires some form of garbage collection, but not necessarily mark-sweep

   C. Allows for manual memory management

   D. Does not address memory management at all

16. Complete the following sentence. Mark-sweep garbage collection…

   A. Can identify unused objects, even if they refer to each other

   B. Cannot collect objects that refer to each other cyclically

   C. Is the fastest garbage collection system

   D. Runs every three seconds, in a separate system-level thread

17. When will the object created as myObject become eligible for collection?

```
class example
{
    public static void main( String args[] )
    {
        UseObject();
    }
```

```
private void UseObject()
    {
        String anObject = AllocateObject();
        System.out.println( anObject );
    }

private String AllocateObject()
    {
            String myObject = new String( "When will I be deleted?" );
        return myObject;
    }
};
```

A. When the AllocateObject() function completes

B. When the call to System.out.println() completes

C. When the UseObject() function completes

D. When the main program completes

18. When might the soft reference *theSoftReference* be automatically cleared?

```
class example
{
        SoftReference    theSoftReference;

public static void main( String args[] )
    {
        theSoftReference =
            new SoftReference( AllocateObject(), null );
        UseObject();
    }

private void UseObject()
    {
        String anObject = (String) theSoftReference.get();
        System.out.println( anObject );
    }

private String AllocateObject()
    {
            String myObject = new String( "When will I be deleted?" );
        return myObject;
    }
};
```

A. After UseObject() returns

B. After calling the get() function in UseObject()

C. As soon as AllocateObject() returns

D. Just before UseObject() is called

SUN CERTIFIED PROGRAMMER®

7

Overloading/ Overriding Runtime Type and Object Orientation

Τhe questions on the Java Programmer Certification Exam test both your general understanding of object-oriented programming and your knowledge of Java's implementation of these concepts. Object-oriented programming in Java has many similarities to programming in other object-oriented languages, but it has a number of syntactic differences from other languages like C++. In this chapter, I will address how to recognize properly coded overridden and overloaded methods. In addition, I will enumerate the valid—and invalid—techniques to invoke a superclass's constructor from the subclass using the *super()* method.

Before delving into the dos and don'ts specific to Java, we will first look at object-oriented programming in general. Encapsulation, the visibility of an implementation to outside classes, is at the core of object-oriented design. You consider encapsulation issues when creating classes and determining whether your methods and instance variables are *public, private,* and so on. The other object-oriented concept to be covered is the often-confused difference between *is a* and *has a* relationships. An understanding of encapsulation, as well as *is a* and *has a* relationships, is very important because the choices for some questions will all be syntactically correct. The correct answer to the question will depend on the appropriate application of these concepts.

CERTIFICATION OBJECTIVE 7.01

Encapsulation in Object-Oriented Design

Two design goals of encapsulation in object-oriented design are modularity and appropriate visibility. Modular classes are as independent (or loosely coupled) as is feasible. In other words, your code should be separated into different classes so that it only knows as much as is necessary about your other code. There are no right or wrong ways to write modular code, but there are several guidelines that will help you to better understand this concept.

Visibility is the accessibility of methods and instance variables to other classes and packages. When implementing a class, you determine your methods' and instance variables' visibility keywords as *public, protected,* or *package*, based on this object-oriented concept. For example, Java has rules stating when a *protected* method may be accessed. Deciding whether *protected* is appropriate is an encapsulation issue.

Writing Modular Code

As stated earlier, modular code keeps implementations isolated so that they depend on other code as little as possible. Though modular code doesn't affect how well your code executes, you will get many benefits by writing code this way. Consider the following code excerpt that is not modular.

```
public class Company
{
  private Vector employeeNames;
  private Vector vendorNames;

  public Company()
  {
    employeeNames = new Vector();
    vendorNames = new Vector();
  }

  public void addEmployee( String empName)
  {
      employeeNames.add( empName);
  }

  public void addVendor( String vendName)
  {
    vendorNames.add( vendName);
  }
}
```

Company contains the implementation of adding employees and vendors in the same class. What would happen if the preceding code excerpt were representative of a large application with many programmers? If the application needed modifications to both the vendor and employee code, and the modifications were assigned to different programmers, then the programmers would have a very difficult task working together. They could easily erase or clobber each other's code because they would have to modify the same class.

The representations of employees and vendors should be separated from each other. *Company* should still be able to access information about both, but there is no reason to keep the employee list and the vendor list implementations so closely coupled. To illustrate this point, we'll modify the design to expand the code into three classes.

Company.java

```
public class Company
{
  private Employees employees;
  private Vendors vendors;

  public Company()
  {
    employees = new Employees();
    vendors = new Vendors();
  }

  public void addEmployeeName( String empName)
  {
    employees.addEmployeeName( empName);
  }

  public void addVendorName( vendName)
  {
    vendors.addVendorName( vendName);
  }
}
```

Employees.java

```
public class Employees
{
  private Vector employeeNames;

  public Employees()
  {
    employeeNames = new Vector();
```

```
    }

    public void addEmployeeName( String empName)
    {
      employeeNames.add( empName);
    }
}
```

Vendors.java

```
public class Vendors
{
    private Vector vendorNames;

    public Vendors()
    {
      vendorNames = new Vector();
    }

    public void addVendorName( String vendName)
    {
      vendorNames.add( vendName);
    }
}
```

The problem where two programmers work on the same class is now
solved. One programmer can work on *Vendors* while the other works
on *Employees*. Another benefit of this change is that *Vendors* and *Employees*
can undergo substantial revision without affecting any other class but
themselves. For example, the programmer that is working on *Vendors* could
change the representation of the *vendorNames* from a *Vector* to a *String* array
without having an impact on either *Company* or *Employees*.

This example illustrates a key distinction in encapsulation: the implementation
versus the interface. By interface I don't necessarily mean a Java *interface*,
though many interfaces to implementations are defined as such. I am referring
to a conceptual interface that outside classes use to access internal data. In the
preceding example, the *Vendors* programmer can modify *vendorNames* (the
implementation) without changing how other classes access *addVendorName*
methods (its interface). As long as the interface's parameter list and return type

doesn't change, you can change your implementation without affecting other classes in your application.

Knowing What Visibility Is Appropriate

As we have seen, making your code modular allows outside code to talk to your class' interface without having to know or depend on the implementation. Though modularity helps enforce the use of an interface, programmers may still be able to circumvent how you intended them to use your code. The following example defines a class *EmployeeInfo* and another class, *Accessor*, which uses *EmployeeInfo*.

EmployeeInfo.java

```java
public class EmployeeInfo
{
  public String firstName;
  public String lastName;
  public int salary;

  public EmployeeInfo() {}

  //Define the interface (accessor) methods for EmployeeInfo
  public void setFirstName( String fName)
  {
    firstName = fName.trim();  //remove any leading or trailing spaces
  }

  public void setLastName( String lName)
  {
    lastName = lName().trim();  //remove any leading or trailing spaces
  }

  public void setSalary( int sal)
  {
    if (sal > 0) //can't have a negative salary
      salary = sal;
  }
}
```

Accessor.java

```
public class Accessor
{
  public static populateData( EmployeeInfo eInfo)
  {
    eInfo.firstName = "  Sarah ";
    eInfo.lastName = "  Grande";
    eInfo.setSalary( -50000);
  }
}
```

Although I intended the accessor methods *(setSalary(), setFirstName(), and setLastName())* to be the interface to *EmployeeInfo*, another programmer evidently thought differently when writing *Accessor*. Because I gave others the ability to directly access my instance variables, I opened the door to letting them use my class in an unintended way. As a result, I gave my instance variables a visibility that is inappropriate to my goal of having others access my class only through the accessor methods.

One quick fix to EmployeeInfo is to change the visibility of the instance variable from *public* to *private*. This change is fine, but I would like to show you a different technique. Java allows you to divide the interface from the implementation more explicitly by defining an *interface* for the implementation class. The following code excerpt illustrates this facility.

EmployeeInfo.java

```
public interface EmployeeInfo
{

  public void setFirstName( String fName);
  public void setLastName( String lName);
  public void setSalary( int sal);
}
```

EmployeeInfoImpl.java

```
public class EmployeeInfoImpl implements EmployeeInfo
{
  private String firstName;
```

```
private String lastName;
private int salary;

private EmployeeInfoImpl() {}

public static EmployeeInfo create()
{    return (EmployeeInfo)(new EmployeeInfoImpl());

}

//Define the interface (accessor) methods for EmployeeInfo
public void setFirstName( String fName)
{
  firstName = fName.trim();  //remove any leading or trailing spaces
}

public void setLastName( String lName)
{
  lastName = lName.trim();   //remove any leading or trailing spaces
}

public void setSalary( int sal)
{
  if (sal > 0) //can't have a negative salary
    salary = sal;
}
}
```

By providing the *EmployeeInfo* interface, we have explicitly defined which methods are intended for outside access. In fact, we have it set up so that an outside class cannot even create an *EmployeeInfoImpl* instance, because its constructor is declared *private*. Thus, we have enforced that others go through the *EmployeeInfo* interface and we have completely hidden the implementation outside *EmployeeInfoImpl.*

Designing and Implementing Tightly Encapsulated Classes

Building on the distinctions of appropriate visibility and modularity, we will implement the framework of an object-oriented system. Here we will not have any code with which to work. Rather, we will only have a high-level description of the real-world model that we will make. The description of our application follows:

```
Create an object-oriented model for an inventory system.
The inventory has products and orders. Each product has a
name and a price. An order has one or more items in it.
These order items have to know what product is ordered
and the quantity of items ordered. Finally, an outside
system needs some mechanism of placing a new order and
determining that order's total cost.
```

This high-level design only mentions a few of the components necessary for a fully functional inventory system, but it is sufficient for a simple object-oriented application.

Designing for Modularity

We will make this system modular by dividing the inventory system into separate concepts and determining their relationships with each other. We will not decide how these concepts will be implemented at this point because that introduces a level of detail that is not yet necessary. The goal is to understand how the objects relate in the real world. Once we know that, we can express that relationship in Java.

When talking about the inventory system, we are describing something that appears, at least indirectly, to contain all the other concepts mentioned. In other words, the inventory has a list of available products rather than the available products having an inventory. Also, the inventory system contains a list of orders, not vice a versa. To take this idea of containment further, each order contains a list of the items in that order, and each order item contains exactly one product.

Stating the containment relationships of each concept gives us an insight into an approach for modularity. The concepts that we discussed earlier (inventory, orders, and so on) are contained and are containers at some point, so it would be best to refer to them as independent entities. Other concepts that we did not mention, such as the product's price, are so integral to another concept (in this case, the product) that it would not be very useful to separate them into their own objects.

Designing for Appropriate Visibility

Now that we have determined how we want this system modularized, we will determine the information in each object that we want to be visible to other objects. The key here is to know what information each object will need to perform the tasks requested. For our design, we need the objects to be sufficiently visible for an outside system to create a new order and determine the order's cost.

To create a new order, an outside system will need to be able to tell the inventory system to do so. We also need the inventory system to place that order in the list of orders known by the inventory system. Furthermore, the order needs to be able to create a new item for each product in the order and add the order item to the list of items known by the order. The design didn't specifically state what information it would provide when creating new orders, but we have to know the products ordered and the number of items ordered. Therefore, we will assume that is the information provided.

Determining an order's cost doesn't really require anything out of the inventory system. The outside system just needs to query the order itself. To figure this calculation, the order needs to access the number of products in each item and the item's products. The order will then need to retrieve the product's price.

Writing Encapsulated Classes

Given the visibility and modularity required for our object-oriented inventory system, we can now write the code. We can also use the description of our system from the previous two sections to comment our code so that other programmers will understand our design justification.

The code in this section is somewhat over-commented, but it should help you understand how a conceptual design is transformed into working code. I have also left out most of the class constructors and all of the method bodies. Other accessor methods that are not required for this limited example are omitted as well. Thus, this code is incomplete and will not compile.

InventorySystem.java

```java
package com.acme.inventorysystem;

import java.util.Vector;

public class InventorySystem
{
  /** The internal representation of the available products is private
    * because its implementation is irrelevant to outside classes.
    */
  private Vector availableProducts;

  /** The internal representation of the orders is private
    * because its implementation is irrelevant to outside classes.
    */
  private Vector currentOrders;

  /** createNewOrder() is public because outside systems need to be able
    * to create new orders. We assume that the outside system will pass
    * in the products ordered and the number of items ordered. This
    * constructor should also add the new instance to currentOrders.
    */
  public Order createNewOrder( Product [] products, int [] numItemsOrdered)
  {
    /* Body omitted */
    return null;
  }
}
```

Order.java

```
package com.acme.inventorysystem;

import java.util.Vector;

public class Order
{
  /** The internal representation of the orderItems is private
    * because its implementation is irrelevant to outside classes.
    */
  private Vector orderItems;

  /** The constructor has default (package) visibility because
    * we do not want the outside system to create an order
    * without going through the InventorySystem's createNewOrder().
    * We do want other classes in this package to access it though.
    */
  Order(Product [] products, int [] numItemsOrdered)
  { /* Body omitted */ }

  /** computeCost() is public because the outside system needs to be
    * able to determine the cost of an order.
    */
  public double computeCost()
  {
    /* Body omitted */
    return 0.0;   }
}
```

OrderItem.java

```
package com.acme.inventorysystem;

import java.util.Vector;
public class OrderItem
{
  /** getProduct() has default visibility because Order, another
    * class in this package needs access, but classes in
    * the outside system should not access this directly. We do
    * allow other classes in this package to access this, however.
    */
```

```
  protected Product getProduct()
  {
    /* Body omitted */
    return null;
  }

  /** numberOrdered() has default visibility because Order, another class
   * in this package needs access, but classes in the
   * outside system should not access this directly. We do
   * allow other classes in this package to access this, however.
   */
  protected int numberOrdered()
  {
    /* Body omitted */
    return 0;
  }
}
```

Product.java

```
package com.acme.inventorysystem;

 import java.util.Vector;

public class Product
{
  /** getCost() is protected because Order, another class in this package
   * needs access, but classes in the outside system should not access
   * this directly.
   */
  protected double getCost()
  {
     /* Body omitted */
     return 0.0;
  }

  /** getName() is protected because though other classes in this package
   * may need access, but the outside system should not access this directly.
   */
  protected String getName()
  {
    /* Body omitted */
    return null;
  }
}
```

Having implemented the inventory system with the precise modularity and visibility required by the design, there is one more suggestion to mention. Though visibility suitable to your design is important, so is maintenance. You might want an outside system to access the name and cost of *Product* in the future, so it might not be a bad idea to make those accessor methods public. Otherwise, you will have to change the code later. Appropriate visibility still applies here, though what is appropriate may be what you anticipate users will need to access for the life of your code.

on the **!** ob

A knowledge of object-oriented techniques, including encapsulation, is essential to working on a software development team. Many productivity studies have shown that the difference between programmers that know these techniques and those who don't is up to tenfold. There are many excellent books about object-oriented design on the market.

Benefits of Encapsulation

Because we wrote the inventory system with tightly encapsulated classes, we receive many benefits that will pay off later. We have hidden the implementation details of each class, and that will help if we need to *maintain* the code. For example, if we needed to change how we represented the *OrderItem* list in *Orders*, we would only have to change *Orders*. It is much easier to modify one class than having to propagate changes throughout our inventory system.

Another benefit of encapsulation is *extensibility*, or the ease with which we can add to our existing code. If we had implemented the inventory system as one class, we would have to consider the ramifications to the entire system when adding functionality because we would have had interdependent code. Making a change in a large body of code also increases the chances that you will introduce a bug when adding a feature. For our code, suppose we needed to add billing statements to our inventory system. All we would have to do is to add a new *BillingStatement* class that has access to the *Orders* on the statement. We would not need to concern ourselves with the effect of this change on *OrderItem*, *Product*, or *InventorySystem* because we have written modular code.

A final benefit from encapsulation is code *clarity*. Our code is very easy to understand for a new programmer because the code is divided along conceptual lines. Reading through large sections of code that serves many purposes is difficult because you cannot be sure what purpose each piece of code serves. How our code is meant to be used is also clear because we make explicit visibility rules that enforce when instance variables and methods are accessible.

CERTIFICATION OBJECTIVE 7.03

is a and *has a* **Class Relationships**

An often misunderstood distinction in object-oriented programming, and on the Java certification exam, is the difference between *is a* and *has a* class relationships. The confusion of these concepts occurs when programmers have to determine whether one concept is a subclass of the other or is contained by the other. This section will examine two implementations of the same set of classes to illustrate the distinction.

Building.java

```
public class Building
{
  long length;
  long width;

  public Building( long len, long wid)
  {
    length = len;
    width = wid;
  }
```

```
    public long area()
    {
      return length * width;
    }
}
```

OfficeRoom.java

```
public class OfficeRoom extends Building
{
  public Office( long len, wid)
  {
    super( len, wid);
  }
}
```

This first implementation seems reasonable at first glance. We even use inheritance so that we do not have to rewrite the computation of area. This example, however, fails a fundamental rule of inheritance. One class may only be a subclass of another class, or an implementation of an *interface*, if the former *is a* type of the latter. In other words, *OfficeRoom* should not be a subclass of *Building* because an office room is not type of building. Rather, a building *has an* office room.

The problem with this design becomes evident as you extend the functionality of Building. If we added an address and a janitorial service to *Building*, what would that say about an *OfficeRoom*? A room in an office does not usually have its own assigned janitor or address, but *OfficeRoom* would inherit those characteristics from *Building*. We could make the janitor and address attributes *private* so that they would not be visible to *OfficeRoom*, but we would block those characteristics to other potential subclasses of *Building*, like *House* or *Headquarters*, which may need those attributes.

The confusion here occurs because there is some overlapping characteristics between an office room and a building. The relationship is not an *is a* one, however. The key here is to recognize that the wrong relationship between these concepts makes adding a subclass a poor approach. The following code offers an alternative.

Building.java

```java
public class Building
{
  long length;
  long width;

  //The building has a number of office rooms.
  OfficeRoom [] officeRooms;

  public Building( long len, long wid, OfficeRoom [] ors)
  {
    length = len;
    width = wid;
    officeRooms = ors;
  }

  public long area()
  {
    return length * width;
  }
}
```

OfficeRoom.java

```java
public class OfficeRoom
{
  long length;
  long width;

  public Office( long len, wid)
  {
    super( len, wid);
  }

public long area()
  {
    return length * width;
  }
}
```

We see now how to code a *has a* relationship between classes. A *Building* contains (in this case as an array) a number of *OfficeRoom* objects. Now we can modify *Building* without having to consider the effects of *OfficeRoom* because of inheritance. We do have to write the *area* method a second time, but that is a small price to pay. If we wanted to, we could write a superclass, possibly called *InteriorSpace*, for both classes that implements area. Writing such a class is out of the scope of the exam though.

exam
ⓦatch

Ask yourself two questions when determining if the relationship between classes is "is a" or "has a." First ask: "Is the first class (for example, a circle) a type of the latter class (for example, a shape)?" If so, then the relationship is "is a." You also may ask: "Does the first class (for example, a building) contain one or more of the second class' type (for example, rooms)?" If so, then the relationship is "has a."

Now that we have discussed some distinctions in object-oriented design, here are some possible scenario questions and their answers.

QUESTIONS AND ANSWERS

What benefits do you gain from encapsulation?	Ease of code maintenance, extensibility, and code clarity.
What is the object-oriented relationship between a tree and an oak?	An *is a* relationship.
What is the object-oriented relationship between a city and a road?	A *has a* relationship.

FROM THE CLASSROOM

Object-Oriented Design

Is a and *has a* relationships and encapsulation are just the tip of the iceberg when it comes to object-oriented design. Many books and graduate theses have been dedicated to this topic. The reason for the emphasis on proper design is simple: money. The cost to deliver a software application has been estimated to be as much as 100 times more expensive for poorly designed programs. Having seen the ramifications of poor designs, I can assure you this estimate is not far fetched.

Even the best object-oriented designers make mistakes. It is difficult to visualize the relationships between hundreds, or even thousands, of classes. When mistakes are discovered during the implantation (code writing) phase of a project, the amount of code that has to be rewritten can sometimes cause programming teams to start over from scratch.

The software industry has evolved to aid the designer. Visual object modeling languages, such as the Unified Modeling Language (UML), allow designers to design and easily modify classes without having to write code first because object-oriented components are represented graphically. This allows the designer to create a map of the class relationships and helps them recognize errors before coding begins.

Another recent innovation in object-oriented design is design patterns. Designers noticed that many object-oriented designs apply consistently from project to project and that it was useful to apply the same designs because it reduced the potential to introduce new design errors. Object-oriented designers then started to share these designs with each other. Now, there are many catalogs of these design patterns both on the Internet and in book form.

Though passing the Java certification exam does not require you to understand object-oriented design this thoroughly, hopefully this background information will help you better appreciate why the test writers chose to include encapsulation and *is a* and *has a* relationships on the exam.

—*Jonathan Meeks*

Invoking Overridden or Overloaded Methods

Java and other object-oriented languages allow classes to have multiple methods with the same name. Knowing which of the identically named methods is called is frequently asked on the exam. Specifically, the exam tests your knowledge about overloaded and overridden methods. Methods are *overloaded* when there are multiple methods in the same class with the same names but with different parameter lists. Methods in the parent and subclasses with the same name, parameter list, and return type are *overridden*.

Here is an example to illustrate a simple case of overloaded methods.

```
public class MyTest
{
  public void printNumbers( int a, int b)
  {
    System.out.println( a);
    System.out.println( b);
  } .

  public void printNumbers( int a, int b, int c)
  {
    System.out.println( a);
    System.out.println( b);
    System.out.println( c);
  }
}
```

The compiler will know which *printNumbers* to call based on the parameter list. If there are two arguments it will call the former, and if there are three arguments it will call the latter method.

The following is an example to illustrate a simple case of overridden methods.

MyParent.java

```
public class MyParent
{
  public void printClassName ()
  {
    System.out.println( "MyParent");
  }
}
```

MyChild.java

```
public class MyChild extends MyParent
{
  public void printClassName()
  {
    System.out.println( "MyChild");
  }
}
```

The compiler is able to determine which *printClassName* is called depending on the object on which the method is called. If the object is a *MyChild* then the output will be MyChild. If the object is a *MyParent* then the output will be MyParent.

exam
ⓦatch

The rules that determine which overloaded and overridden methods are called are quite tricky. Also, the exam will present methods that will violate the rules and result in compiler errors. Pay very close attention to the next two sections, and note which parameter lists are valid for overloaded and overridden methods because the rules vary for each.

Properly Overridden Methods

The most obvious overridden method is like the one in the previous section where the keywords, the visibility, and the thrown exceptions are identical. (In the previous section there were no exceptions thrown nor special keywords.) The return types and parameter lists must be identical, but other keywords in the method can differ between the parent and the subclass.

An overridden method may be made more *public* than the method in the parent class. It may not be made more *private*, or *restrictive*. In other words, a subclass may not change the interface of the parent class. Therefore, the following code will not compile because *print()* is *private* in the subclass, whereas it is *public* in the superclass.

```
public class MySuperClass
{
  public void print()
  {
  }
}

public class MySubClass extends MySuperClass
{
  private void print()
  {
  }
}
```

The exceptions thrown by a subclass' method may be equal to or fewer than those thrown in the superclass' method. The overridden method must explicitly declare which methods it can throw, however. An overridden method does not *inherit* the exceptions thrown by the superclass.

Although it is fairly simple to realize that an overridden method can have fewer exceptions that in the superclass without adding any new exceptions, there is one subtle case that looks incorrect but actually is a valid overridden method.

```
public class MySuperClass
{
  public void setID( int id) throws Exception
  {
  }
}

public class MySubClass extends MySuperClass
{
  public void setID( int id) throws NullPointerException
  {
  }
}
```

The preceding example looks as if the overridden *setID()* is adding an exception not listed in *MySuperClass*. This is not the case though, because *NullPointerException* is a subclass of *Exception*. Therefore, *NullPointerException* is a subset of all the exceptions that *Exception* includes, so the overridden method does not throw any exception thrown in *MySuperClass* except for *NullPointerException*. When viewed this way it becomes clear that the preceding example illustrates a valid overridden method.

There is one final keyword that may appear in overridden methods and is somewhat of a trick question on the exam: *synchronized*. An overridden method and the method in the superclass may declare their methods *synchronized* independently of one another.

Overridden Methods and Underlying Types

Now that we know which overridden methods are valid, there is some occasional ambiguity as to which method is called.

```
public class A
{
  public void print()
  {
    System.out.println( 'A' );
  }
}

public class B extends A
{
  public void print()
  {
    System.out.println( 'B' );
  }
}

public class Test
{
  public static void main( String [] args)
  {
    A a = new A();
    B b = new B();
    A a2 = new B();
```

```
        a.print();
        b.print();
        a2.print();
    }
}
```

In the preceding example, it is easy to determine that the first two *print()* calls will have *A* and *B* as output, respectively. But what about the third *print()* call? The answer depends on the *underlying type* of the object, or the type of the object that is created. The fact that the object is cast to type *A* is irrelevant. Because the third object is created as type *B*, the *print()* call will call the method in *B* and have *B* as output.

Properly Overloaded Methods

There is only one criterion for determining whether overloaded methods can compile: All of the overloaded methods must have parameter lists that are unique, so that Java can know which method to call. Return types, visibility, thrown exceptions, and keywords play no part in determining valid overloaded methods.

For simple overloaded methods, ones where there are different numbers of parameters, it is easy to determine which overloaded method is called.

```java
public class Test
{
  //first print method
  private void print()
  {
  }

  //second print method
  private void print( int j)
  {
  }

  public static void main( String [] args)
  {
    Test t = new Test();
    t.print( 3);
  }
```

Because there is only one *print()* method with one parameter, it is obvious that the second *print* method will be called in *main()*. When there are overloaded methods that have the same number of parameters and very similar types in the parameter list, determining which methods will be called—or if the code will compile—is more difficult.

```
public class Test
{
  //first print method
  public void print( int a, long b, long c)
  {
  }

  //second print method
  public void print( long a, long b, long c)
  {
  }
}
```

If I were to call *print(1, 2, 3)* what would happen? The answer is that the code would call the first method because the parameters most closely match its parameter list. Java only has to cast two of the three parameter for the first method, but it would have to cast all three from *ints* to *longs* for the second method. If I called *print(1L, 2L, 3L)*, however, the code would call the second method. The first *print()* cannot accept the first parameter in *print(1L, 2L, 3L)* because *long* requires a greater degree of precision than *int*. Java always chooses the overloaded method with the closest matching parameter list that isn't more specific than the parameters allow.

```
public class SecondTest
{
  //first print method
  public void print( int a, long b, long c)
  {
  }

  //second print method
  public void print( long a, int b, long c)
  {
  }
```

```
public static void main( String [] args)
{
   (new SecondTest()).print( 1, 2, 3);
}
}
```

The final scenario to be discussed is when neither overloaded method more closely matches the other. The preceding code example would not compile because the appropriate *print()* method to call is ambiguous. Strangely enough, if we were to change the *print()* call to *print(1L, 2, 3)*, the code would compile because only one of the methods allows a *long* in the first parameter. Thus, it is the method calls themselves that determine overloaded method ambiguity. One exception to this is if the parameter lists are identical. Overloaded methods with identical parameter lists never compile regardless of the method calls to them.

CERTIFICATION OBJECTIVE 7.05

Invoking Parental or Overloaded Constructors

Class constructors are able to call overloaded constructors both in their class and in their superclass. To call another constructor in the same class, you can place a *this()* in the first line of the body in the calling constructor. Placing *this()* in any other place will result in a compiler error.

```
public class MyClass
{
   String title;

   //Calling constructor
   public MyClass()
   {
      this( "Default Title");
      //rest of the body
   }

   //Called constructor
   public MyClass( String t)
```

```
   {
     title = t;
   }
}
```

In the preceding example, the calling constructor calls the second constructor with a default title. The second constructor executes its body before returning, and the calling constructor then executes the remainder of its body.

```java
public class MyClass
{
   int number;

   //Calling constructor
   public MyClass()
   {
     this( "Default Title");
     //rest of the body
   }

   //Called constructor
   public MyClass( int n)
   {
     number = n;
   }
}
```

Note that Java has the same rules for matching the parameter lists for *this()* as it does for other methods. Therefore, the example would not compile. The calling constructor needs to find a single-parameter constructor that accepts a *String*, but the available single-parameter constructor accepts only an *int*.

In addition to being able to call another constructor in the same class, you are also able to call a superclass' constructor from the subclass' constructor. The rules for using *super()* are similar (such a call must also be placed in the first line of the constructor), but there are a few effects that are different from *this()*.

```java
public class MySuper
{
   //first constructor
```

```
        public MySuper()
        {
          System.out.println( "Super1");
        }

        //second constructor
        public MySuper( String title)
        {
          System.out.println( "Super2");
        }
      }

      public class MySub extends MySuper
      {
        //first constructor
        public MySub()
        {
          super( "the title");
          System.out.println( "Sub1");
        }

        //second constructor
        public MySub( String title)
        {
          System.out.println( "Sub2");
        }
      }
```

The first *MySub()* is fairly straightforward. *MySub()* first calls the second constructor in *MySuper* and prints out *MySuper2*, then finishes calling the remainder of the *MySub()* and prints out *MySub1*.

The second *MySub()* is a little less obvious. Every class constructor, when that class extends another, always calls *super()*. If there is not an explicit *super()* call in the constructor, Java will call one with no arguments. So, the second *MySub* constructor first calls the no-args *MySuper()*, prints *MySuper1*, then executes the rest of *MySub*'s second constructor and prints *Sub2*.

exam
ⓦatch

Many people get confused about the differences between this() and super() on the exam because they function similarly. Remember that a constructor always calls super() (possibly implicitly) when that class extends another. this() is never called unless it is explicitly invoked.

If the no-args constructor was not present in *MySuper*, then the code wouldn't compile. This scenario is very easy to overlook on the exam. Even though no no-args *super()* is explicitly called, Java will expect a no-args constructor in the superclass if a subclass' constructor does not explicitly invoke another superclass constructor. Keep in mind that if no constructor is provided for a class then Java will supply a default no-args constructor. When you have written your own constructors, Java will not automatically supply the no-args constructor.

```
public class A
{
  public A( String title)
  {
    System.out.println( "A");
  }
}

public class B extends A
{
  public B( String title)
  {
    System.out.println( "B");
  }
}
```

The preceding code will not compile because *B()* implicitly calls a no-args constructor for *A*, but no no-args version of *A()* is defined. Because we wrote *A(String title)* for *A*, we do not have a default no-args constructor.

Now that you have a better understanding of overriding and overloading methods and constructors, here are some possible scenario questions and their answers.

QUESTIONS AND ANSWERS

What is the one valid criterion that determines if overloaded methods are valid?	The parameter lists for each must be different enough so that finding the matching method for every method call is unambiguous.
What elements of overridden methods must be identical?	The parameter list and the return type.
Which internal constructor invoker may be called implicitly?	super()

CERTIFICATION SUMMARY

This chapter covered both general design considerations of object-oriented programming as well as the finer points of overloaded and overridden methods. An understanding of encapsulation, or the hiding of implementation details to other modules, will not only help you with the encapsulation-specific questions on the exam but also will give you a background understanding of some of the object-oriented techniques that you will find in other questions.

The distinction between *is a* and *has a* relationships will help you answer questions on the exam that ask you to choose the best object-oriented design. These questions can be especially tricky because the code for each answer may compile correctly. This distinction will also prove useful outside the exam, as it is the source of many poor designs.

Overloading and overriding methods may appear similar on the surface, because they both involve multiple methods with the same name, but the rules governing both differ. Overloaded methods must only have unique parameter lists to determine which calls are handled by which methods. Overridden methods must have the same return type and parameter lists, and specific rules determine the allowable differences in method visibility and thrown exceptions.

Finally, you can use *this()* and *super()* in a class constructor to call constructors in the same class or in the parent's class, respectively. It is important to note that *super()* is always called in a constructor when its class extends another and that the default *super()* requires a no-args constructor in the parent class.

TWO-MINUTE DRILL

- ❏ Encapsulated code uses modularity and appropriate visibility to separate the interface from the implementation.

- ❏ In encapsulation, an interface is the methods and instance variables to which other classes and packages have access. The implementation contains the "under the hood" details that are not visible outside that class or package.

- ❏ An *is a* relationship occurs when the child class is a type of the parent class or interface.

- ❏ A *has a* relationship occurs when one class is a part of or contained by the other class.

- ❏ Overloaded methods are methods with the same name in the same class.

- ❏ Overloaded methods only have to have the same method name. The parameter list must vary. The return type, the visibility, and the exceptions thrown may optionally vary.

- ❏ Overridden methods are methods with the same name and parameter list that exist in different classes in a class hierarchy.

- ❏ Overridden methods must have the same method name and parameter list. The accessibility of an overriding method (the method in the child class) may not be more restrictive.

- ❏ The exceptions thrown by an overriding method must be equal to or a subset of the exceptions thrown by the overridden method.

- ❏ The overridden method that is called is determined by the underlying object's type, not the type of its reference.

- ❏ Use *this()* to call another constructor from the body of a constructor in the same class. The parameters in *this()* must match the parameter list you intend to call.

❑ Use *super()* to call a parental constructor from the body of a constructor in the child class. The parameters in *super()* must match the parameter list you intend to call.

❑ Both *this()* and *super()* must be placed at the first line of the constructor's body, if used at all.

❑ When a constructor does not have an explicit *super()* call, Java will automatically call a no-args *super()*.

❑ You will get a compiler error when you have either an explicit or implicit no-args *super()* call when you do not have a no-args constructor in the parent class. Keep in mind though, that Java will automatically include a no-args constructor when that class doesn't have any other constructor written.

SELF TEST

The following questions will help you measure your understanding of the material presented in this chapter. Read all of the choices carefully, as there may be more than one correct answer. Choose all correct answers for each question.

1. What will happen when you compile and run this program:

    ```
    public class A
    {
      public static void main( String [] args)
      {
        new A().printResult( 1, "abc", 4);
      }
      private void printResult( int a, long b, int c)
      {
        System.out.println( a + b + c);
      }
      private void printResult( long a, String b, int c)
      {
        System.out.println( a + b + c);
      }
    }
    ```

    A. The code will not compile correctly because a long and a String may not be added.
    B. The code will compile and run and will display *1abc4* in the standard output.
    C. The code will compile and run and will display *11234* in the standard output.
    D. The code will compile and will throw a NumberFormatException.

2. All of the following are benefits of encapsulation except what?

    A. Clarity of code.
    B. Code efficiency.
    C. The ability to add functionality later on.
    D. Modification requires less coding changes.

3. What will happen when you compile and run this program?

    ```
    public class MySuper {
        public MySuper(int i) { }
    }
    public class MySub extends MySuper {
        public MySub() {
            super(2);
    ```

```
        public static void main(String args[]) {
            new MySub();
        }
    }
}
```

A. The program does not compile because *MySuper* does not have a no-args constructor.

B. The program compiles but throws a runtime exception when it cannot find the no-args *MySuper* constructor.

C. The program compiles and runs without error.

4. What is the relationship between *Rectangle* and *Square*?

```
public class Rectangle
{
}

public class Square extends Rectangle
{
}
```

A. It's a *has a* relationship.

B. It's an *is a* relationship.

C. It's both an *is a* and *has a* relationship.

D. The relationship is neither an *is a* nor a *has a* relationship.

5. When a subclass' method has the same name, parameter list, and return type as a method in the parent class, this method is said to be what?

A. extended

B. overloaded

C. overextended

D. overridden

6. What code should be inserted in place of XXXXX so that the output of the program is *okay*?

```
public class Test
{
  public static void main( String [] args)
  {
    new Test( 4);
  }
```

```
    public Test()
    {
       System.out.println( "okay");
    }
    public Test( int i)
    {
       XXXXX
    }
}
```

A. *super()*

B. *this*

C. *Test()*

D. *this()*

7. Which of the following must match exactly for overloaded methods to compile correctly?

A. The parameter list.

B. The return type.

C. The exceptions thrown.

D. None of the above.

8. The implementation details of a well encapsulated class should have what accessibility?

A. *public*

B. the default

C. *private*

D. It does not matter.

9. What is the relationship between *Vehicle* and *Engine*?

```
public class Vehicle
{
   private Engine theEngine
}

public class Engine
{
}
```

A. It's a *has a* relationship.

B. It's an *is a* relationship.

C. It's both an *is a* and *has a* relationship.

D. The relationship is neither an *is a* nor a *has a* relationship.

10. What will happen when you compile and run this program:

```
public class Test
{
  public static void main( String [] args)
  {
    new Test().foo( 1, 2);
  }
  private void foo( int a, int b)
  {
    System.out.println( "int");
  }
  private void foo( long a, int b)
  {
    System.out.println( "long");
  }
}
```

A. The code will compile and run and display *int*.

B. The code will compile and run and display *long*.

C. The code will not compile.

D. The code will compile but throw a runtime exception when executed.

11. What will happen when you compile this program?

```
public class Parent
{
  public void execute() throws Exception
  {
    //body omitted
  }
}
public class Child extends Parent
{
  private void execute() throws ClassCastException
  {
    //body omitted
  }
}
```

A. The program will compile successfully.

B. The program will not compile because the *execute()* in the subclass throws a different exception than in the parent class.

C. The program will not compile because the *execute()* in the subclass has less accessibility than in the parent class.

D. The program will not compile because the *execute()* in the subclass has less accessibility *and* throws a different exception than in the parent class.

12. What will happen when you compile and run this program?

```
public class MySuper
{
  public MySuper()
  {
    System.out.println( "MySuper");
  }
}

public class MySub extends MySuper
{
  public static void main( String [] args)
  {
    new MySub();
  }
  public MySub()
  {
    System.out.println( "MySub");
  }
}
```

A. The program will compile and run and will display MySub in the standard output.

B. The program will compile and run and will display MySuper in the standard output.

C. The program will not compile.

D. The program will compile and run and will display MySuper and MySub in the standard output.

13. What will happen when you compile and run this program?

```
public class A
{
  public void baz()
  {
    System.out.println( "A");
  }
```

```
  }
  public class B extends A
  {
    public static void main( String [] args)
    {
      A a = new B();
      a.baz();
    }
    public void baz()
    {
      System.out.println( "B");
    }
  }
```

A. The program compiles and runs and displays *A* in the standard output.

B. The program compiles and runs and displays *B* in the standard output.

C. The program compiles but throws a runtime exception.

D. The program does not compile.

14. What will happen when you compile and run this program?

```
  public class A
  {
    public static void main( String [] args)
    {
      new A().baz( 1, 2);
    }
    private void baz( int a, int b);
    {
      System.out.println( "baz");
    }
    private void foo( int a, int b)
    {
      System.out.println( "first");
    }
    private void foo( int a, int b)
    {
      System.out.println( "second");
    }
  }
```

A. The program compiles and runs and displays *first* in the standard output.

B. The program compiles and runs and displays *second* in the standard output.

C. The program compiles and runs and displays *baz* in the standard output.

D. The program does not compile.

15. The interface methods for a well encapsulated class should have what accessibility?

    A. *public*

    B. *protected*

    C. *private*

    D. It does not matter.

16. What code should be inserted in place of XXXXX so that the output of the program is *good*?

```
public class Parent
{
  public Parent()
  {
    System.out.println( "good");
  }
  public Parent( int j)
  {
    System.out.println( "bad");
  }
}
public class Example extends Parent
{
  public static void main( String [] args)
  {
    new Example();
  }
  public Example()
  {
    XXXXX
  }
}
```

    A. *this()*

    B. *superclass()*

    C. *Parent()*

    D. Leave it blank.

17. What will happen when you compile this program?

```
public class Test
{
  protected void start() throws ClassCastException
  {
    //body omitted
```

```
      }
   }

   public class Child extends Test
   {
     public void start () throws Exception
     {
       //body omitted
     }
   }
```

A. The program will compile successfully.

B. The program will not compile because the *start()* in the subclass throws a different exception than in the parent class.

C. The program will not compile because the *start()* in the subclass is public, whereas it is protected in the parent class.

D. The program will not compile because the *start()* in the subclass has different accessibility *and* throws a different exception than in the parent class.

18. When two or more methods in the same class have the same name, they are said to be what?

A. an implementation detail

B. overridden

C. an interface

D. overloaded

19. What will happen when you compile and run this program?

```
   public class Example
   {
     public static void main( String [] args)
     {
       new Example ().locate( 1.0, 2);
     }
     private void locate ( double a, long b)
     {
       System.out.println( "double-long");
     }
     private void locate ( long a, int b)
     {
       System.out.println( "long-int");
     }
   }
```

A. The code will compile and run and display *double-long*.

B. The code will compile and run and display *long-int*.

C. The code will not compile.

D. The code will compile but throw a runtime exception when executed.

20. What is the relationship between *Movable* and *Bitmap*?

```
public interface Moveable
{
   public void moveObject();
}

public class Bitmap implements Moveable
{
   public void moveObject()
   {
      //body omitted
   }
}
```

A. It's a *has a* relationship.

B. It's an *is a* relationship.

C. It's both an *is a* and a *has a* relationship.

D. The relationship is neither an *is a* nor a *has a* relationship.

8

Inner Classes

I nner classes were an addition to the Java Development Kit 1.1 (JDK1.1). They can increase the clarity of your code by allowing you to create classes close to where they are being used—within another class. This is useful if you have behavior related to a class that shouldn't actually be implemented by that class or is not used by any other class. You can place that behavior in an inner class. Inner classes allow you to group related classes and thus reduce namespace clutter. In this section, we will discuss the different types of inner classes and look at some examples.

CERTIFICATION OBJECTIVE 8.01

Inner Classes

Inner classes are classes defined at a scope smaller than a package. For example, you can define an inner class inside another class, inside a method, and even as part of an expression. Inner classes are classes nonetheless and behave just like any other class. They can extend other classes and they can implement interfaces. There are four types of inner classes:

- Static inner classes (also called nested classes)
- Member inner classes
- Local inner classes
- Anonymous inner classes

Each one of these will be discussed in further detail in the following sections.

Static Inner Classes

Static inner classes are the simplest form of inner classes. They behave much like top-level classes except that they are defined within the scope of another class, namely the enclosing class. For example:

```
package mypackage;
public class EnclosingClass {
```

```
private static int staticvar=0;
public int instancevar=0;

public static class StaticInnerClass {
}
}
```

The fully qualified class name for the inner class in this example is mypackage.EnclosingClass.StaticInnerClass. The Java compiler creates two separate class files for this example: EnclosingClass.class and EnclosingClass$StaticInnerClass.class. Inner classes can not have the same name as the enclosing class.

Static inner classes have no implicit references to instances of the enclosing class and can access only static members and methods of the enclosing class. Because an inner class is defined within the enclosing class, it has access to private static members of the enclosing class. Because the inner class in the previous example is static, it can access only the *staticvar* variable, even though it is private. It cannot access the *instancevar* variable because it is not static, regardless of the fact that it is public.

Static inner classes are often used to implement small helper classes such as iterators. An *iterator* provides the necessary behavior to get to each element in a collection without exposing the collection itself. In classes containing and manipulating collections, it is good practice to return an iterator instead of the collection containing the elements you want to iterate over. This shields clients from internal changes to the data structures used in your classes.

Let's say you want to specify a week as a week number within a year and find out what dates are in that given week. The following example treats a week as a collection of seven days. To find out what dates are in a given week, you create a Week as

```
Week week = new Week(weekNr,year)
```

and then ask the week for the days in that week by calling

```
week.getDays()
```

The return type of the getDays() method is *Iterator*. Iterator is an interface defined in the java.util package. Its interface is defined as follows:

```
package java.util;
public interface Iterator {
    public boolean hasNext();
    public Object next();
    public void remove();
}
```

In the following example, the Iterator interface is realized through the use of a static inner class called DayIterator. The DayIterator class definition is highlighted in the example code. The getDays() method of the Week class creates a DayIterator by passing itself as a parameter to its constructor. The DayIterator uses the week's getWeeknr() and getYear() accessor methods to initialize an instance of GregorianCalendar (also from the java.util package) with the correct year and week. In this example, you can see that static inner classes can implement any arbitrary interface, just like any class can. Because the DayIterator claims to implement the Iterator interface, it must provide implementations for all the methods specified in the Iterator interface. Even though removing a day from a week doesn't make sense, we must still provide an implementation for the Iterator's remove() method. The method's body is left empty. The DayIterator keeps track of the current day of the week in a private member called *index*, which is initialized to zero. As long as this index is less than seven, the DayIterator's hasNext() method will return true, indicating that there are more days to follow in this week. Each time you call the next() method, it uses the Calendar to calculate the Date based on the current value of index, after which it increments the index using index++.

```
import java.util.*;

public class Week {

    private int weeknr;
    private int year;

    public Week(int weeknr, int year) {
        this.weeknr = weeknr;
```

```
        this.year = year;
    }

    public Iterator getDays() {
        return new DayIterator(this);
    }
    public int getWeeknr() {
        return weeknr;
    }

    public int getYear() {
        return year;
    }

    public static class DayIterator implements Iterator {

        private int index = 0;
        private Calendar cal = null;

        DayIterator (Week aWeek) {
            cal = new GregorianCalendar();
            cal.clear();
            cal.set(Calendar.YEAR, aWeek.getYear());
            cal.set(Calendar.WEEK_OF_YEAR, aWeek.getWeeknr());
        }

        public boolean hasNext() {
            return index < 7;
        }

        public Object next() {
            cal.set(Calendar.DAY_OF_WEEK, index++);
            return cal.getTime();
        }

        public void remove() {
            // not implemented
        }
    }

    public static void main(String[] args) {
        // list the days of the week
        if (args.length < 2) {
            System.err.println("Usage: java Week <weeknr> year>");
            System.exit(1);
```

```
    } else {
        try {
            int weeknr = Integer.parseInt(args[0]);
            int year = Integer.parseInt(args[1]);
            Week wk = new Week(weeknr, year);
            for (Iterator i=wk.getDays();i.hasNext();) {
                System.err.println(i.next());
            }
        } catch (NumberFormatException x) {
            System.err.println("Illegal week or year");
        }
    }
}
}
```

The main program of the example shows how to use the getDays() method of the Week class to print all the days of the week. It parses the command line arguments to integer week number and year and creates an instance of Week. The for loop creates an Iterator by calling the getDays() method and will keep looping until the Iterator's hasNext() method returns false. Each object returned by the Iterator is an instance of Date, so the output produced by the following command line:

```
java Week 10 1999
```

is as follows:

```
Sat Feb 27 00:00:00 EST 1999
Sun Feb 28 00:00:00 EST 1999
Mon Mar 01 00:00:00 EST 1999
Tue Mar 02 00:00:00 EST 1999
Wed Mar 03 00:00:00 EST 1999
Thu Mar 04 00:00:00 EST 1999
Fri Mar 05 00:00:00 EST 1999
```

Note that the try-catch block in main is needed to cope with illegal command-line arguments that are not numbers that can be parsed to a valid int. Also note that this example does produce strange results for the first week of the year. This is a Calendar problem and is not related to the use of inner classes, so we made no attempts to fix this problem.

Member Inner Classes

Inner classes defined in an enclosing class without using the static modifier are called *member inner classes*. They are members of the enclosing class just like instance variables. Unlike static inner classes, member inner classes (or simply member classes) can access all members of the enclosing class regardless of their level of protection. In other words, all public, package, protected, and private members are visible to instances of the member class. To gain this access, you must provide an instance of the enclosing class when you create a new instance of a member class. A new syntax was invented for this purpose when they added inner classes to the JDK1.1. This new syntax treats the new operator as if it is a method of the enclosing class. The following is an example:

```
public class EnclosingClass {
    private int instVar = 1;

    public class MemberClass {
        public void innerMethod() {
            // it is OK to do something with instVar here
        }
    }

    public MemberClass createMember() {
        return this.new MemberClass();
    }
}
```

Note how the MemberClass instance is created in the createMember() method. The new operator has to be prefixed with an instance of the enclosing class, in this case *this*. Note that in this particular case, when the enclosing instance is *this*, you don't have to explicitly write it, you simply use *new MemberClass()*. This can be the cause of great confusion because if you need to create an instance of a member class outside of the scope of the enclosing class, you *do* need to use an instance of the enclosing class to create the member instance:

```
EnclosingClass ec = new EnclosingClass();
EnclosingClass.MemberClass mc = ec.newMemberClass();
```

Or, if you're into one-liners:

```
EnclosingClass.MemberClass mc = (new EnclosingClass()).new
EnclosingClass.MemberClass();
```

Another new syntax invented for the use of inner classes in the JDK1.1 has to do with the meaning of the keyword *this*. When in the scope of a member class, *this* refers to the instance of the member class. But how do you refer to the enclosing instance? The answer is to prefix the *this* keyword with the class name of the enclosing instance you want to refer to. The same new syntax applies to the keyword *super*.

```
public class EnclosingClass {

   public class MemberClass {
      public void innerMethod() {
         // 'this' refers to an instance of EnclosingClass.MemberClass
         // 'EnclosingClass.this' refers to an instance of EnclosingClass
         // 'super' refers to the superclass of MemberClass (Object)
         // 'EnclosingClass.super' refers to the superclass of EnclosingClass
      }
   }
}
```

Member classes are compiled to separate class files just like static inner classes, so this example creates a file called EnclosingClass$MemberClass.class in addition to the EnclosingClass.class file. Like static inner classes, member classes cannot have the same name as the enclosing class. In addition, member inner classes cannot have static members. Only interfaces, top-level classes, and static inner classes can have static members.

The following example is a modification of the Week example from the preceding section. We modified it so that the DayIterator class is now a member class that can access the Week's weeknr and year members directly. The DayIterator no longer takes the Week as a constructor argument, and we modified the getDays() method to use the proper this.new syntax.

```java
import java.util.*;
public class Week {
    private int weeknr;
    private int year;

    public Week(int weeknr, int year) {
        this.weeknr = weeknr;
        this.year = year;
    }

    public Iterator getDays() {
        // DayIterator is not static and therefore
        // needs an enclosing instance (this)
        return this.new DayIterator();
    }

    public class DayIterator implements Iterator {

        private int index = 0;
        private Calendar cal = null;

        DayIterator () {
            cal = new GregorianCalendar();
            cal.clear();
            cal.set(Calendar.YEAR, year);
            cal.set(Calendar.WEEK_OF_YEAR, weeknr);
        }

        public boolean hasNext() {
            return index < 7;
        }

        public Object next() {
            cal.set(Calendar.DAY_OF_WEEK, index++);
            return cal.getTime();
        }

        public void remove() {
            // not implemented
        }
    }

    public static void main(String[] args) {
        // identical to main of the Static inner class example
    }
}
```

Local Inner Classes

The preceding two forms of inner classes, static and member inner classes, were both defined at the class scope. You can also define inner classes within the scope of a method, or even smaller blocks within a method. We call this form of inner class *local inner class*. This is by far the least used form of inner classes. There are very few cases where you would ever need a named local inner class because most problems can be solved with the other types of inner classes. In the following example, we placed the complete DayIterator inner class inside the getDays() method of the Week class. Local inner classes, like local variables, can not be declared public, protected, private, or static. Like member inner classes, local inner classes cannot have static members and they cannot have the same name as the enclosing class in which they are defined. Local inner classes can access certain kinds of local variables and method arguments of the enclosing method. Access to local variables and method arguments is restricted. These restrictions are an important certification objective and we will discuss them separately later in this chapter. In this example, the DayIterator's toString() method accesses the local variable of the getDays() method called *text*.

```
import java.util.*;

public class Week {

    private int weeknr;
    private int year;

    public Week(int weeknr, int year) {
        this.weeknr = weeknr;
        this.year = year;
    }

    public Iterator getDays() {
        final String text = "DayIterator for week " + weeknr + " of " + year;
```

```java
class DayIterator implements Iterator {

    private int index = 0;
    private Calendar cal = null;

    DayIterator (Week aWeek) {
        cal = new GregorianCalendar();
        cal.clear();
        cal.set(Calendar.YEAR, aWeek.getYear());
        cal.set(Calendar.WEEK_OF_YEAR, aWeek.getWeeknr());
    }

    public boolean hasNext() {
        return index < 7;
    }

    public Object next() {
        cal.set(Calendar.DAY_OF_WEEK, index++);
        return cal.getTime();
    }

    public void remove() {
        // not implemented
    }

    public String toString() {
        return text;
    }
}
return new DayIterator(this);
}

public int getWeeknr() {
    return weeknr;
}

public int getYear() {
    return year;
}

public static void main(String[] args) {
    // same as before
}
}
```

Anonymous Inner Classes

Anonymous inner classes are local inner classes that don't have a class name. You use an anonymous class when you want to create and use a class but don't want to bother with giving it a name or using it again. In the preceding example, you'll notice that we're using syntax that is different from that of a normal class definition. The keyword *class* is missing, and there are no modifiers (public, protected, and so on). The keywords *extends* and *implements* are missing too. These keywords aren't allowed because we create anonymous inner classes through another extension to the *new* operator syntax. That means the complete class definition is actually part of a Java expression. Right after the *new someClass()* syntax, you write a curly brace and start to write a class definition. It's that simple!

The lack of a class name has a number of implications for the declaration and use of inner classes. You can't define constructors for an anonymous inner class because you can't name them. They must always (implicitly) extend a superclass or implement some interface even though you never use the *extends* or *implements* keywords. Without a superclass or interface, you wouldn't have a class name to refer to for the new operator.

When you compile the preceding source code, the Java compiler creates the files EnclosingClass$1.class, InnerSuperClass.class, and EnclosingClass.class. The Java compiler writes multiple anonymous inner classes in an enclosing class into sequentially numbered class files prefixed with the name of the enclosing class and a dollar sign. Note that when you create anonymous inner classes inside other inner classes, such as member classes or static inner classes, their numeric postfix is appended to the outermost enclosing class, not the inner class in which they are defined. So instead of Outer$Inner$1.class, you'll see Outer$1.class even if the anonymous inner class is defined in the Outer.Inner class.

Anonymous classes are most commonly used in user interface adapters to perform event handling, such as for AWT and Swing events. Here is an example of an event handler for AWT that uses an anonymous inner class to handle a button event.

```java
import java.awt.Frame;
import java.awt.Button;
import java.awt.event.ActionEvent;
import java.awt.event.ActionListener;

public class DemoFrame extends Frame {
    public DemoFrame() {
        addButton("Hello world");
    }

    private void addButton(final String text) {
        Button b = new Button(text);
        b.addActionListener(new ActionListener() {
            public void actionPerformed(ActionEvent e) {
                // handle the button-pressed event
                System.err.println("Button " + text + " pressed");
            }
        });
        add(b);
    }

    public static void main(String[] args) {
            (new DemoFrame()).show();
    }
}
```

In this example, it looks like we create an instance of an ActionListener, but ActionListener is an interface, so how can it be instantiated? It can't. What is really instantiated by the *new ActionListener() {* syntax is the anonymous inner class defined on the fly after the curly brace that implicitly implements the ActionListener interface. Note the absence of the *implements* keyword. Like local inner classes, anonymous inner classes cannot be public, protected, private, or static. The syntax for anonymous inner classes does not allow for any modifiers to be used.

Anonymous inner classes have access to local variables and method arguments governed by the same restrictions as local inner classes. These restrictions are detailed in a later section.

Using anonymous inner classes is most effective when they are small and implement only a single or very few small methods. Reading inline class definitions is difficult and gets very confusing when the definition of the inner class is long. Let's return to our Week example once more.

```java
import java.util.*;

public class Week {

    private int weeknr;
    private int year;

    public Week(int weeknr, int year) {
        this.weeknr = weeknr;
        this.year = year;
    }

    public Iterator getDays() {
        return new Iterator() {
        private int index = 0;
        private Calendar cal = null;

            private Calendar getCalendar () {
                if (cal == null) {
                    cal = new GregorianCalendar();
                    cal.clear();
                    cal.set(Calendar.YEAR, year);
                    cal.set(Calendar.WEEK_OF_YEAR, weeknr);
                }
                return cal;
            }

            public boolean hasNext() {
                return index < 7;
            }

            public Object next() {
                getCalendar().set(Calendar.DAY_OF_WEEK, index++);
                return getCalendar().getTime();
            }

            public void remove() {
                // not implemented
            }
        };
    }

    public static void main(String[] args) {
        // identical to previous examples
    }
}
```

Note that the day iterator is now created as an anonymous inner class implementing the Iterator interface. Because it is anonymous, it does not have a constructor. We had to find another way to initialize our GregorianCalendar object. We chose a technique called *lazy initialization*. By initializing the cal member to null, the getCalendar() method initializes it the first time that it is called by the iterator's next() method.

An alternative to lazy initialization is using an *instance initializer*. An instance initializer is a block of code (not a method!) that automatically runs every time you create a new instance of an object. In effect, it is an anonymous constructor! Of course, instance initializers are rather limited; because they don't have arguments, you can't overload them, so you can have only one of these "constructors" per class. The method definition in the following example replaces the getDays method in the previous example. It initializes the anonymous day iterator using an instance initializer.

```java
public Iterator getDays() {
   return new Iterator() {

      private int index = 0;
      private Calendar cal = new GregorianCalendar();
      { // instance initializer
         cal.clear();
         cal.set(Calendar.YEAR, year);
         cal.set(Calendar.WEEK_OF_YEAR, weeknr);
      } // end instance initializer

      public boolean hasNext() {
         return index < 7;
      }

      public Object next() {
         cal.set(Calendar.DAY_OF_WEEK, index++);
         return cal.getTime();
      }

      public void remove() {
         // not implemented
      }
   };
}
```

The size of the anonymous inner class in this example is borderline acceptable and slightly on the big side. For the day iterator, we prefer to use the first version of the example using static inner classes because this is the simplest form and makes the meaning of the inner class the most explicit.

CERTIFICATION OBJECTIVE 8.02

Inner Class Access to an Enclosing Class

In the preceding sections, you have learned that an inner class has full access rights to its enclosing class. The access rules get slightly more complicated when we look at local inner classes and anonymous inner classes. These can still access all the instance variables and methods of the enclosing class, but because they are defined within the context of a method, you might expect that they could also access local variables and method arguments. This is where the keyword *final* comes in. The rule is that a local or an anonymous inner class can access only those local variables and method arguments that are declared final. This means that you cannot change the value of local variables from within the code of the inner class. They are read-only.

```java
public class MyClass {
    public void enclosingMethod(final String arg1, int arg2) {
        final String local = "A local final variable";
        String nonfinal = "A local non-final variable";
        Object obj = new Object() {
            public String toString() {
                return local + "," + arg1;
            }
        };
    }
}
```

Within the toString() method of the anonymous subclass of Object, we can access both the local variable called *local* and the method argument arg1. We can not access args2 or nonfinal. If you absolutely have to change the value of some variable in the enclosing scope (this should be extremely rare) you can use the following trick:

```
public class MyClass {
    public void enclosingMethod(final String arg1, int arg2) {
        final int[] trick = new int[1];

        Runnable runner = new Runnable() {
            public void run() {
                trick[0] = 5;
            }
        };
    }
}
```

In this example, the array of integers called *trick* is declared final. That means you can never assign another array of integers to the variable trick. But it doesn't mean that its elements are final, so it is perfectly okay to assign a value to the only element in the trick array. Because the trick array is final, it is accessible from within the inner class as well.

QUESTIONS AND ANSWERS

You are defining a local inner class that needs to access an argument of the enclosing method...	Declare the method parameter as final.
You are defining an anonymous inner class that needs constructor behavior...	Use an instance initializer or lazy initialization.
You want to define an inner class that doesn't need direct access to instance variables...	Use a static inner class.
You want to define an inner class that has direct access to the instance variables of the enclosing class...	Use a member inner class.
You need to access the enclosing instance from within a member inner class...	Use the *EnclosingClass.this* syntax.

CERTIFICATION SUMMARY

Inner classes are classes declared within the scope of an enclosing class. There are four kinds of inner classes: static inner classes, member inner classes, local inner classes, and anonymous inner classes. Inner classes have full access rights to the members of the enclosing class, so they can access private members as well as public and protected ones.

Static inner classes can access only static members of the enclosing class. Member inner classes need an instance of the enclosing class when they are created, hence the object.new syntax. To refer to the instance of the enclosing class from within an inner class you use the EnclosingClass.this syntax.

Local and anonymous inner classes can access only those objects declared as final in their enclosing scope. Anonymous inner classes can't have a constructor.

✓ TWO-MINUTE DRILL

❑ Inner classes are declared within the scope of an enclosing class.

❑ There are static, member, local, and anonymous inner classes.

❑ Inner classes have full access rights to the members of the enclosing class.

❑ Static inner classes can access only static members of the enclosing class.

❑ To create an instance of a member inner class, you need a reference to an instance of the enclosing class (new syntax for *new*).

❑   Inside the scope of an inner class, the keyword *this* refers to the instance of the inner class, not the enclosing class. To get a reference to the enclosing instance, prefix *this* with the name of the enclosing class (new syntax for *this* and *super*).

❑   Local and anonymous inner classes can access only *final* local variables from their enclosing scope.

❑   Anonymous inner classes cannot have a constructor.

❑   Local and anonymous inner classes cannot be defined as private, protected, public, or static.

❑   Only top-level classes, interfaces, and static inner classes can have static members.

❑   Anonymous inner classes are often used for event handling in AWT and Swing.

❑   Most inner classes, especially local and anonymous inner classes, should be small to improve readability.

SELF TEST

The following questions will help you measure your understanding of the material presented in this chapter. Read all of the choices carefully, as there may be more than one correct answer. Choose all correct answers for each question.

1. Which of the following statements are correct? (Choose all that apply.)

    A. Inner classes are defined within the scope of another class.

    B. Inner classes can subclass other classes and they can implement interfaces.

    C. Inner classes cannot be static.

    D. There are four different kinds of inner classes: top-level, static, member, and anonymous.

2. The filename(s) generated by the Java compiler for the following code is (are):

    ```java
    public class MyMap implements Map {
        private static class MapEntry {
            ...
        }
        ...
    }
    ```

    A. MyMap.class

    B. MyMap.class and MyMap.MapEntry.class

    C. MyMap.class and MyMap$MapEntry.class

    D. MyMap$MapEntry

3. What happens when you compile the following code?

    ```java
    import java.util.*;

    public class Week {

    private int weeknr;
        private int year;
        private int[] days = {1,2,3,4,5,6,0};

    public Week(int weeknr, int year) {
            this.weeknr = weeknr;
            this.year = year;
        }

    public Iterator getDays() {
    ```

```
        return new DayIterator(this);
    }

public int getWeeknr() {
    return weeknr;
    }

public int getYear() {
    return year;
    }

private static class DayIterator implements Iterator {

private int index = 0;
    private Calendar cal = null;

DayIterator (Week aWeek) {
        cal = new GregorianCalendar();
        cal.clear();
        cal.set(Calendar.YEAR, aWeek.getYear());
        cal.set(Calendar.WEEK_OF_YEAR, aWeek.getWeeknr());
    }

public boolean hasNext() {
        return index < 7;
    }

public Object next() {
        cal.set(Calendar.DAY_OF_WEEK, days[index++]);
        return cal.getTime();
    }

public void remove() {
        // not implemented
    }
    }

public static void main(String[] args) {
    // list the days of the week
    if (args.length < 2) {
        System.err.println("Usage: java Week <weeknr> year>");
        System.exit(1);
    } else {
        try {
            int weeknr = Integer.parseInt(args[0]);
```

```
            int year = Integer.parseInt(args[1]);
            Week wk = new Week(weeknr, year);
            for (Iterator i=wk.getDays();i.hasNext();) {
                System.err.println(i.next());
            }
        } catch (NumberFormatException x) {
            System.err.println("Illegal week or year");
        }
    }
  }
}
```

A. This code compiles, and when it is run it returns the days of the week starting on Sunday instead of Saturday.

B. This code does not compile because the days array is private.

C. This code does not compile because the days array is not static.

D. This code does not compile because the DayIterator class is private.

4. The following code does not compile. Why?

```
public class MyClass {

private class MyRunner implements Runnable {
    public void run() {
        // do something
    }
}

public static void main(String[] args) {
    (new Thread(new MyRunner())).start();
}
}
```

A. You have to create an instance of MyRunner with new MyClass.MyRunner().

B. MyRunner is private.

C. You have to import Thread from java.lang.

D. You have to create an instance of MyRunner with an enclosing instance of MyClassl.

5. Which of the following are correct ways to create an instance of an inner class called Outer.Inner from outside the scope of the Outer class? Assume Inner is a public static inner class that has no defined constructor.

A. Outer.new Inner()

   B. (new Outer()).new Inner();

   C. (new Outer()).new Outer.Inner();

   D. new Outer.Inner();

6. What number is returned by getValue(), assuming the enclosing class creates an instance of Bar using this.new?

```
public class Foo {
    protected int x = 3;
    private int y = 5;
    private class Bar {
        private int x = 8;

    public Bar() {
            Foo.this.x = y;
        }

    public int getValue() {
            return x*y;
        }
    }

    public int getValue() {
        return (new Bar()).getValue();
    }

    public static void main(String[] args) {
        System.err.println((new Foo()).getValue());
    }
}
```

   A. 15

   B. 24

   C. 25

   D. 40

7. Fill in the blank in the following sentence. Only ... can have static members.

   A. top-level classes

   B. top-level classes, interfaces, and static inner classes

   C. top-level classes and interfaces

   D. top-level classes, interfaces, and member classes

8. What is the result of compiling and executing the following code?

```
import java.util.Iterator;
public class Foo {
    public Iterator getIterator() {
        return new public Iterator() {
            public void remove() {}
            public Object next() {return null;}
            public boolean hasNext() {return false;}
        };
    }
}
```

   A. This code returns a new Foo.Iterator when you call getIterator().
   B. This code returns a new Iterator when you call getIterator().
   C. This code doesn't compile because an Iterator interface method is missing.
   D. This code doesn't compile because the syntax of the inner class creation is wrong.

9. What class files are generated when you compile the following code?

```
import java.util.Iterator;
public class Foo {
    public static class Week {
        public Iterator getIterator() {
            return new Iterator() {
                public void remove() {};
                public Object next() {return null;}
                public boolean hasNext() {return false;}
            };
        }
    }
}
```

   A. Foo.class, Foo$1.class, Foo$Week.class
   B. Foo.class, Foo.Week$1.class, Foo$1$Week.class
   C. Foo.class, Foo$Week.class, Foo$Week$1.class
   D. Foo.class, Foo$Week.class, Foo$Week$Iterator.class

10. What class files are generated when you compile the following code?

```
import java.util.HashMap;
public class Foo {
    public static class Week {
```

```
        public HashMap getMap() {
            return new HashMap() {
                public HashMap(int size) {}
                public Object put(Object key, Object value) {}
            };
        }
    }
}
```

A. None, the code doesn't compile.

B. Foo.class, Foo$HashMap.class, Foo$Week.class

C. Foo.class, Foo$Week$1.class, Foo$Week.class

D. Foo.class, Foo$Week.class, Foo$Week$HashMap.class

11. What do you have to change in the following code to make it valid?

```
public class Foo {
    public Runnable getRunnable(String name) {
        return new Thread() {
            public void run() {
                setName(name);
            }
        };
    }
}
```

A. Change the modifier of the run method to protected.

B. Change the return type of getRunnable() to Thread.

C. Declare the name parameter of getRunnable as final.

D. Nothing.

12. What will be the value of *b* after the assignment in the run() method?

```
public class Foo {
    int a = 10;
    int c = 30;
    public Runnable getRunnable() {
        int a = 20;
        return new Thread() {
            public void run() {
                int b = a+c;
            }
        };
    }
}
```

A. 30

B. 40

C. 50

D. This code doesn't compile.

13. What is the correct way to write a constructor for the SubClassOfInner class?

```
class EnclosingClass {
   public class Inner {
      Inner(int a) {}
   }
}

class SubClassOfInner extends EnclosingClass.Inner {
   // how to write a constructor?
}
```

A. There is no correct way to provide a constructor in this scenario.

B. SubClassOfInner(int a) { super(a); }

C. SubClassOfInner(EnclosingClass outer, int a) { outer.super(a); }

D. SubClassOfInner(int a) {EnclosingClass.super(a);}

14. What is wrong with the following code?

```
import java.util.Hashtable;
class Foo {
   String[] keys;
   String[] names;

public Hashtable buildHash(String start) {
      class MyHash extends Hashtable {
         public MyHash() {
            super();
         }

public void initHash(String str) {
            for (int i=0; i < keys.length; i++)
               if (names[i].startsWith(str))
                  put(keys[i], names[i]);
         }
      }
      MyHash h = new MyHash();
      h.initHash(start);
```

```
        return h;
    }
}
```

A. Nothing. This code is correct.

B. The keys and names arrays must be declared public.

C. The start parameter of buildHash must be declared final.

D. The str parameter of initHash must be declared final.

15. Consider the following code. What is printed on stdout?

```
class Foo {
    protected class Bar {
        protected Bar() {
            System.out.println("Foo.Bar");
        }
    }
    private Bar b;
    Foo() {
        System.out.println("Foo");
        b = this.new Bar();
    }
}

class FooToo extends Foo {
    protected class Bar {
        protected Bar() {
            System.out.println("FooToo.Bar");
        }
    }
    public static void main(String[] args) {
        new FooToo();
    }
}
```

A. Nothing. This code is incorrect.

B. Foo
   Foo.Bar

C. Foo
   FooToo.Bar

D. FooToo
   FooToo.Bar

16. Which of the statements about the following code is correct? (Choose all that apply.)

```
public class Foo {
    int var = 10;
    public class Test {
        public static void main(String[] args) {
            System.out.println("Foo$Test: var = " + var);
        }
    }
}
```

A. The result of java Foo$Test is Foo$Test: var = 10.

B. This code does not compile because Foo$Test cannot access the instance variable var.

C. This code does not compile because Foo$Test can't have a static main() method.

D. This code does not compile because you can't access var from a static method.

17. You want to modify some local value defined in the enclosing scope of an anonymous inner class from within that anonymous inner class. What are your options to accomplish this? (Choose all that apply.)

A. Store the value in an array that is declared final and modify the array element.

B. Make sure the value is an object stored in a final local variable and use a method on that object to modify it.

C. This can't be done.

D. Don't define the value as final and simply modify it.

9

Threads

I n this chapter you'll learn all about what threads are and how they can be used to create rich functionality in your programs.

You can think of a thread as a software engine that can process any sequence of instructions. In older languages, such as Basic, there was only one such engine, whereas in modern languages you can specify many, and have each of them run at the same time and independently of each other.

Different modern languages allow multithreading in different ways, and the resulting program is usually tied to the underlying operating system. Java was designed with this in mind from the beginning, and it provides all the necessary tools to use threads easily in a cross-platform way.

Think of a stockbroker application with a lot of complex behavior that the user can choose from. One of the operations could be "download last stock option prices," another could be "check prices for warnings," and a third, time consuming operation could be "analyze historical data for company x."

In a one-thread environment these actions are executed only after the user says so, and strictly one after the other. The next action can be executed only when the previous one has finished. If some historical analysis takes half an hour, and the user selects to perform a download and check afterwards, a warning may come too late to buy or sell some stock.

This application would benefit greatly from multithreading. Ideally, the download and check would be happening continuously in the background (in another thread), and any warning would be communicated instantly. Meanwhile, the user can work with some other options of the application. Another improvement would be to perform the historical analysis in yet another thread, so the user can work with the rest of the application while the results are being calculated.

A good knowledge of how to use threads is essential to implement this kind of behavior in any application. For the certification exam you will be expected to know how to run threads and how to make them co-operate with each other in an effective way.

New Threads

The first step to writing a multithreaded application is to identify the different series of instructions that will be executed by the different threads. In Java you provide these instructions in a *public void run()* method; this method is executed when the thread is started.

There are two ways of creating a thread: extending the thread class and implementing the Runnable interface.

Creating a Thread by Extending the Thread Class

Extending the thread class is the easiest way to create a thread. Quite often, the behavior that you want to perform in a separate thread is tightly related to an object, and the main reason to create the object is to have it execute that parallel behavior only once. In this case you can keep things easy by declaring the behavior in a new class that extends Thread.

Declaring

The Thread class has a public void run() method. You can override this method to include your functionality as part of an extended Thread class:

```
public class MyThread extends Thread{
    public void run(){
        // Your instructions here
    }
}
```

Note the signature of run() specifies that it doesn't throw any checked exceptions. This means that your run method cannot do it either. The compiler will complain if there are any uncaught checked exceptions.

Instantiating

Once you have the class, you get an instance of it, typically by calling the no parameter constructor:

```
- MyThread testThread=new MyThread();
```

You can use any constructor that you define in your extended class. As in any other classes, the default constructor for the superclass (Thread()) will be called automatically.

Creating a Thread by Implementing the Runnable Interface

A class that implements the Runnable interface can extend any other class, and its main purpose may be unrelated to any thread behavior. Additionally, an instance of this class can be the target of one or more threads throughout its life. It is a lot more flexible than extending Thread, but it requires an extra step.

Defining

The Runnable interface defines only one method:

```
- public void run();
```

You can write a class that implements the method, as shown in the following example:

```
public class MyRunnable implements Runnable{
    public void run(){
        // Your instructions here
    }
}
```

In the same way as the run method of Thread, this method should not throw any checked exceptions.

Instantiating

Once you have a class, you have to create an instance of it by calling any constructor that you have defined, or the default:

```
- MyRunnable firstRunnable=new MyRunnable();
```

This instance of your class will constitute the target of the thread. Now that you have the instance, you create a Thread object by passing the target as a parameter:

```
- Thread testThread=new Thread(firstRunnable);
```

You should always be very clear about which classes have the run methods that you want to execute. It is possible, but serves no purpose, to have an instance of a Thread (not subclassed) with no Runnable target; in the same way it is possible to override public void run() in Thread and then pass a target to the constructor.

Starting an Instance of a Thread

Whether you created it from a subclass of Thread or from a Runnable target, the instance of Thread that you now have does nothing different from any other object. It has variables that you can access and methods that you can call, but it is not doing anything on its own. It is ready to run, but it is not running yet, and it won't do so until you tell it to start running. You do this by calling the start() method on the Thread instance:

```
testThread.start();
```

This starts a new flow of execution with your instructions and returns immediately. From that moment onward, the instructions that you specified in the run method will be executing in parallel to whatever follows the start() method call.

In the case of using a Runnable target, its run method is not called directly, but it is called by the default run method of the Thread instance. So the effect is the same; there is now a separate thread executing instructions in the run method that you specified.

You can call start() only once on a thread. If you try to start a thread that has already been started, you will get an IllegalThreadStateException. If you think you need to start a thread more than once, consider implementing the Runnable interface. Using the Runnable interface, you can create and start as many threads as you want with the same target.

Threads in the Running State

It is in the running state that most things of interest happen to threads. They execute their run methods concurrently with other threads, they cooperate, share resources, and even compete with each other to get their own tasks done as soon as possible.

Because there is a limited number of CPUs in a computer (usually just one) and instructions have to be performed one at a time, threads have to take turns to run. Usually they are switching so fast between each other that the user gets the impression of true parallelism; refer to the scheduling section later in this chapter for more on this.

For the moment, remember that there is never a guarantee that a thread will execute a series of instructions in one go; it may be switched at any time and get its turn later. If there is more than one CPU available, threads may run truly in parallel.

As a thread executes instructions, any variables that it declares within the method (the so-called automatic variables) are stored in a private area of memory, which other threads cannot access. This allows any other thread to execute the same method on the same object at the same time without having its automatic variables unexpectedly modified.

Threads can access an object's variables and methods as long as they have a reference to them and the accessibility rules from the current class are followed. So, more than one thread can read and modify variables, or call methods, in the same object. This is the way in which threads share and transfer complex information between each other.

on the job

You can get a reference to the currently running thread by calling the static method Thread.currentThread(). While developing and testing, it is usually easier to skip a proper debugging tool and just include some instances of System.out.println in your code, including Thread.currentThread(). Even more useful is to dump the stack trace of the current thread by calling the static method Thread.dumpStack().

Sleeping Threads and Interruptions

Sometimes there is a need to delay any further execution of the current thread for a while. Let's discuss why this is needed and how to put threads to sleep.

Think of a thread that runs in a loop, downloading the latest stock prices and analyzing them. Downloading prices one after another would be a waste of time as most of them would be quite similar. More important, it would be incredibly wasteful because it would consume too much bandwidth.

The simplest way to solve this problem is to include a delay of five minutes after each download. You can do this in Java by calling the sleep(long n) method of Thread. This is a static method that will make the current thread go to sleep for the specified number of milliseconds, as follows:

```
- Thread.sleep(5*60*1000);
```

That will make the current thread sleep for five minutes, while other threads keep running.

While a thread is sleeping, a different thread may interrupt it by using the Thread instance method interrupt():

```
- sleepingThread.interrupt();
```

If a thread has been interrupted, an internal flag (in the interrupted Thread instance) is set to indicate this, and the sleeping thread wakes up prematurely. The sleep() method will throw an exception immediately when this happens. The thread will never go to sleep if the flag was already set when sleep was called, and will throw the exception instead.

Because of this exception, the sleep call is typically surrounded inside a try/catch block, as follows:

```
try{
   Thread.sleep(sleepingTime);
}catch(InterruptedException e){
   // do something about it
}
```

InterruptedException is a checked exception, so the compiler will complain if you don't catch it or specify that the current method throws it.

You should be aware of the context on which the thread will run, and be able to predict if it is going to be interrupted. If you are quite sure that no other thread is going to interrupt yours, or you don't care about exiting gracefully, it is common to not take any action on the catch section. In this example it is a good opportunity to break out of the loop. The run method for this thread would look like the following:

```
public void run(){
    while(true){
        //download stock prices
        // Analyze and report
    try{
        Thread.sleep(5*60*1000);
        } catch(InterruptedException e){
            break;
        }
    }
}
```

In this example, the thread would download, report, and then go to sleep for five minutes; afterwards (if not interrupted) it would do the loop again.

During the sleeping state, the thread doesn't get a turn at the CPU. It becomes a candidate for running only after the sleep period has elapsed or the thread is interrupted.

Note that there is no instance version of sleep; you cannot make other threads go to sleep.

At any moment a thread can check its own interrupted status by using the static method:

```
Thread.interrupted(); // Returns boolean
```

This method will automatically clear the flag.

Any thread can check another's interrupted status by using the instance method:

```
otherThread.isInterrupted(); // Returns boolean
```

This method, contrary to interrupted(), does not affect the flag in any way. The only way to change a thread's interrupted status from a different thread is to call interrupt() on the target thread.

Note that as soon as the InterruptedException is raised the flag is cleared, so you have to self-interrupt if you want to set the flag again, maybe for some other lines of code to take care of it.

CERTIFICATION OBJECTIVE 9.04

Concurrent Access Problems and Solutions

This section deals with the problems that can arise when different threads access the same information and explains how to use the *volatile* and *synchronized* keywords to avoid these problems.

It is when sharing resources that complexities arise when using threads, and usually we want threads to share information to some degree. One important point to keep in mind is that there is no guarantee that two lines of code will be executed by the CPU one after the other. A different thread may take its turn, even with the following instruction:

```
- i++;
```

Incrementing a member variable is executed by the CPU not in one step, but in three:

```
- bring i to register
- add 1 to register
- store register onto i
```

The CPU may swap over to a different thread at any time between these steps, especially with code like the following:

```
- r=query.getNext();
- name=r.getName();
- address=r.getAddress();
- etc..
```

Without proper protection, a supposedly co-operating thread may modify some variables at the wrong moment, therefore upsetting the results of the unsuspecting thread.

The following sections discuss the two ways of solving these problems. They apply to two different scenarios.

Using volatile to Transmit Single Variables Between Two Threads

Consider the situation in which one thread generates a value (it could be a reference to an object) to be processed by a second thread. The threads have to use a particular member variable to which they both have access. The first thread sets the value, and sometime later the second thread gets the value and does something with it.

Both threads could do this writing and reading from the same object, for example:

```
public class Transfer{
   private Object value; // does it need to be volatile?
   public set(value){
      this.value=value;
   }
   public Object get(){
      return value;
   }
}
```

Unfortunately this is not guaranteed to work. The reason is speed optimization. Threads are allowed to keep copies of member variables in their local memory without necessarily checking to find out if the local copy is current. Because of this, the first thread may not really write the value to the member variable, and the second thread may not re-read the member variable once it has a copy. If there is only one thread dealing with the affected member variables, then this works all right. The local copies are always current, so there is no rush to use the (slower to access) member variables.

In this kind of situation, to make threads aware that some variables may be used by other threads you have to use the *volatile* keyword as a modifier of the member variable definition. For these variables, the threads will never use local copies; they will always use shared memory for reading and writing.

Using volatile variables on their own is quite limited. If you think about it, when you want to transfer two or more variables there is a risk that the reading will be done while the writing (of all of the variables) hasn't finished.

Using synchronized to Transmit Groups of Variables Among Multiple Threads

When there is a group of variables that should be made "exclusive use" for a thread, there is a very flexible way of doing so. This involves using the *synchronized* keyword without a need for marking volatile variables.

Consider an application where a thread modifies a status object every few seconds, and another thread analyzes this information when needed, always expecting it to be the last status generated. The code could look like this:

```
public class StatusInfo{
    private float temperature, pressure, nitroConcentration;
    public void update(float temperature, float pressure, float
    nitroConcentration){
        this.temperature=temperature;
        this.pressure=pressure;
        this.nitroConcentration=nitroConcentration;
    }
    public void analyze(){
        if(isDangerousCombination(temperature,pressure,nitroConcentration))
            stopQuemicalManufacture();
    }
}
```

Without coordinating the access to the object, the analyzer thread might see the status object in mid-modification, when some of the variables are new and some old.

This is highly undesirable, even more so because there is no way to predict when these inconsistencies might happen. It depends on the odd chance that the CPU switches to the analyzer thread just at the wrong moment. If the chance is very low, the software might seem to work all right while testing, even make it through to a live product, only to fail later for no apparent reason.

The solution to guarantee a safe behavior is to "lock" the object while it is being modified, so that the analyzer thread cannot read the information until the current modifications are finished.

In Java this is achieved with synchronized blocks of code. A thread can only enter a synchronized block if it can lock on the object. Otherwise, the thread gets stuck at the entrance of the synchronized block, and it will only get in when the owner of the lock releases it. Many threads may be stuck in this way, but they will get the lock only one at a time, in an orderly fashion.

When many threads are trying to get a lock and it becomes available, only one of them will get it, but which one exactly varies between different systems. You should not make your code dependent on the particular order in which the threads will get the locks.

You could make the previous code safe by synchronizing the update and analyze methods. You add the synchronized keyword to the method declaration:

```
public class StatusInfo{
    private float temperature, pressure, nitroConcentration;
    // The synchronized makes it multithreaded safe
    public synchronized void update(float temperature, float pressure, float nitroConcentration) {
        this.temperature=temperature;
        this.pressure=pressure;
        this.nitroConcentration=nitroConcentration;
    }
    // The synchronized makes it multithreaded safe
    public synchronized void analyze() {
    if(isDangerousCombination(temperature,pressure,nitroConcentration);
        stopQuemicalManufacture();
    }
}
```

In this way, when the status thread enters the update method, it acquires the lock of the StatusInfo object, and it releases it when the method is finished. In the same way, the analyzer thread would acquire the lock upon entering the analyze() method, and it would release it upon finishing.

When either of the threads wants to get the lock but it is already taken, the thread goes from the running state to the *blocked* state. In this state the thread does nothing, it is simply stuck until the lock is released. Only after the lock is released does the thread go back to the running state, continuing in the normal way.

In Java, every object can be used to synchronize. Synchronized methods always try to get the lock of the current object. You can lock on any one by specifying that a block of code is synchronized on some particular object in the following way:

```
void notFullySynchronizedMethod(){
   // Unsynchronized instructions here
   synchronized(otherObject){
      //Safe instructions here
   }
   // More unsynchronized instructions here
}
```

Note that a synchronized method is just a shortcut for specifying the whole contents of the method as being synchronized on the *this* object, such as:

```
public void analyze() {
   synchronized(this) {
      if(isDangerousCombination(temperature, pressure,
      nitroConcentration) {
         stopQuemicalManufacture();
      }
   }
}
```

When accessing variables from synchronized blocks, there is no need to use the volatile keyword. The Java Virtual Machine (JVM) automatically does any refreshing that is needed when entering and exiting synchronized blocks.

CERTIFICATION OBJECTIVE 9.05

Signaling with wait, notify, and notifyAll

This section discusses the signaling system available to Java threads to ensure some order or execution between them.

As discussed previously, a different thread can interrupt a sleeping thread. This can be used to coordinate at what moment a thread executes some action. Unfortunately this is focused on the thread, and usually we want to make a signal according to the object that we are dealing with (that is, the object that is ready for further processing). Even more, the intended purpose of interrupting a thread is typically to suggest that it should stop executing as soon as possible, regardless of what it was doing at that moment, not to use it as a general purpose flag.

Using *wait*, *notify*, and *notifyAll* signaling is a more object-oriented approach than interrupting threads, because it is based on the objects that the threads are dealing with.

Using wait and notify by Two Interdependent Threads

Following is an example of two threads that depend on each other to proceed with their execution, and how to use *wait* and *notify* to make them interact safely and at the proper moments.

Think of a computer-controlled machine that cuts pieces of fabric into different shapes, and an application that allows users to specify a shape and have it cut. The current version of the application has only one thread, which first asks the user for instructions and then directs the hardware to cut that shape, repeating the cycle afterwards.

```
public void run(){
   while(true){
      // Get shape from user
      // Calculate machine steps from shape
      // Send steps to hardware
   }
}
```

This makes the user waste some time while the machine is working, and while there are other shapes to define. Some improvement is required.

A simple solution is to separate the process in two different threads, one of them interacting with the user and another managing the hardware. The user thread would send the instructions to the hardware thread and then go back to query the user immediately. The hardware thread would receive the instructions from the user thread and it would start directing the machine immediately.

Both threads would use a common object to communicate, which would hold the current design being processed.

An initial sketch of the methods used by the threads would look like the following:

```
public void userLoop(){
    while(true){
        // Get shape from user
        // Calculate machine steps from shape
        // Modify common object with new machine steps
    }
}
public void hardwareLoop(){
    while(true){
        // Get steps from common object
        // Send steps to hardware
    }
}
```

The problem now is to get the hardware thread to process the machine steps as soon as they are available. Also, the user thread should not overwrite them until they have all been sent to the hardware. The solution is to use wait and notify and to synchronize some of the code.

The methods wait() and notify() are instance methods of Object. In the same way that every object has a lock, every object has a list of threads that are waiting for a signal related to the object. A thread gets on this list by executing the wait() method of the object. From that moment, it doesn't execute any further instructions until some other thread calls the notify() method of the same object. If many threads are waiting on the same object, only one will be chosen to get out of the list and proceed with its execution. If there are no threads waiting then no particular action is taken.

A waiting thread can be interrupted in the same way as a sleeping thread, so you have to take care of the exception:

```
try{
    wait();
    } catch(InterruptedException e){
        // Do something about it
    }
}
```

For a thread to call wait() or notify(), the thread has to be the owner of the lock for that object. When the thread waits, it temporarily releases the lock for other threads to use, but it will need it again to continue execution. It is common to find code such as the following:

```
synchronized(this){ // At this point the thread has the lock
   try{
       wait(); // the thread releases the lock and waits
       // To continue the thread needs the lock,
       // so it may block until it gets it.
   } catch(InteruptedException e){}
}
```

This waits until other threads' calls notify on the *this* object, and:

```
synchronized(this){
   notify();
}
```

This notifies any thread currently waiting on the *this* object.

The lock can be acquired much earlier, maybe in the calling method. Note that if either wait or notify does not own the lock, they will throw an IllegalMonitorStateExeption. This exception is not a checked exception, so you don't have to catch it explicitly, but note that you should always be clear if a thread has the lock of an object or not, so this exception should never be thrown.

In the fabric example, the way to use these methods is to have the hardware thread wait on the shape to be available, and the user thread to notify after it has written the steps.

The machine steps may comprise global steps, such as moving the required fabric to the cutting area, and a number of substeps, such as the direction and length of a cut. As an example they could be:

```
int fabricRoll;
int cuttingSpeed;
Point startingPoint;
float[] directions;
float[] lengths;
..etc
```

It is important that the user thread does not modify the machine steps while the hardware thread is using them, so this reading and writing should be synchronized.

The resulting code would look like the following:

```
public void userLoop(){
    while(true){
        // Get shape from user
        synchronized(this){
            // Calculate new machine steps from shape
            notify();
        }
    }
}
public void hardwareLoop(){
    while(true){
        synchronized(this){
            wait();
            // Send machine steps to hardware
        }
    }
}
```

After wrapping up the methods userLoop and hardwareLoop on the same object, we still have to create threads to execute these methods. A quick way of doing this is to use inner classes, like the following:

```
public class FabricStation    {
    public static void main(String[] args){
        final FabricStation station = new FabricStation();
        (  new Thread(){    public void run(){
                                station.userLoop();    }
                             }    ).start();
        (  new Thread(){  public void run()  {
                                station.hardwareLoop();    }
                             }    ).start();
    }
    // Machine step variables as above
    // hardwareLoop method as above
    // userloop method as above
}
```

The hardware thread, once started, will immediately go into the waiting state, and will wait patiently until the user sends the first notification. At that point it is the user thread that owns the lock for the object, so the hardware thread gets stuck for a while. It is only after the user thread abandons the synchronized block that the hardware thread can really start processing the machine steps.

While one shape is being processed by the hardware, the user may interact with the system and specify another shape to be cut. When the user is finished with the shape and it is time to cut it, the user thread attempts to enter the synchronized block, maybe blocking until the hardware thread has finished with the previous machine steps. When the hardware thread has finished, it repeats the loop, going again to the waiting state (and therefore releasing the lock). Only then can the user thread enter the synchronized block and overwrite the machine steps with the new ones.

Having two threads is definitely an improvement over having one, although in this implementation there is still a possibility of making the user wait. A further improvement would be to have many shapes in a queue, therefore reducing the possibility of requiring the user to wait for the hardware.

There is a second form of wait that accepts a number of milliseconds as a maximum time to wait. If the thread is not interrupted, it will continue normally whenever it is notified or the specified timeout has elapsed. This normal continuation consists of getting out of the waiting state, but to continue execution it will have to get the lock for the object:

```
// the thread gets the lock
synchronized(this){
   // The thread releases the lock and
   // waits to be notified
   // But only for a maximum of two seconds
   // The thread reacquires the lock
   // More instructions here
   wait(2000);
}
```

Using notifyAll when Many Threads May Be Waiting

In some applications, you would want to notify all of the threads that are waiting on a particular object. If so, you just have to call the method notifyAll() on the object:

```
- targetObject.notifyAll(); // Will notify all waiting threads
```

All of the threads will be notified and start competing to get the lock. As the lock is used and released by each thread, all of them will get into action without a need for further notification.

An object can have many threads waiting on it, and using notify() will affect only one. Which one depends on the JVM implementation, so you should never rely on a particular thread being notified in preference.

When you want to notify one thread or several, and there might be a lot more waiting, the only way to do this is by using notifyAll. You should be careful in this case, and make sure that all the unwanted threads recognize that the notification was not for them and make them go back to the waiting state as soon as possible. Typically these threads would be waiting in a loop while the conditions are not appropriate for them to proceed.

In this example there is one writer and many readers. At any given moment many readers may be waiting.

```
public class MultipleWriters{
    private Object item;
    public synchronized void write(Object o) throws
    InterruptedException{
        while(item!=null) wait();
        item=o;
        notify(); // single writer, notifying one
                  // reader is sufficient
    }
    public synchronized Object read() throws
    InterruptedException {
        while(item==null)
            wait();

        Object myItem=item;
        item=null;
        notifyAll(); // multiple readers, notifyAll ensures
                     // writer notification
        return myItem;
    }
}
```

Note that if the read() method where to use notify instead of notifyAll() when the writer is waiting, a fellow reader may be notified, instead of the intended waiting writer. The fellow reader would see that the transfer item is null and would go back to wait, and the writer would never get notified.

The preceding example would be simple to adapt to multiple writers; change the *notify* in write to notifyAll to ensure that one of the readers is notified.

When Threads Freeze: Deadlock

Considering that threads sometimes get stuck for a while trying to get a lock, it is easy to get into the situation where one thread has a lock and wants another lock that is currently owned by another thread that wants the first lock.

This is called *deadlock*, or deadly embrace. In its simplest form there are only two threads participating, as in the following example:

```
public class DeadlockRisk{
    private static class Resource{
        public int value;
    }
    private resourceA=new Resource();
    private resourceB=new Resource();
    public int read(){
        synchronized(resourceA){ // May deadlock here
            synchronized(resourceB){
                return resourceB.value+resourceA.value;
            }
        }
    }

    public void write(int a, int b){
        synchronized(resourceB){ // May deadlock here
            synchronized(resourceA){
                resourceA.value=a;resourceB.value=b;
            }
        }
    }
}
```

If there are two different threads that may read and write independently, there is a risk of deadlock at the commented lines. The reader thread will have resourceA and the writer thread will have resourceB, and both will get stuck forever waiting for the other to back down.

Code like this almost never results in deadlock because the CPU has to switch from the reader thread to the writer thread in a very particular moment, and the chances of deadlock occurring are very small. The application may work fine 99.9 percent of the time.

The preceding simple example is easy to fix; just swap the order of locking for either the reader or the writer. More complex embraces can take a long time to figure out.

Deadlock is one of those problems that are difficult to cure, especially because things just stop happening and there are no friendly exception stack traces to study. They might be difficult, or even impossible to replicate, because they always depend on what many threads may be doing at a particular moment in time.

The best way to avoid deadlocked applications is to plan in advance. A well-designed application will never have the possibility of deadlock happening. You have to consider all the different paths that a thread will follow, and the different combinations of locks that it will acquire in each path. This tree of paths can be combined with the trees for other threads, making it easy to detect possible deadlocks, and if they appear, the design can be changed before it is too late.

For simple applications it is generally a good idea to use blocks that are mostly synchronized on the *this* object. This way all the synchronized code can be found on the same file. Try to keep locks on objects for the minimum amount of time possible. Also, it is generally a good idea to avoid circular *paths of execution* where threads may go from object to object only to call the same objects again.

In six words: To avoid deadlocks, keep it simple.

CERTIFICATION OBJECTIVE 9.07

Scheduling: Problems and Solutions

As noted earlier in the chapter, it is not possible to predict when the currently executing thread will be swapped for a different one, and which thread will be chosen next. It all depends on the JVM and the underlying operating system. Even so, there are some sure ways of getting your threaded application to perform reliably on any platform.

The first thing to consider is, "When does the current thread lose its turn at the CPU?" A thread will always lose its turn when calling the yield(), which is a static method of Thread:

```
Thread.yield(); // will give up the turn on the CPU
```

Using yield() is always a conscious decision by the programmer; it is used to give up the turn voluntarily.

Note that yield is a static method of Thread. If you have a reference to a thread (otherThread) and you call yield on it (otherThread.yield()), what actually happens is that the current thread will yield, not the other one. No thread can make another thread yield.

Besides yielding, the turn is always given up when the current thread sleeps, waits, or does a blocking input/output (I/O) operation. Blocking I/O operations are, for example, the ones that read information from a stream, and after some information arrives from the stream, the thread will attempt to get turns off the CPU again.

In most systems the turn is also lost when a higher priority thread becomes a candidate to run (either after starting, waking up, being notified, or returning from a blocking I/O), but this behavior is not guaranteed for all systems.

There are some systems that will also forcefully switch to another thread if the turn is not given up after some amount of time. This is the so-called "time-slicing." You should be careful about making any assumptions. Many programs work fine in one system because, by luck, they rely on time-slicing not occurring, or the opposite, they work fine by relying on time-slicing always occurring. It is only when these programs are tested on different systems that the problems arise.

The second thing to consider is which thread will be the next to execute. Java allows the programmer to specify the priorities of threads. The intention of the priorities is to suggest that no lower priority thread executes while a higher priority one needs executing, although this is not guaranteed either.

The method setPrority(int n) of thread instances accepts an integer between 1 and 10. For clarity, Thread has the static final ints MIN_ PRIORITY, NORM_PRIORITY, and MAX_PRIORITY, which are 1, 5, and 10 respectively. It is used as follows:

```
- realTimeThread.setPriority(Thread.MAX_PRIORITY); // For example to control hardware
```

You can change the priority of a thread while it is running; see the section on thread groups and security for more on this.

In practice, the least forgiving scheduling algorithm that you may find is the prioritized round-robin: switching is done on yielding, sleeping, waiting, and blocking I/O. The next thread is higher in priority or, if there is not a higher one, the next in a circular list of highest priority threads.

The most friendly is the pre-emptive prioritized time-slicing round-robin scheduling algorithm: switching is done on yielding, sleeping, waiting, and blocking I/O. When another thread becomes the highest priority thread or timeout is exceeded, the next thread is next in a circular list of highest priority threads.

Applications that rely on a system with time-slicing scheduling may have threads hogging the CPU when this is not available. Conversely, but even worse, applications that rely on a no-time-slicing system may produce corrupted data and deadlocks when moved on to a time-slicing system.

If there is a need for priorities, you should consider the whole picture, the purpose of each thread, how often will they be running, and the real time constraints they might have. You should also take into account the different threads that are already running on the JVM when your application is first called, because your threads may have to compete with them:

- **main**   calls your *public static void main(String[])* method, priority 5
- **Finalizer**   priority 8
- **Reference handler**   priority 10
- **Signal dispatcher**   priority 5
- **AWT-Windows**   priority 5
- **AWT-EventQueue-0**   calls processEvent(AWTEvent) methods, priority 6
- **SunToolkit.PostEventQueue-0**   priority 5
- **ScreenUpdater**   calls paint(Graphics) methods, priority 4

For most applications, there is no need to think about priorities because NORM_PRIORITY will be used for all your threads. In general, just by inserting yields in loops that are going to be running for seconds or more, your application will run fine across different platforms.

on the **Job**

When running functions triggered by the user it is easy to end up having the DispatchThread running for a few seconds. During this time, the graphical user interface (GUI) seems unstable (native components get refreshed, but paint() methods don't get called) and the GUI doesn't respond to any more actions. On these occasions, the users will get a better experience if the action is performed in a separate, lower priority thread, even if it only lasts for some seconds. This is at the cost of explicitly taking care of concurrent access problems.

CERTIFICATION OBJECTIVE 9.08

Thread Groups and Security

As the name indicates, a ThreadGroup provides a way of managing groups of threads.

A Thread always has a parent ThreadGroup. You can specify it when creating the thread, otherwise the one that the current thread belongs to will be used. Similarly, a ThreadGroup also belongs to another ThreadGroup, except for the root one, which is created by the JVM.

You can perform some operations on a ThreadGroup that will propagate to all its related Threads and ThreadGroups recursively, such as getting a list of active threads or mass interrupting. A ThreadGroup also has a priority, which none of its Threads can surpass.

When discussing the previous topics, the issue of security was ignored for simplicity's sake. When you are programming normal applications this is not a concern, but if they are servlets or applets then there might be a security manager to restrict some operations. This varies greatly from system to system and affects methods that are not used often, such as setPriority() or setDaemon().

The method setDaemon is an instance method of Thread and it is used as follows:

```
- backgroundHelpThread.setDaemon(true);
```

Its purpose is for telling the JVM that the thread is to be used for servicing other non-daemon threads. When the JVM detects that there are no more non-daemon threads running on the system, it discards the daemon threads and exits.

The End of the Thread

The job of a programmer is never finished. Even after you have all your threads working fine there is the detail of how to finish.

If it is fine to just pull the plug on the whole application, you can call System.exit(n), but usually you would want some clean up, saving and closing of files, or any other "end of the day" activity. Note that, depending on the system, servlets and applets can have threads started, and if not stopped correctly, they would always be consuming memory resources.

A well-behaved thread has a predictable exit point, either by returning normally from the run method or by throwing an unchecked exception. In either case, the thread is no longer running and no longer consuming resources. This can be ensured by detecting InterruptedExceptions or the interrupted() flag and exiting gracefully when either one is detected.

Unfortunately this is not always possible. Most blocking I/O operations don't respond to interrupt() signals, and neither do threads that are trying to acquire a lock. In the case of blocking I/O, a graceful exit can be ensured by closing the underlying stream from a different thread; the I/O method will raise an appropriate exception. Other cases may be difficult or impossible to cancel.

Also note that there is no need to stop threads that you have set as Daemon, because these will be discarded by the JVM without your help.

Now that you have a better understanding of Java Threads, here are some possible scenario questions and their answers.

QUESTIONS AND ANSWERS

I'm migrating a Java1.1 application to Java2.0. The method stop() is called on some threads. What is this all about?	stop(), suspend(), and resume() are deprecated in Java2.0 because they are deadlock prone. Use interrupt() and other case-specific alternatives to stop the threads safely.
I'm writing a complex web of waiters and notifiers. Why not always use notifyAll instead of notify? There would be one less method to remember.	It is a good idea to make software maintainable, and by using notifyAll when there will never be more than one thread waiting, you would have the maintainer of your code looking for ghosts.
I'm using a third party package that doesn't respond to interrupts, and there is nothing that I can "close." What can I do?	Not much. A way to minimize the waste of resources is to call the offending methods from a separate thread. This way you can lose the reference to it when you decide that it will not respond anymore.
I'm using plenty of yield()s and the whole application is crawling. What is going on?	Yielding has an overhead and you are using too many. Calling it more than a few times a second produces no benefit and it can make this overhead evident.

CERTIFICATION SUMMARY

This chapter contains all the required information regarding the use of threads that you will need to apply on the Certification Exam.

You were shown how to create threads both by extending Thread and by implementing Runnable, and how to start them. To share information effectively, threads use synchronized blocks of code. To coordinate activity through time, they use the wait/notify model.

You also learned how threads can go through different states between the new and dead states, and when threads go in and out of the sleeping, waiting, blocking on I/O, and acquiring a lock states.

TWO-MINUTE DRILL

- ❑ Your threads can be extensions of Thread by overriding its public void run() method.
- ❑ They can also be Threads with a Runnable target.
- ❑ You can start a Thread only once, but you can create many with the same Runnable target.
- ❑ Sleeping is used to delay execution for some amount of time, and no locks are released.
- ❑ The intended use of interrupt() is signaling to a thread that it should stop running as soon as possible.
- ❑ Threads on the wait and sleeping state can be interrupted, but not so the ones in blocking I/O and the ones getting a lock.
- ❑ Synchronized blocks of code get "exclusive use" of an object.
- ❑ The synchronized wait() method is used to wait for a signal related to a particular object.
- ❑ The synchronized notify() method is used to send such a signal to one and only one of the threads that are waiting for it.
- ❑ The synchronized method notifyAll() works in the same way as notify, only it sends the signal to all of the threads waiting on the object.
- ❑ The use of yield() is recommended to avoid hogging the CPU in non-time-slicing systems.
- ❑ To avoid deadlock, keep things simple.

SELF TEST

The following questions will help you measure your understanding of the material presented in this chapter. Read all of the choices carefully, as there may be more than one correct answer. Choose all correct answers for each question.

I. The following code tries to create a Thread by passing a Runnable target:

```
Runnable target=new XXXX();
Thread MyThread=new Thread(target);
```

Which of the following classes can be used to create the target, so that the preceding code compiles correctly?

A. public class MyRunnable extends Runnable{public void run(){}}

B. public class MyRunnable extends Object{public void run(){}}

C. public class MyRunnable implements Runnable{public void run(){}}

D. public class MyRunnable extends Runnable{void run(){}}

E. public class MyRunnable implements Runnable{void run(){}}

2. You have a class that looks like this:

```
public class MyRunnable implements Runnable{
    public void run(){
        // some code here
    }
}
```

What would be the proper way to create and start a new thread to run this code?

A. new Runnable(MyRunnable).start();

B. new Thread(MyRunnable).run();

C. new Thread(new MyRunnable()).start();

D. new MyRunnable().start();

3. In the following method:

```
public void printAll(String[] lines){
    for(int i=0;i<lines.length;i++){
        System.out.println(lines[i]);
        // add line here
    }
}
```

Assuming that the thread is not interrupted, which of the following lines would ensure that no more than one line is printed each second? (Choose all that apply.)

A. try{Tread.sleep(1100);}catch(InterruptedIOException e){}

B. Thread.sleep(1000);

C. try{Thread.sleep(1000);}catch(InterruptedException e){}

D. try{Thread.sleep(1100);}catch(IOException e){}

E. try{Thread.sleep(900);}catch(InterruptedException e){}

4. What would be the output of the following thread?

```
public class MyThread extends Thread{
    public void run(){
        try {
        for(int i=1;i<5;i++) {
            System.out.print(i+" ");
            if(i>2)
                interrupt();

            sleep(1000);
            if(interrupted())
                break;
        }
        }catch(InterruptedException e) {
            System.out.print("caught ");}
        }
    }
}
```

A. 1

B. 1 2

C. 1 2 3

D. 1 caught

E. 1 2 caught

F. 1 2 3 caught

G. None of the above.

5. What is the purpose of the volatile keyword?

A. To mark methods as being of exclusive use of a thread.

B. To mark variables that may change at any time.

C. To mark variables as being of exclusive use of a thread.

D. To mark variables that can be used to synchronize on.

E. To mark methods that may be called at any time.

6. You have an object that is used to contain two values. Which of the following methods in its class can prevent concurrent access problems? (Choose all that apply.)

   A. public int read(int a, int b){return a+b;}
      public void set(int a, int b){this.a=a;this.b=b;}

   B. public synchronized int read(int a, int b){return a+b;}
      public synchronized void set(int a, int b){this.a=a;this.b=b;}

   C. public int read(int a, int b){synchronized(a){return a+b;}}
      public void set(int a, int b){synchronized(a){this.a=a;this.b=b;}}

   D. public int read(int a, int b){synchronized(a){return a+b;}}
      public void set(int a, int b){synchronized(b){this.a=a;this.b=b;}}

   E. public synchronized(this) int read(int a, int b){return a+b;}
      public synchronized(this) void set(int a, int b){this.a=a;this.b=b;}

   F. public int read(int a, int b){synchronized(this){return a+b;}}
      public void set(int a, int b){synchronized(this){this.a=a;this.b=b;}}

7. What is the purpose of notifying a thread that is in the wait state?

   A. To prevent it getting turns at the CPU.
   B. To make it throw an InterruptedException.
   C. To set the notified flag.
   D. To signal that it should proceed in executing instructions.
   E. To signal that there are no more instructions to execute.

8. Which of the following are methods of the Object class? (Choose all that apply.)

   A. notify();
   B. notifyAll();
   C. isInterrupted();
   D. synchronized();
   E. interrupt();
   F. wait(long msecs);
   G. sleep(long msecs);
   H. yield();
   I. synchronized(Object lock);

9. What would be the result of trying to compile and run the following program?

```
public class WaitTest{
    public static void main(String[] args){
        System.out.print("1 ");
        synchronized(args){
            System.out.print("2 ");
            try{
                args.wait();
            }catch(InterruptedException e){
            }
        }
        System.out.print("3 ");
    }
}
```

   A. It will fail to compile because the IllegalMonitorStateException of wait is not dealt with.
   B. It will compile and the output would be: 1 2 3.
   C. It will compile and the output would be: 1 3.
   D. It will compile and the output would be: 1 2.
   E. It will compile and throw, and at run time it will throw an IllegalMonitorStateException when trying to wait.
   F. It will fail to compile because it has to be synchronized on the *this* object.

10. After calling the following method, when will the thread become a candidate to get another turn at the CPU? (Assume that it is properly synchronized and the exception is caught.)

```
wait(2000);
```

   A. After the thread is interrupted, the thread is notified, or two seconds have elapsed.
   B. After the thread is interrupted or two seconds after the thread is notified.
   C. Two seconds after the thread is notified or interrupted.
   D. After the thread is interrupted, or two seconds have elapsed.

11. When should notifyAll be used instead of notify?

   A. When there is one thread waiting for notification on the specific object.
   B. When all the objects that the thread has locked should be notified.
   C. When many threads are waiting on a waitAll method for the specified object.
   D. When there might be more than one thread waiting for notification on the specified object.
   E. When all waiting threads on the system should be notified.
   F. When there might be one thread waiting for notification on the specific object.

12. What will be the output of the following program?

    ```
    public class ThreadTest extends Thread {
        public static void main(String[] args){
            new ThreadTest(1);
            new ThreadTest(2);
            System.out.println("main ");
        }
        private int val;
        private ThreadTest(int val) {
            this.val = val;
            start();
        }
        public void run(){System.out.print(val+" ");}
    }
    ```

    A. 1 2 main
    B. 2 1 main
    C. main 1 2
    D. main 2 1
    E. 1 main 2
    F. 2 main 1
    G. Any of the above.
    H. None of the above.

13. One of your threads (called backgroundThread) does some lengthy numerical processing. What would be the proper way of setting its priority to ensure that the rest of the system is very responsive while the thread is running? (Choose all that apply.)
    A. backgroundThread.setPriority(Thread.LOW_PRIORITY);
    B. backgroundThread.setPriority(Thread.MAX_PRIORITY);
    C. backgroundThread.setPriority(1);
    D. backgroundThread.setPriority(Thread.NO_PRIORITY);
    E. backgroundThread.setPriority(Thread.MIN_PRIORITY);
    F. backgroundThread.setPriority(Thread.NORM_PRIORITY);
    G. backgroundThread.setPriority(10);
    H. backgroundThread.setPriority(0);

14. What factors affect the resulting priority of a thread after using setPriority(int n)? (Choose all that apply.)
    A. The priority of the thread that started it.
    B. The current maximum priority of the thread group to which it belongs.
    C. The current minimum priority of the thread group to which it belongs.
    D. The security manager installed.
    E. The current priority of the thread that calls setPriority.

15. Which method can be called on a Thread instance to make sure it never again receives a turn at the CPU?
    A. yield(0);
    B. exit(0);
    C. yield();
    D. setDaemon();
    E. setDaemon(0);
    F. interrupt();
    G. None of the above.

10

The java.lang.Math Class

T he Math class is part of the java.lang package and encapsulates basic mathematical operations such as absolute value, sine, cosine, tangent, and square root.

The Math class also defines two approximations of the mathematical constants *pi* and *e*. Math.PI is a double value that is close to the ratio of a circle's circumference to its diameter. Math.E is a double value that is close to the base of the natural logarithms. The signatures of them are as follows:

- public final static double Math.PI
- public final static double Math.E

Because all methods of the Math class are defined as static, it's unnecessary to create an instance to access the functionality. In fact it's not possible to extend or create an instance of the Math class.

The certification exam will not contain questions that require you to verify the result of calling methods such as Math.log(35.6). The exam may test your knowledge of the Math class method signatures. You may have to know, for instance, that Math.round() could take a float or a double as an input parameter and returns an int or a long.

The java.lang package defines classes used by all Java programs. The package defines class wrappers for all primitive types such as Boolean, Byte, Character, Double, Float, Integer, Long, Short, and Void as well as Object, the class from which all Java classes inherit.

The package also contains the Math class, which is used to perform basic mathematical operations.

CERTIFICATION OBJECTIVE 10.01

Methods of the java.lang.Math Class

The methods of the Math class are static and are accessed like any static method, through the class name.

The following sections describe the Math methods and include examples of how to use them.

abs

The abs method returns the absolute value of the argument. The method is overloaded to handle an int, a long, a float, or a double argument. In all but two cases, the returned value is non-negative. If the argument is equal to Integer.MIN_VALUE or Long.MIN_VALUE, then the returned result is the same as the argument, which is less than zero. Invoking Math.abs(99) returns 99, whereas invoking Math.abs(-99) returns 99. The signatures of the abs method are as follows:

- public static int abs(int a)
- public static long abs(long a)
- public static float abs(float a)
- public static double abs(double a)

ceil

The ceil method returns the smallest double that is greater than or equal to the argument and equal to the nearest Integer value. In other words, the argument is rounded up to the nearest Integer equivalent. The signature of the ceil method is as follows:

- public static double ceil(double a)

All the following calls to Math.ceil() return the double value 9.0: Math.ceil(9.0), Math.ceil(8.4), and Math.ceil(8.8).
All the following calls to Math.ceil() return the double value −9.0: Math.ceil(-9.0), Math.ceil(-9.4), and Math.ceil(-9.8).

floor

The floor method returns the largest double that is less than or equal to the argument and equal to the nearest Integer value. In other words, the argument is truncated to the nearest Integer equivalent. The signature of the floor method is as follows:

- public static double floor(double a)

All the following calls to Math.floor() return the double value 9.0: Math.floor(9.0), Math.floor(9.4), and Math.floor(9.8).

All the following calls to Math.floor() return the double value −9.0: Math.floor(-9.0), Math.floor(-8.4), and Math.floor(-8.8).

max

The max method compares the two arguments and returns the greater value. This method is overloaded to handle int, long, float, or double arguments. If the input parameters are the same, max returns a value equal to the two arguments. The signatures of the max method are as follows:

- public static int max(int a, int b)
- public static long max(long a, long b)
- public static float max(float a, float b)
- public static double max(double a, double b)

Invoking Math.max(1024, -5000) returns 1024.

min

The min method compares the two arguments and returns the lesser value. This method is overloaded to handle int, long, float, or double arguments. If the input parameters are the same, min returns a value equal to the two arguments. The signatures of the min methods are as follows:

- public static int min(int a, int b)
- public static long min(long a, long b)
- public static float min(float a, float b)
- public static double min(double a, double b)

Invoking Math.min(0.5, 0.0) returns 0.0.

random

The random method returns a random double that is greater than or equal to 0.0 and less than 1.0. The random method does not take any parameters. The signature of the random method is as follows:

- public static double random( )

round

The round method returns the closest Integer to the argument. The algorithm is to add 0.5 to the argument and truncate to the nearest Integer equivalent. This method is overloaded to handle a float or a double argument. The signatures of the round method are as follows:

- public static int round(float a)
- public static long round(double a)

Ceil, floor, and round all take floating-point arguments and return Integer equivalents. If the number after the decimal point is less than 0.5, Math.round(arg) is equal to Math.floor(arg). If the number after the decimal point is greater than or equal to 0.5, Math.round(arg) is equal to Math.ceil(arg).

sin

The sin method returns the sine of an angle. The argument is a double representing an angle in radians. Degrees can be converted to radians by using Math.toRadians(arg). The signature of the sin method is as follows:

- public static double sin(double a)

Invoking Math.sin(Math.toRadians(90.0)) returns 1.0.

cos

The cos method returns the cosine of an angle. The argument is a double representing an angle in radians. The signature of the cos method is as follows:

- public static double cos(double a)

Invoking Math.cos(Math.toRadians(0.0)) returns 1.0.

tan

The tan method returns the tangent of an angle. The argument is a double representing an angle in radians. The signature of the tan method is as follows:

- public static double tan(double a)

Invoking Math.tan(Math.toRadians(45.0)) returns 1.0.

sqrt

The sqrt method returns the square root of a double. NaN is returned if the argument is NaN or less than zero. NaN is a bit pattern that denotes "not a number." The mathematical square root function returns a complex number (comprised of real and imaginary parts) when the operand is negative. The java.lang.Math.sqrt() function returns NaN instead of an object representing a complex number. The signature of the sqrt method is as follows:

- public static double sqrt(double a)

Invoking Math.sqrt(9.0) returns 3.0.

acos

The acos method returns the arc cosine of the angle. The argument is a double representing an angle in radians. The method is defined only for an input angle in the range of 0.0 through PI. The signature of the acos method is as follows:

- public static double acos(double a)

asin

The asin method returns the arc sine of the angle. The argument is a double representing an angle in radians. The method is defined only for an input angle in the range of –PI/2 through PI/2. The signature of the asin method is as follows:

- public static double asin(double a)

atan

The atan method returns the arc tangent of the angle. The argument is a double representing an angle in radians. The method is defined only for an input angle in the range of –PI/2 through PI/2. The signature of the atan method is as follows:

- public static double atan(double a)

atan2

The atan2 method returns the Polar coordinate equivalent of the input Cartesian coordinate. The arguments represent a location in a rectangular plane. The signature of the atan2 method is as follows:

■ public static double atan2(double a, double b)

exp

The exp method returns the value of the constant *e* raised to the power of the input parameter. The mathematical constant *e* is represented by the constant approximation Math.E. The signature of the exp method is as follows:

■ public static double exp(double a)

log

The log method returns the logarithm of the input parameter. The calculated logarithm uses the constant *e* as the base. The method is defined for an argument greater than 0.0. The signature of the log method is as follows:

■ public static double log(double a)

pow

The pow method returns the first argument raised to the power of the second argument. This method will throw an ArithmeticException if the first argument is 0.0 and the second argument is not greater than 0.0, or if the first argument is less than 0.0 and the second argument is not equal to a whole number. The signature of the pow method is as follows:

■ public static double pow(double a, double b)

Invoking Math.pow(2, 3) returns 8. You can calculate the result by multiplying (2 * 2 * 2).

rint

The rint method returns the closest Integer equivalent to the argument. When there are two Integer equivalent values of equal distance from the argument, the even Integer equivalent is returned. The signature of the rint method is as follows:

- public static double rint(double a)

Invoking Math.rint(12.9) returns 13.0.

Both the following calls to Math.rint() return the double value 8.0: Math.rint(7.5) and Math.rint(8.5).

toDegrees

The toDegrees method takes an argument representing an angle in radians and returns the equivalent angle in degrees. The signature of the toDegrees method is as follows:

- public static double toDegrees(double a)

Invoking Math.toDegrees(Math.PI * 2.0) returns 360.0.

toRadians

The toRadians method takes an argument representing an angle in degrees and returns the equivalent angle in radians. This method is useful for converting an angle in degrees to an argument suitable for use with the trigonometric methods (cos, sin, tan, acos, asin, and atan). The signature of the toRadians method is as follows:

- public static double toRadians(double a)

Invoking Math.toRadians(360.0) returns 6.283185, which is 2 * PI.

Now that you have a better idea of the methods of the Math class, here are some possible scenario questions and their answers.

QUESTIONS AND ANSWERS

Calling Math.ceil(-16.3) results in what value?	-16.0
What is the correct signature for the random method?	static double random()
Calling Math.floor(10.125) results in what value?	10.0
The result obtained from calling Math.random() is never equal to 1.0?	True
Calling Math.max(-5, -10) results in what value?	-5
Math.min is overloaded only for float and double.	False
Calling Math.round(26.51) results in what value?	27

CERTIFICATION SUMMARY

The Math class is used to perform mathematical operations in a platform-independent way and has unlimited scientific and business applications.

As the Math class relates to the certification exam, you will not be expected to reproduce complicated mathematical algorithms in your head or know the cosine of an angle. You should, however, know all the method signatures shown in Table 10-1.

You should also know how to calculate the result of calling abs(), ceil(), floor(), max(), min(), and round() with any given values.

You should count on missing some questions on the exam. One key to passing is to not miss any questions testing your ability to remember method signatures or to follow simple algorithms. The questions on the Math class fall into the category of simple, as long as you've spent the time to commit to memory the Math class methods and their calling signatures.

There is ample time to take the test and you are allowed to use scratch paper to work out results. It is suggested that you use the scratch paper to draw a number line for all questions involving ceil, floor, max, min, round, or rint.

static int abs(int a)	static long abs(long a)
static float abs(float a)	static double abs(double a)
static double ceil(double a)	static double floor(double a)
static int max(int a, int b)	static long max(long a, long b)
static float max(float a, float b)	static double max(double a, double b)
static int min(int a, int b)	static long min(long a, long b)
static float min(float a, float b)	static double min(double a, double b)
static double random()	static int round(float a)
static long round(double a)	static double sin(double a)
static double cos(double a)	static double tan(double a)
static double sqrt(double a)	

Graph the number or numbers from the question.

```
| - - - - - - - - - | - - - - - - - - - | - - - | - - - - - | - - - - - - - - - |
-4.0              -3.0              -2.0  -1.7    -1.0                0.0
```

If the number from the question is −1.7, then the following answers should be automatic:

■ What is Math.ceil(-1.7)? The answer is found by moving to the right to the first Integer equivalent.

■ What is Math.floor(-1.7)? The answer is found by moving to the left to the first Integer equivalent.

■ What is Math.round(-1.7)? The answer is found by selecting the closest Integer equivalent.

■ What is Math.rint(-1.7)? The answer is found by selecting the closest Integer equivalent.

If the question involves two numbers and Math.min() or Math.max(), the number furthest to the left on the number line is the min and the number furthest to the right on the number line is the max.

This may appear like overkill, but the goal is to not miss any questions that should be givens.

TWO-MINUTE DRILL

- ❑ Abs is overloaded to take an int, long, float, or a double.
- ❑ Abs can return a negative if the argument is the minimum int or long.
- ❑ Max is overloaded to take int, long, float, or double arguments.
- ❑ Min is overloaded to take int, long, float, or double arguments.
- ❑ Random returns a value greater than or equal to 0.0 and less than 1.0.
- ❑ Random does not take any arguments.
- ❑ Ceil, floor, and round all return Integer equivalent doubles.
- ❑ Round is overloaded to take a float.
- ❑ Sin, cos, and tan take a double angle in radians.
- ❑ Sqrt can return NaN if the argument is NaN or less than zero.

SELF TEST

The following questions will help you measure your understanding of the material presented in this chapter. Read all of the choices carefully, as there may be more than one correct answer. Choose all correct answers for each question.

1. Calling Math.abs(10.4) returns which value?

   A. 10.0

   B. 10.4

   C. 11.0

   D. −10.4

2. Which answer best describes the result of running the following program?

```
public class AbsExample {
        public static void main(String args[]) {
        float x = -5.6f;
        float absX = Math.abs(x);
        System.out.println("The abs of " + x + " is " + absX);
    }
}
```

   A. A compiler error occurs at line four.

   B. The abs of −5.6 is 5.6.

   C. The abs of −5.6 is −5.6.

   D. The abs of −5.6 is −5.

3. Calling Math.ceil(-5.5) results in which value?

   A. −5.5

   B. −5.0

   C. −6.0

   D. −4.0

4. To better understand how the ceil method works, the following program is written to output the index of the values array when the ceil method return is the same as the input parameter. Which answer best describes the result of running the program?

```
public class CeilExample {
    public static void main(String args[]) {
        float values[] = {1.0f, 1.2f, 1.4f, 1.6f, 1.8f, 2.0f};
        float ceilValues[] = new double[values.length];
        for (int i = 0; i < values.length; i++) {
```

```
            ceilValues[i] = Math.ceil(values[i]);
        }
        for (int i = 0; i < values.length; i++) {
            if (values[i] == ceilValues[i]) {
                System.out.println(i);
            }
        }
    }
}
```

A. 0, 5

B. 0, 1, 2, 3, 4, 5

C. Runs, but no output is written

D. Compile error at line six

5. Calling Math.ceil(25.9) results in which value?

   A. 25.9

   B. 30.0

   C. 25.0

   D. 26.0

6. The result of calling Math.floor(-0.5) is what value?

   A. 0.0

   B. −1.0

   C. 1.0

   D. 0.5

7. Running this program yields which of the following?

```
public class FloorExample {
    public static void main(String args[]) {
        double values[] = {-2.3, -1.0, 0.25, 4};
        int cnt = 0;
        for (int i = 0; i < values.length; i++) {
            if (Math.floor(values[i]) == Math.ceil(values[i])) {
                ++cnt;
            }
        }
        System.out.println("The results are the same " + cnt + " time(s)");
    }
}
```

A. The results are the same 0 time(s).

B. The results are the same 2 time(s).

C. The results are the same 4 time(s).

D. A compiler error at line six.

8. Calling Math.floor(96.4) yields which result?

A. 96.4

B. 95.0

C. 96.0

D. 97.0

9. Which of the following are valid calls to Math.max? (Choose all that apply.)

A. Math.max(1, 4)

B. Math.max(2.3, 5)

C. Math.max(1, 3, 5, 7)

D. Math.max(-1.5, -2.8f)

10. Calling Math.max(8.2, 6.9) returns which value?

A. 8.2

B. 8.0

C. 6.9

D. 7.0

11. Calling Math.min(8.2, 6.9) returns which value?

A. 8.2

B. 8.0

C. 6.9

D. 7.0

12. What output is produced running the following program?

```
public class MinDouble1 {
    public static void main(String args[]) {
        double setA[] = {1.1, 1.5, -3.6};
        double setB[] = {1.1, 1.4, 3.6};
        for (int i = 0; i < setA.length; i++) {
            if (Math.min(setA[i], setB[i]) ==
```

```
            Math.max(setA[i], setB[i])) {
                System.out.println("Min and Max are the same at " + i);
            }
        }
    }
}
```

A. Min and Max are the same at 0.

B. Min and Max are the same at 1.

C. Min and Max are the same at 2.

D. A compiler error at line six.

13. Calling Math.min(1, 8.25) returns which type and value?

A. int 1

B. long 1L

C. float 1.0f

D. double 1.0

14. Running this program yields which of the following?

```
public class RandomExample {
    public static void main(String args[]) {
        if(Math.random() >= 5.0) {
            System.out.println(
            "The number is greater than or equal to 5.0");
        }
        else {
            System.out.println(
            "The number is less than 5.0");
        }
    }
}
```

A. The number is greater than or equal to 5.0.

B. The number is less than 5.0.

C. Either A or B.

D. A compiler error at line three.

15. The following program is run three times on the same platform. What statements are true?

```
public class RandomExample {
    public static void main(String args[]) {
        double seed = Math.PI;
        Math.random(seed);
```

```
for (int i = 0; i < 10; i++) {
    System.out.println(Math.random());
}
}
}
```

A. Each run produces the same 10 random numbers.

B. Each run produces a different set of 10 random numbers.

C. The seed value is added to each random number.

D. A compiler error occurs at line four.

16. What statements are true about the result obtained from calling Math.random()? (Choose all that apply.)

A. The result is less than 0.0.

B. The result is greater than or equal to 0.0.

C. The result is less than 10.0.

D. The result is greater than 1.0.

17. Calling Math.round(99.2) returns which result?

A. 99.0

B. 100.0

C. 99

D. 100

18. For which arguments are the results from round and floor the same? (Choose all that apply.)

A. −1.3

B. 0.4

C. 6.2

D. −2.7

E. 100

19. Calling Math.round(9.5) returns which result?

A. 9

B. 9.5

C. 10

20. If you wanted to plot the curve of the sine function from 0 to 360 degrees, using the sin method, what other Math methods would you likely use?

A. abs

B. min

C. toRadians

D. toDegrees

E. random

21. Choose all the valid sin method signatures.

    A. static double sin(double a)

    B. static float sin(float a)

    C. static double sin(double a, double b)

    D. static float sin(float a, float b)

22. For which ranges of values is the sin method defined? (Choose all that apply.)

    A. greater than or equal to 0.0

    B. –PI / 2 through PI / 2

    C. 0.0 through 360.0

23. What is the result of running the following program?

```
public class TanExample {
    public static void main(String args[]) {
        double angle = Math.PI / 4;
        if (Math.tan(angle) == (Math.sin(angle) / Math.cos(angle))) {
            System.out.println("tan(a) = sin(a) / cos(a)");
        }
        else {
            System.out.println(Math.tan(angle));
        }
    }
}
```

    A. tan(a) = sin(a) / cos(a)

    B. 1.0

    C. PI

    D. 360.0

24. What are the valid signatures for the sqrt method?

    A. static int sqrt(int a)

    B. static long sqrt(long a)

    C. static float sqrt(float a)

    D. static double sqrt(double a)

25. What value is returned from calling Math.sqrt(0.0)?

    A. 0.0

    B. NaN

    C. ArithmeticException is thrown

    D. A compiler error is generated by calling Math.sqrt(0.0)

26. What is the result of running the following program?

    ```
    public class SqrtExample {
        public static void main(String args[]) {
            double value = -9.0;
            System.out.println("The sqrt of "
                + value + " is "
                + Math.sqrt(value));
        }
    }
    ```

    A. The sqrt of −9.0 is 3.0

    B. The sqrt of −9.0 is −3.0

    C. The sqrt of −9.0 is NaN

    D. A compiler error at line seven

11

Strings

In the early days of computing, working with information systems could often mean confronting rows of toggle switches. Obviously, this wasn't exactly user-friendly. In response, the designers of today's systems try to create them so that they can interact with users in their native languages. This demands the ability to process strings of text characters, or *strings* as they are commonly known throughout the industry. Like many other computer languages, Java has facilities to create and modify strings, to display them on the screen, or to write them to files. Many of the commands are similar to other programming languages such as C++, Basic, or Pascal. For example, consider the following program:

```
public class Test
{
  public static void main(String args[])
  {
    String w = "Welcome to ";
    String j = "Java ";
    float v = 1.2f;      String txt;      txt = w + j + v + ".";
    System.out.println(txt);
  }
}
```

This program combines the strings *Welcome to* and *Java* with the text representation of the number 1.2 and a period, and then prints the entire line. A similar program could be written in many computer languages. However, there are many Java-specific operations occurring behind the scenes that should be understood to pass the certification exam. (For instance, in the preceding example, five blocks of character storage are allocated, even though only three string variables are referenced.)

CERTIFICATION OBJECTIVE 11.01

Creating and Working with Strings in Java

A string variable is used to store a string of text characters in Java. Strings can store uppercase and lowercase letters, numbers, punctuation, and white space. Because all characters are stored in Unicode, a two-byte character encoding system that includes thousands of international language symbols, a string can hold text from writing systems used all over the world. However, programmers who are used to C or C++ will find that strings are twice as long.

For example, the contents of the string "Hello, world." will be 26 bytes long, because it holds thirteen two-byte characters. There is no limitation in Java on the length of a string, however, the operating system may impose limitations.

Creating a string can be deceptively simple. For example:

```
String myname = "Joe";  // initialized to Joe
```

However, strings are not simple variables, such as integers or floats. They are Java classes, and part of the java.lang package library. They can be constructed like any other object. For example, the preceding code is simply shorthand for the following:

```
String myname = new String("Joe");  // also initialized to Joe
```

Java programmers use methods within the String class to work with string variables. For example, there is a method in the String class named concat(), which can be used to combine strings. The following code is an example of string concatenation.

```
String a = "hello ";
String b = "world";
String c;c = a.concat(b);
```

Java provides shortcuts to string concatenation by overloading the + (plus) operator. The following instructions have the same effect:

```
String a = "hello ";
String b = "world";
String c; c = a + b;
```

It is important to be aware, however, that the + operator is merely a shortcut to other method calls, just as the equal sign can be used as a shortcut to calling a string constructor directly.

exam
ⓦatch

If a string appears on either side of the + operator, the result is a String, and the non-String type operand is converted to a String at runtime. The certification test often has a code sample in which a number is concatenated to a String, so it is important for the examinee to understand that this is allowed.

Note that string concatenation is actually done using StringBuffer objects, not the concat() method of the String class.

Despite a few shortcuts provided by the Java language, strings are objects, and the String class is just another class. Strings can be the arguments of methods or they can be returned by methods. They can be used in arrays or in other classes.

As a footnote, realize that String conversion from other classes is done using the method toString(). This method is built into the Object class and, as such, is present in every object.

Storage for Strings and String Immutability

Many programmers with backgrounds in other languages but new to Java are confused when they look at the methods of the String class. None of the methods defined actually change the referenced string object, they just return another string object. For instance, in the string concatenation example earlier, the statement c = a.concat(b) doesn't change either of the string variables *a* or *b*. It creates a new string, and assigns that string to *c*.

It's important to understand that in the Java programming language, once a string is created, it is immutable. Its contents can never be changed. There is no method that changes the contents of a string; there are only methods that take the source string as input and return another string. Strings in Java are not data structures that can be operated on, they can only be referenced.

The reason for this is that a String object is not the string itself, it is just a reference to an in-memory location that contains a string of characters. The following source code provides an example of storage allocation for strings.

```
String a = "hello";
String b = "hello";
String c = "hello";
```

To save space and reduce complexity, even though three strings are initialized, the Java compiler creates only a single memory space for storing the text *hello*. As shown in Figure 11-1, that memory space is shared by all three strings, and the variables *a*, *b*, and *c* are simply pointers to that space.

FIGURE 11-1

Memory space is shared by
all three strings

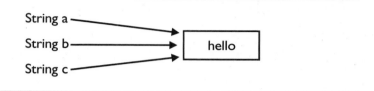

Any changes to a single string would clearly affect all three. Therefore, by disallowing the direct manipulation of strings, the Java environment prevents changes in one string from impacting others.

String references can, however, be reassigned. Consider the following example:

```
String a = "hello";
String b = "hi"; String c;c = a;c = b;
```

Two areas in memory are allocated for string storage. The first holds *hello* and the second holds *hi*, and the string variable *c* points to first one and then the other, as shown in Figure 11-2.

Understanding string storage also explains some idiosyncrasies in string comparison in Java. Consider the following:

```
public class Test {
   public static void main(String args[]) {
      String a = "java";
      String b = "java";
      String x = "ja";
      String y = "va";
      String c;
      c = x + y;
      if (a==b) {
         System.out.println("a and b are the same object");
      } else {
         System.out.println("a and b are not the same object");
      } if (b==c) {
         System.out.println("a and c are the same object");
      } else {
         System.out.println("a and c are not the same object");
      }
   }
}
```

When this Java source code is executed, the contents of the String variables a, b, and c will be the same: the string "java." However, they will

FIGURE 11-2

At first String c references the same space as String a; when String c is reassigned, it points to the same space as String b

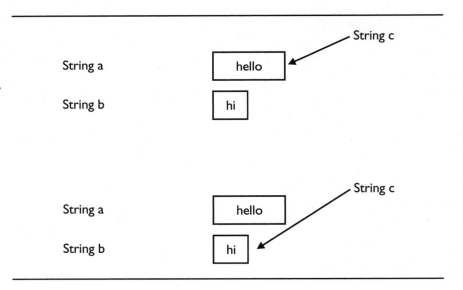

not all point to the same memory location, and thus the second comparison will fail, and the program will print out:

```
a and b are the samea and c are not the same.
```

Even though the contents of *a* and *c* are the same, the word *java*, the string objects *a* and *c* do not point to the same memory location, so the comparison will fail. When the if statements are reached, the internal memory structures associated with these variables will look like Figure 11-3.

The == operator is not the appropriate operator to use to determine the equality of string contents. Instead, the equals() method should be used. It is highly likely, however, that the certification exam will have questions on code samples similar to the preceding example to ensure that the examinee has an understanding of how strings are allocated.

Programmers with a background in C may be concerned about needlessly creating strings. In a case where a string variable is reused over and over, the contents in many of the steps along the way may be lost. For example:

```
String y = "yes";
String n = "no";
String m = "maybe";String s = "I vote " + y;
String s = "I vote " + n;
String s = "I vote " + m;
```

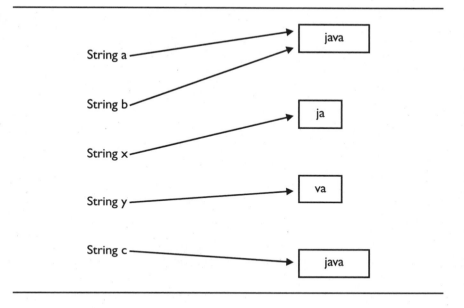

FIGURE 11-3

Strings a and b are allocated at compile time, have the same value, and reference the same memory space; String c is allocated at run time and is stored in a separate space

In the preceding example, the strings I vote yes, I vote no, and I vote maybe are created. The memory contents then look like Figure 11-4.

Is this a memory leak? In a language such as C, if the reference to a string is lost, it's then impossible to free its memory contents. This means that during the execution of the program, the first two strings, I vote yes, and I vote no, would continue to take up memory. Although a few short bytes

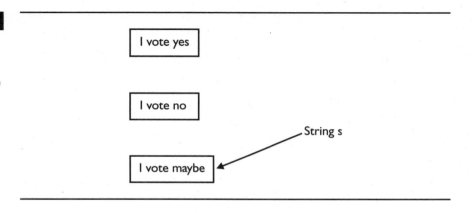

FIGURE 11-4

At the end of the code sample, there's no reference to either of the first two strings may not seem that important, if the routine was called over and over again in a multi-tasking operating system, it could eventually consume all of the available memory and bring the system down. C programmers are constantly on the lookout for this type of situation.

This isn't a problem in Java, however. Java has automatic garbage collection, which means that if memory is allocated but then later a reference to that memory is lost, the runtime environment will reclaim that memory and allow it to be reused by the operating system. Although deallocating and reallocating strings, as in the source code shown earlier, is not particularly efficient, reusing strings is not and can never be a source of memory leaks, thanks to Java's automatic garbage collection.

on the !job

The + operator in Java is "overloaded" to perform either addition or String concatenation. Some languages allow developers to overload operators, but Java does not. The + operator, however, is a special case. When two operands of the + operator are of a primitive numeric type, the + is taken to be a "Binary Plus Operator." If instead one or both of the operands is of type String, the + is taken to be a "String Concatenation Operator." Not only can we combine Strings with it, but also we can use it to combine Strings with other object types, primitive types, or even null. If only one operand is a String, the other is converted to a String at runtime, regardless of its type.

How does this happen? The concatenation is implemented using the StringBuffer class (discussed in the next section). When the String Concatenation Operator is encountered, a StringBuffer is instantiated and its append() method is called once for each operand, with the respective operand passed in as a parameter. Then, the StringBuffer's toString() method is called. So, this code:

```
str = "A" + 2 + "Z";
```

will be compiled as if it was:

```
str = new  StringBuffer().append("A").append(2)
   .append("Z").toString();
```

Using the StringBuffer Class

The main problem with a string class based upon immutable string contents is that certain types of problems can be solved much more easily and efficiently if a string can be directly modified. Java provides an alternate class, StringBuffer, for these types of situations. A StringBuffer is a string that can be modified. StringBuffers are used internally to implement many of the methods in the String class.

Every StringBuffer can hold only a certain amount of characters upon creation. This is known as its *capacity*. A StringBuffer has a default capacity of 16 characters, but the programmer typically defines the capacity upon creation. For example, the following line creates an empty StringBuffer with a capacity of 100 characters.

```
StringBuffer b = new StringBuffer(100);
```

A StringBuffer can also be created from an existing string.

```
StringBuffer b = new StringBuffer("hello");
```

This creates a StringBuffer with a capacity of five that contains the string *hello*. Unlike a string, however, the text *hello* can be changed.

StringBuffer capacity is not particularly important however, as StringBuffers grow when characters are added beyond their initial capacity. Setting sufficient capacity is simply a matter of efficiency; changing the capacity of a StringBuffer requires allocating and deallocating additional memory, which can be an expensive operation.

Here is a common example from Sun that highlights the differences between strings and StringBuffers:

```
public String reverseIt(String source) {
    int c, len = source.length();
    StringBuffer dest = new StringBuffer(len);
    for (c = (len - 1); c >= 0; c--) {
        dest.append(source.charAt(c));
    }
    return dest.toString();
}
```

The preceding method reverses the characters in a string. A StringBuffer, dest, is created to hold the intermediate results. The for loop takes characters from the end of the string to the beginning, using the charAt() method of the String class, and appends them to the end of the StringBuffer using the append() method of that class. The StringBuffer is then converted to a string using the toString method, and returned. Because StringBuffers can be modified, it's the best class to use to store intermediate string operations.

If the code had been written using the String object internally instead of StringBuffers, it would have required allocating a single character string for every character in the source string. This would have run much slower. StringBuffers make the code much more efficient.

It should be noted also that the StringBuffer class is thread-safe and its methods are synchronized. If methods are called on the same string by multiple threads, then one method call must finish before another is begun. This prevents the two threads from getting unexpected results.

exam
ⓦatch

String and StringBuffer are not the same class, and the exam will definitely ask questions that test that this is understood. Look out for code samples that try to use StringBuffer methods on String variables and vice versa. These code samples are invalid and will not even compile. The toString() method must be used to convert a StringBuffer to a String before string methods can be used on it.

CERTIFICATION OBJECTIVE 11.04

Constructors and Methods for the String Class

A string can be constructed and initialized using either a String value, a String variable, or a StringBuffer object. The following constructors are frequently used to create String objects.

Syntax	Description	Example
String()	Initializes and constructs a String object containing no characters. It is the same as String("");	String();
String(String value)	Initializes and constructs a String object. The contents are a copy of the passed String.	String("Hello world.");
String(StringBuffer buffer)	Initializes and constructs a String object. The contents are identical to the sequence of characters stored in the StringBuffer object.	String(new StringBuffer("Text"));

One could easily go through a large Java program and never find a formal String constructor. Professional Java programmers typically just create strings at compile time (using the = operator or by specifying a string literal) and pass the references back and forth between their objects.

Some of the methods that are typically used for working with strings are described in the following sections.

equals(string str)

The equals method of the String class is the preferred way to check for string equality. (The == operator will not accurately test the contents.) The method returns true if the contents of the target string are identical to the source string or false otherwise. The match is case sensitive, so differences in case will return false. A null argument will also return false.

```
String x = "hello";
String y = "HellO";
if ((x.equals(y) == false){
    System.out.println("the two strings are not equal");
    System.out.println("- equals() is case sensitive");
}
```

equalsIgnoreCase(string str)

The equalsIgnoreCase method allows programmers to determine the equality of strings without taking case into account. The method returns true if the two strings are identical, even if the case is different. Otherwise, the method returns false. A null argument will also return false.

```
String x = "hello";
String y = "HellO";
if (x.equalsIgnoreCase(y)) {
    System.out.println("the two strings are equal -
    equalsIgnoreCase() is case insensitive");
}
```

compareTo(string str)

If the target string is earlier in the alphabet than the referenced string, this method returns a negative number. If the string is later in the alphabet, it returns a positive number. If the string is identical, then a zero is returned. This method is commonly used in sorting operations. Comparisons are based upon Unicode representations of the characters.

```
String s1 = "one";
String s2 = "two";
String s3 = "three";
if (s1.compareTo(s2) < 0) {
    // returns true, because the string "one" appears
    // before "two" in the alphabet
    System.out.println("one appears before two");
}
if (s2.compareTo(s3) > 0) {
    // returns true, because the string "two"
    // appears after "three" in the alphabet
    System.out.println("three appears before two");
}
```

toUpperCase()

The toUpperCase method returns a string identical to the original string, except that any lowercase characters are changed to uppercase. The original string is unchanged, of course, only the string returned is different. (Note: If the string is already uppercase, a reference to the original string is returned.)

```
String s1 = "HELLO WORLD";
String s2 = "hello world";
if (s1.equals(s2.toUpperCase()) = true) {
   System.out.println("String s1 is equal to an
   uppercase version of string s2");
}
```

toLowerCase()

The toLowerCase method returns a string identical to the original string, except that any uppercase characters are changed to lowercase.

```
String s1 = "HELLO WORLD";
String s2 = "hello world";if (s2.equals(s1.toLowerCase())
= true) {
        System.out.println("A lowercase version of string
s1 is equal to string s2");
   }
```

charAt(int index)

The charAt method returns the character at the specified position in the string. The position is zero-based, so that s.charAt(0) returns the first character in the string, s.charAt(1) is the second character, and so on until s.charAt(s.length()-1), which returns the last character.

```
String s = "hello world";
char c1, c2, c3;c1 = s.charAt(0);  // returns "h"
c2 = s.charAt(3);  // returns "l"
c3 = s.charAt(10); // returns "d"
```

substring(int start, int end)

The substring method returns a portion of a string from within another string. The substring call has two forms. The first method call accepts one argument and returns the remainder of the string from the indicated character. The second method call requires two arguments and returns the portion of the string from the first indicated position to the character before the second indicated position.

The arguments are zero-based, so that the first character is referenced as position 0, and the last character is referenced as length()-1. Figure 11-5 is a graphical representation of this.

```
s1 = "wired".substring(2);    // s1 is set to "red"
s2 = "substring".substring(3,6);   // s2 is set to "str"
```

indexOf(char ch), indexOf(char ch, int index), indexOf(String s), indexOf(String s, int index)

The indexOf method searches a string for a character or string and, if found, returns the first position at which the target character (or characters) is found. Like other methods, the location is zero-based, so that a returned position of zero would indicate that the target was found at the beginning of the original string. If the target character or string is not found, the method returns a −1. The match is case sensitive.

```
String s = "Welcome to Java 1.2";
int x1, x2, x3, x4;
x1 = s.indexOf("W"); // returns 0, first position
x2 = s.indexOf("e"); // returns 1, second position
// (e appears twice in the string, but IndexOf
// only returns the first occurrence)

x3 = s.indexOf("J");    // returns 11
x4 = s.indexOf("1");    // returns 16
x5 = s.indexOf("java"); // returns -1 because the match
                        //fails (case insensitive)
```

The indexOf method can also accept a second parameter indicating the position with which to begin the search. This can be used to find all of the occurrences of a certain character or string.

FIGURE 11-5	
A graphical representation of the argument	wi[red] 01234 "wired" .substring(2,4) returns "red" "substring" .substring(3,5) returns "str" sub[str]ing 012345678

---

lastIndexOf(char ch)

The lastIndexOf method, like indexOf, searches a string for a character and, if found, returns the first position at which the target character is found. However, unlike indexOf, the search starts at the end of the string. As with indexOf, the method can also be called with a second parameter to begin the search at another location. (Although the search still continues from the end and goes to the beginning.)

```
String s = "hello world";
int x1, x2;
x1 = s.lastindexOf("l"); // Returns 9, the
    //position of last l, right before world

x2 = s.lastIndexOf("o",5) // Returns 4, because the
    // search starts at the 5th position
```

startsWith(string str)

The startsWith method of the String class tests whether the string begins with a specific sequence of characters. An alternate method call begins the test using a specific offset, and is similar to substring.

```
public class Test {
    public static void main(String args[]) {
        String s = "knowledge";
        if(s.startWith("know")==true) { // returns true
            System.out.println("knowledge begins with know");
        }
        if (s.startsWith("led",4)==true) { // returns true
            System.out.println("knowledge from the fourth
                character on includes led");
        }
    }
}
```

trim()

The trim method is used to remove white space from the beginning and ending of a string. White space includes not only spaces but any control characters as well (ASCII characters such as tabs or form feeds). The returned string will still contain white space within the string; only leading and trailing white space will be removed.

```
String s1 = " trim() method removes leading and
    trailing white space ";

String s2;
s2 = s1.trim();

// this line will print "trim() method removes
// leading and trailing white space";
System.out.println(s2);
```

exam
Watch

Passing the Java certification exam requires the ability to read short segments of Java code and to quickly identify what principles of the language are being tested in the question. This is much more important than knowing syntax. For example, there probably won't be a question that asks, "What is the syntax of the charAt() method?" But there may be a question that shows a code sample that uses both charAt() and indexOf() on a string variable and then asks what results are returned. Understanding syntax wouldn't be enough to answer the question.

CERTIFICATION OBJECTIVE 11.05

Constructors and Methods for the StringBuffer Class

StringBuffers, like strings, can hold a series of String characters. However, individual characters within the string can be changed. StringBuffers also have an attribute named *capacity*, which is the maximum number of characters that the StringBuffer can hold. This capacity will grow if characters are appended and the length of the string grows beyond the current capacity.

The following constructors are frequently used to create StringBuffer objects.

Syntax	Description	Example
StringBuffer()	Initializes and constructs an empty StringBuffer object with a default capacity of 16 characters. It is the same as StringBuffer(16);	StringBuffer();
StringBuffer(int capacity)	Initializes and constructs an empty StringBuffer object with the specified capacity.	StringBuffer(100);
StringBuffer(String value)	Initializes and constructs a StringBuffer object. The contents are identical to the passed string, and its capacity is equivalent to the length of the String argument.	StringBuffer("Hello world.");

Some of the methods that are typically used for working with StringBuffers are described in the following sections. Methods that act upon StringBuffers are often destructive (the contents may be changed).

capacity()

The capacity() method of the StringBuffer class returns the current capacity of the StringBuffer object.

```
String s = "hello world";
int c;
StringBuffer buf = new StringBuffer(s);
c = buf.capacity; // c will be set to 11
```

reverse()

The reverse() method reverses the contents of the referenced StringBuffer object.

```
StringBuffer buf = new StringBuffer("hello");
buf.reverse();
System.out.println(buf.toString()); // prints out the
                                    // text 'olleh'
```

Note that like most objects, the StringBuffer class has a toString() method that can be used to return a String value.

setCharAt(int index, char ch)

The setCharAt method of the StringBuffer class changes a character at a specific position to another character. The arguments are a position within the StringBuffer and a character. The positional argument, like most other String and StringBuffer positions, is zero-based, so that 0 is the first character of the StringBuffer.

```
StringBuffer buf = new StringBuffer("java");
buf.setCharAt(0,"J");
buf.setCharAt(2,"V");System.out.println(buf.toString());  //
prints "JaVa"
```

append(object obj)

The append method appends, in order, the character sequence from the target object to the end of the referenced StringBuffer. This method is usually called with a string as the argument, but the method is overloaded to support ints, floats, and character arrays. The capacity of the StringBuffer object will grow to accommodate the added characters.

```
StringBuffer buf = new StringBuffer("Test");
buf.append("ing");

// prints "Testing"
System.out.println(buf.toString());

buf.append(123);

// prints "Testing123"
System.out.println(buf.toString());
```

insert(int index, object obj)

The insert method of the StringBuffer class inserts characters into the object at a specific position. It takes two arguments, a position and an object— typically a string, though the method is overloaded to support many other arguments such as ints, floats, characters, and character arrays. The second object is converted to a sequence of characters, and those characters are inserted at the position specified by the first argument. Like all positional arguments, it is zero-based. See Figure 11-6 for an example.

```
StringBuffer buf = new StringBuffer("mod");
buf.insert(1,"eth");
System.out.println(buf.toString());  // prints method
```

FIGURE 11-6

An example of the
preceding argument

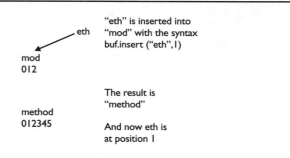

"eth" is inserted into
"mod" with the syntax
buf.insert ("eth",1)

mod
012

The result is
"method"

method
012345

And now eth is
at position 1

delete(int start, int end)

The delete method deletes characters from within a StringBuffer. It takes two
arguments, a starting position and an ending position. The ending position
is actually the character after the last character to be deleted. If the ending
position is beyond the end of the string, all characters after the starting
position are removed. If the starting and ending position are the same, no
characters are deleted. The positional arguments, like all others in the String
and StringBuffer objects, are zero-based. Thus, zero references the first character
in the String, and one less than the length of the StringBuffer represents the
last character in the string. Figure 11-7 is a picture of this example.

```
public class Test {
    public static void main(String args[]) {
        StringBuffer buf =
            new StringBuffer("We'll delete characters from this
                sentence");
        buf.delete(0,13);
        buf.delete(10,99);
        System.out.println(buf.toString()); // displays
"characters"
    }
}
```

length()

The length method returns the length of the StringBuffer's character
content. If the StringBuffer is empty, the method will return a zero.

```
StringBuffer buf = new StringBuffer("");
// prints "The length is 0"
System.out.println("The length is " + buf.length());
```

FIGURE 11-7

A representation of the argument

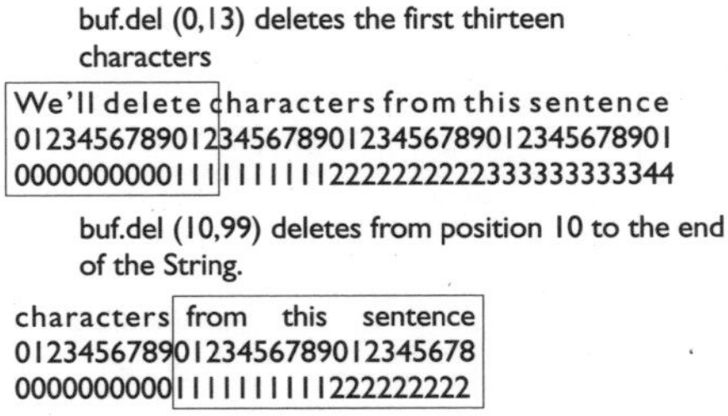

buf.del (0,13) deletes the first thirteen characters

```
We'll delete characters from this sentence
012345678901234567890123456789012345678901
000000000011111111112222222222333333333344
```

buf.del (10,99) deletes from position 10 to the end of the String.

```
characters from   this   sentence
01234567890123456789012345678
0000000000111111111122222222
```

QUESTIONS AND ANSWERS

How do I convert numeric or date variables to Strings? Does Java have a function that you have to call to perform the conversion?	The Object class has a method named toString(), which generates a string value from the object. Every class in Java inherits from this class, and most classes override this method to provide some type of meaningful value. But for any complex formatting, you'll probably want to use the Format classes of the java.text package.
What's the easiest way to place debugging statements within a program?	Use a statement such as: System.out.println("Your name is "+name+" and your age is "+age+".");. In Java, if a string appears on either side of a + operator, the result is a string. Java calls the toString() method (see the above question) on any other non-string objects to get a String result.
Why do positions for the substring(), charAt(), and other String and StringBuffer methods start at zero, rather then one?	The Java programming language has its roots in C. In C, Strings are arrays of characters, and the first element of all arrays is zero. Java adopted the same convention to make transitioning easier for C programmers. (Often, it makes learning to use these methods more difficult for the rest of us! After all, we'd expect substring(1,3) to refer to the first three characters, not just the second and third.)
If Strings are immutable (i.e. can't be changed), how can they be concatenated together using the '+' operator?	True, String variables are not actually combined. The Java compiler uses StringBuffers to implement the concatenation. A new String object is created that holds the results of the operation.
Given that toString() can be used to convert a number to a string, what's the easiest way to convert a string back to a number?	Four of the "type wrapper" classes, Integer, Double, Float, and Long, have static methods for converting strings to numbers. For example, to return a floating point value from a string, use the expression "Float.valueOf(s)."

CERTIFICATION SUMMARY

Almost all programming languages have facilities for working with strings of characters. However, strings in Java have some special properties that should be understood before taking the Java certification test. Strings in Java are implemented using the String class of the java.lang package.

After a string is constructed, its contents can never be changed. The String object itself may be reassigned to another set of contents, but its individual contents may not be changed. This is known as string immutability. String contents are also shared at compile time; String objects that are defined with the same contents will reference the same location. This is another reason that strings are immutable. Strings have a few simple constructors, and several methods that can be used to return uppercase or lowercase strings, trimmed strings, lengths, the positions of found characters, or other information. There is also an equals method that must be used to determine whether strings are equal.

A second class, the StringBuffer class, provides the ability to work with text on a character-by-character basis. In this class, the text is not immutable and can be changed. StringBuffers have a specific capacity that is defined at creation time, but this can be extended automatically. StringBuffers are typically constructed from Strings, and are converted back to Strings using the toString() method. The class has methods for appending, inserting, and deleting characters.

 # TWO-MINUTE DRILL

- ❑ String operations are carried out by the String class, which can be found in the java.lang package.
- ❑ In Java, strings are immutable. Their contents can never be changed. None of the methods for the String class change the actual contents of the string, they only return new values.
- ❑ Text for strings defined at compile time with identical contents may share the same memory space.
- ❑ Strings can be constructed by the syntax String s = new String(<"text">), but are typically initialized at compile time using the syntax "String s = <text>".

❑   Strings can be concatenated with the overloaded + operator; the result is a string. Operands are converted to String type at runtime.

❑   The equals() method is used to compare two strings and determine if they are identical. The == operator should not be used, as it will determine only if the two string variables reference the same object.

❑   The indexOf() and lastIndexOf() methods of the String class can be used to search a string's contents for a specific character or sequence of characters.

❑   A second class, StringBuffer, is used for operations that require working with strings on a character-by-character basis. StringBuffers are not immutable; their contents can be changed.

❑   StringBuffers are initialized with a certain character capacity. If this capacity is exceeded, the StringBuffer object automatically grows.

❑   The setCharAt(), insert(), delete(), and append() methods are used to work with individual characters and strings of characters in StringBuffers.

❑   All positional arguments for methods in the String or StringBuffer classes are zero-based. The first character is referenced as zero.

SELF TEST

The following questions will help you measure your understanding of the material presented in this chapter. Read all of the choices carefully, as there may be more than one correct answer. Choose all correct answers for each question.

1. Which of the following methods would be used to concatenate the text string *World* to an existing String variable that contains the characters *Hello*?

   A. trim

   B. insert

   C. append

   D. None of these

2. Will the following code compile?

   ```
   public class Test
   {
     public static void main(String args[])
     {
         String a  = "foo";
         String b = "bar";
         a = a + b;
     }
   }
   ```

   A. Yes

   B. No

3. When the following fragment of code is executed, what will the output be?

   ```
   public class Test {
      public static void main(String args[]) {
          String a = "Java is ";
          String b = a;a += "Great.";
          if (a == b) {
              System.out.println("a and b are the same");
          }
          else {
              System.out.println("a and b are not the same");
          }
      }
   }
   ```

A. a and b are the same

B. a and b are not the same

4. When the following fragment of code is executed, what will the output be?

```
public class Test {
    public static void main(String args[]) {
        String a = "JAVA IS GREAT";
        String b = a.toUpperCase();
        if (a == b) {
            System.out.println("a and b are the same");
        }
        else {
            System.out.println("a and b are not the same");
        }
    }
}
```

A. a and b are the same

B. a and b are not the same

5. Which of the following is true about the StringBuffer class in Java?

A. StringBuffer objects have a specific character capacity.

B. StringBuffer objects inherit all of the methods of the String class.

C. The contents of StringBuffer variables can be initialized using the = operator.

D. The contents of StringBuffer objects can be compared using the == operator.

6. When the following fragment of code is executed, what will the output be?

```
public class Test
{
    public static void main(String args[])
    {
        String a = "Java";
        System.out.println(a.length);
    }
}
```

A. 3

B. 4

C. 5

D. This code will not compile.

7. When the following fragment of code is executed, what will the output be?

```
String a = "Java";
    System.out.println(a.length());
```

   A. 3

   B. 4

   C. 5

   D. This code will not compile.

8. When the following fragment of code is executed, what will the output be?

```
String a = "Java is great.";
    System.out.println(a.charAt(a.length()));
```

   A. "."

   B. "t"

   C. "J"

   D. The code will generate an exception.

9. When the following fragment of code is executed, what will the output be?

```
String a = "Java is great.";
    System.out.println(a.indexof("i"));
```

   A. 5

   B. 6

   C. 7

   D. The code will generate an exception.

10. When the following fragment of code is executed, what will the output be?

```
public class Test {
   public static void main(String args[]) {
       String a = "Java is great.";
       String b = a.toString();
       if (a==b) {
          System.out.println("A is the same as B");
       }
       else {
          System.out.println("A is not the same as B");
       }
       if (a.equals(b)) {
          System.out.println("A equals B");
       }
       else {
```

```
                    System.out.println("A does not equal B");
            }
        }
    }
```

A. A is the same as B
   A equals B

B. A is not the same as B
   A equals B

C. A is the same as B
   A does not equal B

D. A is not the same as B
   A does not equal B

11. Will the following line of code compile?

```
    String a = "There are " + 99 + " bottles of beer on the wall." ;
```

A. Yes

B. No

12. Will the following code fragment compile?

```
    class MyObject
        {
            public static void main(String[] arg)
            {
                MyObject mo = new MyObject();
                String a = "My object is " +  mo;
            }
        }
```

A. Yes

B. No

13. Which of the following statements is *not* true?

A. Strings can be initialized using the = operator.

B. The toString() method can be used to return a String value from a StringBuffer object.

C. All strings are terminated with a null (ASCII 0) character.

D. It is impossible to change the contents of a String object.

14. What is the output of the following Java program?

```
public class foo {
   public static void main(String[] args) {
      String a = " java ";
      String b = " java";
      if (a.trim() == b.trim()) {
         System.out.println("a == b");
      }
      if (a.trim().equals(b.trim())) {
         System.out.println("a equals b");
      }
   }
}
```

   A. The program will not compile.
   B. a == b
   C. a equals b
   D. Both B and C.

15. What is the output of the following code fragment?

```
String a = "xxxJava is great.xxx";

      System.out.println(a.substring(0, a.lastIndexOf('x') - 2));
```

   A. "xxxJava is great."
   B. "xxxJava is great.xx"
   C. "xxxJava is grea"
   D. "x"

16. Which of the following is not the appropriate way to construct and initialize a string?

   A. String s = "test";
   B. String s = new String "test";
   C. String s = new String();
   D. String s = new String("test");

17. When the following code fragment is executed, what will be the result?

```
public class Test
{
   public static void main(String args[])
   {
```

```
        String s1 = new String ("one");
        StringBuffer s2 = new StringBuffer("three");s1.append("1");
        s2.append("2");if (s1.equals(s2))
            System.out.println("The two strings are equal");
    }
  }
```

A. It will print "The two strings are equal."

B. There will not be any output.

C. An exception will be thrown at line five.

D. The code will not compile.

18. How many bytes of storage are required to store each character in a string?

    A. 1

    B. 2

    C. 3

    D. 4

    E. The number of bytes depends upon the character.

19. What will the output of this code fragment be?

    ```
    StringBuffer b = new StringBuffer("abcdefg");
    b.delete(3,6);
    b.append("hij");
    System.out.println(b.toString());
    ```

    A. abcghij

    B. abcdefghij

    C. abfghij

    D. abchij

    E. The code will not compile.

20. If a StringBuffer is constructed with the following syntax, what will the original capacity be?

    ```
    StringBuffer buf = new StringBuffer("Test");
    ```

    A. 4

    B. 16

    C. 32

    D. Unlimited

12

The java.util Package

T here are many useful classes in the java.util package, but for the exam you will need to know only about collections. Collections are new for Java 2.0, and they are extremely useful when dealing with sets of data. There are several different types of collections, each slightly different in behavior. For the exam, you will need to know the interfaces and classes and the behavior they deliver.

Collections Overview

In a general sense, a collection is an element used to store data. For Java, a *collection* is an object used to store other objects, similar to an array. Two common examples of collections are Hashtables and Vectors. Don't worry if you haven't heard of these or used them before; they will be covered later in the chapter.

An array can store primitives or objects, but collections can store only objects in Java. Primitive types cannot be added to a collection, so it is necessary to use the wrapper classes such as Integer and Double in lieu of primitives. The following is a simple example of a Hashtable using a wrapper class:

```
import java.util.*;
class CollectionTest {
    public static void main (String [] args) {
        Hashtable ht = new Hashtable();
        ht.put("Key1",new Integer(12));
    }
}
```

The preceding code is easy to analyze. It first creates a Hashtable object, then adds an Integer object with the key Key1.

Three elements make up collections.

■ **Interfaces**   Define the methods that each type of collection must implement

- **Implementations**   Actual classes such as Hashtable and Vector
- **Algorithms**   Methods that store, retrieve, and manipulate elements in a collection

Collectively, these elements create what is known as the *collections framework*. The collections framework did not exist in the Java Development Kit 1.1 (JDK 1.1), though it did have some of the same classes such as Vector and Hashtable. The new collections framework is very powerful, and gives the following benefits as outlined by Sun Microsystems:

- *Reduces programming effort*   Methods such as sorting algorithms are already written.
- *Increases program speed and quality*   Let's face it, unless you are some kind of super-programmer you will not be able to make a faster sorting routine than what you find in the Java Collections application programming interface (API).
- *Allows interoperability among unrelated APIs*   Programmers can use their classes with other classes that use the collections framework.
- *Reduces the effort to learn and use new APIs*
- *Reduces the effort to design new APIs*   The architecture is already designed and method names are already chosen for you.
- *Fosters software reuse*   Classes that use the collections framework can be used in any class that uses collections in its methods.

Collections may possess the four properties shown in Table 12-1. These are the properties you must know to differentiate collection types.

	Property	Description
TABLE 12-1 The Four Properties of Collections	Sorted	Ascending order, sorted naturally using the equals() object method. An example is a Membership list.
	Ordered/Unordered	Collection keeps an order determined by where the object is placed in the collection. For example, a deck of cards is ordered.

	Property	Description
TABLE 12-1 The Four Properties of Collections *(continued)*	Allows duplicates	Duplicate objects can be added to the collection. An example is a collection of hockey cards.
	Uses keys	A key object is used to reference the stored object. For example, names of people are stored by social insurance number.

CERTIFICATION OBJECTIVE 12.02

Collection Interfaces and Classes

The interfaces in the collections framework are the foundation of collections. By using these interfaces, collections can be passed into other methods regardless of the details of a particular collection.

Six interfaces make up the core collections framework. Some of these interfaces extend other interfaces to form a hierarchy, as shown in the following illustration:

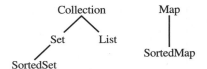

Notice Map and SortedMap do not extend the Collection interface. Map and SortedMap are still known as collections, even though in strict Java terms they are not Collection types.

Each of the interfaces also has an abstract class that has some of the methods already programmed. For example, the Collection interface has a class called AbstractCollection, and the Set interface has a class called AbstractSet. We will now examine the interfaces individually.

Collection Interface

The Collection interface is general in its handling of groups of objects. In theory it accepts any group of objects, regardless of whether duplicates are present, and stores them as unordered. This is "in theory" because the Collection interface is not implemented by any functional class.

exam
ⓦatch

The exam will not question you on methods within each type of collection, or on how to implement the collections framework. However, it is a good idea to at least be familiar with the methods to gain a better understanding of what collections are all about. It is recommended that you run through the method descriptions to get an idea of how the collection classes work. There is nothing worse than taking an exam on a topic you partially comprehend. On the other hand, do not try to memorize these methods. Instead, learn the types of collections and their behavior. You will need to know which classes and interfaces are sorted, which are ordered, which allow duplicates, and which use keys.

Add and Remove Methods

The add and remove methods are used to add and remove individual elements to and from the collection. If the set has successfully changed, the method will return true.

This adds the specified element to the collection:

```
boolean add(Object element)
```

This removes the specified element from the collection:

```
boolean remove(Object element)
```

Query Methods

The query methods are used to find out information about a collection.

This returns the number of elements in this set (its cardinality):

```
int size()
```

This returns true if this set contains no elements:

```
boolean isEmpty()
```

This returns true if this set contains the specified element:

```
boolean contains(Object element)
```

Iterator Methods

A simple explanation of an iterator is an object that contains methods that allow a programmer to iterate through the data one element at a time.

The iterator() method returns an Iterator object from the collection. The methods in the Iterator interface follow.

```
Iterator iterator()
```

This returns true if the iteration has more elements:

```
boolean hasNext()
```

This returns the next element in the iteration:

```
Object next()
```

This removes from the underlying collection the last element returned by the iterator:

```
void remove()
```

Group Methods

Group methods deal with entire collections. With these, it is possible to perform queries or add or remove one or more elements with one method call.

This returns true if the collection contains all of the elements in the specified collection:

```
boolean containsAll(Collection collection)
```

This appends all of the elements in the specified collection to the specified collection:

```
boolean addAll(Collection collection)
```

This removes all of the elements from this collection:

```
void clear()
```

This removes from this collection all of its elements that are contained in the specified collection:

```
void removeAll(Collection collection)
```

This retains only the elements in this collection that are contained in the specified collection:

```
void retainAll(Collection collection)
```

There are no functional classes that implement the Collection interface directly. AbstractCollection implements the interface, but it is abstract and therefore not functional.

on the job *Some programmers have wondered why the methods do not follow standard JavaBean methodology of using the is, has, set, and get prefixes. The reason this was not followed is because a collection is not a bean and therefore does not need to stick to this methodology. Instead, it follows the common naming convention of earlier collections, such as Hashtable.*

Set

A Set does not allow duplicate objects to enter the collection of elements. The Set interface contains all the methods of the Collection interface (see the following illustration) and does not add any new methods. The difference is the add() and addAll() methods check for duplication of objects using the equals() method on each object.

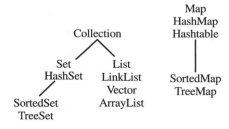

The only functional class in the Java API that directly implements the Set interface is HashSet. Let's look at the HashSet class in use.

```
import java.util.*;
class SetTest {
    public static void main (String [] args) {
        HashSet hs = new HashSet();
        hs.add("Hockey Game");
        hs.add("Poker");
        hs.add("Solitaire");
        hs.add("Hockey Game");
        System.out.println(hs);
    }
}
```

The preceding code attempts to add the string *Hockey Game* twice to the Set. The code compiles fine, but let's take a look at the output.

```
C:\Java projects\SetTest>java SetTest
[Hockey Game, Poker, Solitaire]
```

As you can see, the program runs fine but it does not add the String object Hockey Game more than once, because sets may not contain duplicates. The add() method actually returns a boolean value of *false* if the object already exists in the set, so it is possible to see if an object failed to be added. And, as is characteristic of Sets, the collection is unsorted and unordered.

on the
Üob

You may want to make your own type of collection using the collections framework. To do this, you will need to implement the collections interfaces. If your new class will not use one of the predefined operations in the interface, you have the option of throwing an UnsupportedOperationException. For example, if your collection is read-only, you could throw this exception if the method add() is used. This will signal to any methods using your collection class that this operation is not available.

Sorted Set

The SortedSet interface is similar to the Set interface, except that the elements in the set are stored in ascending order. Once again, the elements are nonduplicating. The SortedSet interface includes all of the methods of Set because it extends Set, but also adds a few more to take advantage of the fact that it is sorted.

This returns the first (lowest) element currently in this sorted set:

```
Object first()
```

This returns the last (highest) element currently in this sorted set:

```
Object last()
```

This returns a view of the portion of this sorted set whose elements range from fromElement, inclusive, to toElement, exclusive:

```
SortedSet subSet(Object fromElement, Object toElement)
```

This returns a view of the portion of this sorted set whose elements are strictly less than toElement:

```
SortedSet headSet(Object toElement)
```

This returns a view of the portion of this sorted set whose elements are greater than or equal to fromElement:

```
SortedSet tailSet(Object fromElement)
```

The TreeSet class is the only class to implement this interface directly. Let's examine the TreeSet class in some code.

```
import java.util.*;
class SortedSetTest {
    public static void main (String [] args) {
        SortedSet set = new TreeSet();
        set.add("Hockey Game");
        set.add("Chess");
        set.add("Checkers");
        set.add("Blackjack");
```

```
                          System.out.println(set);
                          SortedSet end = set.tailSet("Checkers");
                          System.out.println(end);
             }
      }
```

This code adds several String objects to TreeSet and outputs it to the screen. It then uses the tailSet() method and prints the result to the screen.

```
C:\Java projects\SetTest>java SortedSetTest
[Blackjack, Hockey Game, Checkers, Chess]
[Checkers, Chess]
```

The tailSet() method pulled out the elements that were equal to or less than the element specified as an argument in the method. Notice that the set is in ascending order even though the elements were added randomly.

List

A List is ordered. This allows a List to maintain an order as objects are added and removed from the collection. This is not the same as sorted! Sorted objects form a hierarchy based on how the objects compare to each other, such as alphabetical sorting.

A List can also contain duplicate entries of objects. The List interface adds several methods, all of which deal with the List collection being ordered. The added methods contain an index or index numbers that are used to specify a certain ordered object in the List.

This inserts the specified element at the specified position in the List:

```
void add(int index, Object element)
```

This appends all of the elements in the specified collection to the end of the List in the order that they are returned by the specified collection's iterator:

```
boolean addAll(int index, Collection collection)
```

This returns the element at the specified position in the List:

```
Object get(int index)
```

This searches for the first occurrence of the given argument, testing for equality using the equals method:

```
int indexOf(Object element)
```

The following returns the index of the last occurrence of the specified object in the List:

```
int lastIndexOf(Object element)
```

This removes the element at the specified position in the List:

```
Object remove(int index)
```

This replaces the element at the specified position in the List with the specified element:

```
Object set(int index, Object element)
```

There are also methods for working with an iterator subset of the collection, as we saw previously with Sets. In this case, it is called a ListIterator. The following returns a ListIterator object of the elements in this list (in the proper sequence):

```
ListIterator listIterator()
```

This returns a ListIterator object of the elements in this list (in the proper sequence), starting at the specified position in this list:

```
ListIterator listIterator(int startIndex)
```

This returns a view of the portion of this list between the specified fromIndex, inclusive, and toIndex, exclusive:

```
List subList(int fromIndex, int toIndex)
```

Three functional classes implement the List interface:

- **LinkedList** This implements all optional list operations and accepts null. Also, methods to add and get methods at the beginning or end of the list are provided, so this class may also be used as a stack, queue, or double-ended queue (deque).

■ **Vector**   A growable array of objects.

■ **ArrayList**   This class is roughly equivalent to Vector, except that it is unsynchronized.

Let's examine the Vector class in a simple example.

```
import java.util.*;
class VectorTest {
    public static void main (String [] args) {
        Vector v = new Vector();
        v.add("Zak");
        v.add("Gordon");
        v.add(0, "Duke");
        v.add("Lara");
        System.out.println(v);
        String name = (String)v.get(2);
        System.out.println(name);
    }
}
```

The preceding code creates a Vector and adds several names to it. Notice the third name, Duke, is added with an index variable. This inserts it in the 0 slot in the List, which is the first slot. The class also uses the get() method to retrieve a name, using the index 2. Also notice that to retrieve the object from the list, it is necessary to cast the object to a string, as you can see in the code. The output from this program is as follows:

```
C:\JAVA\BOOKTEST>java VectorTest
[Duke, Zak, Gordon, Lara]
Gordon
```

This code shows that the elements retain the order in which they are placed into the list. The List is guaranteed to keep this order, but a Set has no guarantee of keeping this order over time.

Map

The Map interface does not extend the Collection interface, so in strict terms it is not a Collection type. In general terms, however, it is part of the collections architecture.

A Map stores objects that are identified by unique keys. A Map may not store duplicate keys. It can, however, store duplicate objects. Objects are stored in Map collections in no particular order.

Two common collections directly implement the Map interface:

- Hashtable

- HashMap

The HashMap class is roughly equivalent to Hashtable, except that it is not synchronized for threads and it permits null values to be stored. The Hashtable was present in the JDK 1.1, however it did not use the same collections framework as Java 2.0, and hence it did not implement the Map interface. The overall functionality of Hashtable is the same, and it has been reworked so that it is now a Map.

We saw a demonstration of a Hashtable earlier in this chapter, so we will instead examine the HashMap class. Let's examine a piece of code that stores several objects then retrieves them using keys.

```
import java.util.*;
class HashMapTest {
    public static void main (String [] args) {
        HashMap hm = new HashMap();
        hm.put("Game1","Tic Tac Toe");
        hm.put(null, "Chess");
        hm.put("Game3", "Checkers");
        hm.put("Game3", "Hockey Game");
        hm.put("Game4", "Chess");
        System.out.println(hm);
        String title = (String)hm.get("Game3");
        System.out.println(title);
    }
}
```

The preceding code adds several String objects to the HashMap using keys, which are also Strings. Although the key is a String in this example, it is possible to use any object as a key. Notice that it attempts to place two titles under the same key, Game3. This code will compile successfully, but the output might be unexpected. Looking at the preceding code, which title will it display, Checkers or Hockey Game?

```
C:\JAVA\MAPTEST>java HashMapTest
{Game4=Chess, Game3=Hockey Game, Game1=Tic Tac Toe,
null=Chess}
Hockey Game
```

As we can see it stored Hockey Game, so the last object to be added under a key will be stored. The code shows that null can be used for objects or keys. Also, notice the objects are stored in no particular order. Objects may be duplicated in this set, as shown by the String Chess.

The Map interface defines several methods that manipulate objects using keys. This removes all mappings from this map:

```
void clear()
```

This returns true if this map contains a mapping for the specified key:

```
boolean containsKey(Object key)
```

The following returns true if this map maps one or more keys to the specified value:

```
boolean containsValue(Object value)
```

This returns a set view of the mappings contained in this map:

```
Set entrySet()
```

This compares the specified object with this map for equality:

```
boolean equals(Object o)
```

This returns the value to which this map maps the specified key:

```
Object get(Object key)
```

This returns the hash code value for this map:

```
int hashCode()
```

This returns true if this map contains no key-value mappings:

```
boolean isEmpty()
```

This returns a set view of the keys contained in this map:

```
Set keySet()
```

This associates the specified value with the specified key in this map:

```
Object put(Object key, Object value)
```

This copies all of the mappings from the specified map to this map:

```
void putAll(Map t)
```

The following removes the mapping for this key from this map, if present:

```
Object remove(Object key)
```

This returns the number of key-value mappings in this map:

```
int size()
```

This returns a collection view of the values contained in this map:

```
Collection values()
```

Sorted Map

SortedMap is similar to Map, except the objects are stored in ascending order according to their keys. Like Map, there can be no duplicate keys and the objects themselves may be duplicated. One very important difference with SortedMap objects is that the key may not be a null value.

TreeMap is the only core API class to implement the SortedMap interface directly, so let's examine this in some code.

```
import java.util.*;
class TreeMapTest {
    public static void main (String [] args) {
        Map titles = new TreeMap();
        titles.put(new Integer(2),"Tic Tac Toe");
        titles.put(new Integer(3), "Checkers");
        titles.put(new Integer(1), "Hockey Game");
        titles.put(new Integer(4), "Chess");
        System.out.println(titles);
    }
}
```

Notice the order of the keys before the program is executed. Now let's examine the output:

```
C:\JAVA\BOOKTEST>java TreeMapTest
{1=Hockey Game, 2=Tic Tac Toe, 3=Checkers, 4=Chess}
```

This output demonstrates that SortedMap collections are automatically sorted in ascending order by the key. In this case we used Integer objects as keys. Because it uses the object equals() method, it sorted in numerical order.

The SortedMap interface uses all the methods in the Map interface, as well as the following, which returns the comparator associated with this sorted map, or null if it uses its keys' natural ordering:

```
Comparator comparator()
```

This returns the first (lowest) key currently in this sorted map:

```
Object firstKey()
```

This returns a view of the portion of this sorted map whose keys are strictly less than toKey:

```
SortedMap headMap(Object toKey)
```

This returns the last (highest) key currently in this sorted map:

```
Object lastKey()
```

This returns a view of the portion of this sorted map whose keys range from fromKey, inclusive, to toKey, exclusive:

```
SortedMap subMap(Object fromKey, Object toKey)
```

The following returns a view of the portion of this sorted map whose keys are greater than or equal to fromKey:

```
SortedMap tailMap(Object fromKey)
```

Table 12-2 shows a summary of the collection interfaces.

| TABLE 12-2 | | Summary of Collection Interfaces | | |

Interface	Sorted	Ordered	Uses Keys	No Duplicates
Set				X
SortedSet	X			X
List		X		
Map			X	
SortedMap	X		X	

EXERCISE 12-1

Creating a Domain Name Server

Create a program that uses a collection to store three Internet Protocol (IP) addresses and their respective domain names. It will, in effect, be a domain name server. The class should look up the domain name as a string and return the IP address, also a string.

1. Decide the properties of the domain name server that you will be creating. In this case, it is a non-sorted, non-duplicating, unordered collection using keys.

2. Choose the appropriate collection type. In this case, Hashtable is the best choice.

3. Your final program can look something like this:

```
import java.util.*;

class GetHost {
    public static void main (String [] args) {
        Map addresses = new Hashtable();
        addresses.put("java.sun.com","192.18.97.137");
        addresses.put("www.syngress.com",
            "204.146.80.99");
        addresses.put("www.madeupsite.com",
            "216.65.63.102");
        String hostName = (String)
            addresses.get(args[0]);
        System.out.println(hostName);
    }
}
```

Methods in the Collections Class

The Collections class contains static methods that perform operations on various collections. The operations usually perform some type of sorting routine on the collection. The methods use one of the collection interfaces as the argument in the method—sometimes as general as a Collection object or as specific as SortedMap. The good thing about this is if you decide to make your own type of collection and use one of the interfaces in the collection architecture, your collection should work flawlessly with the static methods in the Collections class!

Let's look at an example of the shuffle() method to demonstrate how easy these methods are to use. The shuffle method takes a List object, such as a Vector, and shuffles the contents randomly.

```
import java.util.*;
class CardShuffle {
    public static void main (String [] args) {
        Vector deck = new Vector();
        deck.add("2 of hearts");
        deck.add("3 of diamonds");
        deck.add("4 of hearts");
        deck.add("5 of clubs");
        System.out.println(deck);
        Collections.shuffle(deck);
        System.out.println(deck);
    }
}
```

Using the Collections methods is extremely easy. As you can see in line 10, the line that actually shuffles our deck of cards is trivial to write. You can save yourself immeasurable time using the Collections class. The output from this program is as follows:

```
C:\JAVA\BOOKTEST>java CardShuffle
[2 of hearts, 3 of diamonds, 4 of hearts, 5 of clubs]
```

```
[4 of hearts, 5 of clubs, 2 of hearts, 3 of diamonds]

C:\JAVA\BOOKTEST>java CardShuffle
[2 of hearts, 3 of diamonds, 4 of hearts, 5 of clubs]
[4 of hearts, 5 of clubs, 2 of hearts, 3 of diamonds]

C:\JAVA\BOOKTEST>java CardShuffle
[2 of hearts, 3 of diamonds, 4 of hearts, 5 of clubs]
[3 of diamonds, 2 of hearts, 4 of hearts, 5 of clubs]
```

The program was run three times to demonstrate how random it may or may not be. There is an additional shuffle() method that lets you seed the number with a random object of your own. By the way, the reason the shuffle() method works only with a list is because List is the only object that is ordered. Using shuffle() on any other type would be meaningless. For example, if it were a Sorted collection, as soon as the items were shuffled they would go back to ascending order.

exam
Ⓦatch

It is important to know about the methods in the Collections class for the real world because they can save you valuable programming time and the methods are very efficient. For the exam, you will not need to know the methods or how to implement them.

Let's quickly cover some of the more notable methods contained in the Collections class. The following searches the specified list for the specified object using the binary search algorithm:

```
static int binarySearch(List list, Object key)
```

This searches the specified list for the specified object using the binary search algorithm:

```
static int binarySearch(List list, Object key, Comparator c)
```

This copies all of the elements from one list into another:

```
static void copy(List dest, List src)
```

This returns an enumeration over the specified collection:

```
static Enumeration enumeration(Collection c)
```

The following replaces all of the elements of the specified list with the specified element:

```
static void fill(List list, Object o)
```

This returns the maximum element of the given collection, according to the natural ordering of its elements:

```
static Object max(Collection coll)
```

This returns the maximum element of the given collection, according to the order induced by the specified comparator:

```
static Object min(Collection coll)
```

This returns the minimum element of the given collection, according to the natural ordering of its elements:

```
static Object max(Collection coll, Comparator comp)
```

This returns the minimum element of the given collection, according to the order induced by the specified comparator:

```
static Object min(Collection coll, Comparator comp)
```

This returns an immutable list consisting of *n* copies of the specified object:

```
static List nCopies(int n, Object o)
```

This reverses the order of the elements in the specified list:

```
static void reverse(List l)
```

This returns a comparator that imposes the reverse of the natural ordering on a collection of objects that implement the Comparable interface:

```
static Comparator reverseOrder()
```

This randomly permutes the specified list using a default source of randomness:

```
static void shuffle(List list)
```

The following randomly permutes the specified list using the specified source of randomness.

```
static void shuffle(List list, Random rnd)
```

This sorts the specified list into ascending order, according to the natural ordering of its elements:

```
static void sort(List list)
```

This sorts the specified list according to the order induced by the specified comparator:

```
static void sort(List list, Comparator c)
```

Storing and Sorting Strings

Create a program to store a list of strings, then sort the strings in reverse alphabetical (descending) order.

1. Decide the appropriate type of collection to use for a list of names. In this case, Vector sounds good because it will keep them ordered, but not in ascending order.

2. Use the Collections methods for sorting. Use sort() to sort the names in the natural alphabetic order, then use reverse() to reverse the order.

3. The code should look something like this:

```
import java.util.*;
class Reverse {
    public static void main (String [] args) {
        Vector names = new Vector();
        for(int i = 0;i<args.length;i++)
            names.add(args[i]);
        Collections.sort(names);
        Collections.reverse(names);
        System.out.println(names);
    }
}
```

Now that you have a better idea of collections, here are some possible attributes for a collection, followed by the correct collection interface:

Non-duplicating, unordered collection	Set
Duplicating, ordered collection	List
Duplicating, with keys	Map
Non-duplicating, sorted collection	SortedSet
Duplicating collection sorted by keys	SortedMap

CERTIFICATION SUMMARY

The main information that you should concentrate on from this chapter are the four properties that collections may possess: sorting, ordered collections, allowing duplicates, and using keys. You should also know the interfaces and classes that make up the collections framework.

✓ TWO-MINUTE DRILL

- ❑ A Set can store only unique objects, not duplicates.
- ❑ A List keeps the objects in a definite order.
- ❑ A Map stores objects according to keys.
- ❑ SortedSet stores objects in ascending order without duplicates.
- ❑ SortedMap stores objects in ascending order using keys.
- ❑ SortedSet can't contain objects that are null.
- ❑ SortedMap can't contain keys that are null.
- ❑ HashSet implements the Set interface.
- ❑ TreeSet implements the SortedSet interface.
- ❑ LinkedList, Vector, and ArrayList implement List.
- ❑ HashMap and Hashtable implement the Map interface.
- ❑ TreeMap implements the SortedMap interface.

SELF TEST

The following questions will help you measure your understanding of the material presented in this chapter. Read all of the choices carefully, as there may be more than one correct answer. Choose all correct answers for each question.

1. Which of the following properties apply to a deck of cards?
   A. Ordered
   B. Sorted
   C. Duplicating
   D. Uses keys

2. Which of the following properties apply to a list of phone numbers in a directory? (Choose all that apply.)
   A. Ordered
   B. Sorted
   C. Duplicating
   D. Uses keys

3. Which of the following interfaces form the framework for a nonduplicating, unsorted, unordered collection?
   A. List
   B. Map
   C. Set
   D. Collection

4. Which of the following classes directly implement the Set interface?
   A. Vector
   B. LinkedList
   C. HashSet
   D. Hashtable

5. Which of the following classes would be appropriate to use for a list of one-of-a-kind baseball cards? Keep in mind that you are not interested in sorting these or in their order.
   A. Vector
   B. TreeMap
   C. Hashtable

   D. TreeSet

   E. HashSet

6. Which of the following interfaces form the framework for a nonduplicating, sorted collection?

   A. SortedList

   B. SortedMap

   C. SortedSet

   D. List

7. Which of the following classes directly implement the SortedSet interface?

   A. Vector

   B. LinkedList

   C. HashSet

   D. TreeSet

   E. Hashtable

8. You are creating a program that stores a list of the members in your Monday night bowling league. It would be nice to have them stored alphabetically. Which of the following classes would you use?

   A. Vector

   B. TreeMap

   C. Hashtable

   D. TreeSet

   E. HashSet

9. Which of the following interfaces form the framework for a duplicating, ordered, unsorted collection?

   A. List

   B. Map

   C. Set

   D. Collection

10. Which of the following classes directly implement the List interface? (Choose all that apply.)

   A. Vector

   B. LinkedList

   C. HashSet

   D. TreeSet

   E. Hashtable

11. Which of the following classes would be appropriate to use for a deck of cards?

    A. Vector
    B. TreeMap
    C. Hashtable
    D. TreeSet
    E. HashSet

12. Which of the following interfaces form the framework for an unsorted, unordered collection that uses keys to access the elements?

    A. List
    B. Map
    C. Set
    D. Collection

13. Which of the following classes directly implement the Map interface? (Choose all that apply.)

    A. Vector
    B. LinkedList
    C. HashSet
    D. Hashtable
    E. HashMap

14. Which of the following methods are part of the Map interface? (Choose all that apply.)

    A. get()
    B. add()
    C. set()
    D. put()
    E. remove()

15. Which of the following classes would be appropriate to use for a telephone directory listing?

    A. TreeMap
    B. Vector
    C. Hashtable
    D. TreeSet
    E. HashSet

16. Which of the following interfaces form the framework for a sorted collection that uses keys?

   A. SortedList

   B. SortedMap

   C. SortedSet

   D. List

   E. Map

17. Which of the following classes directly implement the SortedMap interface?

   A. Vector

   B. ArrayMap

   C. HashMap

   D. Hashtable

   E. TreeMap

18. A coworker has left a printout of some code on your desk. You examine the code:

```
import java.util.*;
class Inventors {
    public static void main (String [] args) {
        Set dir = new TreeSet();
        dir.put("Jon G.", "555-5553");
        dir.put("Al E.", "555-1978");
        dir.put("Tom E.", "555-1330");
        dir.put("Jimmy W.", "555-7165");
        System.out.println(dir);
    }
}
```

What will the output of this program be when it is compiled and run?

   A. {Al E.=555-1978, Jimmy W.=555-7165, Jon G.=555-5553, Tom E.=555-1330}

   B. { Jon G.=555-5553, Al E.=555-1978, Tom E.=555-1330, Jimmy W.=555-7165}

   C. The program won't compile because of line four.

   D. The program won't compile because of lines five through eight.

   E. Something else will prevent the program from compiling.

19. You are attempting to create a computerized fortune-teller that can read Tarot cards. Your prototype program looks like this:

```
import java.util.*;
class MadameCthulhu {
    public static void main (String [] args) {
        Map tarot = new HashMap();
        tarot.put("Lovers", "you will have romance");
        tarot.put("Justice", "justice will be yours at last");
        tarot.put("The Fool", "beware what your friends tell you");
        tarot.put("Death", "you better make a will");
        Collections.shuffle(tarot);
        String card = (String)tarot.firstKey();
        String prediction = (String)tarot.get(card);
        System.out.println("Madam Cthulhu has picked " + card);
        System.out.println("She says " + prediction + "!");
    }
}
```

Which lines will prevent this code from compiling successfully? (Choose all that apply.)

A. `Map tarot = new HashMap();`

B. `Collections.shuffle(tarot);`

C. `String card = (String)tarot.firstKey();`

D. `String prediction = (String)tarot.get(card);`

E. Lines 5–8

20. You are attempting to create a class that will store an alphabetized list of your comic collection. Here is your prototype code so far:

```
import java.util.*;
class ComicBooks {
    public static void main (String [] args) {
        Map comics = new TreeMap();
        comics.put(new Integer(404),"Batman:Year One pt 1");
        comics.put(new Integer(437),"Batman:Year Three pt 2");
        comics.put(new Integer(461),"Batman:Once upon a time");
        comics.put(new Integer(459),null);
        System.out.println(comics);
    }
}
```

What will occur when this class is compiled and run?

A. It will not compile because an Integer object can't be used as a key.

B. It will not compile because Map objects can't store null values.

C. It will not compile because SortedMap objects can't store null values.

D. It will compile and run fine.

13

The java.awt Package: The Basics

T he java.awt package is the part of the Java application programming interface (API) that declares graphical components. An application developer uses these graphical components to construct the graphical user interface (GUI) of an application.

This chapter covers the Component, Container, and LayoutManager classes and the relationships among them.

CERTIFICATION OBJECTIVE 13.01

java.awt Basics

The java.awt package of the Java Development Kit (JDK) provides developers with widgets to construct graphical user interfaces. The three main types of classes within the java.awt package are components, containers, and layout managers. Each type of class has a special relationship to the other two.

- *Component* is the base class and provides functionality for defining the appearance of the widget, the response (if any) to various events, and, finally, the instructions on how to render itself.

- *Containers* are specialized components that hold other components. Because containers themselves are components, you can nest containers to achieve a desired layout.

- *Layout managers* are those classes that are responsible for laying out all components within a container, a process that includes sizing and positioning. A layout manager is associated with a container and a reference to that layout manager is held as a member of the container class.

exam
ⓦatch

The key points on the exam concerning the basics of the java.awt package will be the usage of the Component, Container, and LayoutManager classes and the relationships between them.

Overview

The principal classes of the java.awt package are components, containers, and layout managers. Each plays a fundamental role in the presentation layer of any Java applet or application. The following section provides a brief overview of these class types.

Component Overview

The subclasses of java.awt.Component are those classes that make up the visual components of Java. The java.awt.Component class is the ultimate superclass for all nonmenu graphical widgets. Even Swing components descend from java.awt.Component. All Swing components inherit from javax.swing.JComponent. JComponent is a subclass of java.awt.Component, so it follows that Swing components contain the inherited functionality of their Abstract Window Toolkit (AWT) predecessors.

Container Overview

Containers are components that are capable of holding other components. Because containers are components, you can nest containers within each other. This process of nesting containers can be carried out indefinitely and can be used to implement a variety of layouts.

LayoutManager Overview

Layout managers are responsible for sizing and positioning components within a container. If the LayoutManager attribute of a container is set to null then that container uses absolute positioning to lay out the components that it contains. Absolute positioning means that each component is placed and sized at the coordinates as defined by the getBounds() method.

Components

Components are those objects in the Java Development Kit that render graphical widgets. Every type of component inherits from java.awt.Component and thus inherits all of the methods necessary to render itself. They also inherit the methods for capturing and processing events such as mouse movement and keyboard activity.

Key Methods of Components

Component classes have many methods to perform those tasks that components must do. There are, however, certain methods that deserve closer attention as they perform some of the key functionality.

Remember that the Component class of the java.awt package is the ultimate superclass for all nonmenu graphical components.

EVENTS   The ability to efficiently process events within AWT components improved greatly with the release of the Java Development Kit Version 1.1. In that version the event delegation model was introduced. This gave developers the ability to have components register an interest in certain events rather than simply propagate an event notification message up through the container hierarchy. There are several types of events that exist within the Java Event Framework. They include Mouse, Window, MouseMotion, Key, Focus, and others.

The way that a component registers for receiving certain events has two parts. First, the component that wishes to receive events declares that it implements the appropriate interface. For example, if a class wished to receive Key events then the class declaration would take the following form:

```
public class SomeKeyEventInterestedClass implements KeyListener
```

The interface to implement a type of event always follows the naming convention of *EventType*Listener. Consequently, the Key event interface is named KeyListener, the MouseMotion event interface is named MouseMotionListener, and so on.

By declaring that a class implements an event listener's interface, the methods of that interface must be defined. In the case of our class declaration, the class would have to implement the keyPressed(), keyReleased(), and keyTyped() methods.

After the class that wishes to receive events has implemented all necessary methods, the final step is to register that class as an event listener in the component that will produce the event. This registration is done by calling the appropriate add listener method in the event producing class. The methods for adding event listeners follows the naming convention of add*EventType*Listener(). In the case of our key event listener, we would call the method addKeyListener(SomeKeyEventInterestedClass) in the class that will produce the event.

The addEventTypeListener() method adds an instance of a listener class to the list of listener classes that will be notified when that event type occurs.

VISUAL SETTINGS Each component can customize its visual representation in a variety of ways. The most common properties of a component that are modified are its colors, fonts, and dimensions.

There are two methods for setting the color of a component. These methods are setForeground() and setBackground(). The setForeground() method defines the color that will be used to draw items in the foreground of the component; the text, for example. The setBackground() method defines the color that will be used to draw the background of the component. As expected, the two methods getForeground() and getBackground() return the current color settings.

For example, to set the color of the foreground of a component to red and the background to black, you would add the following code within the component's class:

```
this.setForeground( Color.red );
this.setBackground( Color.black );
```

If either the foreground color or the background color is not set using these methods then the appropriate color setting of the parent component is used.

The java.awt.Component class provides a method for changing the font. This method is called setFont() and must be passed a java.awt.Font object in the method call. To retrieve the current font, the getFont() method may be called.

For example, to set the font of a component you would make the following call from within the component's class:

```
this.setFont( new Font( "SanSerif", Font.PLAIN, 14 ) );
```

As with the colors of the component, if a font is not explicitly specified then the font of the parent component is inherited.

The dimensions of a component refer to its physical geometry on the screen. There are several methods for setting and retrieving the location and size of a component.

For setting or retrieving the dimensions of the component, you use setSize() and getSize() respectively. For setting the dimensions, you can pass either two integers representing the width and height or a java.awt.Dimension object. The getSize() method only returns a java.awt.Dimension object.

To set or retrieve the current location of the component within the container, you call setLocation() and getLocation() respectively. The location of a component is defined relative to the upper-left corner of the component. For setting the location, you may pass in either two integer parameters representing the x and y coordinates of the upper-left corner or a java.awt.Point object. The getLocation() method only returns a java.awt.Point object.

For example, to create a Label within an application that will sit at location x = 100, y = 100, have a width of 300, and a height of 50, you use the following code:

```
Label label = new Label( "A Label" );
label.setLocation( 100,100 );
label.setSize( 300,50 );
```

There are also methods that perform all of these tasks in one call. These methods are setBounds() and getBounds(). These methods pass and return the entire physical geometry of the component all at once. For the setBounds() methods you can pass either four integers representing the x and y coordinates and the width and height or pass one java.awt.Rectangle object. The getBounds() method only returns a java.awt.Rectangle object.

Before you get too excited about this absolute control over the location and size of a component, it is only fair to warn you that all of these settings may be ignored by the layout manager of the container within which this component resides. It is at the layout manager's discretion to pay attention to all or some of these geometry settings or to ignore them completely.

RENDERING   Each component contains methods for rendering (or painting) itself. The most common experience with rendering methods is the process of overriding the paint(Graphics g) method of java.awt.Component so that you can define your own rendering characteristics. The other common methods are update(Graphics g) and repaint(). Of these three, only repaint() may be called directly from within an application. The other two are invoked by the system.

The Component class of the java.awt package is the ultimate superclass for all nonmenu graphical components.

The paint(Graphics g) method is where all rendering takes place. When implementing your own paint(Graphics g) method, you use the graphics context provided to set the colors, the fonts, and to draw the various parts of the component.

The update(Graphics g) method is called automatically when you (or the system) invokes the repaint() method. The most common experience with the update(Graphics g) method is to override it to call the paint(Graphics g) method. By using this technique, one can reduce or eliminate flickering when a component is redrawn. This flicker is caused by the default implementation of the update() method. Normally, the update() method calls the clearRect() method to erase the drawing space prior to drawing. This process may cause the appearance of flickering while drawing. By overriding the update() method to call the paint() method, the flickering is usually reduced.

The update() method of java.awt.Component clears the drawing rectangle prior to rendering the component. This causes flickering under certain circumstances. To alleviate this, it is customary to override the update() method in your custom component such that it calls paint() directly and does not clear the screen.

When a component is to be rendered, the methods are invoked in the following order:

- repaint()
- update(Graphics g)
- paint(Graphics g)

Using Components

Like other Java classes, you use components by instantiating them. After instantiating them you modify their characteristics and add them to a container. The container, by way of its layout manager, will size and position that component within itself.

Creating Components

Invariably, there will come a time when the Java GUI components provided with the JDK will not be suitable for a certain task. This unsuitability may result from a component simply not possessing the necessary functionality for your needs or the absence of a component that makes sense within the desired context. You can create your own components to fit those requirements.

When it comes to creating new components, you as a developer have two choices: either extend (or subclass) an existing component, or create a new component from scratch. The main advantage of extending an existing component is that you inherit all of the functionality of that class and you only need to add whatever new functionality is desired. In contrast, by creating a new component from scratch, you must implement a variety of methods that are necessary to allow the component to render itself, as well as other functions.

The following sections cover both methods of creating components.

EXTENDING EXISTING COMPONENTS The easiest way to create your own component is to subclass or extend an existing component. In this manner, you inherit the characteristics of the component and modify it to suit your requirements.

```java
import java.awt.*;

public class MyLabel extends java.awt.Label {
    public MyLabel(String text) {
        super(text);
        this.setBackground(Color.black);
        this.setForeground(Color.white);
        this.setFont(new Font(
            "monospaced",Font.PLAIN,14));
    }
}
```

In this example, we extend an existing component subclass, Label, and create a new component that inherits all of the functionality of the Label class. Our new class, named MyLabel, constructs a Label and sets the background to black and the foreground to white. It also sets the font to an appointed fixed-width font as designated by your system.

It is interesting to note the absence of a default constructor in our MyLabel class. Because we did not choose to provide one in MyLabel, you can't create a new instance by calling a constructor with no arguments. In actuality, there are three constructors in the parent class of java.awt.Label. Because we have implemented only one of those three, the other two may not be used to create an instance of MyLabel. In other words, non-private methods and members will be inherited but constructors will not.

The inability to inherit constructors from the parent class applies if at least one constructor is defined in your extending class. If no constructors are implemented in your extending class then a default constructor with no arguments is created that invokes the constructor of the superclass that also takes no arguments.

To demonstrate this, we will create a class that will generate a frame and add several instances of the MyLabel class within it. A frame is a top-level container that is used to hold components. This frame is defined by the java.awt.Frame class. We will go into further detail on the Frame class shortly.

```java
import java.awt.*;

public class MyLabelExample {
    public static void main(String[] args) {
        Frame f = new Frame("FlowLayout Example");
        f.setBounds(0,0,300,300);
        f.setLayout(new FlowLayout());
        MyLabel label1 = new MyLabel("Small Label");
        MyLabel label2 = new MyLabel("A Very Very
            Very Large Label" );
        MyLabel label3 = new MyLabel("Java Rules");
        f.add(label1);
        f.add(label2);
        f.add(label3);
        f.setVisible(true);
    }
}
```

The preceding code, when compiled and executed, will produce a frame as shown in Figure13-1.

CREATING NEW COMPONENTS   Another way to create new components is to do so from scratch. This allows you, the developer, maximum flexibility over the functionality of your component, but it is a little more work than simply extending an existing component.

The most common way to create a new component is to create a class that extends the java.awt.Component itself. This has the advantage of being a lightweight and not needing a native peer to render itself. Basically this

FIGURE 13-1

MyLabel examples
in a frame

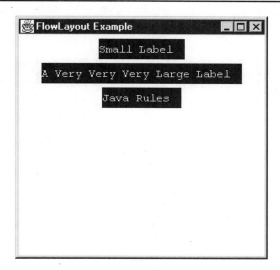

means that your new component will look the same across all platforms that
support the Java Virtual Machine.

There are two requirements for creating a new component in this
manner. The first requirement is that you must provide a constructor in
your component. You can either implement a constructor or allow the
virtual machine to create a default constructor with no arguments. The
other requirement is providing a means for the component to render
itself. This entails overriding the paint() method of the java.awt.
Component superclass and implementing the code that will draw the
component on the screen.

Containers

Containers are special components that can contain other components.
Components are added to a container by way of one of the add() methods.
Each container utilizes a layout manager (discussed later) to size and
position those components within it.

The add() method, with all of its overloaded forms, is used to add component instances to the container.

Key Methods of Containers

Several methods are defined by the various containers. Of these, the most important are the methods that deal with adding components as well as performing the layout and sizing of components.

The add() method of the java.awt.Container class is overloaded with several different methods. These give the container a great deal of flexibility when adding components to its collection. The add() methods are the following:

- **add(Component component, int index)**   This adds the specified component and inserts it into the specified position. Although the results of an invalid index vary from one layout manager to another, the general result is an exception of some sort.

- **add(Component component)**   This method adds the specified component as the last object in the container.

- **add(Component component, Object constraints)**   This add() method is special in the fact that it provides the constraints object for those layout managers that require it. In fact, this method calls the addLayoutComponent() method of the container's layout manager.

- **add(Component component, Object constraints, int index)**   This add() method provides the necessary information for those layout managers that require both a constraints object and an index to properly layout the component.

The layout and sizing of methods is supported by several methods of java.awt.Container. The first of which is the setLayout(LayoutManager) method. This method allows you to set the layout manager that will be responsible for the sizing and positioning of components within the container.

Types of Containers

Because the java.awt.Container class is an abstract class, you cannot instantiate one directly. Instead, there are several subclasses of Container that you can use. These subclasses are described in the following sections.

PANEL   Panel is by far the simplest and most common of the Container classes. If no LayoutManager is specified then the FlowLayout manager is used by default.

SCROLLPANE   ScrollPane is a container that provides optional scroll bars to gain access to the part of the container that is presently off the viewable area. The scroll bars may be included as always on or on an as needed basis. Figure 13-2 shows a ScrollPane that contains the license agreement bundled with the latest Java 2 Development Kit.

FIGURE 13-2

ScrollPane is a subclass of
the class Container

WINDOW   The java.awt.Window class is a container with no decorations such as borders or menu bars. The Window container is a top-level container.

A typical use of the java.awt.Window class is to present a splash or an About screen from an application. Such screens usually do not need the decorations and controls associated with an application frame.

If no LayoutManager is specified for the Window container then a BorderLayout manager is used by default.

FRAME   The java.awt.Frame class is a container that has decorations such as borders, titles, and menu bars. The Frame container is a top-level container.

If no LayoutManager is specified, a BorderLayout manager is used by default.

Figure 13-3 shows a blank frame. This illustrates the basic components of graphical representation of the Frame class. Notice the standard window management controls at the top of the frame as well as the border. The border surrounding the frame can be used to resize the frame during execution. Of course, this resizing behavior can be disabled from within the program.

FIGURE 13-3

A blank frame

Figure 13-4 illustrates the window management menu of the Frame class as it appears on the Windows platform.

Layout Managers

Layout managers are responsible for positioning and sizing components within a container. The type of layout manager of the parent container determines where a component gets positioned within that container.

Layout managers free the developer of having to calculate positions and sizes of each component. Given the fact that different platforms render each component differently, the task of manually calculating the appropriate size and position of a component such that the appearance of the application remains more or less the same across platforms would be a daunting one indeed.

Fortunately, the layout managers are able to handle these tasks for the developer. Each layout manager knows how to position each of the components within the container and repositions them (if necessary) when the size of the parent container changes during runtime.

A frame with the window management menu

Layout Manager Interfaces

A class that wishes to perform the role of a layout manager must either implement java.awt.LayoutManager or java.awt.LayoutManager2. Both of these interfaces define those methods necessary to determine how to position and size components within a container.

The java.awt.LayoutManager interface defines the following methods for implementing classes:

- **addLayoutComponent(String name, Component comp)**   This method is used by those layout managers that use a name to determine in which section of the container the component will be placed.

- **removeLayoutComponent(Component comp)**   This method is implemented by those layout managers that need to be able to remove a component from a container.

- **preferredLayoutSize(Container cont)**   This method is called to provide the dimensions necessary to render the given container. It is up to the implementing layout manager to determine how those dimensions are calculated. Some layout managers step through each component and calculate the dimensions and position of each one, and other layout managers simply return the current size of the container.

- **minimumLayoutSize(Container cont)**   This method should be implemented by layout managers to return the minimum size necessary to render the container.

- **layoutContainer(Container cont)**   This method is where most of the action takes place. It is here that the implementing layout manager class will size and position each component with the specified container.

The java.awt.LayoutManager2 interface is a subinterface of the java.awt.LayoutManager interface. The main difference is that LayoutManager2 provides for the sizing and positioning of components based upon a constraints object. The LayoutManager2 interface also adds the following methods to implement:

- **addLayoutComponent(Component component, Object constraints)**   This will add the specified component to the container. The constraints object will dictate to the layout manager how to render the component.

- **maximumLayoutSize(Container container)**   This method introduces the concept of a maximum size to a container. If implemented by the layout manager, the container will not exceed the size returned.

- **getLayoutAlignmentX(Container container)**   This method returns a float value representing the alignment of the container specified along the horizontal axis. The range of values for the return type is 0.0 to 1.0. Those values nearer to 0.0 mean an alignment more towards the left edge of the container. Those values nearer to 1.0 mean an alignment more towards the right edge of the container. A value of 0.5 means it is centered.

- **getLayoutAlignmentY(Container container)**   This method returns a float value representing the alignment of the container specified along the vertical axis. The range of values for the return type is 0.0 to 1.0. Those values nearer to 0.0 mean an alignment more towards the top edge of the container. Those values nearer to 1.0 mean an alignment more towards the bottom edge of the container. A value of 0.5 means it is centered.

- **invalidateLayout(Container container)**   This method will tell the layout manager that the current information about the layout of the specified container is no longer valid and should be purged from any cached information.

Types of Layout Managers
There are a variety of predefined layout managers in the Java Development Kit. Each one performs its role of sizing and positioning components in

different ways. The following sections outline the predefined layout managers of the JDK.

GRIDLAYOUT   The java.awt.GridLayout layout manager is a class that implements the LayoutManager interface. This layout manager arranges components in a grid within a container. Each cell in the grid is of equal dimensions. The GridLayout manager ignores the preferred size of each component and resizes them to exactly fit each cell's dimensions. As each component is added to the container, the GridLayout manager inserts them across each column until that row is filled and then starts at the first column of the next row.

It should be noted that explicitly setting the number of columns and rows either in the constructor or by calling the setRows() and setColumns() methods does not guarantee that you will get the expected number of columns. Due to the nature of the GridLayout class, the number of columns is calculated by the number of rows and the number of components added. The number of columns specified is respected only if the number of rows is not specified.

The following is an example of the GridLayout manager. Figure 13-5 is a visual representation.

```
import java.awt.*;

public class GridLayoutExample
{
    public static void main( String args[] )
    {
        Frame f = new Frame( "GridLayout Example" );
        f.setBounds( 0,0,300,300 );
        f.setLayout( new GridLayout( 3,3 ) );
        for( int i = 1; i <= 9; i++ )
        {
            Button b = new Button( "Button "+i );
            f.add( b );
        }
        f.setVisible( true );
    }
}
```

FIGURE 13-5

A GridLayout example

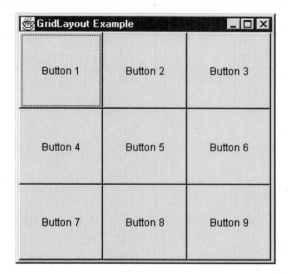

This class will generate a frame divided into a grid with nine cells, with three cells per row. Each cell in the grid is of equal dimensions. When the frame is resized, all of the cells resize proportionally to remain the same size as each other.

FLOWLAYOUT   FlowLayout is a class that implements the LayoutManager interface. This layout manager arranges components within the container from left to right. When the container runs out of room on the current row, FlowLayout resumes positioning components on the next row. The FlowLayout manager respects the preferred size of each component.

The following is an example of FlowLayout. Figure 13-6 is a visual representation.

```
import java.awt.*;

public class FlowLayoutExample
{
    public static void main( String args[] )
```

```
      {
          Frame f = new Frame( "FlowLayout Example" );
          f.setBounds( 0,0,300,300 );
          f.setLayout( new FlowLayout() );
          for( int i = 1; i < 10; i++ )
          {
              Button b = new Button( "Button "+i );
              f.setSize( 100,25 );
              f.add( b );
          }
          f.setVisible( true );
      }
  }
```

This class will generate a frame containing nine buttons. Each row of buttons is centered on the vertical axis of the frame. As you resize the frame, notice that the buttons are rearranged into new rows or placed into existing rows as dictated by the size of each button and the size of the frame itself.

BORDERLAYOUT   The java.awt.BorderLayout class implements the LayoutManager2 interface. The BorderLayout layout manager divides the

A FlowLayout example

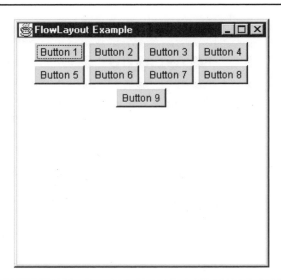

container into five areas. These areas are NORTH, SOUTH, EAST, WEST, and CENTER. The name of the area indicates where the component will be placed. All directional references are relative to the top of the container, which is considered NORTH.

The following is an example of BorderLayout. Figure 13-7 is a visual representation.

```java
import java.awt.*;

public class BorderLayoutExample
{
    public static void main( String args[] )
    {
        Frame f = new Frame( "BorderLayout Example" );
        f.setBounds( 0,0,300,300 );
        f.setLayout( new BorderLayout() );

        Button north = new Button( "North" );
        Button south = new Button( "South" );
        Button east = new Button( "East" );
        Button west = new Button( "West" );
        Button center = new Button( "Center" );

        f.add( BorderLayout.NORTH, north );
        f.add( BorderLayout.SOUTH, south );
        f.add( BorderLayout.EAST, east );
        f.add( BorderLayout.WEST, west );
        f.add( BorderLayout.CENTER, center );

        f.setVisible( true );
    }
}
```

In this example we create five buttons, label them in a descriptive manner, and insert them into the five different sections of the container. This example allows you to view the distinctive behavior of the BorderLayout class.

Any component placed within the NORTH or SOUTH areas of the container are resized to fill the entire width of the container. The preferred height of the component is maintained.

FIGURE 13-7

A BorderLayout example

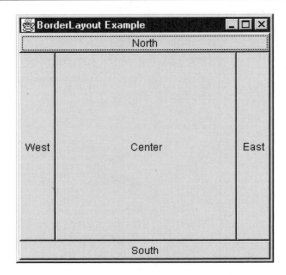

Any component placed within the EAST or WEST areas of the container are resized to fill the entire height of the container. The preferred width of the component is maintained.

Any component placed within the CENTER section of the container is resized to fill whatever space is left over after the other four sections have positioned components. The preferred size of any component in this CENTER section is ignored completely.

GRIDBAGLAYOUT   The java.awt.GridBagLayout class implements the LayoutManager2 interface. The GridBagLayout layout manager allows the placement of components that are aligned either vertically or horizontally without constraining those components to be the same height or width.

The GridBagLayout accomplishes this by defining a dynamic grid of cells. The constraints object that is passed when the component is added to the container determines how many cells the component encompasses.

The following is an example of the GridBagLayout layout manager.
Figure 13-8 is a visual representation.

```java
import java.awt.*;

public class GridBagLayoutExample
{
    public static void main( String args[] )
    {
        Frame f = new Frame( "GridBagLayout Example" );
        f.setBounds( 0,0,300,300 );
        GridBagLayout gb = new GridBagLayout();
        GridBagConstraints c = new GridBagConstraints();
        f.setLayout( gb );
        Button b = null;
        c.fill = GridBagConstraints.BOTH;

        b = new Button( "Button 1" );
        c.gridwidth = 1;
        c.gridheight = 1;
        gb.setConstraints( b, c );
        f.add( b,c );

        b = new Button( "Button 2" );
        c.gridwidth = 1;
        c.gridheight = 1;
        gb.setConstraints( b, c );
        f.add( b,c );

        b = new Button( "Button 3" );
        c.gridwidth = GridBagConstraints.REMAINDER;
        gb.setConstraints( b, c );
        f.add( b,c );

        b = new Button( "Button 4" );
        c.gridwidth = GridBagConstraints.RELATIVE;
        gb.setConstraints( b, c );
        f.add( b,c );

        b = new Button( "Button 5" );
        c.gridwidth = GridBagConstraints.REMAINDER;
        gb.setConstraints( b, c );
        f.add( b,c );
```

```
        b = new Button( "Button 6" );
          c.gridwidth = 1;
          gb.setConstraints( b, c );
          f.add( b,c );

          b = new Button( "Button 7" );
          c.gridwidth = GridBagConstraints.REMAINDER;
          gb.setConstraints( b, c );
          f.add( b,c );

          f.setVisible( true );
      }
  }
```

In this example we place seven buttons in three rows. Two of the buttons span multiple cells in the grid. There is no limit to the amount of complexity with which the grid can be defined and the components added. By virtue of this complexity the GridBagLayout is the most flexible of the layout managers but is also the hardest to master.

A GridBagLayout example

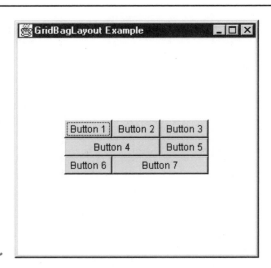

CARDLAYOUT The java.awt.CardLayout class implements the LayoutManager2 interface. The CardLayout layout manager treats each component as a card, with only one card being visible at any given time. Whichever component was added first will be visible first when the container is displayed.

The following is an example of the CardLayout layout manager. Figure 13-9 is a visual representation.

```java
import java.awt.*;
import java.awt.event.*;

public class CardLayoutExample {
    public static void main(String args[]) {
        Frame f = new Frame( "CardLayout Example" );
        f.setSize(300,100);
        f.setLayout(new CardLayout());
        /* Make a final copy of the reference to the Frame for
         *  the anonymous inner class below. */
        final Frame f1 = f;
        for(int i = 1; i <= 5; i++) {
            Button b = new Button( "Button "+i );
            b.setSize( 100,25 );
            b.addActionListener(
                new ActionListener() {
                    public void actionPerformed(ActionEvent ae) {
                        CardLayout cl = (CardLayout)f1.getLayout();
                        cl.next( f1 );
                    }
                }
            );
            f.add( b,"button"+i );
        }
        f.setVisible( true );
    }
}
```

FIGURE 13-9

A CardLayout example

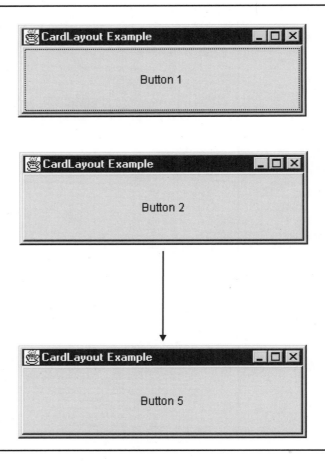

In this example we create a frame with a layout manager of CardLayout. We then add five buttons to this frame. Each button is assigned an anonymous action listener class that will receive the action event when the button is clicked and initiate the viewing of the next button in the card layout. This process cycles over when the last button is reached.

NO LAYOUTMANAGER (null)   If the LayoutManager is set to null for a container then absolute positioning is used to layout the components. Each component will be sized and positioned according to its own parameters. The preferred size and position of the component will be respected.

The following is an example of a frame with its layout manager attribute set to null. Figure 13-10 is a visual representation.

```java
import java.awt.*;

public class NullLayoutExample {
    public static void main(String[] args) {
        Frame f = new
            Frame("No LayoutManager Example");
        f.setSize(300,300);
        f.setLayout(null);
        Button b1 = new Button("Button1");
        b1.setBounds(50,50,100,100 );
        Button b2 = new Button("Button2");
        b2.setBounds(100,100,100,100);
        Button b3 = new Button("Button3");
        b3.setBounds(150,150,100,100);
        f.add(b1);
        f.add(b2);
        f.add(b3);
        f.setVisible(true);
    }
}
```

FIGURE 13-10

An example of a LayoutManager set to null

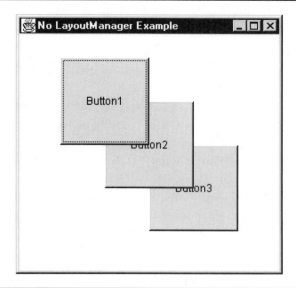

QUESTIONS AND ANSWERS

Describe the relationship between components and containers.	A component is a class that represents a widget. A container is a special kind of component that can contain other components.
Describe the relationship between containers and layout managers.	The container holds a collection of components. The layout manager of the container is responsible for sizing and positioning those components.
How does a child component get its color settings if it does not explicitly set them itself?	The child component inherits the color settings from the parent component.
You wish to create a top-level container that the user can resize. Which container do you use?	Frame. It is a top-level container that provides handles for resizing the Frame object.
You wish to create a splash screen that contains no decorations or menu bars. Which container do you use?	Window. It is a top-level container that has no decorations or menus.
Which of the layout managers provided in the JDK always respects the preferred size of the components within the container?	FlowLayout
Which of the layout managers provided in the JDK always ignores the preferred size of the components within the container?	GridLayout and CardLayout
Which of the layout managers only allows one component to be visible at any given time?	CardLayout

In the preceding example you can see how the preferred size and position of each component is respected. In this case it results in an overlap of components. Resizing the container has no effect on the components it contains.

Now that you have a better understanding of components, containers, and layout managers, here are some possible scenario questions and their answers.

CERTIFICATION SUMMARY

All nonmenu graphical widgets of the Java Development Kit extend from java.awt.Component. As a result, they all inherit the methods of that class. You can use any of the existing components or create your own. You can create new components by extending an existing component or from scratch by extending from java.awt.Component directly.

Containers are a special type of component that can contain other components. Because containers are components themselves, you can create nested containers.

Layout managers are responsible for the sizing and positioning of components within a container. Each layout manager handles this responsibility differently. If the layout manager attribute of a container is set to null then absolute positioning is used to render components within a container.

on the
!
() o b

An application's GUI design has far-reaching implications beyond initial development. The ease of use and layout of a GUI will influence the success of an application just as much as the functionality behind it. It is therefore imperative that a GUI behave and respond in a way that the user expects. It is with this in mind that layout managers were designed. Layout managers free the developer from having to worry about the look and feel of the application from platform to platform. Layout managers will automatically size and position components according to whatever constraints they are under. A number of layout managers are included with the java.awt package as shipped from Sun Microsystems. If one of them does not suit your particular needs, you have a couple of options. First, you can try to achieve your layout needs by nesting containers within each other. Nested containers, when properly implemented, can yield complex layouts without the need to create a brand new layout. If nested containers is not the answer, creating a new layout may be the solution.

TWO-MINUTE DRILL

❑ The java.awt.Component class is the abstract superclass for nonmenu graphical components.

❑ You can create a new component by extending an existing component subclass or by extending the java.awt.Component class directly.

❑ A container is a type of component that contains other components.

❑ A container is itself a subclass of component, so it is possible to nest containers within one another.

❑ A container uses a layout manager to position the components that it contains.

❑ The layout manager for a container determines the size and position of each component within a container.

❑ If no layout manager is specified for a container then absolute positioning is used to determine each component's position.

❑ The java.awt.LayoutManager2 interface provides for positioning and sizing components within a container according to a constraints object.

SELF TEST

The following questions will help you measure your understanding of the material presented in this chapter. Read all of the choices carefully, as there may be more than one correct answer. Choose all correct answers for each question.

1. Which of the following statements are true of the java.awt.Component class? (Choose all that apply.)
   A. It is the ultimate superclass for all nonmenu graphical components.
   B. It contains methods for handling events.
   C. It contains methods for rendering.

2. Which method is used to set the background color of a component?
   A. setColor(Color c)
   B. setBackground(Color c)
   C. setBackgroundColor(Color c)
   D. setForegroundColor(Color c)

3. Assume that you have a Panel, named p1, with a layout manager of BorderLayout. The background color of this panel is explicitly set to black and the foreground color is explicitly set to white. Now also assume that a new Panel, named p2, with a layout manager of FlowLayout is added to the first panel in the CENTER area. This new panel p2 has a foreground color that is explicitly set to red, but no background color is set. A label with some text in it is added to this second panel. No colors are set for this label. Which of the following sentences are accurate? (Choose all that apply.)
   A. The label text is white in color.
   B. The label text is red in color.
   C. The layout manager of panel p2 overrides the layout manager of panel p1.
   D. The panel p2 has a background color of black.
   E. The label in panel p2 fills the entire area of panel p2.

4. Suppose you extend the class java.awt.Button with a new class called NewButton. NewButton defines the following constructors:
```
public NewButton( String label ) { ... }
public NewButton( String label, Color color ) { ... }
```
   Now by definition the Button class has the following constructors:
```
public Button() { ... }
public Button( String label ) { ... }
```

Based upon this information, which statements that attempt to instantiate NewButton will compile? (Choose all that apply.)

A. NewButton nb = new NewButton("Start");

B. NewButton nb = new NewButton("Start", 4);

C. NewButton nb = new NewButton();

D. NewButton nb = new NewButton("Start", new Color(255,255,255));

5. Which of the following method signatures are correct for the setSize() method of Component? (Choose all that apply.)

A. setSize(int width, int height)

B. setSize(int x, int y, int width, int height)

C. setSize(Dimension dim)

D. None of the above.

6. The getSize() method of Component returns what data?

A. A single int.

B. A Dimension object.

C. A Rectangle object.

7. Which of the following method signatures are correct for the setLocation () method of Component? (Choose all that apply.)

A. setLocation (int width, int height)

B. setLocation (int x, int y, int width, int height)

C. setLocation (Point p)

D. setLocation(Dimension dim)

E. None of the above.

8. The getLocation() method of Component returns what data?

A. A single int.

B. A Dimension object.

C. A Point object.

9. Which of the following method signatures are correct for the setBounds () method of Component? (Choose all that apply.)

   A. setBounds (int width, int height)
   B. setBounds (int x, int y, int width, int height)
   C. setBounds (Point p)
   D. setBounds (Rectangle rect)
   E. None of the above.

10. The getBounds() method of Component returns what data?

    A. A Dimension object.
    B. A Rectangle object.
    C. A Point object.

11. Which methods are defined by java.awt.Container? (Choose all that apply.)

    A. add(Component c, index index)
    B. add(int index, Component c)
    C. add(Component c)
    D. add(Component c, Object constraints, Container parent)
    E. add(Component c, Object constraints)

12. Which of the following containers are top-level containers? (Choose all that apply.)

    A. Panel
    B. ScrollPane
    C. Window
    D. Frame

13. What is the default layout manager for a Panel container?

    A. BorderLayout
    B. CardLayout
    C. GridLayout
    D. GridBagLayout
    E. FlowLayout
    F. null

14. What is the default layout manager for a Frame container?

    A. BorderLayout

    B. CardLayout

    C. GridLayout

    D. GridBagLayout

    E. FlowLayout

    F. null

15. What is the default layout manager for a Window container?

    A. BorderLayout

    B. CardLayout

    C. GridLayout

    D. GridBagLayout

    E. FlowLayout

    F. null

16. Which of the following are valid area designations for the java.awt.BorderLayout layout manager? (Choose all that apply.)

    A. NORTH

    B. SOUTH

    C. TOP

    D. EAST

    E. MIDDLE

    F. CENTER

17. As part of your GUI design, you wish to have a dialog that contains five buttons arranged vertically. These buttons must take up all of the space provided by the container of the dialog. These buttons are allowed to vary in size but must be the same size as each other no matter how the dialog is resized. Which strategy would you use?

    A. Create a FlowLayout instance and pass that instance to the setLayout() method of the dialog's container. Then add each of the five buttons in turn to that container by calling the add(Component c) method for that container.

    B. Create a BorderLayout instance and pass that instance to the setLayout() method of the dialog's container. Then add each of the five buttons in turn to that container by calling the add(Component c) method for that container.

    C. Create a GridLayout instance using the constructor GridLayout(5,1) and pass that instance to the setLayout() method of the dialog's container. Then add each of the five buttons in turn to that container by calling the add(Component c) method for that container.

    D. null (no LayoutManager)

18. Assume that you have a Frame with a layout manager of FlowLayout. The alignment of the layout manager is LEFT. Which one sentence accurately describes the rendering of a Button added to this Frame?

    A. The Button is at the top of the Frame. Its width is that of the entire Frame and its height is the preferred height of that Button.

    B. The Button fills the entire Frame.

    C. The Button is at the top left of the Frame and both its height and width are of the preferred size.

    D. The Button is at the top right of the Frame and both its height and width are of the preferred size.

19. Assume that you have a panel that has a GridLayout as its layout manager. Which of the following statements is true regarding the placement of components within that container?

    A. The components are placed top to bottom, then left to right.

    B. The components are placed right to left, then top to bottom.

    C. The components are placed left to right, then top to bottom.

20. The number of columns and rows in a GridLayout are dictated by either setting them in the constructor or by calling the setRows() and setColumns() methods.

    A. True

    B. False

21. Which of the following LayoutManagers will respect all dimensions of a component's preferred size?

    A. FlowLayout

    B. GridLayout

    C. BorderLayout

    D. None of the above

JAVA™
SUN CERTIFIED PROGRAMMER®

14

The java.awt Package: Event Handling

CERTIFICATION OBJECTIVES

T he Java 2 event model is a key part of the Java programming language. Although normally associated with graphical components, any object can be implemented to generate or receive events. The event model allows components to publish information about their state to other objects by generating *event objects* and delivering them to *event listeners*.

Java Event and Event Listener Basics

The Java event mechanism consists of three participants:

- The event source
- The event object
- The event listener

In a nutshell, *event sources* create *event objects* and deliver them to *event listeners*. The event object is the medium used by the event source to deliver pertinent information about a change in state to the event listeners.

Event Objects

An event object embodies information related to a particular type of event. At a minimum, an event object contains a reference to the object that caused the event (the event source). Usually, the event object also contains other data such as mouse position or a timestamp.

All event objects are defined in event classes that subclass java.util.EventObject. EventObject defines the following method used to get a reference to the source of the event:

```
public Object getSource();
```

The class of the event defines the event type. For instance, the class FooEvent defines events of type Foo. The following is an example implementation of FooEvent:

```
public class FooEvent extends java.util.EventObject{
    public FooEvent(Object source){
        super(source);
    }
}
```

Event Sources

An event source is a component or object that generates events. Event sources have the following responsibilities:

- Provide methods that allow objects to add and remove themselves as listeners.

- Maintain a list of interested event listeners.

- Contain logic to create and deliver event objects of the appropriate type (class) to all interested event listeners.

An event source does not have to subclass any specific class or implement any specific interface. Additionally, an object can act as the source of multiple event types, provided that it fulfills the preceding responsibilities for each type.

The following is an example of a partial implementation of a class that generates Foo events:

```
public class FooEventGenerator{
    public void addFooListener(FooListener l){
        //Code to add listener to the list of listeners.
        ....
    }
    public void removeFooListener(FooListener l){
        // Code to remove listener from the list of listeners.
        ....
    }
```

```
private void notifyFooListeners(){
    // Create a FooEvent with this as the source.
    FooEvent fooEvent = new FooEvent(this);
    // Deliver the event.
    ....
    }
}
```

Event Listeners

For an object to receive a particular type of event, the object must implement the appropriate *listener interface.* All listener interfaces are subclasses of java.util.EventListener. EventListener does not define any methods and is used strictly as a marker interface. Each specialized listener interface defines at least one method that is used to deliver an event object to the listener. The method or methods defined in the listener interface normally take one parameter that is a subclass of EventObject. The following is an example definition of a FooEvent listener interface:

```
public interface FooListener extends java.util.EventListener{
    public void handleFooEvent(FooEvent evt);
};
```

The following is an example of how to write a class that implements the FooListener interface:

```
public class FooTest implements FooListener{
    // Implement the FooListener interface.
    public void handleFooEvent(FooEvent evt){
        System.out.println("Received FooEvent!");
    }
}
```

To receive events, event listeners must first register with an event source. Event listeners register for events using a well-known method provided by the event source. For example, instances of FooTest could register to receive FooEvents like this:

```
FooEventGenerator eventSource = new FooEventGenerator();
FooTest listener = new FooTest();
eventSource.addFooListener(listener);
```

Instances of FooTest could then unregister to receive FooEvents like this:

```
eventSource.removeFooListener(listener);
```

From the perspective of the event listener, events occur asynchronously. All events are delivered in the event source's thread of execution. Another way to think of this is that the event source *pushes* events to the event listeners.

The java.awt.event Package

The java.awt.event package contains all of the events and corresponding event listener interfaces associated with AWT components. *Adapter classes* are also provided to help the programmer develop classes that implement the event interfaces.

The AWTEvent class

All event classes defined in the java.awt.event package are subclasses of java.awt.AWTEvent, which is itself a subclass of java.util.EventObject. Note that AWTEvent is in the java.awt package, not the java.awt.event package. AWTEvent defines the following methods:

- **public int getID()**   Returns the event's integer event type.
- **protected void consume()**   Consumes the event.
- **protected boolean isConsumed()**   Tests to see if this event has been consumed.
- **public String paramString()**   Provides useful debug information.

Each AWTEvent has an integer *event type*. The event type is used to distinguish between events that share the same class but have a different purpose. For instance, a Mouse event is generated when a mouse button is pressed and released. The event type provided by the MouseEvent object can be used to determine which is the case.

AWT events can be consumed using the consume() method. This keeps them from being further processed by their underlying event source.

Events in the java.awt.event Package

Events in the java.awt.event package can be classified as either *semantic* or *low-level*. Semantic events occur as the result of a combination of low-level events. Semantic events tend to be associated with the primary purpose of the component that sources them. Take the semantic event ActionEvent for example. Button components fire Action events when the button is activated (pressed). TextField components fire Action events when the user enters text and then presses the ENTER key. Low-level events, on the other hand, are finer grained than semantic events and tend to occur at a higher frequency. For example, a TextField fires the low-level KeyEvent whenever the user presses any key, not just after the user presses the ENTER key.

Semantic Events

ActionEvent, ItemEvent, and TextEvent are the only semantic events defined in the java.awt.event package. They provide a high-level view into the component that sources them. For example, a Button component generates an ActionEvent when it is selected and is also enabled. This keeps the programmer from having to deal with combinations of low-level events, such as MouseEvents, directly. The following class hierarchy displays the semantic events defined in the java.awt.event package:

```
java.awt.AWTEvent
   |
   +-java.awt.event.ActionEvent
   |
   +-java.awt.event.ItemEvent
   |
   +-java.awt.event.TextEvent
```

ACTIONEVENT   ActionEvents occur as a result of the following actions:

- An item is double-clicked in a List component.
- A Button is selected.
- A MenuItem is selected.
- The ENTER key is pressed in a TextField component.

Each action event object contains a *command string* that can be accessed using the following method:

- **public String getActionCommand()**   Returns the command string for this ActionEvent object.

The command string contains data about the source or cause of the event. An Action event that is the result of a Button being activated contains the Button's text. An Action event that is the result of the ENTER key being pressed in a TextField component returns the entered text. Similarly, the text that represents a MenuItem or item in a List component is returned when a MenuItem or List is the source of the Action event.

The following method provides information about modifier keys, such as SHIFT or ALT, that were held down at the time of the event.

- **public int getModifiers()**   Returns the integer modifier field for this ActionEvent object.

The integer modifier field can be tested against public static values defined in ActionEvents that represent the various keys.

TEXTEVENT   TextEvents occur as a result of the following actions:

- Text is changed in a TextField component.
- Text is changed in a TextArea component.

ITEMEVENT   ItemEvents occur as a result of the following actions:

- A Check box is selected or cleared.
- A CheckboxMenuItem is selected or cleared.
- An item is selected in a Choice component.

■ An item or items is selected in a List.

ItemEvent provides the following methods:

■ **public Object getItem()** Returns the object affected by the selection. Note that this is not the same as the source component, but an object that represents the item that was selected in the source component. For example, getItem() would return a String that represents an item in a List.

■ **public ItemSelectable getItemSelectable()** Returns an ItemSelectable interface on the source component.

■ **public int getStateChange()** Returns an int value that is either ItemEvent.SELECTED or ItemEvent.DESELECTED.

Low-Level Events

The following hierarchy displays the low-level events defined in the java.awt.event package. The majority of these events are component events; that is, they subclass java.awt.event.ComponetEvent. The remaining events are AdjustmentEvent, InputMethodEvent, and InvocationEvent. InputMethodEvent and InvocationEvent are rarely used and will not be discussed in detail.

```
+-java.awt.AWTEvent
     |
     +-java.awt.event.InvocationEvent
     |
     +-java.awt.event.AdjustmentEvent
     |
     +-java.awt.event.InputMethodEvent
     |
     +-java.awt.event.ComponentEvent
          |
          +-java.awt.event.ContainerEvent
          |
          +-java.awt.event.FocusEvent
          |
          +-java.awt.event. PaintEvent
          |
          +-java.awt.event.WindowEvent
```

```
        |
        +-java.awt.event.InputEvent
                |
                +-java.awt.event.MouseEvent
                |
                +-java.awt.event.KeyEvent
```

COMPONENTEVENT   A component generates a ComponentEvent when the component's size, position, or visibility has changed. ComponentEvents are for notification purposes only. The AWT automatically adjusts the size, position, and visibility of components internally.

ComponentEvent defines the following method to get the source component of the event:

■ **public Component getComponent()**   Returns the event source as a Component.

The component returned by the getComponent() method is the same object that is returned by the getSource() method defined in EventObject. This is simply a convenience method that returns the source as a component, so that you do not have to cast the object returned by the getSource() method. ItemEvent, WindowEvent, and ContainerEvent provide similar methods (getItemSelectable(), getWindow(), and getContainer()) for the same purposes.

Note that ComponentEvent is a base class for many other low-level event classes.

CONTAINEREVENT   A *container* component, such as Panel, generates a ContainerEvent as a result of a child component being added or removed from the container. ContainerEvents are for notification purposes only. The AWT automatically handles changes to the contents of a Container component internally.

ContainerEvent defines the following methods:

■ **public Component getChild()**   Gets the affected child component.

■ **public Container getContainer()**   Returns the event source as a Container.

FOCUSEVENT   A component generates a FocusEvent when it gains or loses keyboard focus. The event ID is set to either FOCUS_GAINED or focus lost. There are two types of focus events, permanent and temporary. Permanent focus events indicate that another component has gained the focus, whereas temporary focus events indicate that the component has lost focus temporarily due to window deactivation or scrolling. FocusEvent defines the following method:

■ **public boolean isTemporary()**   Returns *true* if the focus was lost temporarily.

INPUTEVENT   InputEvent is an abstract class that serves as the base class for MouseEvent and KeyEvent. InputEvent defines the following method to determine the time of the event:

■ **public long getWhen()**   Returns a timestamp.

InputEvent provides the following methods that are used to determine modifier keys that were pressed when the event was generated:

■ **public int getModifiers()**   Returns the integer modifiers flag.
■ **public boolean isAltDown()**   Tests for the ALT key.
■ **public boolean isAltGraphDown()**   Tests for the ALT-GRAPH key.
■ **public boolean isControlDown()**   Tests for the CTRL key.
■ **public boolean isMetaDown()**   Tests for the META key.
■ **public boolean isShiftDown()**   Tests for the SHIFT key.

Input events are delivered to listeners before they are handled by their source component. This allows listeners and component subclasses to *consume* the event to keep the event from being processed in the default manner by the source. For example, consuming a mouse press event from a Button component will prevent the Button from being activated. InputEvent overrides the consume() method defined in AWTEvent and changes its visibility from *protected* to *public*. This allows listeners from other packages to consume the event.

KEYEVENT   A component generates Key events when it has the current input focus and the user presses a key. There are two basic types of Key events: *key pressed* events and *key typed* events. *Key typed* events are higher-level than key pressed events, and only occur when a logical sequence or combination that represents a character has been completed. For example, pressing SHIFT-A results in key typed event with the character *A*. The event type of a key typed event is KEY_TYPED.

KeyEvent provides the following method to get the character represented by a key typed event:

- **public char getKeyChar()**   Returns the character represented by a key typed event.

Key pressed events occur for keys that don't have an associated character, or that must be used in combination with other keys to form a logical character. These are keys such as function keys, up and down arrow keys, and the SHIFT key. The event types for key pressed events are KEY_PRESSED and KEY_RELEASED.

KeyEvent provides the following method, which returns a *virtual key code* constant that represents the key:

- **public int getKeyCode()**   Returns a virtual key code constant that represents the key.

Many virtual key code constants are defined in KeyEvent as public static int variables.

MOUSEEVENT   A component generates Mouse events in the following situations:

- A mouse button is pressed while the cursor is over the component.

■ A mouse button is released while the cursor is over the component.

■ A mouse button is clicked (pressed and released) while the cursor is over the component.

■ When the cursor enters or exits the component's boundaries.

■ Additionally, the component generates special *mouse motion events* in the following situations:

  ■ The mouse is moved while it is over the component.

  ■ The mouse is dragged (moved while a button is pressed) while it is over the component.

Mouse Motion events are special because they are delivered using a listener interface that is different from normal Mouse events. A separate interface is used because mouse motion events occur at a high volume and frequency, but are superfluous to a listener that is only interested in mouse-clicks. Therefore, it would be inefficient to deliver events for every movement of the cursor.

Mouse events contain information about click activity and cursor location. The methods pertaining to click activity are as follows:

■ **public int getClickCount()**   Returns the number of mouse-clicks.

■ **public boolean isPopupTrigger()**   True if the button pressed is the pop-up menu trigger for this platform.

The getClickCount() method is useful for testing for double-clicks. The isPopupTrigger() is necessary due to platform differences.

The getModifiers() method and *modifier flags*, defined in InputEvent, can be used to determine which mouse button was clicked. For example, the following code tests for a right mouse-click:

```
public void mouseClicked(MouseEvent e)
   if((e.getModifiers() & InputEvent.BUTTON3_MASK) != 0){
      System.out.println("Right Mouse Button Clicked!");
   }
}
```

MouseEvent defines the following methods to determine cursor location:

- **public int getX()**   Gets the x coordinate.
- **public int getY()**   Gets the y coordinate.
- **public Point getPoint()**   Gets the x and y coordinates as a Point object.
- **public void translatePoint(int x, int y)**   Translates the x and y coordinates by the given amount.

All coordinates are relative to the source component's coordinate system. The translatePoint() method is used to convert the coordinates to another coordinate system, such as that of the source component's container.

Note that there is no separate MouseMotionEvent class. MouseEvent objects are used for all Mouse Motion events, but as mentioned earlier, are delivered using a separate listener interface.

WINDOWEVENT   A window generates Window events in the following situations:

- A window is about to close.
- A window is opened or closed.
- A window is activated or deactivated.
- A window is iconified or de-iconified.

WindowEvent provides the following method to determine the window that caused the event:

- **public Window getWindow()**   Gets the source window.

ADJUSTMENTEVENT   ScrollBar and ScrollPane objects generate Adjustment events when their scroll position changes. Scrolling is handled internally by these components, so Adjustment events won't be discussed in detail.

PAINTEVENT   Paint events are used internally to ensure serialization of paint operations in the AWT event thread. They are not intended to be used like other events and will not be discussed here. Note that there is no corresponding listener interface for PaintEvent.

Implementing the Listener Interfaces

A listener class must implement the appropriate listener interface to receive a particular type of event. The java.awt.event package contains 13 listener interfaces. Table 14-1 is a summary of the events and their corresponding listener interfaces. Note that MouseEvent has two corresponding listener interfaces.

Each listener interface has one or more methods that must be implemented. In most cases, the methods in the listener interface determine

Event	Listener Interface
ActionEvent	ActionListener
AdjustmentEvent	AdjustmentListener
AWTEvent	AWTEventListener
ComponentEvent	ComponentListener
ContainerEvent	ContainerListener
FocusEvent	FocusListener
InputMethodEvent	InputMethodListener
ItemEvent	ItemListener
KeyEvent	KeyListener
MouseEvent	MouseListener MouseMotionListener
TextEvent	TextListener
WindowEvent	WindowListener

TABLE 14-1 Events and Their Listener Interfaces

the event type of the event. For example, MouseListener defines the following methods:

```
public void mouseClicked(MouseEvent e)
public void mousePressed(MouseEvent e)
public void mouseReleased(MouseEvent e)
public void mouseEntered(MouseEvent e)
public void mouseExited(MouseEvent e)
```

These methods correspond to the mouse event types MOUSE_CLICKED, MOUSE_PRESSED, MOUSE_RELEASED, MOUSE_ENTERED, and MOUSE_EXITED, respectively.

Listener Methods

Table 14-2 summarizes the listener interfaces and their corresponding methods.

To receive a particular type of event, an object must implement the appropriate listener interface and register as an event listener with the event source. It is usually a good idea to use the semantic events when possible, because they are typically easier to use and are more efficient. For instance, assume you want to know when a user presses a Button component. It is best to implement the ActionListener interface and not the MouseListener interface. This is because only one event will be delivered when the button is pressed. If you implement MouseListener, three events will be delivered, *mouse pressed, mouse released,* and *mouse clicked.*

The following is an example of how to implement the ActionListener interface using an inner class. The implementation is then registered with both a Button and a TextField to receive action events.

```
import java.awt.*;
import java.awt.event.*;

public class Foo extends Frame {
    public Foo() {
        final TextField text1 = new TextField();
```

```
        final Button button1 = new Button("Select Me!");
        ActionListener l = new ActionListener() {
           public void actionPerformed(ActionEvent e) {
              if(e.getSource() == button1) {
                 System.out.println("Button selected!");
              }
              else if(e.getSource() == text1) {
                 String text2 =
                    ((TextField)e.getSource()).getText();
                 String text3 = e.getActionCommand();
                 System.out.println("Text from ActionEvent
                    : " + text2);
                 System.out.println("Text from TextField :
                    " + text3);
              }
           }
        };
        button1.addActionListener(l);
        text1.addActionListener(l);
        setLayout(new GridLayout(2,1));
        add(button1);
        add(text1);
        pack();
        show();
     }

     public static void main(String args[]) {
        new Foo();
     }
  }
```

The Button fires an action event only when it is selected, and the TextField fires Action events only when the user presses ENTER. Consequently, the number of events being delivered is significantly less than if MouseListener and KeyListener had been implemented.

Note that TextField and Button are declared as final. This is necessary because they are being accessed from within an inner class.

Additionally, two different techniques for obtaining the text entered into the TextField are demonstrated. One uses the getCommandString() method provided by ActionEvent, and the other uses the getSource() method provided by EventObject to get a reference to the TextField and query it directly.

Listener Interface	Methods
ActionListener	actionPerformed(ActionEvent e)
AdjustmentListener	adjustmentValueChanged(AdjustmentEvent e)
ComponentListener	componentResized(ComponentEvent e) componentMoved(ComponentEvent e) componentShown(ComponentEvent e) componentHidden(ComponentEvent e)
ContainerListener	componentAdded(ContainerEvent e) componentRemoved(ContainerEvent e)
FocusListener	focusGained(FocusEvent e) focusLost(FocusEvent e)
ItemListener	itemStateChanged(ItemEvent e)
KeyListener	keyTyped(KeyEvent e) keyPressed(KeyEvent e) keyReleased(KeyEvent e)
MouseListener	mouseClicked(MouseEvent e) mousePressed(MouseEvent e) mouseReleased(MouseEvent e) mouseEntered(MouseEvent e) mouseExited(MouseEvent e)
MouseMotionListener	mouseDragged(MouseEvent e) mouseMoved(MouseEvent e)
TextListener	textValueChanged(TextEvent e)
WindowListener	windowActivated(WindowEvent e) windowClosed(WindowEvent e) windowClosing(WindowEvent e) windowDeactivated(WindowEvent e) windowDeiconified(WindowEvent e) windowIconified(WindowEvent e) windowOpened(WindowEvent e)

TABLE 14-2

Listener Interfaces and Their Methods

Using Adapter Classes to Implement Listener Interfaces

You may have noticed that certain listener interfaces, such as MouseListener and WindowListener, have quite a few methods. In many cases, you will only be interested in receiving certain event types but would still have to provide implementations for *all* methods in the listener interface. Of course, you could provide empty implementations for the methods of no interest, but that would be both painful and messy. Enter *adapter classes*.

Adapter classes are classes that implement a particular listener interface with empty implementations. This means that you can subclass an adapter and then override only the methods that you are interested in. The following example uses a MouseAdapter to listen for mouse-clicks that occur on a TextField, and then print out the location of the mouse cursor at the time of the click.

```
import java.awt.*;
import java.awt.event.*;
public class MouseDemo extends Frame
{
  public static class MouseListenerImpl extends MouseAdapter{
  public void mouseClicked(MouseEvent e){
     System.out.println("MouseEvent " + e.paramString() );
  };
}

public MouseDemo() {
   TextField text = new TextField();
   text.addMouseListener(new MouseListenerImpl());
   add(text);
   pack();
   show();
  }
  public static void main(String args[]) {new MouseDemo();}
}
```

It is common to use an anonymous inner class to specialize an adapter class. The following example uses an anonymous inner class to specialize WindowAdapter to exit an application when the user selects the Close button of the application's frame (window):

```
import java.awt.*;
import java.awt.event.*;

public class WindowTest{
    public static void main(String[] args){
        WindowListener closeListener = new WindowAdapter(){
            public void windowClosing(WindowEvent e){
                System.exit(0);
```

```
                }
            };
            Frame f = new Frame();
            f.addWindowListener(closeListener);
            f.pack();
            f.show();
        }
    }
```

Note that we override *windowClosing()* and not *windowClosed()*. Window closed event types only occur when dispose() is called on a window.

Table 14-3 summarizes the event adapter classes and their corresponding listener interfaces.

Enabling Events

Events can be explicitly enabled or disabled by subclasses of java.awt.Component using the following method along with event masks defined in java.awt.AWTEvent:

```
protected void enableEvents(long eventsToEnable)
```

Component automatically enables processing of an event type such as MouseEvent when the appropriate listener interface (in this example MouseListener or MouseMotionListener) is added. The only time this method is useful is when subclasses want to have event types delivered to processEvent() regardless of whether or not a listener is registered.

TABLE 14-3	Adapter Class	Listener Interface
Adapter Classes and Their Listener Interfaces	ComponentAdapter	ComponentListener
	ContainerAdapter	ContainerListener
	FocusAdapter	FocusListener
	KeyAdapter	KeyListener
	MouseAdapter	MouseListener
	MouseMotionAdapter	MouseMotionListener
	WindowAdapter	WindowAdapterListener

Event Naming

You may have noticed a naming convention for the AWT events, listeners, and adapters. For each event class there is a corresponding listener interface, and optionally, an event adapter. Additionally, there are methods used to add and remove listeners to the event source (Component). The naming convention is as follows:

Event Class	event nameEvent
Listener Interface	event nameListener
Adapter Class	event nameAdapter
Add Method	addlistenerInterface name
Remove Method	removelistenerInterface name

Let's use Window events as an example:

Event Class	WindowEvent
Listener Interface	WindowListener
Adapter Class	WindowAdapter
Add Method	addWindowListener
Remove Method	removeWindowListener

Note that there are a couple of exceptions to the naming conventions:

- Mouse Motion Listener corresponds to a MouseEvent, not a MouseMotionEvent.

- PaintEvent has no associated listener interface because it is primarily used to internally serialize paint requests.

- InvocationEvent has no associated listener interface. Invocation events are used to run a piece of code in the AWT event thread using the invoke() and invokeAndWait() methods. This is more of a utility than a part of the AWT event system, so invocation events were not discussed in this chapter.

It is important that you remember these exceptions to the naming conventions for the exam.

Now that you have a better idea of the java.awt package, here are some possible scenario questions and their answers.

QUESTIONS AND ANSWERS

What is the primary requirement for an object that wants to receive a certain type of event?	The object must implement the appropriate listener interface.
Which event types provide information about the time the event was generated?	KeyEvent and MouseEvent.
How do you get a reference to the event source? Is there more than one way to do this?	Use the getSource() method defined in EventObject. Also, other event classes provide more specialized versions. Examples are getWindow(), getComponent() , getContainer(), and getItemSelectable().

CERTIFICATION SUMMARY

The Java 2 event model consists of event sources, event objects, and event listeners. Event listeners must implement the appropriate listener interface and then register themselves as listeners with the event source.

AWT events can be classified as either semantic or low-level. Semantic events are more commonly used than low-level events. The three semantic events are ActionEvent, ItemEvent, and TextEvent.

Because all events are subclasses of EventObject, the source of the event can be obtained using the getSource() method.

Adapter classes provide empty implementations for many of the listener interfaces. This makes it easy to implement a listener interface by simply subclassing the appropriate adapter class.

TWO-MINUTE DRILL

❑ The three semantic events are ActionEvent, ItemEvent, and TextEvent.

❑ An object must implement the appropriate listener interface to receive a certain type of event.

❑ AWT events have an integer *event type* associated with them. This type can be accessed using the getID() method defined in AWTEvent.

❑ In many cases, you do not need to explicitly check the event type because there is a one-to-one mapping of event types to methods in the corresponding listener interface.

❑ AWT events can be consumed using the protected consume() method defined in AWTEvent. InputEvent subclasses AWTEvent and changes the visibility of consume() to public.

❑ Listeners of the Input events (MouseListener, MouseMotionListener, and KeyListener) process their corresponding events before the source component handles them. This allows them to consume the event, effectively hiding it from the source component.

❑ MouseEvent has two associated listeners: MouseListener and MouseMotionListener.

❑ The following components generate Action events: Button, List, MenuItem, and TextField.

❑ Subclasses of TextComponent (TextField and TextArea) generate TextEvents.

❑ InputEvent provides the getModifiers() method, which returns the modifier flags for that event. These flags can be tested against public *modifier mask* values defined in InputEvent. The modifier flags represent keys (such as SHIFT or ALT) that were pressed at the time of the input event. InputEvent also provides tester methods for many of these flags. Examples would be the isShiftDown() and isAltDown() methods.

❑ InputEvent provides the getWhen() method that can be used to get a timestamp representing the time that the event occurred.

❏ MouseEvent defines the getClickCount() method to test for double-clicks.

❏ MouseEvent provides the following methods to determine the mouse cursor position at the time of the mouse event: getX(), getY(), and getPoint().

❏ Adapter classes are provided for many of the listener interfaces. Adapter classes provide empty implementations of all of the methods in a listener interface. It is common practice to use an inner class (usually anonymous) to specialize an event adapter.

SELF TEST

The following questions will help you measure your understanding of the material presented in this chapter. Read all of the choices carefully, as there may be more than one correct answer. Choose all correct answers for each question.

1. Which is the best way to receive events when a Button component is activated (pressed)?
   A. Create an implementation of ButtonListener and add it as a listener to the Button component by invoking addButtonListener().
   B. Create an implementation of ActionListener and add it as a listener to the Button component by invoking addActionListener().
   C. Subclass ActionAdapter and override the actionPerformed() method. Then, add an instance of the subclass as a listener to the Button component by invoking addActionListener().
   D. Subclass MouseAdapter and override the mouseClicked() method. Then, add an instance of the subclass as a listener to the Button component by invoking addMouseListener().

2. Which of the following events are subclasses of InputEvent? (Choose all that apply.)
   A. MouseEvent
   B. WindowEvent
   C. MouseMotionEvent
   D. KeyEvent

3. Can an object be an event source and an event listener for the same type of event?
   A. Yes
   B. No

4. If you wanted to ensure that only numeric characters were entered in a TextField component, what is the best approach?
   A. Subclass KeyAdapter and implement the keyTyped() method to invoke the consume() method on any event representing a non-numeric character.
   B. Subclass KeyAdapter and implement the keyPressed() method to consume all events.
   C. Subclass KeyAdapater and implement the keyTyped() method to invoke setKeyChar(null) on any event representing a non-numeric character.
   D. Subclass KeyEvent and implement the keyTyped() method to consume any event representing a non-numeric character using the consume() method.

5. Which of the following events are paired with their appropriate listener interfaces?

   A. MouseEvent, Mouse Listener

   B. MouseMotionEvent, MouseListener

   C. MouseMotionEvent, MouseMotionListener

   D. InputEvent, InputListener

6. Which event classes support the getWhen() method? (Choose all that apply.)

   A. MouseEvent

   B. WindowEvent

   C. ActionEvent

   D. KeyEvent

7. How would you determine the time at which a MouseEvent was generated?

   A. Implement the MouseListener interface and call System.getCurrentTimeMillis() from within the implemented methods.

   B. Invoke the getTime() method on the MouseEvent object.

   C. Invoke the getWhen() method defined in the MouseAdapter class.

   D. Invoke the getWhen() method on the MouseEvent object.

8. Which of the following event classes are subclasses of ComponentEvent?

   A. TextEvent

   B. ActionEvent

   C. MouseEvent

   D. WindowEvent

9. A Mouse listener can keep other MouseListeners from receiving a Mouse event by invoking the consume() method on the MouseEvent object.

   A. True

   B. False

10. Which listener interfaces are paired with the appropriate event class?

    A. TextListener, TextFieldEvent

    B. MouseMotionListener, MouseMotionEvent

    C. ActionListener, ActionEvent

    D. KeyListener, KeyPressedEvent

11. Which of the following are valid uses for the flags returned by the getModifiers() method defined in InputEvent? (Choose all that apply.)

    A. Determining which mouse button caused a Mouse event.

    B. Determining whether the ALT key was pressed at the time of a Key event.

    C. Determining whether a Mouse event was caused by a double-click.

    D. Determining whether the SHIFT key was pressed at the time of a Key event.

12. Which listener interface would you implement to determine when components were added to a Panel?

    A. ComponentListener

    B. ContainerListener

    C. ActionListener

    D. InputListener

13. Which of the following is not true about adapter classes?

    A. They implement their corresponding listener interface.

    B. They provide empty implementations for every method in their corresponding interface.

    C. They are only useful for interfaces with more than one method.

    D. Using an adapter class is more efficient because only the methods that you override are invoked by the event source.

14. Which of the following listener interfaces have an associated adapter class? (Choose all that apply.)

    A. KeyListener

    B. ItemListener

    C. MouseListener

    D. ActionListener

    E. TextListener

15. Why does it not make sense to have an ActionAdapter class?

    A. Because ActionEvent is a low-level event.

    B. Because ActionListener is rarely used by developers.

    C. Because the ActionListener interface only defines one method.

    D. Because ActionListener serves only as a base interface for the other AWT listener interfaces and should not be implemented directly.

16. Which of the following properly implements the mouseClicked() method of MouseListener to print the (x, y) coordinates of a mouse-click? (Choose all that apply.)

    A.
```
public void mouseClicked(MouseEvent e){
    Point point = e.getPoint();
    System.out.println("Mouse click at (" + point.x + "," + point.y + ")");
};
```

    B.
```
public void mouseClicked(MouseEvent e){
    System.out.println("Mouse click at (" + e.getX() + "," + e.getY() + ")");
};
```

    C.
```
public void mouseClicked(MouseEvent e){
    System.out.println("Mouse click at (" + e.x + "," + e.y + ")");
};
```

    D.
```
public void mouseClicked(MouseEvent e){
    int x;
    int y;
    e.translatePoint(x,y);
    System.out.println("Mouse click at (" + x + "," + y + ")");
};
```

17. To enable events for a component, you must first invoke enableEvents() with the appropriate flags.

    A. True

    B. False

A

Self Test Answers

Chapter 1 Self Test

1. The following source file is given the name FirstClass.java.

```
import java.*;
public class FirstClass {}
public interface Second {}
abstract class SecondClass {}
```

What error will the compiler likely generate?

A. Package java not found in import.

B. Public class FirstClass must be defined in a file called FirstClass.java.

C. Public interface Second must be defined in a file called Second.java.

D. Class SecondClass may not be defined as abstract.

E. None. The file will compile fine.

C. There can be only one public class or interface per source file. *A* is not the answer because, although it does not end up importing any classes, it still compiles fine. *B* is not the answer because the filename matches the class name. *D* is not the answer because an abstract class is perfectly legal.

2. You have just entered some Java code into a source file. You now wish to save and compile it. Which of the following will work? (Choose all that apply.)

A. Save it in a file called MyClass.jav and compile with javac MyClass.jav.

B. Save it in a file called 1999Work.java and compile with javac 1999Work.java.

C. Save it in a file called MyClass.java and compile with javac MyClass.

D. Save it in a file called MyClass.java and compile with javac MyClass.java.

B, D. You must save it with the extension and specify the java extension when compiling. *B* works because numbers are allowed for the filename; however, if there was a public class this would not work because classes cannot be named with numbers. *A* does not work because it ends with *jav*. *C* does not work because the suffix *java* must be included when compiling.

3. Examine the following code:

```
import java.util.Vector;
public Vector v = new Vector();
class Test {
    public static void main (String [] args) {
        System.out.println("Good luck");
    }
}
```

What will happen if we try to compile and run this code?

A. The code will compile and run fine.

B. The code will compile fine, but an error will occur when the class is instantiated.

C. The code won't compile.

    C. The Vector variable is declared outside of a class, which is illegal.

4. You have just created a few classes in a source file called Server.java. There is a main class called Server, which begins the program. The top of this file has the line:

```
package com.syngress;
```

The classpath environment setting is properly set so it will look in c:\Java Packages for packages, and there is a subdirectory structure of c:\Java Packages\com\syngress\Server. Which of the following procedures will work?

A. You place the classes in the directory Server, and type the following:

```
c:\Java Packages\com\syngress\Server>java Server
```

B. You place the classes in the directory syngress, and type the following:

```
c:\Java Packages\com\syngress\Server>java com.syngress.Server
```

C. You place the classes in the directory syngress, and type the following:

```
c:\Java Packages\com\syngress>java Server
```

D. You place the classes in the directory Server, and type the following:

```
c:\>java com.syngress.Server
```

E. None of the above

    B. *B* works just fine, because you can run the class from any prompt. *A* is incorrect because the classes must be in the directory syngress. *C* will not work because you must specify com.syngress.Server. *D* will not work for the same reason that *A* does not work.

5. Which of the following top-level class definitions are legal? (Choose all that apply.)

A. private class A {}

B. class B {}

C. public class C {}

D. final class Class {}

E. abstract class E;

F. final abstract class F {}

    B, C, D. *A* is wrong because a class cannot be private. *E* is wrong because there must be curly braces instead of the semicolon, even for an abstract class. *F* is not legal because a final class can't be extended

6. Which of the following interface declarations are legal?

A. public interface A {int a();}

B. public interface B implements A {}

C. interface C {int a;}

D. private interface D {}

E. abstract interface E {}

A. *A* contains a legal method definition for an interface. *B* will not work because interfaces can only extend interfaces. *C* will not work because integers must be initialized in an interface. *D* will not work because an interface can't be private. *E* is wrong because interfaces can't be abstract.

7. You have just created a class that extends a Runnable interface.

```
public class Century implements Runnable {
    public void run () {
        for (int year = 1900;year < 2000;year++) {
            System.out.println(year);
            try {Thread.sleep(1000);} catch(InterruptedException e) {}
        }
        System.out.println("Happy new millenium!");
    }
}
class CountUp {
    public static void main (String [] args) {
        Century ourCentury = new Century();
        // INSERT POINT
    }
}
```

You now wish to begin the thread from another class. Which is the proper code, placed in the second class at the insert point, to begin the thread?

A. Thread t = new Thread(this);
t.start();

B. Thread t = new Thread(ourCentury);
ourCentury.start();

C. Thread t = new Thread(this);
t.start(ourCentury);

D. Thread t = new Thread(this);
ourCentury.run();

E. Thread t = new Thread(ourCentury);
t.start();

E. A thread object must be made, using the Thread() constructor, which accepts a Runnable interface as an argument. The next line starts the thread running.

8. Which of the following methods will compile properly when inserted into a class? (Choose all that apply.)

   A. public static final synchronized getPrice() {}

   B. public abstract int getPrice();

   C. public static final int getPrice() {}

   D. public final static int getPrice(int unit) {}

   E. protected volatile int getPrice() {}

   F. protected int static getPrice(int unit) {}

   B. *C* and *D* will not compile because they have no return value. *A* has no return type specified. *E* uses a variable keyword *volatile*. In *F*, the return type *int* must come directly before the identifier.

9. We would like to create a valid main() method that we can use to start a class from the command line. Which of these candidates will work? (Choose all that apply.)

   A. static public void main(String [] args) {}

   B. public static int main(String [] args) {}

   C. public static void main(String args []) {}

   D. public static void main(String [] contract) {}

   A, C, D. *A* works even though the keywords are in an unusual order. *C* works even though the array is defined in a different manner. *D* works even though the array is not identified as *args*. *B* does not work because it has a return type of *int*.

10. A summer student has just finished creating a class and wants you to review it:

```
class DataServer extends Server{
    public String serverName;
    public DataServer () {
        serverName = "Customer Service";
        super(serverName);
    }
}
```

What do you tell the programmer?

   A. The code will compile and run fine.

   B. The code will compile fine, but an error will occur when the class is instantiated.

   C. The code won't compile because the String serverName must be static.

   D. The code won't compile because of something in the DataServer() method.

   D. The super() method must be the first line of code in the constructor method. *B* is wrong because it won't compile at all. *C* is wrong because the DataServer() method is not static, therefore the String serverName may be manipulated within the method.

11. Which of the following variable definitions are legitimate if it is an instance variable? (Choose all that apply.)

    A. protected int a;

    B. transient int b = 3;

    C. public static final int c;

    D. volatile int d;

    E. private synchronized int d;

    A, B, C, D. *E* is incorrect because synchronized is a method keyword only.

12. Which one of these contains only Java keywords?

    A. class, Thread, void, long, if, continue

    B. goto, instanceof, native, finally, default, throws

    C. try, redo, throw, final, volatile, transient

    D. true, throws, super, implements, do

    E. null, byte, break, switch

    B. In *A*, Thread is a class and not a keyword. In *C*, redo is completely made up. In *D*, true is not a keyword but rather a literal, as is null in *E*.

13. Study the following class definition carefully:

    ```
    public class Test {
        public int t = 4;
        public static void main (String [] args) {
            new Test().NumberPlay();
        }
        public void NumberPlay() {
            int t = 2;
            t = t + 5;
            this.t = this.t - 2;
            t = t - this.t;
            System.out.print(t + " ");
            System.out.println(this.t);
        }
    }
    ```

    What is the output of this code going to be?

    A. 2 5

    B. −9 0

    C. 0 −9

    D. 5 2

E. 7 2

F. 2 7

D. In the code, *this.t* refers to the class member, and *t* refers to the local variable.

14. Assuming the array is declared as a class member, which of the following will declare an array of five elements?

A. int [] a = {23, 22, 21, 20, 19}

B. int [] array;

C. int array [] = new int[5];

D. int a [] = new int(5);

C. *A* does not work because there are no semicolons after the statement. *B* will declare an array but it does not initialize it with five integers. *D* does not work because the size of the array must be declared in square brackets.

15. Examine the following code:

```
public class LocalTest {
    public static void main(String [] args) {
        int i;
        System.out.print("int i = " + i);
        i = 20;
    }
}
```

If you try to compile and run this class, what will happen?

A. It will compile, but will produce an interpreter error when executed.

B. It will compile and output '0' to the screen.

C. It will not compile and will give a compiler error.

D. None of the above.

C. *A* does not work because the compiler will recognize that a local variable is being used before it is initialized. *B* does not work because local variables are not given default values.

16. Your manager has given you some insect population data.

Bees: 48057800

Ants: 2147483648

Spiders: 12934853

Mosquitoes: 35247914580

You are thinking of using the int data type to store these figures. Determine which of these insect populations could be stored in an int type.

A. Spiders

B. Bees, Spiders

C. Bees, Spiders, Ants

D. Mosquitoes, Bees, Spiders, and Ants

B. An integer has a maximum value of $2^{31} - 1$ (or 2147483647).

17. Examine the following code:

```
public class CheckDefault {
    private static boolean test;
    public static void showTest() {
        System.out.println(test);
    }
}
```

If we invoke the static method showTest(), what will the output be?

A. true

B. false

C. none, the class will not compile

B. A boolean variable is given a default of false.

18. Here are two literal numbers: 0x001B and 033. What are these numbers equal to?

A. 21 and 33

B. 21 and 27

C. 27 and 33

D. 33 and 33

E. 27 and 27

E. The first is a hexadecimal number and the second is octal.

19. We are given a two-dimensional array named *a* with the hypothetical dimensions *x* by *y*. In this example, *x* represents the size of the first array, and *y* represents the size of the second dimension of arrays. The value of *x* is 10. Which of the following can we use to determine the value of *y*?

A. a.length();

B. a.size();

C. a[0].length;

D. a.length(10);

E. a[].length;

C. *A* does not work because length is a variable and not a method. *B* does not work because there is no such size method. *D* does not work for the same reason that *A* does not work. *E* does not work because you must refer to the length of a specific array index.

20. Examine the following code:

```
import java.util.Date;
public class Y2K {
    public static void main(String [] args) {
        Date date;
        if (date == null)
            System.out.println("date is null");
    }
}
```

What will happen when we try to compile and run this class?

A. It will compile, but will produce an interpreter error when executed.

B. It will compile and output *date is null* to the screen

C. It will not compile and will give a compiler error.

D. None of the above.

C. The variable *date* is not initialized, so if we attempt to use the local variable *date* in any way, this will not compile.

Chapter 2 Self Test

1. A trading firm, Gardener, Ross, and Cunningham, has hired you to improve the code for its systems. They have an object that contains the names of their employees on the trading floor. The company representative, Sally Ross, is interviewing you for some consulting work. She shows you two objects:

```
package payroll;
class EmployeeNames{
    public static String [] names ={"Ian","Paul","Adam","Jansky"};
    public static String [] getNames() {
        return names;
    }
}
```

And the following:

```
package client;
import payroll.EmployeeNames;
class TraderNames extends EmployeeNames{
    public static String [] traders = {"Marty", "Ziggy", "Niko",
"Chris"};
}
```

She would like to know what will happen when these are compiled and instantiated. What do you tell her?

A. The file with class EmployeeNames will not compile.

B. The file with class TraderNames will not compile.

C. The files will both compile, but an error will occur when the class TraderNames is instantiated.

D. The files will compile, and when either class is instantiated, it will work fine.

B. This file will not compile because it does not have access to the class EmployeeNames. Default protection does not allow classes outside the package to access the class. *A* is incorrect because EmployeeNames is a properly defined class. *C* and *D* are incorrect because of the compile error TraderNames will produce.

2. Sally was obviously impressed by your answer and would like you to examine several other prototypes of their objects:

```
package payroll;
final class EmployeeNames{
    public static String [] names = {"Ian","Paul","Adam","Jansky"};
    public static String [] getNames() {
        return names;
    }
}
```

And the following:

```
package payroll; // New package
class TraderNames extends EmployeeNames{
    public static String [] Traders = {"Marty", "Ziggy", "Niko", "Chris"};
}
```

What do you tell her about the objects this time?

A. The file with class EmployeeNames will not compile.

B. The file with class TraderNames will not compile.

C. The files will both compile, but an error will occur when the class TraderNames is instantiated.

D. The files will compile, and when either class is instantiated, it will work fine.

B. This file will not compile because EmployeeNames is a final class. *A* is incorrect because EmployeeNames is a properly defined class. *C* and *D* are incorrect because of the compile error TraderNames will produce.

3. Sally shows you a third prototype for your opinion:

```
package payroll;
class EmployeeNames{
    public static String [] names = {"Ian","Paul","Adam","Jansky"};
    public static String [] getNames() {
```

```
return names;
     }
 }
```

And the following:

```
package payroll; // New package
abstract class TraderNames extends EmployeeNames{
    public static String [] Traders = {"Marty", "Ziggy", "Niko",
"Chris"};
 }
```

What will you tell her this time?

A. The file with class EmployeeNames will not compile.

B. The file with class TraderNames will not compile.

C. The files will both compile, but an error will occur when the class TraderNames is instantiated.

D. The files will compile, and when either class is instantiated, it will work fine.
   C. The class TraderNames can not be instantiated because it is an abstract class. *A* and *B* are incorrect because they will both compile fine. *D* is incorrect because class TraderNames can not be instantiated.

4. Sally pulls a fourth prototype out of her briefcase. You now begin to suspect that this is just a test to see how well you know your stuff.

```
package payroll;
class EmployeeNames{
    private static String [] names = {"Ian","Paul","Adam","Jansky"};
    public static String [] getNames() {
         return names;
    }
 }
```

And the following:

```
package payroll; // New package
class TraderNames extends EmployeeNames{
    public static String [] Traders =names;
 }
```

What will happen when these classes are compiled and run?

A. The file with class EmployeeNames will not compile.

B. The file with class TraderNames will not compile.

C. The files will both compile, but an error will occur when the class TraderNames is instantiated.

D. The files will compile, and when either class is instantiated, it will work fine.
B. This file will not compile because it does not have access to the array *names*. Private protection does not allow variables outside the class to access the variable. *A* is incorrect because it is a properly defined class. *C* and *D* are incorrect because of the compile error TraderNames will produce.

5. Sally seems very impressed so far, but she wants to be thorough in testing you. She shows you a fifth prototype:

```
package payroll;
public class UserConnection{
    protected final int MAXUSERS = 20;
    public static String getServerName() {
        return "Main Server";
    }
}
```

And the following:

```
package client;
import payroll.UserConnection;
class ServerConnection extends UserConnection{
    public final int MAXCONNECTIONS = MAXUSERS * 10;
}
```

What will happen when these classes are compiled and run?

A. The file with class UserConnection will not compile.

B. The file with class ServerConnection will not compile.

C. The files will both compile, but an error will occur when the class ServerConnection is instantiated.

D. The files will compile, and when either class is instantiated, it will work fine.
D. The files will compile fine. Protected access allows subclasses outside the package to access the variable MAXUSERS. *A*, *B*, and *C* are incorrect because both UserConnection and ServerConnection are properly defined classes that will run properly.

6. After your last answer, she throws you a knowing smile and pulls out a sixth piece of Java code:

```
package payroll;
public class UserConnection{
    final int MAXUSERS = 20;
    public static String getServerName() {
        return "Main Server";
    }
}
```

And the following:

```
package client;
import payroll.UserConnection;
```

```
class ServerConnection extends UserConnection{
     public final int MAXCONNECTIONS = MAXUSERS * 10;
}
```

What will happen when these classes are compiled and run?

A. The file with class UserConnection will not compile.

B. The file with class ServerConnection will not compile.

C. The files will both compile, but an error will occur when the class ServerConnection is instantiated.

D. The files will compile, and when either class is instantiated, it will work fine.

B. This file will not compile because it does not have access to the variable MAXUSERS. Default access does not allow a subclass outside the package to access the variable. *A* is incorrect because UserConnection is a properly defined class. *C* and *D* are incorrect because ServerConnection will not compile and therefore may not be instantiated.

7. She comments that no applicant has done this well so far, as she pulls out a seventh piece of code for examination.

```
package payroll;
public class UserConnection{
     protected int users = 0;
     public static String getServerName() {
          return "Main Server";
     }
}
```

And the following:

```
package client;
import payroll.UserConnection;
class ServerConnection {
   UserConnection u = new UserConnection();
   u.users += 1;
}
```

What will happen when these classes are compiled and run?

A. The file with class UserConnection will not compile.

B. The file with class ServerConnection will not compile.

C. The files will both compile, but an error will occur when the class ServerConnection is instantiated.

D. The files will compile, and when either class is instantiated, it will work fine.

B. This file will not compile because it does not have access to the variable *users*. Protected access does not allow variables outside the package to access the variable. **A** is incorrect because UserConnection is a properly defined class. *C* and *D* are incorrect because ServerConnection will not compile and therefore may not be instantiated.

8. Sally nods her head and passes you another. You feel nervous, and wonder how you are doing so far. She promises there are only two more to go.

```
package server;
public class ServerNames{
      abstract public static String sendName();
}
```

What will happen when the class is compiled and run?

A. The file will not compile.

B. The file will compile, but an error will occur when the class ServerNames is instantiated.

C. The file will compile, and when the class is instantiated, it will work fine.

A. This file will not compile because this class contains an abstract method, but the class itself is not declared as abstract. *B* and *C* are incorrect because class ServerNames will not compile.

9. Sally hands you the final prototype and leans back in her chair.

```
package server;
public class ServerNames{
      protected final int MAXUSERS = 20;
      public final static String sendName() {
            return "Main Server";
      }
}
```

And the following:

```
package client;
import server.ServerNames;
class Retrieve extends ServerNames{
      public final int MAXCONNECTIONS = MAXUSERS * 10;
      public static String sendName(String s) {
            return s;
      }
}
```

What will happen when these classes are compiled and run?

A. The file with class ServerNames will not compile.

B. The file with class Retrieve will not compile.

C. The files will both compile, but an error will occur when the class Retrieve is instantiated.

D. The files will compile, and when either class is instantiated, it will work fine.

D. This file will compile because it has access to the protected variable MAXUSERS. Protected access allows subclasses outside the package to access the variable.

A, B, and *C* are incorrect because ServerNames and Retrieve are properly defined classes that will run properly.

10. You are creating a small class for a call center. The class will keep track of the number of users who log in.

```
class TestServer {
    static int users = 0;
    public void logIn() {
        users += 1;
    }
}
```

What will happen when this class is compiled and run?

A. The file will not compile.

B. The file will compile, but an error will occur when the class is instantiated.

C. The file will compile, and when either class is instantiated, it will work fine.
   C. This class works because a static variable may be modified in an instance method. *A* and *B* are incorrect because the file will compile and run properly.

11. You try another piece of prototype code to test static members.

```
class TestServer {
    int users = 0;
    static public void logIn() {
        users += 1;
    }
}
```

What will happen when this class is compiled and run?

A. The file will not compile.

B. The file will compile, but an error will occur when the class is instantiated.

C. The file will compile, and when either class is instantiated, it will work fine.
   A. This class does not compile because a static method may not modify an instance variable. *B* and *C* are incorrect because the file will not compile.

12. Examine the following piece of code:

```
class TestVariable {
    int users = 1;
    public TestVariable() {
        this(2);
        users += 1;
    }
    public TestVariable(int users) {
        users -= 2;
        this.users += 1;
    }
}
```

The class is instantiated with the following line of code:

```
TestVariable t = new TestVariable();
```

What is the value of users after TestVariable has been instantiated?

A. 5

B. 4

C. 3

D. 2

E. 1

F. The class TestVariable will not compile.

C. The method TestVariable() will invoke the TestVariable(int user) method, which only increments the instance variable by 1 (this.user). The automatic variable *user* does not affect the instance variable *user*. *A, B, D* and *E* are incorrect because of incorrect values for TestVariable. *F* is incorrect because this class compiles.

13. Examine the following piece of code:

```
class TestServer {
    public TestServer() {
        int users = 1;
    }
    public void increment() {
        users = users + 1;
    }
    public static void main(String [] args){
        increment();
        System.out.println("Variable users = " + users);
    }
}
```

What will the output of this class be?

A. Output is 1.

B. Output is 2.

C. The file will compile, but will give an error when run.

D. The file will not compile.

D. This class does not work because the int variable users is only declared as an automatic variable. It should be declared as an instance or static variable. *A, B,* and *C* are incorrect because the compiler will detect there is no class variable declaration named users.

14. Examine the following piece of code:

```
class TestServer {
    final int users = 20;
    public TestServer() {
        int users = this.users * 10;
    }
    public static void main(String [] args){
        System.out.println("Variable users = " + users); .
    }
}
```

What will the output of this class be?

A. Output is 200.

B. Output is 20.

C. The file will compile, but will give an error when run.

D. The file will not compile.

B. The final variable may be used to define other variables. The automatic variable *users* may also be defined. *A* is wrong because it is the automatic variable *users* that is multiplied by 10, not the instance variable. *C* and *D* are incorrect because the class is defined properly and will compile and run fine.

15. Examine the following code:

```
class SuperServer {
    public SuperServer() {
        System.out.print(35);
    }
    public SuperServer(int y) {
        y = y + 2;
        System.out.print(y);
    }
}
class TestServer extends SuperServer{
    public TestServer(int y) {
        y = y * 10;
        System.out.print(y);
    }

    public static void main(String [] args){
        TestServer ts = new TestServer(10);
    }
}
```

What will the output of this class be?

A. 12100

B. 10012

C. 1224

D. 35100

D. The default SuperServer constructor is run first, followed by the TestServer constructor. *A*, *B*, and *C* are incorrect because these numbers will not be produced given the order the constructors are invoked.

16. Examine the following code:

```
class SuperServer {
    public SuperServer() {
        System.out.print(" all ");
    }
    public SuperServer(int y);
        this();
        System.out.println {" good ");
    }
}
class TestServer extends SuperServer{
    public TestServer(int y) {
        System.out.print(" things ");
    }
    public TestServer() {
        super(10);
        System.out.print(" come ");
    }
    public static void main(String [] args){
        TestServer ts = new TestServer(10);
    }
}
```

What will the output of this class be?

A. good things

B. all things come

C. all things

D. all good things

C. The default SuperServer constructor is run first, followed by the code in the TestServer(int y) constructor. *A*, *B*, and *D* are incorrect because these sentences will not be produced given the order the constructors are invoked.

17. Which of the following methods are legal?

```
class Force

{
    public short Jerec() {
        byte Kyle = 20;
        return Kyle;
    }
    public int Pic() {
        long Gorc = 200;
        return Gorc;
    }
    public Boolean Sariss() {
        boolean Boc = true;
        return Boc;
    }
    public long Maw() {
        float Yun = 2000F;
        return Yun;
    }
}
```

A. Jarec

B. Pic

C. Sariss

D. Maw

A. A method with a declared return type of short may return a byte.
B is incorrect because a long is larger than an int, therefore long is an illegal return type. *C* is incorrect because a Boolean object is the declared return type, but the method tries to return a primitive boolean. *D* is incorrect because a long cannot store a float type, therefore a float is illegal as a return value.

18. Which of the following methods are legal?

```
class Music/ {
    public float airbag() {
        long airbag = 1980;
        return airbag;
    }
    public float paranoidAndroid() {
        double paranoidAndroid = 2056;
        return paranoidAndroid;
    }
```

```
        public double subterraneanHomesickAlien() {
            float subterraneanHomesickAlien = 2623.12F;
            return subterraneanHomesickAlien;
        }
        public double letDown() {
            byte letDown = 2000;
            return letDown;
        }
    }
```

A. airbag

B. paranoidAndroid

C. subterraneanHomesickAlien

D. letDown

A, C, and D. All of these methods return types that are smaller than themselves. *B* is incorrect because a double is larger than a float, therefore it is illegal to use it as a return value.

19. You have created some classes for a supermarket database. The following are some of the classes you have created so far:

```
class Food implements Eatable{}
class Vegetable extends Food {}
class GreenPeas extends Vegetable {}
class Meat extends Food {}
```

You have also programmed a method, as follows:

```
public Vegetable getSomething() {
        // returns something here
}
```

Choose all of the legal lines that could be inserted into the method getSomething().

A. return new Vegetable();

B. return new Food();

C. return new Meat();

D. return new GreenPeas();

A and D. Vegetable is of course a legal return type, as is declared in the method getSomething(). GreenPeas is also a Vegetable, since it is a subclass of Vegetable. *B* is incorrect because Food is the superclass of Vegetable. *C* is incorrect because meat is not of type vegetable.

20. You have created some classes for a supermarket database. The following are some of the classes you have created so far:

```
class Food{}
class Vegetable extends Food implements Eatable{}
class GreenPeas extends Vegetable {}
class Meat extends Food implements Eatable{}
```

You have also programmed a method as follows:

```
public Eatable getSomething() {
      // returns something here
}
```

Choose all of the legal lines that could be inserted into the method getSomething().

A. return new Vegetable();

B. return new Food();

C. return new Meat();

D. return new GreenPeas();

A, C, and D. Vegetable, Meat, and GreenPeas are all of type Eatable. GreenPeas inherits the Eatable methods and variables from Vegetable. *B* is incorrect because in this example Food is not implementing Eatable.

Chapter 3 Self Test

1. Your company hired a contractor to write several classes for a sales software package. Unfortunately, his term has expired and now it is up to you to work out any bugs left in the classes. You examine the first class:

```
import java.util.Date;
class  TimeStamp{
    public static void main (String [] args) {
        Date d = new Date();
        addDay(d); // *
    }
    public static void addDay(Date old) {
        long newTime = old.getTime() + 60*60*24*1000;
        old.setTime(newTime);
    }
}
```

When the object *d* is initialized, it stores the current date and time. The date method setTime() will reset the time to whichever value is passed to it. Approximately what value will the Date object *d* have after the method addDay() is run?

A. Approximately the present time.

B. Something other than the present time.

C. Nothing, this class will not compile.

> **B.** The variable *d* is passed by reference to the method addDay(). This method adds one whole day to the present time. *A* is incorrect because the reference variable *old* refers to the exact same object as *d* does, hence it is not passed as a copy. *C* is incorrect because there is nothing wrong with this code.

2. This class was programmed to keep track of inventory using a special numbering system. The convertCode() method creates a unique inventory number:

```
class   Inventory{
     public static void main (String [] args) {
          int code = 237;
          convertCode(code); // *
     }
     public static void convertCode(int inv) {
          inv = inv + 100000;
     }
}
```

What will the variable code equal after the method convertCode() is run?

A. 237

B. 100237

C. Nothing, this class will not compile.

> **A.** The variable code is passed by value to the method convertCode(), so any changes made within the method will not change the original variable. *B* is incorrect because the variable inv behaves like a copy of code. *C* is incorrect because there is nothing wrong with this code.

3. The contractor didn't even have time to compile the next piece of code. You have a feeling that there may be something wrong with this:

```
import java.awt.*;
class CompareTest {
     static public void main(String [] args) {
          Component b = new Button("Exit");
          boolean compare = b.instanceof (Button);
     }
}
```

Which lines do you think contain errors?

A. class CompareTest {

B. static public void main(String [] args) {

C. Component b = new Button("Exit");

D. boolean compare = b.instanceof (Button);

E. Nothing is wrong with this class.

   D. instanceof is an operator, not a method. *A, B,* and *C* are all properly defined class lines.

4. The contractor has started a Ticker class to post the company stock price.

```
import java.awt.*;
class Ticker extends Component {
    public static void main (String [] args) {
        Ticker t = new Ticker();
        // Insert statement here
    }
}
```

Which of the following statements could legally be inserted into this code?
(Choose all that apply.)

A. boolean test = (t instanceof Ticker);

B. boolean test = t.instanceof(Ticker);

C. boolean test = (t instanceof Component);

D. boolean test = t.instanceof(Object);

E. boolean test = (t instanceof String);

   A, C. *A* is correct because class type Ticker is part of the hierarchy of *t*. *C* is also correct because Component is part of the hierarchy of *t*. *B* and *D* are incorrect because the statement is used as a method, which is illegal. *E* is incorrect because the String class is not in the hierarchy of the *t* object.

5. What will the output be when the following code is compiled and executed?

```
class Equals {
    public static void main(String [] args) {
        int x = 100;
        double y = 100.1;
        boolean b = (x = y);
        System.out.println(b);
    }
}
```

A. True

B. False

C. Nothing, the code will not compile.

D. Nothing, the code will compile but not execute.

 C. The code will not compile because in line five, the line will only work if we use (x == y) in the line. The == operator compares values to produce a boolean, and the = operator assigns a value to variables. *A, B,* and *D* are incorrect because the code does not get as far as compiling.

6. Which of the following comparisons are legal to use in code? (Choose all that apply.)

A. 'a' == 'b'

B. 12.1 == 12L

C. 'a' == true

D. 'a' == 12

E. 1 == true

 A, B, D. *A* is correct because any two primitives of the same type are legal to compare. *B* is correct because any number primitives may be compared for equality, even float and integer types. *D* is correct because char primitives may be compared to numbers. *C* and *E* are incorrect because boolean values may only be compared exclusively with each other. It is illegal to compare a boolean with anything but a boolean.

7. What will be the output from the following program?

```
import java.awt.Button;
class CompareReference {
    public static void main(String [] args) {
        Button a = new Button("Exit");
        Button b = new Button("Exit");
        Button c = a;
        System.out.println((a == b) + " " + (a == c));
    }
}
```

A. true false

B. true true

C. false true

D. false false

E. Nothing, this will not compile.

 C. Button *a* and *b* are separate objects, and therefore the reference variables are not equal (false). Button *c* refers to the same object as Button *a*, therefore the reference variables are equal (true). *A, B,* and *D* are incorrect for the same reasons described previously. *E* is incorrect because this is a properly defined class.

8. Which of the following lines of code are illegal? (Choose all that apply.)

    A. x =% 3;

    B. x++;

    C. String animal = "Gray Elephant" – "Gray ";

    D. --y;

    E. String animal = "Gray " + "elephant";

    A, C. *A* is illegal because the shorthand should be %=. *C* is illegal because the – operator may not be used with strings. *B* and *D* are legal because the increment and decrement operators may be used before or after the variable. *E* is legal because the + operator may be used to concatenate two strings together.

9. The following program was written by the contractor to keep track of the number of times people have logged in. What will be the output of the following program?

    ```
    class Logins {
        static int users = 0;
        public static void main (String [] args) {
            System.out.print (++users);
            System.out.print (users++);
        }
    }
    ```

    A. 01

    B. 02

    C. 12

    D. 11

    E. None of the above

    D. The first line increments the variable users by one, then outputs it as 1. The second line outputs the variable, then increments it; hence the value sent to output is 1. *A, B,* and *C* are incorrect for the reasons stated previously.

10. The following program uses bit shifting. What is the output from the following program?

    ```
    class BitShift {
        public static void main(String [] args) {
            int x = 0x80000000;
            System.out.print(x + " and ");
            x = x >> 31;
            System.out.println(x);
        }
    }
    ```

A. -2147483648 and 1

B. 0x8000000 and 0xffffffff

C. −214783648 and -1

D. −1 and −214783648

E. None of the above

C. The >> operator moves bits to the right, keeping the sign bit. The bit transformation looks like this:

before 1000 0000 0000 0000 0000 0000 0000 0000

after 1111 1111 1111 1111 1111 1111 1111 1111

A is incorrect because the >> operator keeps the bit, so it fills up with 1s, as shown. *B* is incorrect because the output method print always displays integers in decimal format. *D* is incorrect because this is the reverse order of the two output numbers. *E* is incorrect because *C* is right.

11. What is the output from the following bit-shift program?

```
class BitShift {
    public static void main(String [] args) {
        int x = 0x80000000;
        System.out.print(x + " and  ");
        x = x >>> 31;
        System.out.println(x);
    }
}
```

A. -2147483648 and 1

B. 0x8000000 and 0x00000001

C. −214783648 and -1

D. 1 and −214783648

E. None of the above

A. The >>> operator moves all bits to the right, including the sign bit. The bit transformation looks like this:

Before: 1000 0000 0000 0000 0000 0000 0000 0000

After: 0000 0000 0000 0000 0000 0000 0000 0001

C is incorrect because the >>> operator moves the sign bit, so it travels right, as shown. *B* is incorrect because the output method print always displays integers in base 10. *D* is incorrect because this is the reverse order of the two output numbers. *E* is incorrect because *A* is right.

12. What is the output from the following program?

```
class Bitwise {
    public static void main(String [] args) {
        int x = 11 & 9;
        System.out.println(x);
    }
}
```

A. 20

B. 9

C. 11

D. 2

B. The & operator produces a 1 bit when both bits are 1. The equation is as follows: 1011 & 1001 = 1001 (or 9 in decimal). *A* is wrong because we are not adding two decimal numbers together. *C* is wrong because we are not choosing one bit or the other. *D* is wrong because we are not choosing only bits that are complements.

13. What is the output from the following program?

```
class Bitwise {
    public static void main(String [] args) {
        int x = 10 | 5;
        System.out.println(x);
    }
}
```

A. 15

B. 0

C. 9

D. 2

A. The | operator produces a 1 bit when one or the other bits are 1. The equation is as follows:

1010 & 0101 = 1111 (or 15 in decimal)

B is wrong because the equation is not using the & operator. *C* and *D* are both incorrect results.

14. What will be the result of compiling and running the following code?

```
class AssignmentOps {
    public static void main(String [] args) {
        int x=2;
        String sup = (>15000)?"Pencil":(>=5)?"Eraser":"Pen";
```

```
                System.out.println(sup);
        }
    }
```

A.   Pencil

B.   Eraser

C.   Pen

D.   This code will not compile

   D. Assignment operators must use a boolean test. The brackets in the code should contain the variable *x*.

   A, B, and *C* are incorrect because this will not compile.

15.   Which of the following are legal lines of code? (Choose all that apply.)

A.   int w = (int)888.8;

B.   byte x = (byte)1000L;

C.   long y = (byte)100;

D.   byte z = (byte)100L;

   A, B, C, D. *A* is correct because when a floating-point number (a double in this case) is casted to an int, it simply loses the digits after the decimal. *B* and *D* are correct because a long can be cast into a byte. If the long is over 127, it reverts back to −128. *C* actually works, even though a cast is not necessary, because a long can store a byte.

16.   Examine the following classes:

```
class Hardware {}
class Monitor extends Hardware{}
class HardDrive extends Hardware{
    public void test() {
        Monitor a = new Monitor();
        Hardware b = new Monitor();
        HardDrive c = (HardDrive)a;
        Monitor d = b;
    }
}
```

Which of the preceding lines are illegal? (Choose all that apply.)

A.   Monitor a = new Monitor();

B.   Hardware b = new Monitor();

C.   HardDrive c = (HardDrive)a;

D.   Monitor d = b;

   C, D. *C* is illegal because the *a* variable is of type Monitor, which is not in the same hierarchy as HardDrive. *D* is illegal because a cast must be used to assign the Monitor variable *d* to Hardware type *b*. *A* and *B* are wrong because they are both legal object declarations.

17. Examine the following code:

```
class StringLiteral {
    public static void main(String[] args) {
        String java = "Java", va = "va";
        System.out.println(java == "Java");
        System.out.println(java == ("Ja"+"va"));
        System.out.println(java == ("Ja"+va));
        System.out.println(java.equals("Ja"+va));
    }
}
```

What will be the order of booleans produced by this program?

A. true true true true

B. true false false true

C. true true false true

D. true false false false

C. Lines four and five compare two strings that are created at compile time with the same string, and therefore equal. Line six compares a string created at runtime, therefore they refer to different objects in memory. Line seven uses the equals() method, which compares the character contents of a two strings. *A, B,* and *D* are incorrect for the preceding reasons.

18. Examine the following code:

```
class Equals {
    public static void main(String [] args) {
        Boolean a = new Boolean(true);
        Boolean b = new Boolean(true);
        System.out.println(a.equals(b));
        System.out.println(a == b);
    }
}
```

What is the order of boolean values produced from this program?

A. true true

B. true false

C. false true

D. false false

B. When the equals() method is used on Boolean objects, it compares the boolean property of the objects (true), but when we compare the reference variables using == it returns false because they are distinct objects.

19. Examine the following code:

```
class ReferenceTest {
    public static void main (String [] args) {
        int a = 1;
        ReferenceTest rt = new ReferenceTest();
        System.out.print(a);
        rt.modify(a);
        System.out.print(a);
    }
    void modify(int number) {
        number = number + 1;
    }
}
```

What will be the output?

A. 12

B. 10

C. 11

D. Nothing, this class will not compile.

C. The variable *a* is passed to the method modify() by value. *A* and *B* are incorrect because the variable *a* is not changed at all within the method modify(). *D* is incorrect because this code compiles fine.

20. Examine the following code:

```
import java.awt.Dimension;
class ReferenceTest {
    public static void main (String [] args) {
        Dimension d = new Dimension(5,5);
        ReferenceTest rt = new ReferenceTest();
        System.out.print(d.height);
        rt.modify(d);
        System.out.println(d.height);
    }
    void modify(Dimension dim) {
        dim.height = dim.height + 1;
    }
}
```

What is the output from this code?

A. 55

B. 56

C. 01

D. 00

E.   Nothing, this class will not compile.

B. When objects such as *d* are passed to a method they are passed by reference, which means any changes to the object within the method change the same object outside the method as well. *A* is incorrect because, unlike primitives, objects are passed by reference. *C* and *D* are incorrect because the width and height are initialized as five. *E* is incorrect because this class is properly defined.

Chapter 4 Self Test

1. Will the following code compile?

```
int I = 1;
long L = 2;
if (I == 1) && (L == 2)
{
      System.out.println("Inside if statement");
}
```

A.   Yes

B.   No

B. The code will not compile because the compiler will not realize that this is a compound expression. For it to work, you need to put a set of parenthesis around all the conditions that are applicable to the if statement.

2. Which parts of a for loop are required? (Choose all that apply.)

A.   Initialization

B.   Condition

C.   Increment

D.   None of the above

D. Even though these are the possible sections of the for statement, none of them are required. If all three are left out, the program execution will enter the loop, and will not exit unless a break statement is used.

3. There is one error in the following code. What is it?

```
for (int I = 0; I < 10;)
{
      if ( I = 0 )
            System.out.print("I equals 1");
      I++;
}
```

A. If *I* is initialized in the for loop, it must be incremented in the for loop.

B. In Java, there must be brackets after an if statement.

C. There is something else wrong with the code.

D. There is nothing wrong with the code.

C. The problem with the code is that there is an assignment in the if statement, as opposed to a relational expression. You should expect questions like this one on the exam. *A* is not correct because it is perfectly legal to increment the variable that is initialized in a for loop. *B* is incorrect because you do not need to use brackets if the body of the if statement is only one line.

4. The use of the break statement causes what to happen when it is unlabeled? (Choose all that apply.)

A. The current iteration of a loop to stop and the next line of code after the loop to start.

B. The current iteration of a loop to stop and the next iteration to start.

C. An exit from all loops.

D. An exit from a switch statement.

A, D. When a break statement is used in an unlabeled manner it has the ability of causing both *A* and *D* to happen. *B* is incorrect, this is what the continue statement does. *C* is incorrect because the unlabeled break statement only affects the innermost loop or switch.

5. What are the valid types for the expression in a switch statement? (Choose all that apply.)

A. int

B. long

C. byte

D. String

A, C. The only valid values for a switch statement are byte, short, int, and char. No objects, floating-point numbers, or boolean values are acceptable in this statement. *B* and *D* are incorrect because they are not one of the four acceptable types (byte, short, int, and char).

6. What will be the value of *I* when it is printed?

```
int I = 0;
outer: while (true) {
    I++;
    inner: for (int j = 0; j < 10; j++) {
        I += j;
        if (j == 3)
            continue inner;
```

```
      break outer;
   }
      continue outer;
}
System.out.println("I is " + I);
```

A. 1

B. 2

C. 3

D. 4

A. I will be incremented by one after it enters the first loop. Then, I will be incremented by zero. The if statement evaluates to false and the continue statement never gets executed. The next line of code tells the program to break out of the outer loop. At the time that I is printed, the value is still 1.

7. You are writing a program that uses a switch statement. You need to have the switch statement do something if there are no matches found for the condition. What Java keyword should you use?

A. case

B. default

C. else

D. do

B. If you need to simulate the else from an if...else statement, you need to use the default keyword in a switch statement. The others are not applicable to that part of a switch statement. *A* is incorrect, the case statement is used to mark the various conditions inside a switch statement. *C* is incorrect, the else keyword is used in conjuction with the if statement, not the switch statement. *D* is incorrect, the do keyword is a looping construct unrelated to switch statements.

8. Which looping construct are you guaranteed to enter?

A. while

B. do-while

C. for

D. None of them

B. Because the condition of the do-while is not checked until after the execution of the loop, you are guaranteed to have it execute at least once. *A* and *C* are incorrect because both while and for loops check the condition before entering the loop, and if the condition is false, the loop body may not be entered.

9. Will the following code compile?

```
int I = 0;
while ( 1 )
{
      System.out.print("I plus one is " + (I + 1));
}
```

A. Yes

B. No

B. Using the integer 1 in the while statement, or any other looping or conditional construct for that matter, will result in a compiler error. You should replace the 1 with the word *true*.

10. What would be the output of the following code block?

```
for (int I = 0; I < 2; I++)
{
      switch (I)
      {
         case 0:  {
                     System.out.println("I is " + I);
                     break;
                  }
         case 1:  {
                     System.out.println("I is " + I);
                     break;
                  }
      }
}
System.out.println("Out of for loop");
```

A. I is 0
   I is 1
   Out of for loop

B. I is 0
   Out of for loop

C. I is 0
   I is 1
   I is 1
   Out of for loop

D. Out of for loop

A. Program control enters the loop with I being set to zero. After the first pass at the switch statement, "I is 1" is printed. At this point, the break statement sends control out of the switch statement, but not out of the loop. The second time through the loop I is 1 and "I is 1" is printed out. Again, the break statement sends control out of the switch, but not out of the for statement. I is incremented but the condition is no longer met. Lastly, "Out of for loop" is printed.

11. What happens if a labeled continue statement is used in a for loop? (Choose all that apply.)

   A. The next line of code after the continue keyword is executed.
   B. The current iteration of the loop stops and the next iteration of the innermost loop starts.
   C. The current iteration of the outermost loop stops.
   D. If a variable is incremented in the labeled for loop, it is incremented.

   D. If a for loop is designed to have a variable incremented in a normal situation, it will have that variable incremented even if a continue statement is used. *A, B,* and *C* are not correct because a labeled continue statement stops the current iteration of all loops up to and including the labeled loop. In the case of a for statement, it performs any predefined calculations on the variables and starts the next iteration of the labeled loop. The labeled loop is not necessarily the outermost loop. *A* is incorrect, because the continue statement always causes a jump in program execution. *B* is correct for an unlabled continue, but incorrect for a labeled continue. Remember the labeled loop may not be the innermost one. *C* is incorrect; the labeled continue stops the current iteration of the labeled loop, which may not be the outer-most one.

12. Write a labeled while loop. Make the label "outer" and provide a condition to check if a variable age is less than or equal to 21. Do not use any extra spaces that you do not need to use.
   Answer: outer:while(age<=21)
   You will be asked to do something like this on the exam. The test is very picky about extra spaces, as well as syntax errors.

13. Will the following code compile?

```
for ( ; ; I++)
{
    int I = 0;
    System.out.println("I is " + I);
}
```

A. Yes

B. No

   B. A variable that is incremented or evaluated in a for loop must be declared before or at the for loop declaration.

14. Will the following code block compile?

```
for ( ; ; )
{
    System.out.println("Inside the loop");
}
```

A. Yes

B. No

   A. This is a valid for loop declaration. It is considered an endless loop and would be equivalent to using the keyword true as the expression.

15. What will be printed after this loop has executed?

```
do
{
    System.out.println("Inside do-while loop");
    break;
} while (false);
```

A. Nothing, it will not compile.

B. "Inside do-while loop" will print once.

C. Nothing, the condition is false.

D. "Inside do-while loop" will print an infinite number of times.

   B. The code compiles fine, so *A* is incorrect, and the condition is not checked until after the first time the phrase is printed, so *C* is incorrect. It is not an endless loop like answer *D* would infer; the break statement is encountered and the condition is false.

16. What is wrong with the following piece of code? (Choose all that apply.)

```
for (int x; ; )
{
    x = 5;
    if (x == 5)
        System.out.println("x is equal to " + x);
    break;
}
```

A. The value of *x* must be assigned in the for loop declaration.

B. The if statement needs to have brackets around its body.

C. If *x* is declared in the for statement, then it must be incremented in the for statement.

D. None of the above is correct.

> **D.** The answer is none of them is correct. On the exam, you must pay close attention to the wording of the question. If you see the words "Choose all that apply" or something of that nature, then that means you can choose one, more than one, all, or none of the answers that are given. *A* is incorrect because it is not necessary for the value of x to be assigned at this point. The value of x only needs to be assigned before the first time it is used, and this is done just before the if statement where it is first used. *B* is incorrect because the body of this if statement is only one line. *C* is incorrect because the three parts of a for statement are independent of each other.

17. What will the output of the program be?

```
for ( int I = 0; I < 2; ++I )
{
        System.out.println("I is ");
}
```

A. I is 1
   I is 2

B. I is 1

C. I is 0
   I is 1

D. I is 0

> **C.** It doesn't matter whether you pre-increment or post-increment the variable in a for loop. It is always incremented after the loop executes and before the expression is evaluated. *A* and *B* are incorrect because the first iteration of the loop I is zero, as it is specified in the initialization part of the if statement. *D* is incorrect because the loop would not terminate here since the condition I < 2 is still true after the increment section of the loop executes (I is then equal to one, which is less than 2).

18. What will be printed from the following code?

```
for (int I = 0; I < 2; I++)
{
        switch (I)
        {
            case 0:  {
                        System.out.println("I is 0");
                        continue;
```

```
                              }
              case 1:    {
                              System.out.println("I is 1");
                              break;
                          }
          }
      }
```

A. I is 0
   I is 1

B. I is 0
   I is 1
   I is 1

C. I is 0

D. Nothing, it will not compile.

A. The code will compile, so *D* is incorrect. The first time through the loop, I is 0. When the switch statement is entered, it goes to the case 0 block and prints out I is 0. When the program encounters the continue statement, it stops the current iteration of the loop and starts the next iteration, which makes *B* incorrect. Upon the second iteration, I is now 1 so it executes the case 1 block. I is 1 is printed out and the program breaks out of the loop, making answer *C* incorrect.

19. Will the following code compile, and if so, what will be printed?

```
int I = 1;
do while (I < 1)
        System.out.println("I is " + I);
while (I > 1);
```

A. The code will not compile.

B. I is 1 is printed once.

C. Nothing is printed.

D. I is 1 is printed twice.

C. The code will compile, so answer *A* is incorrect. There are two different looping constructs in this problem. One is a do-while loop and the other is a while loop. The body of the do-while is only a while loop, so you do not need brackets. You are assured that the while loop will be checked at least once. The first time it is checked, I is not less than one so nothing is printed. Then, the do-while condition is checked and it too evaluates to false, so the do-while loop ends and nothing is ever printed out, making answers *B* and *D* incorrect.

20. Will the following code compile, and if so, what will be printed?

```
int I = 0;
label: if (I < 2)
        {
                System.out.println("I is " + I);
                I++;
                continue label;
        }
```

A. It will not compile.

B. I is 1 will be printed.

C. I is 0.
   I is 1 will be printed.

D. None of the above.

A. The code will not compile because a continue statement has to be in a looping construct. Since it won't compile, the other answers, *B*, *C*, and *D*, are incorrect.

Chapter 5 Self Test

1. Given the following program:

```
public class MyProgram {
   public void main(){
      try {
         System.out.println("Hello World ");
      }
   }
}
```

A. The program will compile correctly.

B. The program will not compile because there is no catch clause.

C. The program will not compile because there is no catch clause and because there is no finally clause.

D. The program will not compile because main does not specify any exceptions but there is a try block.

C. Although neither catch nor finally is required, you are required to provide at least one of them with a try clause.

2. Given the following program:

```
public class MyProgram {
   public static void main(String args[]){
      try {
```

```
              System.out.print("Hello world ");
          }
          finally {
              System.out.print("Finally executing ");
          }
      }
  }
```

What will the output of this program be?

A. Nothing. The program will not compile because no exceptions are specified.

B. Nothing. The program will not compile because no catch clauses are specified.

C. Hello world

D. Hello world Finally executing

  D. The program will first execute the try block, printing "Hello world" and will then execute the finally block, printing "Finally executing." Answer *C* is incorrect because it does not account for the execution of the finally block. Answer *B* is incorrect because a catch clause is not required when a finally block is present.

3. Given the following program:

```
public class MyProgram {

public static void throwit()
    {
      throw new RuntimeException();
    }
    public static void main(String args[]){
        try {
            System.out.println("Hello world ");
            throwit();
            System.out.println("Done with try block ");
        }
        finally {
            System.out.println("Finally executing ");
        }
    }
  }
```

Which answer most closely indicates the behavior of the program?

A. The program will not compile.

B. The program will print "Hello world," then will print that a RuntimeException has occurred, then will print "Done with try block," and then it will print "Finally executing."

C. The program will print "Hello world," then will print that a RuntimeException has occurred, and then it will print "Finally executing."

D. The program will print "Hello world," then will print "Finally executing," then it will print that a RuntimeException has occurred.

D. Once the program throws a RuntimeException that is not caught, the finally block will be executed and the program will be terminated. If a method does not handle an exception, the finally block is executed before the exception is propagated. Answer *C* is incorrect because nothing will execute after a program is terminated by a runtime exception. Answer *B* is incorrect because no part of the try block is executed after an exception is thrown from within it.

4. Given that EOFException and FileNotFoundException are both subclasses of IOException, which statement is most true concerning the following code?

```
System.out.println("Start ");
try {
    System.out.println("Hello world");
    throw new FileNotFoundException();
}
System.out.println(" Catch Here ");
catch(EOFException e) {
    System.out.println("End of file exception");
}
catch(FileNotFoundException e) {
    System.out.println("File not found");
}
```

A. The code will not compile.
B. The code will print File Not Found.
C. The code will print End of file exception.
D. The code will print Start Hello world Catch Here File not found.

A. Catch clauses must immediately follow try blocks. If they do not, a compile error will result. All other answers are wrong because the program cannot run if it does not compile.

5. Given that EOFException is a subtype of IOException, what can be said about the following code?

```
try {
    throw new EOFException();
}
catch(IOException e) {
    System.out.println("IO Exception caught ");
}
```

A. The code will not compile.
B. The code will run and print "IO Exception Caught."
C. The thrown exception will be ignored because there is no catch clause for it.

D. The thrown error will propagate up the call stack and the program will terminate.
B. Because the catch clause is coded to catch a supertype of the thrown exception, it will catch the exception and execute the catch clause. Answer *C* is incorrect because thrown exceptions are never ignored; if they are checked exceptions they must be handled and if they are unchecked they will terminate the program. Answer *D* is incorrect because, as stated in answer *B*, the catch clause will catch the exception because the exception is a subtype of the type in the catch clause.

6. Which methods are available in all Exceptions? (Choose all that apply.)

   A. toString
   B. retry
   C. printStackTrace
   D. getMessage
   A, C, and **D.** There is no retry method in an exception object.

7. Which class is a base class for all Exceptions?

   A. String
   B. Error
   C. Throwable
   D. RuntimeException
   C. All Exception types derive from class Throwable. Answer *B* is incorrect because Error is a subclass of Throwable. Answer *D* is incorrect because RuntimeException is a subtype of Exception, but Exception is a base type for many other exception types.

8. Unhandled checked exceptions:

   A. Terminate the application
   B. Are ignored at runtime
   C. Cause the program to not compile
   D. Are handled automatically by the Java VM
   C. Java programs must provide handlers for all checked exceptions to compile. Answers *A* and *D* are wrong because the program cannot run if it does not compile. Answer *B* is wrong because checked exceptions must be handled at some point.

9. Unhandled unchecked exceptions:

   A. Terminate the application
   B. Are ignored
   C. Cause the program to not compile

D. Are handled automatically by the Java VM

A. If not handled, unchecked exceptions terminate the application. Answer *B* is wrong because exceptions must be handled at some point. Answer *C* is incorrect because a program need not, and typically does not, provide handlers for unchecked exceptions to compile. Answer *D* is incorrect because no exceptions are automatically handled by the Java VM.

10. Given that EOFException and FileNotFoundException are subtypes of IOException, what can be said about the following code?

```
try {
    throw new FileNotFoundException();
}
catch(IOException e) {
    System.out.println("IO Exception caught");
}
catch(EOFException e) {
    System.out.println("EOF Exception caught");
}
```

A. The code will not compile.

B. The code will print "IO Exception Caught."

C. The thrown exception will propagate up the call stack.

D. The code will print "EOF Exception caught."

A. Catch clauses for the most specific classes must be listed before those of their supertype. All other answers are incorrect because the code cannot run if it does not compile, so there can be no runtime behavior.

11. Exceptions that are not RuntimeExceptions or Errors:

A. Must be either caught or specified

B. Need not be caught or specified

C. Must not be caught

D. Must not be specified

A. Non-runtime exceptions are checked exceptions and checked exceptions must be either caught or specified. All other answers contradict Java's catch or specify requirement and are therefore incorrect.

12. RuntimeExceptions:

A. Must be either caught or specified

B. Need not be caught or specified

C. Must not be caught

D. Must not be specified

B. Runtime exceptions are an exception to Java's catch or specify rule. They may be caught or specified but need not be. Answers *A*, *C*, and *D* are incorrect because the question asked about unchecked exceptions, not checked ones.

13. RuntimeExceptions usually:

A. Cannot be caught

B. Are just like other exceptions

C. Represent program bugs

D. Must be specified

C. Runtime errors usually occur because of bugs in your program. Typically, your code does not catch a runtime error. Runtime errors are an exception to Java's catch or specify rule, so they need not be caught or specified. Answer *A* is incorrect because any exception can be caught with a catch clause. Answer *B* is incorrect because RuntimeExceptions are special in that they are exempt from the catch or specify requirement. Answer *D* is incorrect because RuntimeExceptions need not be specified.

14. Finally clauses:

A. Are executed only after a try block executes with no exceptions

B. Are only executed if an exception is thrown but no matching catch clause is found

C. Are always executed after try and catch blocks

D. Are only executed if a catch clause is executed in the current method

C. Finally clauses are always executed. If a try block executes with no exceptions, the finally clause is executed immediately after the try block. If the try block generates an exception, the finally block executes after the catch clause completes, if there is a catch clause available in the current method. If there is no catch clause, the finally block is executed and the exception is propagated up the call stack. Answers *A*, *B*, and *D* are all incorrect because a finally block always executes at some point.

15. Overridden methods:

A. May add exceptions from new hierarchies to the method's exception specification

B. May not add exceptions from new hierarchies to the method's exception specification

C. May not throw exceptions

D. May only throw RuntimeExceptions

B. When you override a method, you may specify no exceptions or you may specify subtypes of exceptions thrown by the overridden method. You can not specify any exceptions that are not the same type as, or a subtype of, exceptions specified by the overridden method. Answer *A* is incorrect because it contradicts this rule. Answer *C* is incorrect because overridden methods may throw exceptions. Answer *D* is incorrect because there is no requirement that overridden methods, in general, may only throw RuntimeExceptions.

16. An exception object's getMessage method:

    A. Returns the exact type of the exception object

    B. Prints the name of the method in which the object was instantiated

    C. Returns a string containing an explanation of the exception

    D. Returns the string, if any, that was passed to the constructor of the object
    D. All other answers are incorrect because they do not accurately describe the behavior of the getMessage method.

17. An exception object's fillInStackTrace method:

    A. Changes the object's origin point to reflect the location where the object was created

    B. Prints a stack trace from the object's original origin

    C. Prints a stack trace from the object's current location

    D. Returns an object of type Throwable and changes the object's origin point to reflect the current location
    D. Answer **D** accurately describes the behavior of the fillInStackTrace method. Answer *A* is incorrect because fillInStackTrace changes the origin point to reflect the current location, not the original location. It is the original origin that is replaced. Answers *B* and *C* are incorrect as this method does not print anything.

18. The following code fragment:

    ```
    class MySpecialRunException extends RuntimeException {
        public MySpecialRunException() {}
        public MySpecialRunException(String s) { super(s); }
    }
    ```

    A. Will prevent a code module from compiling

    B. Creates a type of checked exception

    C. Creates a type of unchecked exception

    D. Will compile but not run
    C. By subclassing Java's RuntimeException class, you are creating a special type of unchecked exception for your application. Answer *A* is incorrect as there are no mistakes that would prevent a successful compile. Answer *D* is incorrect because there is nothing that will prevent this code from executing. Answer *B* is incorrect because we are subclassing an unchecked exception, so that's what this new type will be.

19. The following code fragment:

    ```
    class MySpecialException extends Exception {
        public MySpecialException() {}
        public MySpecialException(String s) { super(s); }
    }
    ```

A. Will prevent a code module from compiling

B. Creates a type of checked exception

C. Creates a type of unchecked exception

D. Will compile but not run

   B. By subclassing Java's Exception class, or any of its subclasses other than RuntimeException, you are creating a special type of checked exception for your application. Answer *A* is incorrect as there are no mistakes that would prevent a successful compile. Answer *D* is incorrect as there is nothing that will prevent this code from executing. Answer *C* is incorrect because we are subclassing a checked exception, so that's what this new type will be.

20. Which of the following is not an advantage of exception handling?

   A. Exception handling improves code organization by separating a method's error handling code from the body of the method.

   B. Exception handling allows a method to defer the handling of its errors to a previously called method.

   C. Exception handling improves an application's performance.

   D. Exception handling allows similar errors to be handled by a single handler.

   C. Error handling does not improve an application's performance. Answers *A*, *B*, and *D* represent the three primary benefits of exception handling.

Chapter 6 Self Test

1. What does a Java programmer have to do to release an object that is no longer needed?

   A. Use the delete statement

   B. Call the finalize() method for the object

   C. Call System.gc()

   D. Nothing

   D. In Java, the programmer does not have to perform any special actions to delete an object that is no longer in use. Rather, the system will automatically detect that the object is no longer used, and will collect the object. *A* is not correct, as there is no delete statement in Java. *B* is not correct, as the finalize() method of an object is called automatically by the system and is never called by the programmer directly. *C* is not correct; although calling System.gc() might cause the object to be collected, it is not required for the object to be collected.

2. Can a Java application run out of memory?

   A. Yes, if there are too many soft references

   B. Yes, if there are too many strong references

   C. Yes, if you do not override the finalize() method for an object

   D. No, garbage collection ensures that there will be enough memory

   B. Yes, if there are too many strong references. The garbage collection system attempts to remove objects from memory when they are not used. However, if you maintain too many live objects (strongly referenced from other live objects) then the system can run out of memory. *A* is not correct because soft references are designed for memory-sensitive caching mechanisms; the objects they refer to would be deleted before the system runs out of memory. *C* is not correct, as you do not have to override the finalize() method at all for most objects. *D* is not correct, as garbage collection cannot ensure that there is enough memory, only that the memory that is available will be managed as well as possible.

3. When should you directly invoke the garbage collection system?

   A. Before entering a time-critical section of code

   B. Before attempting a large number of allocations

   C. After leaving a method with a large number of temporary objects

   D. Never, garbage collection is automatic

   A. Before entering a time-critical section of code. One disadvantage of a garbage collection system is that it is unpredictable when the system will have to go looking for more memory. Because looking for more memory can take time, it can be a good idea to request a garbage collection before executing time-critical code. This way, if the code allocates any objects, the allocation should execute as quickly as possible.

   B isn't a bad answer, but if you need memory at any point when performing a large number of allocations, then you will probably free up enough memory to satisfy all of them. *C* isn't a bad answer, but there isn't really a penalty to pay for having unused objects on the heap until you need more memory. *D* isn't a bad answer either, in that you never really have to call garbage collection directly, but your program might perform better if you do.

4. Complete the following sentence. Garbage collection…

   A. Is faster than hand-written memory management

   B. Is available only in the Java language

   C. Is more reliable than hand-written memory management

D. Uses less memory than hand-written memory management

C. Garbage collection is more reliable than hand-written memory management. Garbage collection is designed to eliminate errors in memory management. It does not attempt to address memory usage or performance. *A* isn't a good answer because garbage collection will generally be slower overall than hand-written memory management. *B* isn't a good answer because garbage collection has been available in a variety of languages for a number of years. Garbage collection doesn't attempt to reduce the amount of memory that an object takes, so *D* isn't a good answer either.

5. Complete the following sentence. Soft references...

A. Were added in JDK 1.1
B. Require the use of reference queues
C. Allow for memory-sensitive caching algorithms
D. Allow for recovery of previously deleted objects

C. Allow for memory-sensitive caching algorithms. Soft references were introduced in Java 1.2 to enable the creation of memory-sensitive caches. Soft references allow unreferenced objects to remain in memory as long as the memory is not needed for another use.
A isn't correct because soft references weren't introduced until the 1.2 Java release. *B* isn't correct because you can use soft references with reference queues by checking the results of the get() method for null. Because there is no mechanism for recovering objects that have already been deleted, *D* isn't correct.

6. Complete the following sentence. Phantom references...

A. Are used to manage memory allocated with native code through the JNI interface
B. Prevent memory from being reused
C. Allow the recovery of previously deleted objects
D. Are interchangeable with weak references

B. Phantom references prevent memory from being reused. Phantom references control the reuse of memory that was occupied by objects that have been deleted. *A* isn't the right answer: there is no direct mechanism in Java for managing memory allocated through JNI code. *C* isn't correct because there is no way that a deleted object can be recovered once it has been deleted. Phantom and weak references are similar in a number of respects, but aren't interchangeable, so *D* isn't correct.

7. Complete the following sentence. Using weak references...
   A. Allows an object to be collected when not used
   B. Allows an object to be tracked even after collected
   C. Is required for complex Java programs
   D. Allows for memory sensitive caches
      A. Allows an object to be collected when not used. The purpose of weak references is to allow you to keep track of an object, but not prevent that object from being collected. *B* is not correct, as weak references do not allow you to track an object after it has been collected. When the object is collected the weak reference will be set to null automatically. *C* is not correct because many applications, even complex ones, will have no need for weak references. In fact, weak references weren't added to Java until release 1.2, and certainly a lot of complex programs were written before that! *D* isn't correct because soft references are a better choice for memory-sensitive caches, as they provide the hints to the garbage collection system that the object should only be removed from memory when memory is required.

8. Complete the following sentence. Reference queues...
   A. Are required for soft references
   B. Are required for strong references
   C. Are required for phantom references
   D. Are never required for any reference type
      C. Are required for phantom references. Reference queues provide a means of determining when a reference has become invalidated. Because phantom references always return null, even when valid, the only means of determining that they are invalid is through the use of reference queues.
      A isn't correct because soft references do not require the use of reference queues. The references can be tested for null to determine if the reference is invalid. *B* isn't correct because strong references aren't created directly by the programmer and can't be associated with a reference queue. *D* isn't correct because as we have seen reference queues are required for phantom references.

9. Complete the following sentence. The get() method on a Reference object...
   A. Always returns the referent object
   B. Returns the referent object until it is collected, then returns null
   C. Returns the referent object until clear() is called

D. Returns the referent object only for soft and weak references

D. This one is tricky, but the important thing to remember is that phantom references never return the referent object, they always return null. The fourth answer hints that we should be considering phantom references as well as soft and weak ones, and so the correct answer is that the get() method returns the referent object only for soft and weak references. This means that *A* isn't correct, as PhantomReference objects never return the referent object. *B* also isn't correct because PhantomReferences will not return the referent object even if the object hasn't been collected yet. *C* isn't correct for the same reason: PhantomReferences will return null both before and after clear() is called. If PhantomReferences aren't considered, then the answers would be different.

10. Complete the following sentence. The clear() method…

A. Is called automatically when the reference is created
B. Is called automatically for all references when the reference is enqueued
C. Is called automatically for soft and weak references only when they are enqueued
D. Is called automatically for phantom references only when they are enqueued

C. The clear() method is automatically called for soft and weak references when they are added to their reference queues. For phantom references, however, you have to make sure to call clear when removing the reference from the queue to free the object's memory. *A* isn't correct because the clear() method isn't called when the reference is created. This would make the reference somewhat useless, as it would never track an object! *B* isn't correct, as the clear() method is only called for soft and weak references. *D* isn't correct because the clear() method is never automatically called for phantom references.

11. Complete the following sentence. Calling the *new* statement for an object…

A. Creates a new soft reference to the object
B. Creates a new weak reference to the object
C. Creates a new phantom reference to the object
D. Creates a new strong reference to the object

D. The *new* statement is a part of the original memory model for the Java language that did not include soft, weak, or phantom references. It always creates a strong reference to the object. *A, B,* and *C* are all incorrect because reference objects have to be created directly by the programmer. The new statement will always create a strong reference; all other reference types have to be created from this strong reference.

12. Prior to Java 1.2, all references were what?

    A. Strong
    B. Weak
    C. Soft
    D. Phantom

    A. Prior to Java 1.2, all references were strong. The Java memory model was enhanced in release 1.2 by the addition of soft, weak, and phantom references.

13. Complete the following sentence. The Reference class…

    A. Can be subclassed to make your own custom reference types
    B. Has four subclasses: StrongReference, WeakReference, SoftReference, and PhantomReference
    C. Cannot be subclassed by Java programmers
    D. Is used directly to manage memory for an object

    C. the Reference class cannot be subclassed by Java programmers. The Reference class is a special class in Java, tied very directly to the internals of the Java virtual machine. As such, the individual programmer can't subclass the Reference class—at least not without rewriting the Java virtual machine! *A* isn't correct because even if you did subclass the Reference class, the virtual machine won't know about the new subclass, and so it wouldn't do anything. *B* isn't correct because strong references aren't a subclass of the reference class. Strong references are built into the virtual machine. *D* isn't correct because the Reference class is abstract and can't be directly created; you have to create a subclass of the Reference class instead.

14. Complete the following sentence. Calling Runtime.gc()…

    A. Guarantees enough memory for the next memory allocation request
    B. Always frees up some memory, but may not free enough for the next allocation request
    C. May have no effect, based in the virtual machine implementation
    D. Should be performed before every memory allocation request

    C. Calling Runtime.gc() may have no effect, based on the virtual machine implementation. The Runtime.gc() (or the equivalent System.gc()) calls are requests to the virtual machine to run a garbage collection pass. The implementation of this call depends upon the virtual machine you are running under, and may have no effect. *A* isn't correct, as there is never a guarantee that there will be enough memory for the next allocation request; this will always depend upon the size of the request and the amount of memory available to the virtual machine. *B* is not correct because the call may do nothing if it is not implemented in your virtual machine. *D* is not correct because invoking Runtime.gc() before every memory allocation request would only add unnecessary overhead to your application without any benefits.

15. Complete the following sentence. The Java Virtual Machine specification...

A. Requires mark-sweep garbage collection

B. Requires some form of garbage collection, but not necessarily mark-sweep

C. Allows for manual memory management

D. Does not address memory management at all

B. Requires some form of garbage collection, but not necessarily mark-sweep. The Java Virtual Machine specification requires that the virtual machine support garbage collection, but does not require that this garbage collection be implemented using the mark-sweep algorithm. It is true, however, that the mark-sweep algorithm is by far the most popular implementation, and is the implementation in Sun's JDK. *A* isn't correct because the virtual machine specification doesn't address how to implement memory management, only that memory management must be provided. The virtual machine specification does not allow any form of manual memory management, however, so *C* isn't correct. *D* isn't correct because the specification clearly addresses the need for automatic memory management.

16. Complete the following sentence. Mark-sweep garbage collection...

A. Can identify unused objects, even if they refer to each other

B. Cannot collect objects that refer to each other cyclically

C. Is the fastest garbage collection system

D. Runs every three seconds, in a separate system-level thread

A. Can identify unused objects, even if they refer to each other. One advantage of the mark-sweep memory management algorithm is the ability to identify cycles of objects that refer only to each other internally. This allows these cyclically-referenced objects to be collected and the memory recovered. *B* isn't correct, as mark-sweep is specifically designed to collect objects that refer to each other cyclically. *C* isn't correct, as mark-sweep may not be the fastest garbage collection system. The time it takes to evaluate objects to find out which objects are really live imposes some overhead on the performance of the garbage collector. *D* isn't correct, although it could be for some implementation; mark-sweep will generally run when needed to free up memory, rather than regularly in another thread.

17. When will the object created as myObject become eligible for collection?

```
class example
{
    public static void main( String args[] )
    {
        UseObject();
    }
}
```

```
private void UseObject()
    {
        String anObject = AllocateObject();
        System.out.println( anObject );
    }

private String AllocateObject()
    {
            String myObject = new String( "When will I be deleted?" );
        return myObject;
    }
};
```

A. When the AllocateObject() function completes

B. When the call to System.out.println() completes

C. When the UseObject() function completes

D. When the main program completes

C. When the UseObject() function completes. The object is eligible for collection after the *last* reference that refers to it is dropped. For this code, the last reference is the anObject reference, which is dropped when the UseObject() function completes. *A* isn't correct, as the object reference is returned from the function. This increases the number of references to the object, so the object isn't freed even though the myObject references go out of scope. *B* isn't correct because the reference to the object is not dropped after the last usage of the reference, but rather when the scope that reference is in completes. *D* isn't correct, although the object may well not be collected until the program completes, as it is eligible for deletion as soon as the last reference is dropped.

18. When might the soft reference *theSoftReference* be automatically cleared?

```
class example
{
        SoftReference    theSoftReference;

public static void main( String args[] )
    {
        theSoftReference =
            new SoftReference( AllocateObject(), null );
        UseObject();
    }

private void UseObject()
    {
        String anObject = (String) theSoftReference.get();
        System.out.println( anObject );
    }
```

```
private String AllocateObject()
    {
                String myObject = new String( "When will I be deleted?" );
        return myObject;
    }
};
```

A. After UseObject() returns
B. After calling the get() function in UseObject()
C. As soon as AllocateObject() returns
D. Just before UseObject() is called

D. Just before UseObject() is called. Remember that the soft reference will be automatically cleared when the object that it refers to is collected. So, we have to figure out when the object might be collected. The object that is created in the AllocateObject() function has a strong reference only up until the point that the soft reference is created. It is not the creation of the soft reference that drops the strong reference, but rather the fact that the result of the AllocateObject() function is not assigned to a strong reference. It is instead passed in as the first argument to the SoftReference constructor, so once that constructor returns, all strong references to the object will have been dropped. *A* isn't correct because the object may have been collected before that point. The same applies to *B*, but it is also important to note that calling the get() function has no effect on the state of the object. *C* isn't correct either. Even though there are no explicit strong references to the object outside the AllocateObject() function, there is an implicit one that is passed into the SoftReference constructor. The object will not be eligible for collection until this strong reference is dropped, which occurs after the constructor returns.

Chapter 7 Self Test

1. What will happen when you compile and run this program:

```
public class A
{
  public static void main( String [] args)
  {
    new A().printResult( 1, "abc", 4);
  }
  private void printResult( int a, long b, int c)
  {
    System.out.println( a + b + c);
  }
  private void printResult( long a, String b, int c)
  {
    System.out.println( a + b + c);
  }
}
```

A. The code will not compile correctly because a long and a String may not be added.

B. The code will compile and run and will display *1abc4* in the standard output.

C. The code will compile and run and will display *11234* in the standard output.

D. The code will compile and will throw a NumberFormatException.

B. The first argument is acceptably cast to a long. Adding a String to an int or a long functions as string concatenation. *A* is incorrect because a String and a long may be added. *C* incorrectly describes the effect of adding a String to a long and int. *D* is incorrect because it runs without error.

2. All of the following are benefits of encapsulation except what?

A. Clarity of code.

B. Code efficiency.

C. The ability to add functionality later on.

D. Modification requires less coding changes.

B. Encapsulation does not make code run any better. It only keeps code more organized. *A, C,* and *D* are incorrect because all are direct benefits of code organization.

3. What will happen when you compile and run this program?

```
public class MySuper {
    public MySuper(int i) { }
}
public class MySub extends MySuper {
    public MySub() {
        super(2);
        public static void main(String args[]) {
            new MySub();
        }
    }
}
```

A. The program does not compile because MySuper does not have a no-args constructor.

B. The program compile but throws a runtime exception when it cannot find the no-args MySuper constructor.

C. The program compiles and runs without error.

C. MySuper does not need a no-args constructor because MySub() explicitly calls the MySuper constructor with an argument. *A* and *B* are incorrect because they assume that MySuper needs a no-args constructor.

4. What is the relationship between Rectangle and Square?

```
public class Rectangle
{
}

public class Square extends Rectangle
{
}
```

   A. It's a *has a* relationship.
   B. It's an *is a* relationship.
   C. It's both an *is a* and *has a* relationship.
   D. The relationship is neither an *is a* nor a *has a* relationship.

   B. Because Square extends Rectangle, and a square is a type of rectangle, the relationship is *is a*. *A, C,* and *D* are incorrect because they claim other relationships exists or that no relationship exists.

5. When a subclass' method has the same name, parameter list, and return type as a method in the parent class, this method is said to be what?

   A. extended
   B. overloaded
   C. overextended
   D. overridden

   D. Overridden methods have the same name, parameter list, and return type in the subclass as in the parent class. *A* applies to a parent-child class relationship, *B* refers to methods in the same class, and *C* is a nonsensical term.

6. What code should be inserted in place of XXXXX so that the output of the program is *okay*?

```
public class Test
{
  public static void main( String [] args)
  {
    new Test( 4);
  }
  public Test()
  {
    System.out.println( "okay");
  }
  public Test( int i)
  {
```

```
            XXXXX
        }
    }
```

A. `super()`

B. `this`

C. `Test()`

D. `this()`

   D. this() is used within a constructor to call another constructor in the same class. *A* is incorrect because super() is used to invoke constructors in the parent class. *B* is incorrect because this is used to get a reference to your class. *C* will not compile.

7. Which of the following must match exactly for overloaded methods to compile correctly?

   A. The parameter list.

   B. The return type.

   C. The exceptions thrown.

   D. None of the above.

   D. Only the method name must match exactly for overloaded methods. Therefore, *A, B,* and *C* are incorrect.

8. The implementation details of a well encapsulated class should have what accessibility?

   A. public

   B. the default

   C. private

   D. It does not matter.

   C. private keeps other classes from viewing the implementation details, which is a primary goal of encapsulated classes. *A* will allow any class to see the details. *B* will allow other classes in its package to see the details.

9. What is the relationship between Vehicle and Engine?

```
public class Vehicle
{
    private Engine theEngine
}

public class Engine
{
}
```

A. It's a *has a* relationship.
B. It's an *is a* relationship.
C. It's both an *is a* and *has a* relationship.
D. The relationship is neither an *is a* nor a *has a* relationship.

A. Vehicle contains an instance variable pointing to an Engine reference, and a vehicle contains an engine. *B, C,* and *D* are incorrect because they state that other relationships exist or no relationship exists at all.

10. What will happen when you compile and run this program:

```
public class Test
{
  public static void main( String [] args)
  {
    new Test().foo( 1, 2);
  }
  private void foo( int a, int b)
  {
    System.out.println( "int");
  }
  private void foo( long a, int b)
  {
    System.out.println( "long");
  }
}
```

A. The code will compile and run and display *int.*
B. The code will compile and run and display *long.*
C. The code will not compile.
D. The code will compile but throw a runtime exception when executed.

A. Though both methods seem like they could accept the method call, foo(1, 2) will print *int* because Java chooses the parameter list that is closest to the parameters in the call. foo(1, 2) would have to cast the first parameter from int to long in the second method, but no casting is needed for the first overloaded method. *B* is incorrect because it assumes the second method is called. *C* and *D* are incorrect because they claim that the code will not compile and run, respectively.

11. What will happen when you compile this program?

```
public class Parent
{
  public void execute() throws Exception
  {
```

```
      //body omitted
    }
  }
public class Child extends Parent
{
  private void execute() throws ClassCastException
  {
    //body omitted
  }
}
```

A. The program will compile successfully.

B. The program will not compile because the execute() in the subclass throws a different exception than in the parent class.

C. The program will not compile because the execute() in the subclass has less accessibility than in the parent class.

D. The program will not compile because the execute() in the subclass has less accessibility *and* throws a different exception than in the parent class.

C. The only problem with this code is that the subclass version of execute() is private, whereas it is public in the parent class. Throwing a different exception is fine as long as the exception in the subclass is a subset of that in the parent class. *A, B,* and *D* are incorrect because they all state that the throws cause is part of the problem or that there is no problem at all.

12. What will happen when you compile and run this program?

```
public class MySuper
{
  public MySuper()
  {
    System.out.println( "MySuper");
  }
}

public class MySub extends MySuper
{
  public static void main( String [] args)
  {
    new MySub();
  }
  public MySub()
  {
    System.out.println( "MySub");
  }
}
```

A. The program will compile and run and will display MySub in the standard output.

B. The program will compile and run and will display MySuper in the standard output.

C. The program will not compile.

D. The program will compile and run and will display MySuper and MySub in the standard output.

> **D.** MySub() implicitly calls super(), which in turn calls the MySuper(). *A* is incorrect because it does not account for MySuper() being called. *B* is incorrect because it does not account for MySub() being called. *C* is incorrect because the program compiles successfully.

13. What will happen when you compile and run this program?

```
public class A
{
  public void baz()
  {
    System.out.println( "A");
  }
}
public class B extends A
{
  public static void main( String [] args)
  {
    A a = new B();
    a.baz();
  }
  public void baz()
  {
    System.out.println( "B");
  }
}
```

A. The program compiles and runs and displays *A* in the standard output.

B. The program compiles and runs and displays *B* in the standard output.

C. The program compiles but throws a runtime exception.

D. The program does not compile.

> **B.** Though the object is cast as type A, the underlying type of the object upon which baz() is called is type B. *A* claims that the method is called based on the type to which the object is casted. *C* and *D* claim that there are runtime and compilation errors, respectively.

14. What will happen when you compile and run this program?

```
public class A
{
  public static void main( String [] args)
  {
    new A().baz( 1, 2);
  }
  private void baz( int a, int b);
  {
    System.out.println( "baz");
  }
  private void foo( int a, int b)
  {
    System.out.println( "first");
  }
  private void foo( int a, int b)
  {
    System.out.println( "second");
  }
}
```

A. The program compiles and runs and displays *first* in the standard output.
B. The program compiles and runs and displays *second* in the standard output.
C. The program compiles and runs and displays *baz* in the standard output.
D. The program does not compile.
   D. Even though foo() is never called, both parameter lists are identical. Therefore, we know that the parameter lists can never be distinguished one from the other. *C* is wrong because the code doesn't compile. *A* and *B* are also incorrect because foo() is never called.

15. The interface methods for a well encapsulated class should have what accessibility?

A. public
B. protected
C. private
D. It does not matter.
   A. public allows other classes to see the methods through which they are supposed to receive access. *C* is the preferred visibility, what implementation details. *B* limits the accessibility to classes in the package or its subclasses.

16. What code should be inserted in place of XXXXX so that the output of the program is *good*?

```
public class Parent
{
  public Parent()
  {
    System.out.println( "good");
  }
  public Parent( int j)
  {
    System.out.println( "bad");
  }
}
public class Example extends Parent
{
  public static void main( String [] args)
  {
    new Example();
  }
  public Example()
  {
    XXXXX
  }
}
```

A. this()

B. superclass()

C. Parent()

D. Leave it blank.

D. Leaving it blank would cause super() to be called automatically by the constructor.
A would result in an error because the constructor would invoke itself. *B* is not syntactically correct. *C* is an invalid call to the Parent constructor.

17. What will happen when you compile this program?

```
public class Test
{
  protected void start() throws ClassCastException
  {
    //body omitted
  }
}

public class Child extends Test
{
  public void start () throws Exception
```

```
   {
       //body omitted
   }
}
```

A. The program will compile successfully.

B. The program will not compile because the start() in the subclass throws a different exception than in the parent class.

C. The program will not compile because the start() in the subclass is public, whereas it is protected in the parent class.

D. The program will not compile because the start() in the subclass has different accessibility *and* throws a different exception than in the parent class.

B. The problem here is that the exception in Child is more general than the one thrown in the parent class. Thus, the exception in Child is not a subset of the one thrown in Test. *A* is incorrect because the program will not compile. *C* is incorrect because the subclass is more accessible. *D* is incorrect for the same reason.

18. When two or more methods in the same class have the same name, they are said to be what?

A. an implementation detail

B. overridden

C. an interface

D. overloaded

D. Methods in the same class with the same name are overloaded. *A* and *C* refer to term used in encapsulation. *B* refers to methods with the same name in different classes.

19. What will happen when you compile and run this program?

```java
public class Example
{
    public static void main( String [] args)
    {
        new Example ().locate( 1.0, 2);
    }
    private void locate ( double a, long b)
    {
        System.out.println( "double-long");
    }
    private void locate ( long a, int b)
    {
        System.out.println( "long-int");
    }
}
```

A. The code will compile and run and display *double-long*.

B. The code will compile and run and display *long-int*.

C. The code will not compile.

D. The code will compile but throw a runtime exception when executed.

    A. 1.0 matches the double parameter in the first locate(), and 2 is cast up to a long. *B* is incorrect because 1.0 cannot automatically be cast to a double. *C* and *D* are incorrect because the code runs and compiles fine.

20. What is the relationship between Movable and Bitmap?

```
public interface Moveable
{
   public void moveObject();
}

public class Bitmap implements Moveable
{
   public void moveObject()
   {
     //body omitted
   }
}
```

A. It's a *has a* relationship.

B. It's an *is a* relationship.

C. It's both an *is a* and *has a* relationship.

D. The relationship is neither an *is a* nor a *has a* relationship.

    B. Implementing an interface is another type of an *is a* relationship. *A* and *C* are incorrect because the type Movable does not contain a Bitmap. *D* is incorrect because the relationship is *is a*.

Chapter 8 Self Test

1. Which of the following statements are correct? (Choose all that apply.)

A. Inner classes are defined within the scope of another class.

B. Inner classes can subclass other classes and they can implement interfaces.

C. Inner classes cannot be static.

D. There are four different kinds of inner classes: top-level, static, member, and anonymous.

    A and **B** are correct. *C* is incorrect because there are static inner classes. *D* is incorrect because top-level classes are not inner classes, and the local inner class is missing.

2. The filename(s) generated by the Java compiler for the following code is (are):

```
public class MyMap implements Map {
    private static class MapEntry {
        ...
    }
    ...
}
```

A. MyMap.class
B. MyMap.class and MyMap.MapEntry.class
C. MyMap.class and MyMap$MapEntry.class
D. MyMap$MapEntry

C is correct because inner classes compile to separate files, and their filenames are prefixed with the name of the enclosing class followed by a dollar sign. *A* is incorrect because inner classes are compiled into their own file. *B* is incorrect because the inner class name is separated from the enclosing class name with a period and it should be a dollar sign. *D* is incorrect because the class file for the enclosing class is missing.

3. What happens when you compile the following code?

```
import java.util.*;

public class Week {

private int weeknr;
    private int year;
    private int[] days = {1,2,3,4,5,6,0};

public Week(int weeknr, int year) {
        this.weeknr = weeknr;
        this.year = year;
    }

public Iterator getDays() {
        return new DayIterator(this);
    }

public int getWeeknr() {
        return weeknr;
    }

public int getYear() {
        return year;
    }
```

```java
private static class DayIterator implements Iterator {

private int index = 0;
      private Calendar cal = null;

DayIterator (Week aWeek) {
        cal = new GregorianCalendar();
        cal.clear();
        cal.set(Calendar.YEAR, aWeek.getYear());
        cal.set(Calendar.WEEK_OF_YEAR, aWeek.getWeeknr());
    }

public boolean hasNext() {
        return index < 7;
    }

public Object next() {
        cal.set(Calendar.DAY_OF_WEEK, days[index++]);
        return cal.getTime();
    }

public void remove() {
        // not implemented
    }
 }

public static void main(String[] args) {
      // list the days of the week
      if (args.length < 2) {
         System.err.println("Usage: java Week <weeknr> year>");
         System.exit(1);
      } else {
         try {
            int weeknr = Integer.parseInt(args[0]);
            int year = Integer.parseInt(args[1]);
            Week wk = new Week(weeknr, year);
            for (Iterator i=wk.getDays();i.hasNext();) {
               System.err.println(i.next());
            }
         } catch (NumberFormatException x) {
            System.err.println("Illegal week or year");
         }
      }
   }
 }
```

A. This code compiles, and when it is run it returns the days of the week starting on Sunday instead of Saturday.

B. This code does not compile because the *days* array is private.

C. This code does not compile because the *days* array is not static.

D. This code does not compile because the DayIterator class is private.

C is the correct answer because static inner classes can access only static members of the enclosing class. The day array is not static, so it cannot be accessed from within a static inner class. B is incorrect because static inner classes have full access rights to static members of the enclosing class, so if days were declared as private static, DayIterator could have accessed it. D is incorrect because static inner classes are allowed to be private.

4. The following code does not compile. Why?

```
public class MyClass {

private class MyRunner implements Runnable {
    public void run() {
        // do something
    }
}

public static void main(String[] args) {
    (new Thread(new MyRunner())).start();
}
}
```

A. You have to create an instance of MyRunner with new MyClass.MyRunner().

B. MyRunner is private.

C. You have to import Thread from java.lang.

D. You have to create an instance of MyRunner with an enclosing instance of MyClassl.

D is the correct answer. MyRunner is a member class and needs an enclosing instance to be created. In this example, you can create one as in:
(new Thread((new MyClass()).new MyRunner())).start();

5. Which of the following are correct ways to create an instance of an inner class called Outer.Inner from outside the scope of the Outer class? Assume Inner is a public static inner class that has no defined constructor.

A. Outer.new Inner()

B. (new Outer()).new Inner();

C. (new Outer()).new Outer.Inner();

D. new Outer.Inner();

    D is the only correct answer. Because Inner is a static inner class, it does not need an instance of the Outer class to be created, which renders *C* invalid. *C* would have been correct if the inner class were not static. *B* is incorrect because Inner has to be prefixed with Outer, as in *C*. *A* is syntactically incorrect.

6. What number is returned by getValue(), assuming the enclosing class creates an instance of Bar using *this.new*?

```
public class Foo {
    protected int x = 3;
    private int y = 5;
    private class Bar {
        private int x = 8;

    public Bar() {
            Foo.this.x = y;
        }

    public int getValue() {
            return x*y;
        }
    }

    public int getValue() {
        return (new Bar()).getValue();
    }

    public static void main(String[] args) {
        System.err.println((new Foo()).getValue());
    }
}
```

    A. 15
    B. 24
    C. 25
    D. 40

    D is the correct answer. The line Foo.this.x = y in the Bar constructor changes the value of the member *x* of the *enclosing* class to become 5. However, the expression x*y in getValue() uses the member *x* declared in the *inner* class, which has the value 8. 8*5 = 40.

7. Fill in the blank in the following sentence. Only ... can have static members.

    A. top-level classes
    B. top-level classes, interfaces, and static inner classes
    C. top-level classes and interfaces
    D. top-level classes, interfaces, and member classes
    B is the correct answer.

8. What is the result of compiling and executing the following code?

```
import java.util.Iterator;
public class Foo {
    public Iterator getIterator() {
        return new public Iterator() {
            public void remove() {}
            public Object next() {return null;}
            public boolean hasNext() {return false;}
        };
    }
}
```

    A. This code returns a new Foo.Iterator when you call getIterator().
    B. This code returns a new Iterator when you call getIterator().
    C. This code doesn't compile because an Iterator interface method is missing.
    D. This code doesn't compile because the syntax of the inner class creation is wrong.
    D is the correct answer. You cannot use modifiers in the creation of anonymous inner classes, and the parentheses on Iterator are missing.

9. What class files are generated when you compile the following code?

```
import java.util.Iterator;
public class Foo {
    public static class Week {
        public Iterator getIterator() {
            return new Iterator() {
                public void remove() {};
                public Object next() {return null;}
                public boolean hasNext() {return false;}
            };
        }
    }
}
```

A. Foo.class, Foo$1.class, Foo$Week.class

B. Foo.class, Foo.Week$1.class, Foo$1$Week.class

C. Foo.class, Foo$Week.class, Foo$Week$1.class

D. Foo.class, Foo$Week.class, Foo$Week$Iterator.class

A is the correct answer. The inner class Week has one anonymous inner class, so you would expect Foo$Week$1.class to be the correct name of the generated class file, in addition to Foo$Week.class and the top-level class Foo.class. However, the compiler ignores the inner classes in the numeric naming scheme of the anonymous inner classes.

10. What class files are generated when you compile the following code?

```
import java.util.HashMap;
public class Foo {
    public static class Week {
        public HashMap getMap() {
            return new HashMap() {
                public HashMap(int size) {}
                public Object put(Object key, Object value) {}
            };
        }
    }
}
```

A. None, the code doesn't compile.

B. Foo.class, Foo$HashMap.class, Foo$Week.class

C. Foo.class, Foo$Week$1.class, Foo$Week.class

D. Foo.class, Foo$Week.class, Foo$Week$HashMap.class

A is the correct answer. Anonymous inner classes cannot define constructors.

11. What do you have to change in the following code to make it valid?

```
public class Foo {
    public Runnable getRunnable(String name) {
        return new Thread() {
            public void run() {
                setName(name);
            }
        };
    }
}
```

A. Change the modifier of the run method to protected.

B. Change the return type of getRunnable() to Thread.

C. Declare the name parameter of getRunnable as final.

D. Nothing

C is the correct answer. Local and anonymous inner classes can access only final local variables and parameters of the enclosing method.

12. What will be the value of *b* after the assignment in the run() method?

```
public class Foo {
    int a = 10;
    int c = 30;
    public Runnable getRunnable() {
        int a = 20;
        return new Thread() {
            public void run() {
                int b = a+c;
            }
        };
    }
}
```

A. 30

B. 40

C. 50

D. This code doesn't compile.

D is correct. This code doesn't compile because at the scope level of the anonymous inner class definition, only the local variable *a* is visible, hiding the instance variable. This local variable has to be declared final to access it from within the run() method.

13. What is the correct way to write a constructor for the SubClassOfInner class?

```
class EnclosingClass {
    public class Inner {
        Inner(int a) {}
    }
}

class SubClassOfInner extends EnclosingClass.Inner {
    // how to write a constructor?
}
```

A. There is no correct way to provide a constructor in this scenario.

B. SubClassOfInner(int a) { super(a); }

C. SubClassOfInner(EnclosingClass outer, int a) { outer.super(a); }

D. SubClassOfInner(int a) {EnclosingClass.super(a);}

C is the correct answer. Because the constructor of Inner needs a handle to an instance of the enclosing class, it must be initialized, but the problem is that you don't have one available in the derived class. The SubClassOfInner inherits only from the inner class, not the enclosing class. The only way to avoid this problem is to pass in the handle to the enclosing instance explicitly and use the object.super() syntax to attach to the handle. Instantiation would work like the following:

```
EnclosingClass ec = new EnclosingClass();
SubClassOfInner sci = new SubClassOfInner(ec, 10);
```

14. What is wrong with the following code?

```
import java.util.Hashtable;
class Foo {
    String[] keys;
    String[] names;

public Hashtable buildHash(String start) {
    class MyHash extends Hashtable {
        public MyHash() {
            super();
        }

public void initHash(String str) {
        for (int i=0; i < keys.length; i++)
            if (names[i].startsWith(str))
                put(keys[i], names[i]);
        }
    }
    MyHash h = new MyHash();
    h.initHash(start);
    return h;
    }
}
```

A. Nothing. This code is correct.

B. The keys and names arrays must be declared public.

C. The start parameter of buildHash must be declared final.

D. The str parameter of initHash must be declared final.

A is correct. The local inner class MyHash has full access to the keys and names arrays, even if they were private, so *B* is wrong. MyHash does not access the start parameter of the buildHash method, so *C* is wrong; start does not have to be declared final. *D* is wrong because initHash is a method of the inner class itself and its parameters don't have to be final (unless of course you have another inner class inside the inner class!).

15. Consider the following code. What is printed on stdout?

```
class Foo {
    protected class Bar {
        protected Bar() {
            System.out.println("Foo.Bar");
        }
    }
    private Bar b;
    Foo() {
        System.out.println("Foo");
        b = this.new Bar();
    }
}

class FooToo extends Foo {
    protected class Bar {
        protected Bar() {
            System.out.println("FooToo.Bar");
        }
    }
    public static void main(String[] args) {
        new FooToo();
    }
}
```

A. Nothing. This code is incorrect.

B. Foo
   Foo.Bar

C. Foo
   FooToo.Bar

D. FooToo
   FooToo.Bar

B is the correct answer. FooToo's default constructor invokes Foo's constructor, which in turn prints "Foo" and creates an instance of Bar. Recall that the class name of Bar in Foo is Foo$Bar and the class name of FooToo's Bar is FooToo$Bar! This means that Foo creates an instance of its own Bar and not the Bar in FooToo, hence the output "Foo.Bar" and not "FooToo.Bar." In effect, with respect to inheritance, the *protected* inner class Bar behaves as if it were *private*.

16. Which of the statements about the following code is correct? (Choose all that apply.)

```
public class Foo {
    int var = 10;
    public class Test {
        public static void main(String[] args) {
            System.out.println("Foo$Test: var = " + var);
        }
    }
}
```

   A. The result of java Foo$Test is Foo$Test: var = 10.
   B. This code does not compile because Foo$Test cannot access the instance variable var.
   C. This code does not compile because Foo$Test can't have a static main() method.
   D. This code does not compile because you can't access var from a static method.
      C and D are correct. This code has two problems. First, Test is a member class and therefore can't have static members and thus no main method. Second, if you were to make the Test class static so that it can have a main(), you wouldn't be able to access the *instance variable* var from the static main() method.

17. You want to modify some local value defined in the enclosing scope of an anonymous inner class from within that anonymous inner class. What are your options to accomplish this? (Choose all that apply.)
   A. Store the value in an array that is declared final and modify the array element.
   B. Make sure the value is an object stored in a final local variable and use a method on that object to modify it.
   C. This can't be done.
   D. Don't define the value as final and simply modify it.
      A and B are correct. A is correct because even though the array itself is final, its elements are not and can therefore be modified from within the anonymous inner class. B is correct because even though the variable referencing the object can't be changed, the object itself can be modified using its own methods or, if it has public non-final members, by changing those members directly. *D* is incorrect because the value has to be declared final if you access it from within an anonymous inner class.

Chapter 9 Self Test

1. The following code tries to create a Thread by passing a Runnable target:

```
Runnable target=new XXXX();
Thread MyThread=new Thread(target);
```

Which of the following classes can be used to create the target, so that the preceding code compiles correctly?

A. public class MyRunnable extends Runnable{public void run(){}}

B. public class MyRunnable extends Object{public void run(){}}

C. public class MyRunnable implements Runnable{public void run(){}}

D. public class MyRunnable extends Runnable{void run(){}}

E. public class MyRunnable implements Runnable{void run(){}}

C. The class correctly implements the Runnable with a public void run() method. *A* is incorrect; interfaces are not extended, they are implemented. *B* is incorrect because even though the class would compile and it has a valid public void run method, it does not implement the Runnable interface, so the compiler would complain when creating a Thread with an instance of it. *D* is incorrect because it tries to extend, not to implement, the Runnable interface. Also, the run method should be public. *E* is incorrect because even if the implementing is done correctly, the run method should be public.

2. You have a class that looks like this:

```
public class MyRunnable implements Runnable{
    public void run(){
        // some code here
    }
}
```

What would be the proper way to create and start a new thread to run this code?

A. new Runnable(MyRunnable).start();

B. new Thread(MyRunnable).run();

C. new Thread(new MyRunnable()).start();

D. new MyRunnable().start();

C. Because your class implements Runnable, an instance of it has to be passed to the Thread constructor, and then the instance of the Thread has to be started. *A* is incorrect. You can't call any constructor of Runnable because Runnable is an interface, and you can't pass a class name to any constructor. *B* is incorrect for the same reason, you can't pass a class name to any constructor. *D* is incorrect because MyRunnable doesn't have a start() method.

3. In the following method:

```
public void printAll(String[] lines){
    for(int i=0;i<lines.length;i++){
        System.out.println(lines[i]);
        // add line here
    }
}
```

Assuming that the thread is not interrupted, which of the following lines would ensure that no more than one line is printed each second? (Choose all that apply.)

A. try{Thread.sleep(1100);}catch(InterruptedIOException e){}

B. Thread.sleep(1000);

C. try{Thread.sleep(1000);}catch(InterruptedException e){}

D. try{Thread.sleep(1100);}catch(IOException e){}

E. try{Thread.sleep(900);}catch(InterruptedException e){}

C. The thread sleeps for one second and the InterruptedException, although ignored, is caught properly. *A* and *D* are incorrect. They would not compile because Thread.sleep may throw an InterruptedException, which is a checked exception, so it has to be dealt with explicitly. Neither IOException or InterruptedIOException extend InterruptedException. *B* is incorrect because it doesn't catch InterruptedException. *E* is incorrect because only 900 milliseconds are guaranteed to have elapsed since the previous print.

4. What would be the output of the following thread?

```
public class MyThread extends Thread{
    public void run(){
        try {
        for(int i=1;i<5;i++) {
            System.out.print(i+" ");
            if(i>2)
                interrupt();

            sleep(1000);
            if(interrupted())
                break;
        }
        }catch(InterruptedException e) {
            System.out.print("caught ");}
        }
    }
}
```

A. 1

B. 1 2

C. 1 2 3

D. 1 caught

E. 1 2 caught

F. 1 2 3 caught

G. None of the above

   F. The thread prints the numbers and in the last loop, when *i* is 3, it will set the interrupted flag. This will force the last of the sleep method calls to throw an InterruptedException immediately and print *caught* after the already printed numbers. *A, B,* and *C* are incorrect because they count on the InterruptedException never being thrown. *D* and *E* are incorrect because they count on the interrupt flag being set before *i* is 3.

5. What is the purpose of the volatile keyword?

   A. To mark methods as being of exclusive use of a thread.

   B. To mark variables that may change at any time.

   C. To mark variables as being of exclusive use of a thread.

   D. To mark variables that can be used to synchronize on.

   E. To mark methods that may be called at any time.

      B. Volatile variables will not be cached on a Thread's private memory. *A* and *E* are incorrect because volatile is not used for methods. *C* is incorrect because access to volatile variables is never exclusive. *D* is incorrect. Variables are not used to synchronize on, objects are.

6. You have an object that is used to contain two values. Which of the following methods in its class can prevent concurrent access problems? (Choose all that apply.)

   A. public int read(int a, int b){return a+b;}
      public void set(int a, int b){this.a=a;this.b=b;}

   B. public synchronized int read(int a, int b){return a+b;}
      public synchronized void set(int a, int b){this.a=a;this.b=b;}

C. public int read(int a, int b){synchronized(a){return a+b;}}
   public void set(int a, int b){synchronized(a){this.a=a;this.b=b;}}

D. public int read(int a, int b){synchronized(a){return a+b;}}
   public void set(int a, int b){synchronized(b){this.a=a;this.b=b;}}

E. public synchronized(this) int read(int a, int b){return a+b;}
   public synchronized(this) void set(int a, int b){this.a=a;this.b=b;}

F. public int read(int a, int b){synchronized(this){return a+b;}}
   public void set(int a, int b){synchronized(this){this.a=a;this.b=b;}}

B, F. By marking the methods as synchronized, the threads will get the lock of the *this* object before proceeding. Only one thread will be either setting or reading at any given moment, thereby assuring that read always returns the addition of a valid pair. *A* is incorrect because it does non-synchronization; therefore there is no guarantee that the values added by the read method belong to the same pair. *C* and *D* are incorrect; only objects can be used to synchronize on. *E* is incorrect because it is not possible to select other objects to synchronize on when marking a method as synchronized. Even using *this* is incorrect syntax.

7. What is the purpose of notifying a thread that is in the wait state?

A. To prevent it getting turns at the CPU.

B. To make it throw an InterruptedException.

C. To set the notified flag.

D. To signal that it should proceed in executing instructions.

E. To signal that there are no more instructions to execute.

D. A waiting thread is waiting for a different thread to signal that it is time to proceed, typically because some data has been made available. *A* is incorrect; a waiting thread is already not taking turns at the CPU. *Notify* takes the thread out of this state and onto a similar state when it tries to get a lock to proceed in executing. *B* is incorrect because interrupt() is used to make it throw an InterruptedException. *C* is incorrect; there is no such flag. *E* is incorrect because notify is used precisely when there are more instructions to execute.

8. Which of the following are methods of the Object class? (Choose all that apply.)

A. notify();

B. notifyAll();

C. isInterrupted();

D. synchronized();

E. interrupt();

F. wait(long msecs);

G. sleep(long msecs);

H. yield();

I. synchronized(Object lock);

A, B, F. They are all related to the list of threads waiting on the specified object. *C, E, G,* and *H* are incorrect answers. isInterrupted() and interrupt() are instance methods of Thread. Sleep and yield are static methods of Thread. *D* and *I* are incorrect; such methods don't exist.

9. What would be the result of trying to compile and run the following program?

```
public class WaitTest{
    public static void main(String[] args){
        System.out.print("1 ");
        synchronized(args){
            System.out.print("2 ");
            try{
                args.wait();
            }catch(InterruptedException e){
            }
        }
        System.out.print("3 ");
    }
}
```

A. It will fail to compile because the IllegalMonitorStateException of wait is not dealt with.

B. It will compile and the output would be: 1 2 3.

C. It will compile and the output would be: 1 3.

D. It will compile and the output would be: 1 2.

E. It will compile and throw, and at run time it would throw an IllegalMonitorStateException when trying to wait.

F. It will fail to compile because it has to be synchronized on the *this* object.

D. 1 and 2 will be printed, but there will be no return from the wait call because no other thread will notify the main thread, so 3 will never be printed. *A* is incorrect; IllegalMonitorStateException is an unchecked exception and doesn't have to be deal with explicitly. *B* and *C* are incorrect; 3 will never be printed. *E* is incorrect because IllegalMonitorStateException will never be thrown because the wait is done on *args* within a block of code synchronized on args. *F* is incorrect because any object can be used to synchronize on, and furthermore, there is no *this* when running a static method.

10. After calling the following method, when will the thread become a candidate to get another turn at the CPU? (Assume that it is properly synchronized and the exception is caught.)

    ```
    wait(2000);
    ```

    A. After the thread is interrupted, the thread is notified, or two seconds have elapsed.

    B. After the thread is interrupted or two seconds after the thread is notified.

    C. Two seconds after the thread is notified or interrupted.

    D. After the thread is interrupted, or two seconds have elapsed.

    A. Either of the three will make the thread become a candidate for running again. *B* and *C* are incorrect because the thread will become a candidate immediately after notification, not two seconds afterwards. *D* is also incorrect because the thread may become a candidate after interruption.

11. When should notifyAll be used instead of notify?

    A. When there is one thread waiting for notification on the specific object.

    B. When all the objects that the thread has locked should be notified.

    C. When many threads are waiting on a waitAll method for the specified object.

    D. When there might be more than one thread waiting for notification on the specified object.

    E. When all waiting threads on the system should be notified.

    F. When there might be one thread waiting for notification on the specific object.

    D. Regardless of how many threads are waiting on notification from the specified object, notifyAll should be used if there is a possibility that there are more threads waiting on the specified object than the one we intended to notify. Just using notify may notify another thread, and the intended thread might never be notified, and so the application may freeze. *A* and *F* are incorrect because if there is or might be only one thread waiting, notify should be used. *B* is incorrect; objects are not notified, threads are. *C* is incorrect because there is no such waitAll method. *E* is incorrect because there is no way of notifying all waiting threads on the system simultaneously.

12. What will be the output of the following program?

    ```java
    public class ThreadTest extends Thread {
        public static void main(String[] args){
            new ThreadTest(1);
            new ThreadTest(2);
            System.out.println("main ");
        }
        private int val;
        private ThreadTest(int val) {
            this.val = val;
            start();
        }
        public void run(){System.out.print(val+" ");}
    }
    ```

A. 1 2 main

B. 2 1 main

C. main 1 2

D. main 2 1

E. 1 main 2

F. 2 main 1

G. Any of the above

H. None of the above

> **G.** It is not possible to tell which will be the output. When exactly threads get a turn at the CPU, in which order, and if they pre-empt the currently running one is JVM/platform dependent. *A, B, C, D, E,* and *F* are incorrect answers because none of them can be guaranteed for all platforms, although for some particular JVM/platforms it is possible to predict their particular outputs. *H* is incorrect because it will always be one of the above, regardless of the platform.

13. One of your threads (called backgroundThread) does some lengthy numerical processing. What would be the proper way of setting its priority to ensure that the rest of the system is very responsive while the thread is running? (Choose all that apply.)

A. backgroundThread.setPriority(Thread.LOW_PRIORITY);

B. backgroundThread.setPriority(Thread.MAX_PRIORITY);

C. backgroundThread.setPriority(1);

D. backgroundThread.setPriority(Thread.NO_PRIORITY);

E. backgroundThread.setPriority(Thread.MIN_PRIORITY);

F. backgroundThread.setPriority(Thread.NORM_PRIORITY);

G. backgroundThread.setPriority(10);

H. backgroundThread.setPriority(0);

> **E, C.** In **E**, the static final int Thread.MIN_PRIORITY is the lowest priority that a Thread can have, and the background thread should have a very low priority or the lowest. Answer **C** is correct because the value of Thread.MIN_PRIORITY is 1, although for clarity it is recommended to use the Thread.MIN_PRIORITY. *A* and *D* are incorrect because there are no such variables in the Thread class. *B* is incorrect; using MAX_PRIORITY would make other threads have less chances of getting a turn of the CPU, even to the point of freezing until the numerical processing is finished. *F* is incorrect because the thread would still compete for the CPU time and even delay other threads. *G* is incorrect because 10 is the value of MAX_PRIORITY, so *i* would be equivalent to answer *B*. *H* is incorrect because the allowed range for thread priorities is 1 through 10.

14. What factors affect the resulting priority of a thread after using setPriority(int n)? (Choose all that apply.)
    A. The priority of the thread that started it.
    B. The current maximum priority of the thread group to which it belongs.
    C. The current minimum priority of the thread group to which it belongs.
    D. The security manager installed.
    E. The current priority of the thread that calls setPriority.
    B, D. When modifying the priority of an already existing thread, the priority cannot be set to anything higher than the current maximum priority of the thread group to which it belongs, and only if the security manager allows it. *A* is incorrect because the priority of the thread that created it is a factor when creating the thread, but not later. *C* is incorrect because there is no such thing as minimum priority for a thread group. *E* is incorrect. Any thread, whatever its priority, can change the priority of another one, provided the security manager allows it.

15. Which method can be called on a Thread instance to make sure it never again receives a turn at the CPU?
    A. yield(0);
    B. exit(0);
    C. yield();
    D. setDaemon();
    E. setDaemon(0);
    F. interrupt();
    G. None of the above
    G. None of these method calls force a thread to never get a turn of the CPU again. *A* is incorrect because yield takes no parameter, and it is a static method, not an instance method. *B* is incorrect; Thread doesn't have an *exit* method. *C* is incorrect because *yield* can be used by the current thread to give up the turn of the CPU, but it will get another turn later. *D* and *E* are incorrect because setting the Deamon state does stop the thread in any way, and further, setting the Daemon state requires one boolean parameter. *F* is incorrect. The interrupted flag of the thread will be set and, if on sleeping or waiting, it will throw an InterruptedException, but it will still get turns at the CPU.

Chapter 10 Self Test

1. Calling Math.abs(10.4) returns which value?

   A. 10.0

   B. 10.4

   C. 11.0

   D. −10.4

   B. 10.4. The abs method returns the absolute value of the expression and the absolute value of 10.4 is 10.4. *A* and *C* are incorrect because abs(x) will return x or −x, depending on the sign of x. *D* is incorrect because the only time abs will return a negative value is if the input parameter is Integer.MIN_VALUE or Long.MIN_VALUE.

2. Which answer best describes the result of running the following program?

   ```
   public class AbsExample {
       public static void main(String args[]) {
           float x = -5.6f;
           float absX = Math.abs(x);
           System.out.println("The abs of " + x + " is " + absX);
       }
   }
   ```

   A. A compiler error occurs at line four.

   B. The abs of −5.6 is 5.6.

   C. The abs of −5.6 is −5.6.

   D. The abs of −5.6 is −5.

   B. The abs of −5.6 is 5.6. The abs method will return the value of the input parameter when the parameter is greater than zero and the negative of the input parameter when the parameter is less than zero. *A* is incorrect. The abs method is overloaded to take a float and return a float. No compiler errors result from line four. *C* and *D* are incorrect because the abs method does not return negative numbers.

3. Calling Math.ceil(-5.5) results in which value?

   A. −5.5
   B. −5.0
   C. −6.0
   D. −4.0

   B. The smallest Integer equivalent that is greater than or equal to −5.5 is −5.0.
   A is incorrect. The result of calling ceil will only return Integer equivalent values. *C* is
   incorrect because −6.0 is less than −5.5. *D* is incorrect because −4.0 is not the smallest
   number greater than −5.5.

4. To better understand how the ceil method works, the following program is written to output
   the index of the values array when the ceil method return is the same as the input parameter.
   Which answer best describes the result of running the program?

```
public class CeilExample {
    public static void main(String args[]) {
        float values[] = {1.0f, 1.2f, 1.4f, 1.6f, 1.8f, 2.0f};
        float ceilValues[] = new double[values.length];
        for (int i = 0; i < values.length; i++) {
            ceilValues[i] = Math.ceil(values[i]);
        }
        for (int i = 0; i < values.length; i++) {
            if (values[i] == ceilValues[i]) {
                System.out.println(i);
            }
        }
    }
}
```

   A. 0, 5
   B. 0, 1, 2, 3, 4, 5
   C. Runs, but no output is written
   D. Compile error at line six

   D. Compile error at line six. The compiler reports that an explicit cast is needed to
   convert a double into a float. The method signature for the ceil method is public static
   double ceil(double a). *A*, *B*, and *C* are incorrect because the program does not compile. If
   the float at line four were changed to double, then *A* would be correct. Calling ceil with an
   Integer equivalent returns the input parameter. Calling Math.ceil(8.0) returns 8.0, whereas
   calling Math.ceil(8.2) returns 9.0.

5. Calling Math.ceil(25.9) results in which value?

   A. 25.9

   B. 30.0

   C. 25.0

   D. 26.0

   D. 26.0. 26 is the closest integer that is greater than 25.9. *B* is incorrect. The ceil method never returns a value rounded to the nearest tenth. *A* is wrong because ceil always returns an Integer equivalent. *C* is incorrect because ceil never returns a value less than the argument.

6. The result of calling Math.floor(-0.5) is what value?

   A. 0.0

   B. −1.0

   C. 1.0

   D. 0.5

   B. −1.0. Floor returns the largest Integer equivalent that is less than or equal to the argument. −1.0 is the largest Integer equivalent that is less than −0.5. *A, C,* and *D* are wrong. The result of calling floor is never greater than the argument.

7. Running this program yields which of the following?

```
public class FloorExample {
    public static void main(String args[]) {
        double values[] = {-2.3, -1.0, 0.25, 4};
        int cnt = 0;
        for (int i = 0; i < values.length; i++) {
            if (Math.floor(values[i]) == Math.ceil(values[i])) {
                ++cnt;
            }
        }
        System.out.println("The results are the same " + cnt + " time(s)");
    }
}
```

   A. The results are the same 0 time(s)

   B. The results are the same 2 time(s)

   C. The results are the same 4 time(s)

   D. A compiler error at line six

   B. The results are the same 2 time(s). When the value is −2.3, Math.floor is −3.0 and Math.ceil is −2.0. When the value is −1.0, Math.floor is −1.0 and Math.ceil is −1.0. When the value is 0.25, Math.floor is 0.0 and Math.ceil is 1.0. When the value is 4, Math.floor is 4.0 and Math.ceil is 4.0. *A* and *C* are wrong because the only time floor and ceil are equal is when argument is an Integer equivalent. *D* is wrong because the program compiles and runs without error. There is nothing wrong with line six. The values are all compatible with a double.

8. Calling Math.floor(96.4) yields which result?

A. 96.4

B. 95.0

C. 96.0

D. 97.0

C. 96.0. Remember the number line; 96.0 is the first number found by moving to the left on the number line from the argument 96.4. *A* is incorrect because floor always returns an integer equivalent. *B* is wrong. 95.0 is not the first number found to the left of 96.4 on the number line. *D* is wrong because the floor method never returns a value greater than the argument.

9. Which of the following are valid calls to Math.max? (Choose all that apply.)

A. Math.max(1, 4)

B. Math.max(2.3, 5)

C. Math.max(1, 3, 5, 7)

D. Math.max(-1.5, -2.8f)

A. Math.max(1, 4), **B.** Math.max(2.3, 5), and **D.** Math.max(-1.5, -2.8f). The max method is overloaded to take two arguments of type int, long, float, and double. *C* is incorrect. Math.max does not take three parameters.

10. Calling Math.max(8.2, 6.9) returns which value?

A. 8.2

B. 8.0

C. 6.9

D. 7.0

A. 8.2. The value of 8.2 is the maximum value given 8.2 and 6.9. *B* and *D* are incorrect. The max method will always return a value equal to one of the two arguments. *C* is incorrect because 8.2 is greater than 6.9.

11. Calling Math.min(8.2, 6.9) returns which value?

A. 8.2

B. 8.0

C. 6.9

D. 7.0

C. 6.9. Regardless of the order in which the arguments appear in the call to min, the lesser value is the min result. 6.9 is less than 8.2. *A* is incorrect because 8.2 is greater than 6.9 and the min method always returns the lesser of the two arguments. *B* and *D* are incorrect. The min method will always return a value equal to one of the two arguments.

12. What output is produced running the following program?

```
public class MinDouble1 {
    public static void main(String args[]) {
        double setA[] = {1.1, 1.5, -3.6};
        double setB[] = {1.1, 1.4, 3.6};
        for (int i = 0; i < setA.length; i++) {
            if (Math.min(setA[i], setB[i]) ==
            Math.max(setA[i], setB[i])) {
                System.out.println("Min and Max are the same at " + i);
            }
        }
    }
}
```

A. Min and Max are the same at 0
B. Min and Max are the same at 1
C. Min and Max are the same at 2
D. A compiler error at line six

A. Min and Max are the same at 0. At the first array location for setA and setB the values are the same. Because the values are the same, the min and the max of two equal values are the same. *B* and *C* are not correct because at the second and third array locations for setA and setB, the values are different. Two numbers that are not equal will result in different min and max values. *D* is not correct because the program compiles and runs without errors.

13. Calling Math.min(1, 8.25) returns which type and value?

A. int 1
B. long 1L
C. float 1.0f
D. double 1.0

D. double 1.0. The 8.25 argument is a double and causes the static double min(double a, double b) method to be called. *A*, *B*, and *C* are incorrect because the return value is a double and not an int, a long, or a float.

14. Running this program yields which of the following?

```
public class RandomExample {
    public static void main(String args[]) {
        if(Math.random() >= 5.0) {
            System.out.println(
            "The number is greater than or equal to 5.0");
        }
        else {
            System.out.println(
            "The number is less than 5.0");
        }
    }
}
```

A. The number is greater than or equal to 5.0
B. The number is less than 5.0
C. Either A or B
D. A compiler error at line three

B. The number is less than 5.0. The random method always returns a value greater than or equal to 0.0 and less than 1.0. The test at line three always fails and line seven is printed out each time the program is executed. *A* and *C* are wrong because the value returned from random is always less than 1.0 and therefore always less than 5.0. *D* is incorrect because the program compiles and executes without any errors.

15. The following program is run three times on the same platform. What statements are true?

```
public class RandomExample {
    public static void main(String args[]) {
        double seed = Math.PI;
        Math.random(seed);
        for (int i = 0; i < 10; i++) {
            System.out.println(Math.random());
        }
    }
}
```

A. Each run produces the same 10 random numbers.
B. Each run produces a different set of 10 random numbers.
C. The seed value is added to each random number.
D. A compiler error occurs at line four.

D. A compiler error occurs at line four. *A* is not correct because the program does not compile or run. If line four is removed, running the program subsequent times produces a different result each time. *B* is not correct because the program does not compile or run. *C* is not correct because a seed is not used in the Java random method.

16. What statements are true about the result obtained from calling Math.random()? (Choose all that apply.)

    A. The result is less than 0.0.

    B. The result is greater than or equal to 0.0.

    C. The result is less than 10.0.

    D. The result is greater than 1.0.

    B, C. The result is greater than or equal to 0.0 and the result is less than 10.0. The range of values returned from random is a value that is greater than or equal to 0.0 and less than 1.0. *A* is wrong because random does not return negative values. *D* is wrong because numbers greater than 1.0 are outside the range of returned values.

17. Calling Math.round(99.2) returns which result?

    A. 99.0

    B. 100.0

    C. 99

    D. 100

    C. 99. The closest integer value is 99. If the argument is greater than or equal to 99.5 and less than 100.5, the result is 100. *A* and *B* are not correct because round returns an integer closest to the argument. *D* is not correct because 99 is closer to 99.2 than 100.

18. For which arguments are the results from round and floor the same? (Choose all that apply.)

    A. –1.3

    B. 0.4

    C. 6.2

    D. –2.7

    E. 100

    B. 0.4, C. 6.2, D. –2.7, and E. 100. Math.round(0.4) is 0 and Math.floor(0.4) is 0.0. Math.round(6.2) is 6 and Math.floor(6.2) is 6.0. Math.round(-2.7) is –3 and Math.floor(-2.7) is –3.0. Math.round(100) is 100 and Math.floor(100) is 100.0. *A* is not correct. Math.round(-1.3) is –1 and Math.floor(-1.3) is –2.0.

19. Calling Math.round(9.5) returns which result?

    A. 9

    B. 9.5

    C. 10

    C. 10. By using the algorithm in which you add 0.5 to the argument and truncating, you get 10. *A* is wrong because round always returns a value greater than or equal to the argument. 9 is definitely less than 9.5. *B* is wrong because round returns an int or a long.

20. If you wanted to plot the curve of the sine function from 0 to 360 degrees, using the sin method, what other Math methods would you likely use?

    A. abs
    B. min
    C. toRadians
    D. toDegrees
    E. random

    C. toRadians. Unless you know, for instance, that 360 degrees is equivalent to two times PI radians, it is necessary to invoke a method to convert the angle into radians before calling sin. The call would look like Math.sin(Math.toRadians(angleInDegrees)). *D* is wrong because the sin method takes an argument in radians and the method toDegrees converts an angle in radians into an angle in degrees. *A, B,* and *E* are wrong because the absolute value of an argument, the minimum of two arguments, and a random value between 0.0 and 1.0 are not necessary to plot the sine of an angle.

21. Choose all the valid sin method signatures.

    A. static double sin(double a)
    B. static float sin(float a)
    C. static double sin(double a, double b)
    D. static float sin(float a, float b)

    A. static double sin(double a). There is only one valid signature for each trigonometric function. The valid signature takes a double argument for an angle in radians and returns a double result. *B, C,* and *D* are incorrect. There are no valid sin method signatures that take a float argument or more than one argument.

22. For which ranges of values is the sin method defined? (Choose all that apply.)

    A. greater than or equal to 0.0
    B. $-PI / 2$ through $PI / 2$
    C. 0.0 through 360.0

    A, B, and **C.** The signature for sin takes a double argument in radians and the function is defined for all real values.

23. What is the result of running the following program?

```
public class TanExample {
   public static void main(String args[]) {
      double angle = Math.PI / 4;
      if (Math.tan(angle) == (Math.sin(angle) / Math.cos(angle))) {
```

```
            System.out.println("tan(a) = sin(a) / cos(a)");
         }
         else {
            System.out.println(Math.tan(angle));
         }
      }
   }
```

A. tan(a) = sin(a) / cos(a)

B. 1.0

C. PI

D. 360.0

A. tan(a) = sin(a) / cos(a). However, you will *not* be expected to answer a question such as this. You will *not* be expected to know that tangent can be defined in terms of sine and cosine or that this example does not work for all values of angle due to round-off errors when dividing. All you need to know is that tan takes a double and returns a double. Knowing the signature of the trigonometric functions will be sufficient.

24. What are the valid signatures for the sqrt method?

A. static int sqrt(int a)

B. static long sqrt(long a)

C. static float sqrt(float a)

D. static double sqrt(double a)

D. static double sqrt(double a). The sqrt method takes a double argument representing an angle in radians and returns the tangent of the angle as a double value. *A*, *B*, and *C* are not correct. The sqrt method is not defined to take an int, a long, or a float.

25. What value is returned from calling Math.sqrt(0.0)?

A. 0.0

B. NaN

C. ArithmeticException is thrown

D. A compiler error is generated by calling Math.sqrt(0.0)

A. 0.0. The sqrt function is defined for all values greater than or equal to 0.0. *B* is incorrect. NaN is returned when the argument is less than 0.0 or NaN. *C* is wrong because Math.sqrt does not throw exceptions. *D* is incorrect. It is syntactically correct to call the sqrt method with any value.

26. What is the result of running the following program?

```
public class SqrtExample {
   public static void main(String args[]) {
      double value = -9.0;
      System.out.println("The sqrt of "
         + value + " is "
         + Math.sqrt(value));
   }
}
```

A. The sqrt of –9.0 is 3.0

B. The sqrt of –9.0 is –3.0

C. The sqrt of –9.0 is NaN

D. A compiler error at line seven

> **C.** The sqrt of –9.0 is NaN. The sqrt method returns NaN whenever the argument is less than 0.0. *A* is not correct because –9.0 is less than 0.0 and sqrt always returns NaN given a negative argument. *B* is not correct because sqrt never returns a negative number. *D* is not correct because the program compiles and runs without errors.

Chapter 11 Self Test

1. Which of the following methods would be used to concatenate the text string *World* to an existing String variable that contains the characters *Hello*?

    A. trim

    B. insert

    C. append

    D. None of these

    > **D.** Strings are immutable. There are no methods that change the contents of an existing String variable. *A, B,* and *C* are incorrect because all of the methods listed apply to StringBuffers, and not Strings.

2. Will the following code compile?

    ```
    public class Test
    {
      public static void main(String args[])
      {
          String a  = "foo";
          String b = "bar";
          a = a + b;
      }
    }
    ```

A. Yes

B. No

A. The code will compile. This code causes a new String object to be created and the object reference of the String object *a* is changed to reference the new string. *B* is incorrect because the code will compile.

3. When the following fragment of code is executed, what will the output be?

```
public class Test {
    public static void main(String args[]) {
        String a = "Java is ";
        String b = a;a += "Great.";
        if (a == b) {
            System.out.println("a and b are the same");
        }
        else {
            System.out.println("a and b are not the same");
        }
    }
}
```

A. a and b are the same

B. a and b are not the same

B. Because operators like += change the object reference, and not the object itself, changes that occur to *a* via these operators do not affect other objects with the same initial reference. *A* is incorrect because the statement *a+= "Great.";* changes the variable's reference, so that it no longer points to the initial string. This makes the comparison fail.

4. When the following fragment of code is executed, what will the output be?

```
public class Test {
    public static void main(String args[]) {
        String a = "JAVA IS GREAT";
        String b = a.toUpperCase();
        if (a == b) {
            System.out.println("a and b are the same");
        }
        else {
            System.out.println("a and b are not the same");
        }
    }
}
```

A. a and b are the same

B. a and b are not the same

A. The toUpperCase() method returns a reference to the original string if it is already in upper case. *B* is incorrect because the a==b comparison succeeds due to *a* and *b* pointing to the same variable.

5. Which of the following is true about the StringBuffer class in Java?

A. StringBuffer objects have a specific character capacity.

B. StringBuffer objects inherit all of the methods of the String class.

C. The contents of StringBuffer variables can be initialized using the = operator.

D. The contents of StringBuffer objects can compared using the == operator.

A. All StringBuffer objects have a set character capacity that is specified when the variable is constructed. *B* is incorrect because StringBuffer is a completely different class from the String class, and does not inherit its methods. *C* is incorrect because the = operator can only be used to initialize Strings, not StringBuffers. *D* is incorrect because the == operator only determines whether object references are equal, and does not test the actual contents.

6. When the following fragment of code is executed, what will the output be?

```
public class Test
{
  public static void main(String args[])
  {
    String a = "Java";
    System.out.println(a.length);
  }
}
```

A. 3

B. 4

C. 5

D. This code will not compile.

D. The length() method is being referenced as an instance variable and not as a method. The correct code to print the length of the string *a* would be:

```
System.out.println(a.length());
```

A, B, and *C* are incorrect because the code will not compile.

7. When the following fragment of code is executed, what will the output be?

```
String a = "Java";
    System.out.println(a.length());
```

A. 3

B. 4

C. 5

D. This code will not compile.

B. The length() method returns the exact number of characters in the string. *A* and *C* are incorrect because the length() method returns a value of 4, not 5 or 3. (There are four characters in the string Java.) *D* is incorrect because the code will compile.

8. When the following fragment of code is executed, what will the output be?

```
String a = "Java is great.";
    System.out.println(a.charAt(a.length()));
```

A. ``.``

B. ``t``

C. ``J``

D. The code will generate an exception.

D. The code will generate an exception. The first character in a Java string is at position 0. The last character is at position length() - 1, so this code will generate a StringIndexOutOfBounds exception. *A, B,* and *C* are incorrect because if an exception is generated when executing the first line, the second will never be reached.

9. When the following fragment of code is executed, what will the output be?

```
String a = "Java is great.";
    System.out.println(a.indexof("i"));
```

A. 5

B. 6

C. 7

D. The code will generate an exception.

A. The first character in a Java string is at position 0, so the indexOf function will parse through the String *a* and find the first *i* at location 5. *B* is incorrect because string indexes in Java are based on zero, not one. *C* is incorrect also, as the indexof() method will return 5, not 7. *D* is incorrect because the code will compile.

10. When the following fragment of code is executed, what will the output be?

```
public class Test {
   public static void main(String args[]) {
      String a = "Java is great.";
```

```
        String b = a.toString();
        if (a==b) {
           System.out.println("A is the same as B");
        }
        else {
           System.out.println("A is not the same as B");
        }
        if (a.equals(b)) {
           System.out.println("A equals B");
        }
        else {
           System.out.println("A does not equal B");
        }
    }
}
```

A. A is the same as B
    A equals B

B. A is not the same as B
    A equals B

C. A is the same as B
    A does not equal B

D. A is not the same as B
    A does not equal B

☑ **A.** Calling the toString() on a String object always returns the object reference of the string itself. After the initialization, *a* and *b* will reference the same String object, therefore the == operator will return true. Because the equals() method evaluates whether the contents of the String object are the same, and both *a* and *b* refer to the same String object, their contents must be the same, so the equals() method will also return true. Answer *B* is incorrect because the a==b comparison will succeed, not fail, due to the String references being the same. *C* is incorrect because the a.equals(b) comparison will succeed due to the contents of the string variables being equal. *D* is incorrect because both comparisons will succeed.

11. Will the following line of code compile?

```
String a = "There are " + 99 + " bottles of beer on the wall." ;
```

A. Yes

B. No

A. Java automatically converts all primitive types to a string when referenced as a string. *B* is incorrect because the code will compile.

12. Will the following code fragment compile?

```
class MyObject
    {
        public static void main(String[] arg)
        {
            MyObject mo = new MyObject();
            String a = "My object is " +  mo;
        }
    }
```

A. Yes

B. No

A. Java automatically converts all other objects to strings using the toString() method when referenced as a string. All classes inherit from the Object class and the Object class defines a default toString() method. All objects have a toString() method that can be called, and all objects can be referenced as strings. *B* is incorrect because the code will compile due to the string concatenation succeeding.

13. Which of the following statements is *not* true?

A. Strings can be initialized using the = operator.

B. The toString() method can be used to return a String value from a StringBuffer object.

C. All strings are terminated with a null (ASCII 0) character.

D. It is impossible to change the contents of a String variable.

C. Strings in Java are not terminated with a null character, as in the C language. *A* is true because strings can be initialized using the = operator. (It is a shortcut to string construction.) *B* is true because a String value can be returned from any object by using the toString() method. The statement in *D* is true because strings are immutable. Their contents can never be changed.

14. What is the output of the following Java program?

```
public class foo {
    public static void main(String[] args) {
        String a = " java ";
        String b = " java";
        if (a.trim() == b.trim()) {
            System.out.println("a == b");
```

```
        }
        if (a.trim().equals(b.trim())) {
            System.out.println("a equals b");
        }
    }
}
```

A. The program will not compile.

B. a == b

C. a equals b

D. Both B and C.

C. The JVM will create two separate strings to hold the result of the a.trim() and b.trim() operations, so the == operator will receive different object references and therefore return false. The result of trimming any string is to return the string with no leading or trailing white space, so because both strings are otherwise identical, both will be returned as *java* and therefore the equals() method will return true. *A* is incorrect because the program will compile. *B* and *D* are incorrect because the two string references will not point to the same location, so the a==b comparison will fail.

15. What is the output of the following code fragment?

```
String a = "xxxJava is great.xxx";

    System.out.println(a.substring(0, a.lastIndexOf('x') - 2));
```

A. "xxxJava is great."

B. "xxxJava is great.xx"

C. "xxxJava is grea"

D. "x"

A. The lastIndexOf() function returns the index of the last *x*, which is also the last character in the string. The substring function returns the portion of the string from the character at index 0 (the first character in the string) to this index - 2, yielding the string in answer *A*. *B*, *C*, and *D* are incorrect because the position returned by the lastIndexOf command, 19, doesn't match any of the answers.

16. Which of the following is not the appropriate way to construct and initialize a string?

A. String s = "test";

B. String s = new String "test";

C. String s = new String();

D.   String s = new String("test");

B. *C* and *D* are incorrect because they are valid constructors for the String class. The Java language also provides programmers with a shortcut to string construction, as shown in *A*. **B** is not valid syntax in any way.

17.   When the following code fragment is executed, what will be the result?

```
public class Test
{
  public static void main(String args[])
  {
    String s1 = new String ("one");
    StringBuffer s2 = new StringBuffer("three");s1.append("1");
    s2.append("2");if (s1.equals(s2))
        System.out.println("The two strings are equal");
  }
}
```

A.   It will print "The two strings are equal."

B.   There will not be any output.

C.   An exception will be thrown at line five.

D.   The code will not compile.

D. There is no append() method for the String class, so the line s1.append("1") will generate an error at compile time. Strings are immutable, so an append() method doesn't make any sense. *A, B,* and *C* are incorrect because the code won't compile.

18.   How many bytes of storage are required to store each character in a string?

A.   1

B.   2

C.   3

D.   4

E.   The number of bytes depends upon the character.

B. All Java characters are two bytes long. *E* would be correct for many other programming languages, but not for Java. *A, C,* and *D* are simply false.

19.   What will the output of this code fragment be?

```
StringBuffer b = new StringBuffer("abcdefg");
b.delete(3,6);
b.append("hij");
System.out.println(b.toString());
```

A. abcghij

B. abcdefghij

C. abfghij

D. abchij

E. The code will not compile.

A. The second line, b.delete(3,6), deletes the characters *def* from the source string, leaving the characters abcg. The next line, b.append("hij"), appends those three characters to the string, which gives the final result, abcghij. *E* is incorrect because there is nothing stopping the code from compiling. *B* and *C* are incorrect because the delete method deleted the characters *def* from the string. *D* is incorrect because the character *g* was never deleted.

20. If a StringBuffer is constructed with the following syntax, what will the original capacity be?

```
StringBuffer buf = new StringBuffer("Test");
```

A. 4

B. 16

C. 32

D. Unlimited

A. 4. When a StringBuffer is constructed using a string as an argument, the capacity is set to the length of the target string. *Test* is four characters in length, so the capacity is initially four. *B* would be correct if no string argument was given, as the default capacity for a StringBuffer is 16. *C* is incorrect; there is no reason why the capacity would be 32. *D* is incorrect because even though the capacities of StringBuffers can grow as the variable grows, all StringBuffer variables have a specific capacity when constructed.

Chapter 12 Self Test

1. Which of the following properties apply to a deck of cards?

A. Ordered

B. Sorted

C. Duplicating

D. Uses keys

A. A deck contains individual cards that, when pulled off the top of the deck one after another, form a definite order. *B* is wrong because a deck of cards is shuffled with no sorting (unless someone is cheating). *C* is incorrect because each card in a deck is unique; therefore, there are no duplicates. *D* is wrong because there is no mapping of keys to refer to the cards in a deck.

2. Which of the following properties apply to a list of phone numbers in a directory? (Choose all that apply.)
    A. Ordered
    B. Sorted
    C. Duplicating
    D. Uses keys
        B and D. B is correct because the names are stored in alphabetical order. **D** is correct because the name acts as the key to retrieve, store, and sort the phone numbers. *A* and *C* are incorrect. *A* is wrong because, although they are sorted, they are not ordered in the sense of keeping a sequence and index of objects in the collection. *C* is incorrect because the phone numbers themselves may be duplicated. It is the key that may not be duplicated. In this case, names may not be duplicated.

3. Which of the following interfaces form the framework for a nonduplicating, unsorted, unordered collection?
    A. List
    B. Map
    C. Set
    D. Collection
        C is correct because a set does not allow duplicate objects to be stored. It also is unsorted and unordered. *A* is wrong because a List allows duplicates. *B* is incorrect because a Map allows duplicates and uses a key, which is not required. *D* is wrong because a Collection is a very general interface that allows anything, including duplicates.

4. Which of the following classes directly implement the Set interface?
    A. Vector
    B. LinkedList
    C. HashSet
    D. Hashtable
        C. HashSet is the only class in the Java API to directly implement the Set interface. *A*, *B*, and *D* are incorrect because they do not use the Set interface.

5. Which of the following classes would be appropriate to use for a list of one of a kind baseball cards? Keep in mind that you are not interested in sorting these or in their order.
    A. Vector
    B. TreeMap
    C. Hashtable

    D. TreeSet

    E. HashSet

    E is correct because a HashSet stores objects in an unordered, unsorted manner without allowing duplicates. *A* is wrong because a Vector keeps objects ordered, which is unnecessary for this example. *B* is wrong because a TreeMap is sorted. *C* is incorrect because Hashtable uses a key to manipulate items, which is unnecessary for this example. *D* is wrong because TreeSet uses the SortedSet interface, hence the objects are sorted.

6. Which of the following interfaces form the framework for a nonduplicating, sorted collection?

    A. SortedList

    B. SortedMap

    C. SortedSet

    D. List

    C is correct because a SortedSet does not allow duplicate objects to be stored, but it has the additional property of being sorted. *A, B,* and *D* are incorrect. *A* is wrong because a SortedList does not actually exist. *B* is incorrect because a SortedMap uses keys, which are not required. *D* is wrong because a List allows duplicates.

7. Which of the following classes directly implement the SortedSet interface?

    A. Vector

    B. LinkedList

    C. HashSet

    D. TreeSet

    E. Hashtable

    D. TreeSet is the only class in the Java API to directly implement the SortedSet interface. *A, B, C,* and *E* are incorrect because they do not use the SortedSet interface.

8. You are creating a program that stores a list of the members in your Monday night bowling league. It would be nice to have them stored alphabetically. Which of the following classes would you use?

    A. Vector

    B. TreeMap

    C. Hashtable

    D. TreeSet

    E. HashSet

D is correct because a TreeSet (SortedSet) sorts items in ascending order, without allowing duplicates. *A* is wrong because a Vector is not sorted (technically you can sort this using the Collections class method sort(), but it does not do it automatically on the fly). *B* and *C* are incorrect because TreeMap and Hashtable use a key to manipulate items, which is unnecessary for a list of names. *E* is not correct because objects placed in a HashSet are not sorted.

9. Which of the following interfaces form the framework for a duplicating, ordered, unsorted collection?
   A. List
   B. Map
   C. Set
   D. Collection
   A is correct because a List allows duplicate objects to be stored, but it has the additional property of being ordered. *B* is incorrect because a Map uses keys, which are not required. *C* is wrong because a Set does not keep track of order. *D* is wrong because a Collection is a very general interface for collections without order.

10. Which of the following classes directly implement the List interface? (Choose all that apply.)
    A. Vector
    B. LinkedList
    C. HashSet
    D. TreeSet
    E. Hashtable
    A and **B.** Both Vector and LinkedList implement the List interface directly. *C, D,* and *E* are incorrect because they do not use the List interface.

11. Which of the following classes would be appropriate to use for a deck of cards?
    A. Vector
    B. TreeMap
    C. Hashtable
    D. TreeSet
    E. HashSet

A is correct because a Vector keeps items ordered. It does allow duplicates, but it is still the best choice for cards, especially if several decks of cards are combined into one. *B* is wrong because a TreeMap is sorted and cards must be able to be shuffled. *C* is incorrect because Hashtable uses a key to manipulate items, which is unnecessary in a deck of cards. *D* is wrong because TreeSet uses the SortedSet interface, hence the objects are sorted. *E* is not quite correct because objects placed in a Set such as HashSet are unordered, so it would be difficult and inaccurate to attempt to use this class for a deck of cards. A real deck of cards is shuffled randomly, yet does have an order.

12. Which of the following interfaces form the framework for an unsorted, unordered collection that uses keys to access the elements?

   A. List
   B. Map
   C. Set
   D. Collection
   B is correct because a Map uses keys to access the elements. It also is unsorted and unordered. *A* is wrong because a List is ordered and does not use a key. *C* is incorrect because a Set does not use a key. *D* is wrong because a Collection is a very general interface that allows anything, including duplicates.

13. Which of the following classes directly implement the Map interface? (Choose all that apply.)

   A. Vector
   B. LinkedList
   C. HashSet
   D. Hashtable
   E. HashMap
   D and E. Hashtable and HashMap both directly implement the Map interface. *A, B,* and *C* are incorrect because they do not use the Map interface.

14. Which of the following methods are part of the Map interface? (Choose all that apply.)

   A. get()
   B. add()
   C. set()
   D. put()
   E. remove()

A, D, and **E.** All of these methods are part of the Map interface. *B* is wrong because add() is used only for classes implementing the Collection interface. *C* is wrong because the set() method is completely made up.

15. Which of the following classes would be appropriate to use for a telephone directory listing?

    A. TreeMap
    B. Vector
    C. Hashtable
    D. TreeSet
    E. HashSet

    A is correct because a TreeMap uses a key (the name) to store other objects (the phone number). The keys will be sorted in ascending order. *B* is wrong because a Vector is not sorted. *C* is incorrect because Hashtable is also unsorted. *D* and *E* are wrong because TreeSet and HashSet do not use keys, hence the phone numbers will not be sorted by name.

16. Which of the following interfaces form the framework for a sorted collection that uses keys?

    A. SortedList
    B. SortedMap
    C. SortedSet
    D. List
    E. Map

    B is correct because a SortedMap stores objects in a sorted collection. *A, C,* and *D* are wrong because these collections do not use keys. *E* is incorrect because a Map is not sorted.

17. Which of the following classes directly implement the SortedMap interface?

    A. Vector
    B. ArrayMap
    C. HashMap
    D. Hashtable
    E. TreeMap

    E. TreeMap is the only class in the Java API to directly implement the SortedMap interface. *A, B, C,* and *D* are incorrect because they do not use the SortedMap interface.

18. A coworker has left a printout of some code on your desk. You examine the code:

```
import java.util.*;
class Inventors {
    public static void main (String [] args) {
        Set dir = new TreeSet();
        dir.put("Jon G.", "555-5553");
        dir.put("Al E.", "555-1978");
        dir.put("Tom E.", "555-1330");
        dir.put("Jimmy W.", "555-7165");
        System.out.println(dir);
    }
}
```

What will the output of this program be when it is compiled and run?

A. {Al E.=555-1978, Jimmy W.=555-7165, Jon G.=555-5553, Tom E.=555-1330}

B. { Jon G.=555-5553, Al E.=555-1978, Tom E.=555-1330, Jimmy W.=555-7165}

C. The program won't compile because of line four.

D. The program won't compile because of lines five through eight.

E. Something else will prevent the program from compiling.

D is correct because TreeSet does not use the method put(), it uses add(). Also, TreeSet does not use keys. *A* is wrong because only TreeMap would cause this output. *B* is wrong because HashMap or Hashtable would give this output. *C* is wrong because this line will compile fine—it is when we try to use the method put() that the compiler complains. *E* is wrong because of the preceding reasons.

19. You are attempting to create a computerized fortune-teller that can read Tarot cards. Your prototype program looks like this:

```
import java.util.*;
class MadameCthulhu {
    public static void main (String [] args) {
        Map tarot = new HashMap();
        tarot.put("Lovers", "you will have romance");
        tarot.put("Justice", "justice will be yours at last");
        tarot.put("The Fool", "beware what your friends tell you");
        tarot.put("Death", "you better make a will");
        Collections.shuffle(tarot);
        String card = (String)tarot.firstKey();
        String prediction = (String)tarot.get(card);
        System.out.println("Madam Cthulhu has picked " + card);
        System.out.println("She says " + prediction + "!");
    }
}
```

Which lines will prevent this code from compiling successfully? (Choose all that apply.)

A. `Map tarot = new HashMap();`

B. `Collections.shuffle(tarot);`

C. `String card = (String)tarot.firstKey();`

D. `String prediction = (String)tarot.get(card);`

E. Lines 5-8.

B and C. B is correct because the shuffle() method requires a List object. HashMap is a Map object and does not implement the List interface. **C** is correct because the method firstKey() is part of the SortedMap interface, not the Map interface. *A* is wrong because this line declares a Map object properly. *D* is wrong because this is the proper way to retrieve an object from a Map collection. The compiler will not complain about this line. *E* is wrong because these lines properly add objects to the HashMap using keys.

20. You are attempting to create a class that will store an alphabetized list of your comic collection. Here is your prototype code so far:

```
import java.util.*;
class ComicBooks {
    public static void main (String [] args) {
        Map comics = new TreeMap();
        comics.put(new Integer(404),"Batman:Year One pt 1");
        comics.put(new Integer(437),"Batman:Year Three pt 2");
        comics.put(new Integer(461),"Batman:Once upon a time");
        comics.put(new Integer(459),null);
        System.out.println(comics);
    }
}
```

What will occur when this class is compiled and run?

A. It will not compile because an Integer object can't be used as a key.

B. It will not compile because Map objects can't store null values.

C. It will not compile because SortedMap objects can't store null values.

D. It will compile and run fine.

D. This is a valid piece of code to output a collection. *A* is wrong because any object can be used as a key. It is primitive types that can't be used as keys. *B* is wrong because Map objects can store null values both as keys and as objects. *C* is wrong because SortedMap objects can store null objects as well. They can't store null values as keys, however.

Chapter 13 Self Test

1. Which of the following statements are true of the java.awt.Component class? (Choose all that apply.)

    A. It is the ultimate superclass for all nonmenu graphical components.

    B. It contains methods for handling events.

    C. It contains methods for rendering.

    A. B. C. The java.awt.Component class is the ultimate superclass for all nonmenu graphical components. The Component class contains methods for both handling events and rendering itself.

2. Which method is used to set the background color of a component?

    A. setColor(Color c)

    B. setBackground(Color c)

    C. setBackgroundColor(Color c)

    D. setForegroundColor(Color c)

    B. The setBackground(Color c) method is used to set the background color of a component. *A* and *C* are incorrect because there are no such methods in components that come with the JDK. *D* is incorrect because that method is used to set the color for those items rendered in the foreground, such as text.

3. Assume that you have a Panel, named p1, with a layout manager of BorderLayout. The background color of this panel is explicitly set to black and the foreground color is explicitly set to white. Now also assume that a new Panel, named p2, with a layout manager of FlowLayout is added to the first panel in the center area. This new panel p2 has a foreground color that is explicitly set to red, but no background color is set. A label with some text in it is added to this second panel. No colors are set for this label. Which of the following sentences are accurate? (Choose all that apply.)

    A. The label text is white in color.

    B. The label text is red in color.

    C. The layout manager of panel p2 overrides the layout manager of panel p1.

    D. The panel p2 has a background color of black.

    E. The label in panel p2 fills the entire area of panel p2.

    B and D. Because the label does not explicitly set a foreground color, it inherits the foreground color of its enclosing container, in this case the red foreground color of its parent panel named p2. The panel p2 does not explicitly set a background color so it inherits the background color of its parent container p1, which has a background color of black.

A is incorrect because the label inherits its foreground color from its parent container, panel p2. *C* is incorrect because layout managers do not override each other in that manner. *E* is incorrect because although panel p1 has a layout manager of BorderLayout and having been inserted into area CENTER makes panel p2 the full size of panel p1, the layout manager of panel p2 is FlowLayout, which means that the label retains its preferred size.

4. Suppose you extend the class java.awt.Button with a new class called NewButton. NewButton defines the following constructors:

```
public NewButton( String label ) { ... }
public NewButton( String label, Color color ) { ... }
```

Now by definition the Button class has the following constructors:

```
public Button() { ... }
public Button( String label ) { ... }
```

Based upon this information, which statements that attempt to instantiate NewButton will compile? (Choose all that apply.)

A. NewButton nb = new NewButton("Start");

B. NewButton nb = new NewButton("Start", 4);

C. NewButton nb = new NewButton();

D. NewButton nb = new NewButton("Start", new Color(255,255,255));

   A and D. Both of these constructors are defined in the NewButton class. *B* will not compile as there is no constructor in the NewButton class with a signature of (String, int). *C* will not compile because constructors are not inherited.

5. Which of the following method signatures are correct for the setSize() method of Component? (Choose all that apply.)

A. setSize(int width, int height)

B. setSize(int x, int y, int width, int height)

C. setSize(Dimension dim)

D. None of the above.

   A and C. Both methods describe valid method signatures for the setSize() method. *B* is incorrect because Component does not have a setSize() method that takes four integer arguments.

6. The getSize() method of Component returns what data?

A. A single int.

B. A Dimension object.

C. A Rectangle object.

   B. The getSize() method of Component returns a Dimension object. *A* is incorrect because a single int would not provide sufficient information to describe the size of an object. *C* is incorrect because a Rectangle also includes information on the position of a component, which is not desired.

7. Which of the following method signatures are correct for the setLocation () method of Component? (Choose all that apply.)

   A. setLocation (int width, int height)

   B. setLocation (int x, int y, int width, int height)

   C. setLocation (Point p)

   D. setLocation(Dimension dim)

   E. None of the above.

   A and **C**. Both methods describe valid method signatures for the setLocation () method. *B* is incorrect because Component does not have a setLocation () method that takes four integer arguments. *D* is incorrect because Component does not have a setLocation () method that takes a Dimension argument.

8. The getLocation() method of Component returns what data?

   A. A single int

   B. A Dimension object

   C. A Point object

   C. The getLocation() method of Component returns a Point object with int members representing the x and y coordinates of the upper-left corner of the component. *A* is incorrect because a single int would be insufficient to describe the current position of the component. *B* is incorrect because the members of Dimension represent width and height, not absolute coordinates.

9. Which of the following method signatures are correct for the setBounds () method of Component? (Choose all that apply.)

   A. setBounds (int width, int height)

   B. setBounds (int x, int y, int width, int height)

   C. setBounds (Point p)

   D. setBounds (Rectangle rect)

   E. None of the above.

   B and **D**. Both methods describe valid method signatures for the setBounds () method. *A* is incorrect because Component does not have a setBounds () method that takes two integer arguments. *D* is incorrect because Component does not have a setBounds () method that takes a Point argument.

10. The getBounds() method of Component returns what data?

    A. A Dimension object

    B. A Rectangle object

    C. A Point object

    B. The getBounds() method of Component returns a Rectangle object. *A* is incorrect because a Dimension object only contains data on the width and height of the component. *C* is incorrect because a Point object only contains coordinates on the position of an object.

11. Which methods are defined by java.awt.Container? (Choose all that apply.)

    A. add(Component c, index index)

    B. add(int index, Component c)

    C. add(Component c)

    D. add(Component c, Object constraints, Container parent)

    E. add(Component c, Object constraints)

    A, C, and **E.** These are all valid methods as defined by the java.awt.Container class. *B* and *D* define methods that are not in java.awt.Container.

12. Which of the following containers are top-level containers? (Choose all that apply.)

    A. Panel

    B. ScrollPane

    C. Window

    D. Frame

    C and **D.** are top-level containers. *A* and *B* are not top-level containers and need to be placed within a parent container.

13. What is the default layout manager for a Panel container?

    A. BorderLayout

    B. CardLayout

    C. GridLayout

    D. GridBagLayout

    E. FlowLayout

    F. null

    E. The FlowLayout is the default layout manager of the Panel container. *A, B, C, D,* and *F* are all incorrect.

14. What is the default layout manager for a Frame container?
    A. BorderLayout
    B. CardLayout
    C. GridLayout
    D. GridBagLayout
    E. FlowLayout
    F. null
    A. The BorderLayout is the default layout manager of the Frame container. *B, C, D, E,* and *F* are all incorrect.

15. What is the default layout manager for a Window container?
    A. BorderLayout
    B. CardLayout
    C. GridLayout
    D. GridBagLayout
    E. FlowLayout
    F. null
    A. The BorderLayout is the default layout manager of the Window container. *B, C, D, E,* and *F* are all incorrect.

16. Which of the following are valid area designations for the java.awt.BorderLayout layout manager? (Choose all that apply.)
    A. NORTH
    B. SOUTH
    C. TOP
    D. EAST
    E. MIDDLE
    F. CENTER
    A, B, D, and **F** are all valid area designations for the BorderLayout layout manager. *C* and *E* are not valid area designations for the BorderLayout layout manager.

17. As part of your GUI design, you wish to have a dialog that contains five buttons arranged vertically. These buttons must take up all of the space provided by the container of the dialog. These buttons are allowed to vary in size but must be the same size as each other no matter how the dialog is resized. Which strategy would you use?

A. Create a FlowLayout instance and pass that instance to the setLayout() method of the dialog's container. Then add each of the five buttons in turn to that container by calling the add(Component c) method for that container.

B. Create a BorderLayout instance and pass that instance to the setLayout() method of the dialog's container. Then add each of the five buttons in turn to that container by calling the add(Component c) method for that container.

C. Create a GridLayout instance using the constructor GridLayout(5,1) and pass that instance to the setLayout() method of the dialog's container. Then add each of the five buttons in turn to that container by calling the add(Component c) method for that container.

D. null (no LayoutManager)

   C. A GridLayout divides the container into equally spaced cells. Each component that is added is resized to fill that cell. The preferred size for each component is ignored. When a container, the dialog in this case, is resized, all components within the container are resized to fit the new cell dimensions. *A* is wrong because a FlowLayout respects the preferred size of each component and would not resize them when the dialog is resized. *B* is wrong because each component is being added to the center part of the container. If a component is already in the center part of the container, it is replaced with the new component. In the end only the fifth button will be visible. *D* is wrong because the lack of a LayoutManager (null) will result in absolute positioning and preferred sizing regardless of the size of the dialog.

18. Assume that you have a Frame with a layout manager of FlowLayout. The alignment of the layout manager is LEFT. Which one sentence accurately describes the rendering of a Button added to this Frame?

   A. The Button is at the top of the Frame. Its width is that of the entire Frame and its height is the preferred height of that Button.

   B. The Button fills the entire Frame.

   C. The Button is at the top left of the Frame and both its height and width are of the preferred size.

   D. The Button is at the top right of the Frame and both its height and width are of the preferred size.

   C. FlowLayout respects the preferred size of each of the components it manages. Because the alignment was set to LEFT, each row of components with the container will start at the left margin of that container. *A* is incorrect because the behavior it describes is indicative of a BorderLayout manager with the component being added to the NORTH section. *B* is incorrect because the behavior it describes is indicative of a BorderLayout manager with the component being added to the CENTER section. *D* is incorrect because although the respecting of the preferred size suggests a FlowLayout manager, the alignment is wrong.

19. Assume you have a panel that has a GridLayout as its layout manager. Which of the following statements is true regarding the placement of components within that container?
   A. The components are placed top to bottom, then left to right.
   B. The components are placed right to left, then top to bottom.
   C. The components are placed left to right, then top to bottom.
   C. When adding components to a container with a layout manager of GridLayout, the components are added from left to right then to the next row. *A* and *B* are incorrect as components are always inserted left to right in a row then down at column one of the next row.

20. The number of columns and rows in a GridLayout are dictated by either setting them in the constructor or by calling the setRows() and setColumns() methods.
   A. True
   B. False
   B is correct. *A* is incorrect because the value passed in the setColumns() is ignored unless the number of rows has not been specified.

21. Which of the following LayoutManagers will respect all dimensions of a component's preferred size?
   A. FlowLayout
   B. GridLayout
   C. BorderLayout
   D. None of the above
   A. The FlowLayout manager class always respects the preferred size of each Component. *B* is wrong because GridLayout ignores the preferred size of each component. *C* is wrong because BorderLayout will ignore at least one dimension of the preferred size of a Component. BorderLayout ignores the preferred height of a component in the EAST and WEST areas of the container, ignores the preferred width of a component in the NORTH and SOUTH areas of the container, and ignores all dimensions of the preferred size in the CENTER area of the container.

Chapter 14 Self Test

1. Which is the best way to receive events when a Button component is activated (pressed)?

   A. Create an implementation of ButtonListener and add it as a listener to the Button component by invoking addButtonListener().

   B. Create an implementation of ActionListener and add it as a listener to the Button component by invoking addActionListener().

   C. Subclass ActionAdapter and override the actionPerformed() method. Then, add an instance of the subclass as a listener to the Button component by invoking addActionListener().

   D. Subclass MouseAdapter and override the mouseClicked() method. Then, add an instance of the subclass as a listener to the Button component by invoking addMouseListener().

   B. Button generates one semantic event, the ActionEvent. You must implement the ActionListener interface and register the implementation as a listener to receive action events through the actionPerformed() method. Answer *A* is incorrect because there is no ButtonListener interface defined in the java.awt.event package. Answer *C* is incorrect because there is no ActionAdapter class defined in the java.awt.event package. Answer *D* is incorrect because it would be inefficient due to the fact that the implementation of MouseListener would be notified on every Mouse event, not just when the button was activated.

2. Which of the following events are subclasses of InputEvent? (Choose all that apply.)

   A. MouseEvent

   B. WindowEvent

   C. MouseMotionEvent

   D. KeyEvent

   A, D. MouseEvent and KeyEvent are the only subclasses of InputEvent in the java.awt.event package. Answer *B* is incorrect because WindowEvent does not subclass InputEvent. Answer *D* is incorrect because there is no MouseMotionEvent. Remember that there is both a MouseListener and a MouseMotionListener listener interface, but both of these receive MouseEvent objects.

3. Can an object be an event source and an event listener for the same type of event?

   A. Yes

   B. No

   A. Yes. As long as the object implements the appropriate interface and also contains the logic to maintain and notify event listeners, this is fine.

4. If you wanted to ensure that only numeric characters were entered in a TextField component, what is the best approach?
   A. Subclass KeyAdapter and implement the keyTyped() method to invoke the consume() method on any event representing a non-numeric character.
   B. Subclass KeyAdapter and implement the keyPressed() method to consume all events.
   C. Subclass KeyAdapater and implement the keyTyped() method to invoke setKeyChar(null) on any event representing a non-numeric character.
   D. Subclass KeyEvent and implement the keyTyped() method to consume any event representing a non-numeric character using the consume() method.
   A. Consuming events that represent non-numeric characters keeps the TextField component from processing the event. Answer *B* is incorrect because all events resulting from keys being pressed would be consumed, and therefore no characters could be entered in the TextField component. Answer *C* is incorrect because your compiler would complain that it cannot convert null to char. Answer *D* is incorrect because keyTyped() is defined in KeyListener, not KeyEvent.

5. Which of the following events are paired with their appropriate listener interfaces?
   A. MouseEvent, Mouse Listener
   B. MouseMotionEvent, MouseListener
   C. MouseMotionEvent, MouseMotionListener
   D. InputEvent, InputListener
   A. MouseEvent is properly paired with MouseListener. Note that MouseEvent could also be properly paired with MouseMotionListener. Answers *B* and *C* are incorrect because there is no MouseMotionEvent defined in the java.awt.event package. Remember that the methods defined in the MouseMotionListener interface all receive MouseEvents as their parameter. Answer *D* is incorrect because there is no InputListener interface defined in the java.awt.event package. InputEvent simply serves as a base class for MouseEvent and KeyEvent.

6. Which event classes support the getWhen() method? (Choose all that apply.)
   A. MouseEvent
   B. WindowEvent
   C. ActionEvent
   D. KeyEvent
   A, D. MouseEvent and KeyEvent both subclass InputEvent and therefore support the getWhen() method. Answers *B* and *C* are incorrect because WindowEvent and ActionEvent are not subclasses of InputEvent.

7. How would you determine the time at which a MouseEvent was generated?
   A. Implement the MouseListener interface and call System.getCurrentTimeMillis() from within the implemented methods.
   B. Invoke the getTime() method on the MouseEvent object.
   C. Invoke the getWhen() method defined in the MouseAdapter class.
   D. Invoke the getWhen() method on the MouseEvent object.
      D. InputEvent defines the getWhen() method that can be used to determine when an event occurred. Because MouseEvent extends InputEvent, MouseEvent also provides this method. Answer *A* is incorrect because System.getCurrentTimeMillis() will simply return the current time, which is not the time that the event was generated. Answer *B* is incorrect because there is no getTime() method defined in MouseEvent. Answer *C* is incorrect because there is no getWhen() method defined in MouseAdapter. Remember that adapter classes simply implement listener interfaces with empty implementations.

8. Which of the following event classes are subclasses of ComponentEvent?
   A. TextEvent
   B. ActionEvent
   C. MouseEvent
   D. WindowEvent
      C, D. MouseEvent is a direct subclass of InputEvent, which is in turn a direct subclass of ComponentEvent. WindowEvent is a direct subclass of ComponentEvent. Answer *B*, ActionEvent, and answer *A*, TextEvent, directly subclass AWTEvent and therefore are not subclasses of ComponentEvent.

9. A Mouse listener can keep other MouseListeners from receiving a Mouse event by invoking the consume() method on the MouseEvent object.
   A. True
   B. False.
      B. False. Consuming an InputEvent object simply keeps the event source from doing any further processing. This does not keep other listeners from receiving the event.

10. Which listener interfaces are paired with the appropriate event class?
    A. TextListener, TextFieldEvent
    B. MouseMotionListener, MouseMotionEvent
    C. ActionListener, ActionEvent
    D. KeyListener, KeyPressedEvent
       C. ActionListener is the listener interface for ActionEvent objects. Answers *A*, *B*, and *D* are incorrect because TextListener, MouseMotionListener, and KeyListener correspond to TextEvent, MouseEvent, and KeyEvent, respectively.

11. Which of the following are valid uses for the flags returned by the getModifiers() method defined in InputEvent? (Choose all that apply.)
    A. Determining which mouse button caused a Mouse event.
    B. Determining whether the ALT key was pressed at the time of a Key event.
    C. Determining whether a Mouse event was caused by a double-click.
    D. Determining whether the SHIFT key was pressed at the time of a Key event.
       A, B, D. InputEvent defines masks for all modifier keys and three mouse buttons. These masks can be bitwise ANDed with the modifier value to test the flags. *C* is incorrect. To determine the number of mouse-clicks that caused a Mouse event, the getClickCount() method can be invoked on the MouseEvent object.

12. Which listener interface would you implement to determine when components were added to a Panel?
    A. ComponentListener
    B. ContainerListener
    C. ActionListener
    D. InputListener
       B. Containers such as Panel generate Container events when child components are either added or removed. Answer *A* is incorrect because Component events are only generated when the Panel's visibility or shape changes, not when its contents are modified. Answer *C* is incorrect because Panel does not generate ActionEvents. Answer *D* is incorrect because there is no InputListener interface defined in the java.awt.event package.

13. Which of the following is not true about adapter classes?
    A. They implement their corresponding listener interface.
    B. They provide empty implementations for every method in their corresponding interface.
    C. They are only useful for interfaces with more than one method.
    D. Using an adapter class is more efficient because only the methods that you override are invoked by the event source.
       D. Just because adapter classes provide an empty implementation for a method does not mean that the event source does not invoke the method. Answers *A*, *B*, and *C* are all true statements about adapter classes.

14. Which of the following listener interfaces have an associated adapter class? (Choose all that apply.)

    A. KeyListener

    B. ItemListener

    C. MouseListener

    D. ActionListener

    E. TextListener

    A, C. KeyAdapter and MouseAdapter are provided for KeyListener and MouseListener, respectively. No adapter classes are provided for *B*, ItemListener; *D*, ActionListener; or *E*, TextListener.

15. Why does it not make sense to have an ActionAdapter class?

    A. Because ActionEvent is a low-level event.

    B. Because ActionListener is rarely used by developers.

    C. Because the ActionListener interface only defines one method.

    D. Because ActionListener serves only as a base interface for the other AWT listener interfaces and should not be implemented directly.

    C. ActionListener only defines one method actionPerformed(ActionEvent e). It would make no sense to provide an adapter. This holds true for TextEvent and ItemEvent also. Answer *A* is incorrect on two counts: one is that ActionListener is actually a semantic event, not a low-level event; the other is that it is perfectly acceptable to have an adapter for low-level events. In fact, all adapters provided in the java.awt.event package are for low-level events. Answer *B* is also incorrect. ActionListener is one of the more commonly implemented (if not the most commonly implemented) listener interfaces. Answer *D* is incorrect because ActionListener is intended to be directly implemented.

16. Which of the following properly implements the mouseClicked() method of MouseListener to print the (x, y) coordinates of a mouse-click? (Choose all that apply.)

    A.

```
public void mouseClicked(MouseEvent e){
    Point point = e.getPoint();
    System.out.println("Mouse click at (" + point.x + "," + point.y +
")");
};
```

B.

```
public void mouseClicked(MouseEvent e){
    System.out.println("Mouse click at (" + e.getX() + "," + e.getY() + ")");
};
```

C.

```
public void mouseClicked(MouseEvent e){
    System.out.println("Mouse click at (" + e.x + "," + e.y + ")");
};
```

D.

```
public void mouseClicked(MouseEvent e){
    int x;
    int y;
    e.translatePoint(x,y);
    System.out.println("Mouse click at (" + x + "," + y + ")");
};
```

A, B. MouseEvent defines two ways of getting the coordinates of the mouse cursor at the time a mouse event was generated: One is to use the getX() and getY() methods to get integer coordinates, and the other is to use getPoint() to get a Point object representing the coordinates. Answer *C* is incorrect because MouseEvent does not have public fields x and y. Answer *D* is incorrect because translatePoint() modifies the MouseEvent object's coordinates by adding x and y parameters to its existing x and y coordinates.

17. To enable events for a component, you must first invoke enableEvents() with the appropriate flags.

A. True.

B. False.

B. False. A component automatically enables a specific event type when the first listener of the appropriate type registers as a listener.

B

About the CD

Installing the Personal Testing Center

T
he CD-ROM included with this book contains a browser-based testing product, the *Personal Testing Center*. The *Personal Testing Center* is easy to install on any Windows 95/98/NT computer.

Double-click on the Setup.html file on the CD to cycle through an introductory page on the *Test Yourself* software. On the second page, you will have to read and accept the license agreement. Once you have read the agreement, click on the Agree icon and you'll see the *Personal Testing Center's* main page.

On the main page, you will find links to the *Personal Testing Center,* to the electronic version of the book, and to other resources you may find helpful. Click on the first link to the *Personal Testing Center* and you will be brought to the Quick Start page. Here you can choose to run the Personal Testing Center from the CD or install it to your hard drive.

Installing the *Personal Testing Center* to your hard drive is an easy process. Click on the Install to Hard Drive icon and the procedure will start for you. An instructional box will appear, and walk you through the remainder of the installation. If installed to the hard drive, the "Personal Testing Center" program group will be created in the Start Programs folder.

Should you wish to run the software from the CD-ROM, the steps are the same as above until you reach the point where you would select the Install to Hard Drive icon. Here, select Run from CD icon and the exam will automatically begin.

To uninstall the program from your hard disk, use the add/remove programs feature in your Windows Control Panel. InstallShield will run uninstall.

Test Type Choices

With the *Personal Testing Center,* you have three options in which to run the program: Live, Practice, and Review. Each test type will draw from a pool of over 280 potential questions. Your choice of test type will depend on whether you would like to simulate an actual Java 2 Programmer exam, receive instant feedback on your answer choices, or review concepts using the testing simulator. Note that selecting the Full Screen icon on Internet Explorer's standard toolbar gives you the best display of the *Personal Testing Center.*

Live

The Live timed test type is meant to reflect the actual exam as closely as possible. You will have 120 minutes in which to complete the exam. You will have the option to skip questions and return to them later, move to the previous question, or end the exam. Once the timer has expired, you will automatically go to the scoring page to review your test results.

Managing Windows

The testing application runs inside an Internet Explorer 4.0 or 5.0 browser window. We recommend that you use the full-screen view to minimize the amount of text scrolling you need to do. However, the application will initiate a second iteration of the browser when you link to an Answer in Depth or a Review Graphic. If you are running in full-screen view, the second iteration of the browser will be covered by the first. You can toggle between the two windows with ALT-TAB, you can click your task bar to maximize the second window, or you can get out of full-screen mode and arrange the two windows so they are both visible on the screen at the same time. The application will not initiate more than two browser windows, so you aren't left with hundreds of open windows for each Answer in Depth or Review Graphic that you view.

Saving Scores as Cookies

Your exam score is stored as a browser cookie. If you've configured your browser to accept cookies, your score will be stored in a cookie named History. If you don't accept cookies, you cannot permanently save your scores. If you delete the History cookie, the scores will be deleted permanently.

Using the Browser Buttons

The test application runs inside the Internet Explorer 4.0 browser. You should navigate from screen to screen by using the application's buttons, not the browser's buttons.

JavaScript Errors

If you encounter a JavaScript error, you should be able to proceed within the application. If you cannot, shut down your Internet Explorer 4.0 browser session and re-launch the testing application.

Practice

When choosing the Practice exam type, you have the option of receiving instant feedback as to whether your selected answer is correct. The questions will be presented to you in numerical order, and you will see every question in the available question pool for each section you chose to be tested on.

As with the Live exam type, you have the option of continuing through the entire exam without seeing the correct answer for each question. The number of questions you answered correctly, along with the percentage of correct answers, will be displayed during the post-exam summary report. Once you have answered a question, click the Answer icon to display the correct answer.

You have the option of ending the Practice exam at any time, but your post-exam summary screen may reflect an incorrect percentage based on the number of questions you failed to answer. Questions that are skipped are counted as incorrect answers on the post-exam summary screen.

Review

During the Review exam type, you will be presented with questions similar to both the Live and Practice exam types. However, the Answer icon is not present, as every question will have the correct answer posted near the bottom of the screen. You have the option of answering the question without looking at the correct answer. In the Review exam type, you can also return to previous questions and skip to the next question, as well as end the exam by clicking the Stop icon.

The Review exam type is recommended when you have already completed the Live exam type once or twice, and would now like to determine which questions you answered correctly.

Questions with Answers

For the Practice and Review exam types, you will have the option of clicking a hyperlink titled Answers in Depth, which will present relevant study material aimed at exposing the logic behind the answer in a separate browser window. By having two browsers open (one for the test engine and one for the review information), you can quickly alternate between the two windows while keeping your place in the exam. You will find that additional windows are not generated as you follow hyperlinks throughout the test engine.

Scoring

The *Personal Testing Center* post-exam summary screen, called Benchmark Yourself, displays the results for each section you chose to be tested on, including a bar graph similar to the real exam, which displays the percentage of correct answers. You can compare your percentage to the actual passing percentage for each section. The percentage displayed on the post-exam summary screen is not the actual percentage required to pass the exam. You'll see the number of questions you answered correctly compared to the total number of questions you were tested on. If you choose to skip a question, it will be marked as incorrect. Ending the exam by clicking the End button with questions still unanswered lowers your percentage, as these questions will be marked as incorrect.

Clicking the End button and then the Home button allows you to choose another exam type, or test yourself on another section.

SUN CERTIFIED PROGRAMMER®

C

About the Web Site

A t Access.Globalknowledge, the premier online information source for IT professionals (http://access.globalknowledge.com), you'll enter a Global Knowledge information portal designed to inform, educate, and update visitors on issues regarding IT and IT education.

Get *What* You Want *When* You Want It

At the Access.Globalknowledge site, you can:

- Choose personalized technology articles related to your interests. Access a new article, review, or tutorial regularly throughout the week, customized to what you want to see.

- Continue your education, in between Global courses, by taking advantage of chat sessions with other users or instructors. Get the tips, tricks, and advice that you need today!

- Make your point in the Access.Globalknowledge community with threaded discussion groups related to technologies and certification.

- Get instant course information at your fingertips. Customized course calendars show you the courses you want, when and where you want them.

- Obtain the resources you need with online tools, trivia, skills assessment and more!

All this and more is available now on the Web at http://access.globalknowledge.com. Visit today!

Glossary

Abstract class   An abstract class is a type of class that is not allowed to be instantiated. The only reason it exists is to be extended. Abstract classes contain methods and variables common to all the subclasses, but the abstract class itself is of a type that will not be used directly.

Abstract method   An abstract method is a method declaration that contains no functional code. The reason for using an abstract method is to ensure that subclasses of this class will include this method. Any concrete class (that is, a class that is not abstract, and therefore capable of being instantiated) must override this method.

Access modifier   An access modifier is a modifier that changes the protection of an element.

Adapter classes   Adapter classes are provided to help the programmer develop classes that implement the event interfaces. Also, adapter classes are classes that implement a particular listener interface with empty methods. This means that you can subclass an adapter and then override only the methods that you are interested in.

Anonymous class   You use an anonymous class when you want to create and use a class but do not want to bother with giving it a name or using it again.

Anonymous inner classes   Anonymous inner classes are local inner classes that do not have a class name. Using anonymous inner classes is most effective when they are small and implement only a single or very few small methods.

API   Application Programmers Interface. This term refers to a set of related classes and methods that work together to provide a particular capability.

Array   Arrays are homogenous data structures implemented in Java as objects. Arrays store one or more of a specific type and provide indexed access to the store.

Automatic variables   Also called method local variables. Automatic variables are variables that are declared within a method and discarded when the method has completed.

AWT   The AWT is Java's Abstract Windowing Toolkit. This is a platform independent API that provides a user interface capability.

Base class   A Base class is a class that has been extended. If class d extends class b, class b is the base class of class d.

Blocked state   A thread that is waiting for a resource, such as a lock, to become available is said to be in a blocked state. Blocked threads consume no processor resources.

Boolean literals   Boolean literals are the source code representation for boolean values. Boolean values can only be defined as either true or false.

BorderLayout layout manager   The BorderLayout layout manager divides the container into five areas. These areas are NORTH, SOUTH, EAST, WEST and CENTER. The name of the area indicates where the component will be placed. All directional references are relative to the top of the container, which is considered NORTH.

Call stack   A call stack is a list of methods that have been called in the order in which they were called. Typically, the most recently called method (the current method) is thought of as being at the bottom of the call stack.

CardLayout layout manager   The CardLayout layout manager treats each contained component as a card, with only one card being visible at any given time. Whichever component was added first will be visible first when the container is displayed.

Casting   Casting is the conversion of one type to another type. Typically, casting is used to convert an object reference to either a supertype or a subtype, but casting can also be used on primitive types.

char   A char is a primitive data type that holds a single character.

Character literals   Character literals are represented by a single character in single quotes, such as 'A'.

Child class   *See* Derived class.

Class   A class is the definition of a type. Classes describe an entity's public interface. *See also* Base class; Derived class; Inner classes.

Class constructors   Class constructors are able to call overloaded constructors both in their class and in their superclass. To call another constructor in the same class, you can place a *this()* in the first line of the body in the calling constructor. Placing *this()* in any other place will result in a compiler error.

Class members   Class members are variables defined at the class level. These include both instance variables and class (static) variables.

Class methods   A class method, often referred to as a static method, may be accessed directly from a class, without instantiating the class first.

Class variable   *See* Static variable.

Collection   A collection is an object used to store other objects. Collections are also commonly referred to as containers. Two common examples of collections are Hashtables and Vectors.

Collection interface   The collection interface defines the public interface that is common to all collection classes.

Collections framework   Three elements (interfaces, implementations, and algorithms) create what is known as the collections framework.

Command string   The command string contains data about the source or cause of an event. An action event that is the result of a Button being activated contains the Button's text. An action event that is the result of the ENTER key being pressed in a TextField component returns the entered text. Similarly, the text that represents a MenuItem or item in a list component is returned when a MenuItem or List is the source of the action event.

Comparison operators   Comparison operators perform a comparison on two parameters and return a boolean value indicating if the comparison is true. For example, the comparison 2<4 will result in true while the comparison 4==7 will result in false.

Components   Components are the base class and provide functionality for defining the appearance of the widget, the response (if any) to various events, and, finally, the instructions on how to render itself. A component generates a ComponentEvent when the component's size, position, or visibility has changed. ComponentEvents are for notification purposes only.

Conditional operators   Conditional operators are used to evaluate boolean expressions, much like if statements, except instead of executing a block of code, a conditional operator will assign a value to a variable.

Constructor   A method of a class that is called when the object is created, or instantiated. Typically, constructors initialize data members and acquire whatever resources the object may require.

Container components   A container component, such as Panel, generates a ContainerEvent as a result of a child component being added or removed from the container. ContainerEvents are for notification purposes only. The AWT automatically handles changes to the contents of a container component internally.

Containers   Containers are specialized components that hold other components. Because containers themselves are components, you can nest containers to achieve a desired layout. In this context, containers are part of the AWT.

Continue statement   The continue statement causes the current iteration of the innermost loop to cease and the next iteration of the same loop to start if the condition of the loop is met. In the case of using a continue statement with a for loop, you need to consider the effects that the continue has on the loop iterator.

Deadlock   Also called deadly embrace. Threads sometimes block while waiting to get a lock. It is easy to get into a situation where one thread has a lock and wants another lock that is currently owned by another thread that wants the first lock. Deadlock is one of those problems that are difficult to cure, especially because things just stop happening and there are no friendly exception stack traces to study. They might be difficult, or even impossible, to replicate because they always depend on what many threads may be doing at a particular moment in time.

Deadly embrace   *See* Deadlock.

Decision statement   The if and switch statements are commonly referred to as decision statements. When you use decision statements in your program, you are asking the program to calculate a given expression to determine which course of action is required.

Declaration   A declaration is a statement that declares a class, interface, method, package, or variable in a source file. A declaration can also initialize the variable, although for class members this is normally done in the constructor method.

Default access   A class with default access needs no modifier preceding it in the declaration. Default access allows other classes within the same package to have visibility to this class.

Derived class A derived class is a class that extends another class. If class d extends class b, then class d "derives" from class b and is a derived class.

Do-while loop The do-while loop is slightly different from the while statement in that the program execution cycle will always perform the commands in the body of a do-while at least once. It does adhere to the rule that you do not need brackets around the body if it is just one line of code.

Encapsulation Encapsulation is the process of grouping methods and data together and hiding them behind a public interface. A class encapsulates methods and the data they operate on.

Event classes All event classes defined in the java.awt.event package are subclasses of java.awt.AWTEvent, which is itself a subclass of java.util.EventObject.

Event objects An event object embodies information related to a particular type of event. At a minimum, an event object contains a reference to the object that caused the event (the event source). Usually, the event object also contains other data such as mouse position or a timestamp.

Event sources An event source is a component or object that generates events. Event sources create event objects and deliver them to event listeners. An event source does not have to subclass any specific class or implement any specific interface. Additionally, an object can act as the source of multiple event types, provided that it fulfills the preceding responsibilities for each type.

Event types An event type is used to distinguish between events that share the same class but have a different purpose.

Exception Exception has two common meanings in Java. First, an Exception is an object type. Second, an exception is shorthand for "exceptional condition," which is an occurrence that alters the normal flow of an application.

Exception handling   Exception handling allows developers to easily detect errors without writing special code to test return values. Better, it lets us handle these errors in code that is nicely separated from the code that generated them and handle an entire class of errors with the same code, and it allows us to let a method defer handling its errors to a previously called method. Exception handling works by transferring execution of a program to an exception handler when an error, or exception, occurs.

Extensibility   Extensibility is a term that describes a design or code that can easily be enhanced without being rewritten.

Final class   The *final* keyword restricts a class from being extended by another class. If you try to extend a final class, the Java compiler will give an error.

Final variables   The final keyword makes it impossible to reinitialize a variable once it has been declared. For primitives, this means the value may not be altered once it is initialized. For objects, the data within the object may be modified, but the reference variable may not be changed. Final variables must be initialized in the same line in which they are declared.

Finalizer   Every class has a special method, called a finalizer, which is called just before an object is reclaimed by the Java VM garbage collector. The JVM calls the finalizer for you as appropriate; you never call a finalizer directly. Think of the finalizer as a friendly warning from the virtual machine. Your finalizer should perform two tasks: performing whatever cleanup is appropriate to the object, and calling the superclass finalizer. If you do not have any cleanup to perform for an object, then you're better off not adding a finalizer to the class.

Floating-point literals   Floating-point literals are defined as double by default, but if you want to specify in your code a number as float, you may attach the suffix *F* to the number.

Floating-point numbers   Floating-point numbers are defined as a number, a decimal symbol, and more numbers representing the fraction.

FlowLayout manager   This layout manager arranges components within the container from left to right. When the container runs out of room on the current row FlowLayout resumes positioning components on the next row.

FocusEvent   A component generates a FocusEvent when it gains or loses keyboard focus. The event ID is set to either FOCUS_GAINED or focus lost. There are two types of focus events, permanent and temporary. Permanent focus events indicate that another component has gained the focus, whereas temporary focus events indicate that the component has lost focus temporarily due to window deactivation or scrolling.

For loop   A flow control statement is used when a program needs to iterate a section of code a known number of times. There are three main parts to a *for* statement. They are the declaration and initialization of variables, the expression, and the incrementing or modification of variables. Each of the sections are separated by semicolons. The for loop is a remarkable tool for developers because it allows you to declare and initialize zero, one, or multiple variables inside the parenthesis after the for keyword.

Garbage collection   The process by which memory requested, but no longer in use, by a Java application is reclaimed by the Java VM.

Generational garbage collectors   Generational garbage collectors make the trade-off of running faster with the cost of leaving garbage lying around longer. With today's large memory machines, this is a very reasonable trade-off to make.

GridBagLayout layout manager   The GridBagLayout layout manager allows the placement of components that are aligned vertically and/or horizontally without constraining those components to be a particular size, height, or width. The GridBagLayout accomplishes this by defining a dynamic grid of cells. The constraints object passed when the component is added to the container determine how many cells the component encompasses.

GridLayout manager   This layout manager arranges components in a grid within a container. Each cell in the grid is of equal dimensions. The GridLayout manager ignores the preferred size of each component and resizes them to exactly fit each cell's dimensions. As each component is added to the container the GridLayout inserts them across each column until that row is filled and then starts at the first column of the next row.

Guarded region   A section of code that is watched for errors to be handled by a particular group of handlers.

HashMap class   The HashMap class is roughly equivalent to Hashtable, except that it is not synchronized for threads and it permits null values to be stored.

Heap   Java manages memory in a structure called a heap. Every object that Java creates is allocated in the heap, which is created at the beginning of the application and managed automatically by Java.

Hexadecimal literals   Hexadecimal numbers are constructed using 16 distinct symbols. The symbols used are 0, 1, 2, 3, 4, 5, 6, 7, 8, 9, A, B, C, D, E, and F.

Identifiers   Identifiers are names that we assign to classes, methods, and variables. Java is a case-sensitive language, which means identifiers must have consistent capitalization throughout. Identifiers can have letters and numbers, but a number may not begin the identifier name. Most symbols are not allowed, but the dollar sign ($) and underscore (_) symbols are valid. *See also* Reference variable.

If statement   If statements test an expression for a boolean result. This is achieved by using one or more of Java's relational operators inside the parenthesis of the statement to compare two or more variables. Also, you can simply use the reserved word *true* as the expression to force execution of the block of code. *See also* Decision statement.

Import statement   Import statements allow us to refer to classes without having to use a fully qualified name for each class. Import statements do not make classes accessible; all classes in the classpath are accessible.

Inheritance   Inheritance is an object-oriented concept that provides for the reuse and modification of an existing type in such a way that many types can be manipulated as a single type. In Java, inheritance is achieved with the extends keyword.

Inner classes   Inner classes are a type of class and follow most of the same rules as a normal class. The main difference is an inner class is declared within the curly braces of a class or even within a method. Inner classes are also classes defined at a scope smaller than a package. *See also* Anonymous inner classes; Local inner classes; Member inner classes; Static inner classes.

InputEvent class   An InputEvent is an abstract class that serves as the base class for MouseEvent and KeyEvent. InputEvent defines the following method to determine the time of the event.

Instance   Once the class is instantiated, it becomes an object. A single object is referred to as an "instance" of the class from which it was instantiated.

Instance initializer   An instance initializer (an alternative to lazy initialization) is a block of code (not a method!) that automatically runs every time you create a new instance of an object. In effect, it is an anonymous constructor. Of course, instance initializers are rather limited; because they do not have arguments, you cannot overload them, so you can have only one of these "constructors" per class.

Instance variable   An instance variable is declared at object level. Instance variables may be accessed from other methods in the class, or from methods in other classes (depending on the access control). Instance variables may not be accessed from static methods, however, because a static method could be invoked when no instances of the class exist. Logically, if no instances exist, then the instance variable will also not exist, and it would be impossible to access the instance variable.

instanceof comparison operator   The instanceof comparison operator is available for object variables. The purpose of this operator is to determine whether an object belongs to a given class (or any of the subclasses). This comparison may not be made on primitive types and will result in a compile-time error if it is attempted.

Interface   An interface defines a group of methods, or a public interface, that must be implemented by any class that implements the interface. An interface allows an object to be treated as a type declared by the interface implemented.

Invocation events   Invocation events are used to run a piece of code in the AWT event thread using the invoke() and invokeAndWait() methods. This is more of a utility than a part of the AWT event system.

Iterator   An iterator provides the necessary behavior to get to each element in a collection without exposing the collection itself. In classes containing and manipulating collections, it is good practice to return an iterator instead of the collection containing the elements you want to iterate over. This shields clients from internal changes to the data structures used in your classes.

Java source file   A file that contains computer instructions written in the Java programming language. A Java source file must meet strict requirements, otherwise the Java compiler will generate errors.

Java Virtual Machine (JVM)   A program that interprets and executes Java byte code and that was generated by a Java compiler. The Java VM provides a variety of resources to the applications it is executing, including memory management, network access, hardware abstraction and so on. Because it provides a consistent environment for Java applications to run in, the Java VM is the heart of the "write once run anywhere" strategy that has made Java so popular.

javac   Javac is the name of the java compiler program. This Java compiler processes the source file to produce a byte code file.

java.lang package   The java.lang package defines classes used by all Java programs. The package defines class wrappers for all primitive types such as Boolean, Byte, Character, Double, Float, Integer, Long, Short, and Void as well as Object, the class from which all Java classes inherit.

JVM   *See* Java Virtual Machine.

Key pressed events   Key pressed events occur for keys that do not have an associated character or that must be used in combination with other keys to form a logical character. These are keys such as function keys, up and down arrow keys, and the SHIFT key. The event types for key pressed events are KEY_PRESSED and KEY_RELEASED.

Key typed events   Key typed events are higher-level than key pressed events, and only occur when a logical sequence or combination that represents a character has been completed. For example, pressing SHIFT-A results in a key typed event with the character *A*. The event type of a key typed event is KEY_TYPED.

KeyEvent   A KeyEvent provides the following method that returns a virtual key code constant that represents the key.

Keywords   Keywords are special reserved words in Java that cannot be used as identifiers for classes, methods, and variables.

Layout managers   Layout managers are those classes responsible for laying out all components within a container, a process that includes sizing and positioning. A layout manager is associated with a container and a reference to that layout manager is held as a member of the container class. Layout managers are responsible for sizing and positioning components within a container. Layout managers free the developer of having to calculate positions and sizes of each component.

Local inner classes   You can define inner classes within the scope of a method, or even smaller blocks within a method. We call this a local inner class. This is by far the least used form of inner classes. There are very few cases where you would ever need a named local inner class because most problems can be solved with the other types of inner classes.

Local variable   A local variable is a variable declared within a method. These are also known as automatic variables. Local variables, including primitives, must be initialized before you attempt to use them (though not necessarily on the same line of code).

Low-level events   In the AWT, low-level events are finer grained than semantic events and tend to occur at a higher frequency.

Mark phase   The mark phase of the mark-sweep garbage collection starts with the root objects and looks at all the objects that each root object refers to. If the object is already marked as being in use, then nothing more happens. If not, then the object is marked as in use and all the objects that it refers to are considered. The algorithm repeats until all the objects that can be reached from the root objects have been marked as in use.

Mark-sweep algorithm   Most Java Virtual Machines (JVMs) implement garbage collection using a variant of the mark-sweep algorithm. This algorithm gets its name from the two passes that it takes over memory. It takes the first pass to mark those objects that are no longer used, and a second pass to remove (sweep) those objects from memory. Mark-sweep starts with the assumption that some objects are always reachable.

Member inner classes   Inner classes defined in an enclosing class without using the static modifier are called member inner classes. They are members of the enclosing class just like instance variables.

Members   Elements of a class, including methods and variables.

Method   A section of source code that performs a specific function, has a name, may be passed parameters and may return a result. Methods are found in classes only.

Method local variables   *See* Automatic variables.

Modifier   A modifier is a keyword in a class, method, or variable declaration that modifies the behavior of the element. *See also* Access modifier.

Modifier flags   The modifier flags represent keys (such as SHIFT or ALT) that were pressed at the time of the input event.

Modular code   Modular code keeps implementations isolated so that they depend on other code as little as possible. Though modular code does not affect how well your code executes, you will get many benefits by writing code this way, including the ability to easily modify, enhance and debug the code

Mouse Motion events   Mouse Motion events are special because they are delivered using a listener interface that is different from normal Mouse events.

Narrowing   The process of modifying a type. For primitives, narrowing means loss of precision, and for objects it means loss of generality.

Native methods   Native indicates that a method is written in a platform-dependent language to perform a platform specific function that cannot be handled in Java. You will not need to know how to use native methods for the exam, other than knowing that *native* is a reserved keyword.

Notify() method   The methods wait() and notify() are instance methods of an object. In the same way that every object has a lock, every object has a list of threads that are waiting for a signal related to the object. A thread gets on this list by executing the wait() method of the object. From that moment, it does not execute any further instructions until some other thread calls the notify() method of the same object.

Object   Once the class is instantiated it becomes an object (sometimes referred to as an instance).

Overloaded methods   Methods are overloaded when there are multiple methods in the same class with the same names but with different parameter lists.

Overridden methods   Methods in the parent and subclasses with the same name, parameter list, and return type are overridden.

Package   A package is an entity that groups classes together. The name of the package must reflect the directory structure used to store the classes in your package. The subdirectory begins in any directory indicated by the class path environment variable.

PaintEvent   Paint events are used internally to ensure serialization of paint operations in the awt event thread. They are not intended to be used like other events.

Panel   A panel is by far the simplest and most common of the AWT container classes.

Parent class   A parent class is a class from which another class is derived. *See also* Base class.

Permanent focus events   Permanent focus events indicate that another component has gained the focus.

Phantom object   A phantom object is one that has been finalized, but whose memory has not yet been made available for another object.

Phantom reference   Phantom references provide a means of delaying the reuse of memory occupied by an object, even if the object itself is finalized. Phantom references are a bit different from soft and weak references. First off, phantom references track memory rather than objects. Secondly, you can never actually get to the object that a phantom reference references.

Primitive literal   A primitive literal is merely a source code representation of the primitive data types.

Primitives   Primitives can be a fundamental instruction, operation, or statement. They must be initialized before you attempt to use them (though not necessarily on the same line of code).

Private members   Private members are members of a class that cannot be accessed by any class other than the class in which it is declared.

Public access   The *public* keyword placed in front of a class allows all classes from all packages to have access to a class.

Public members   When a method or variable member is declared public, it means all other classes, regardless of the package that they belong to, can access the member (assuming the class itself is visible).

Reference   The term reference is shorthand for reference variable. *See* Reference variable.

Reference queue   The reference queue gives you a means for determining in bulk which references have changed. Reference queues give the virtual machine a mechanism for telling you that it has collected an object, or more precisely, that the reference has moved to an invalid state.

Reference variable   A reference variable is an identifier that refers to a primitive type or an object (including an array). A reference variable is a name that points to a location in the computer's memory where the object is stored. A variable declaration is used to assign a variable name to an object or primitive type. A reference variable is a name that is used in Java to reference an instance of a class.

Runtime exceptions   A runtime exception is an exception that need not be handled in your program. Usually, runtime exceptions indicate a program bug. These are referred to as unchecked exceptions, since the Java compiler does not force the program to handle them.

ScrollPane   ScrollPane is a container that provides optional scrollbars to gain access to that part of the container that is presently off of the viewable area. The scrollbars may be included as always on or on an as-needed basis.

Semantic events   Semantic events occur as the result of a combination of low-level events. Semantic events tend to be associated with the primary purpose of the component that sources them. ActionEvent, ItemEvent, and TextEvent are the only semantic events defined in the java.awt.event package.

Shift operators   Shift operators shift the bits of a number to the right or left, producing a new number. Shift operators are used on integer types only.

Soft reference   A soft reference tells the runtime system that we would rather this object not be removed from memory. We do not require that the object not be removed from memory; we just would rather that it not be removed from memory.

SortedMap interface   A data structure that is similar to map except the objects are stored in ascending order according to their keys. Like map, there can be no duplicate keys and the objects themselves may be duplicated. One very important difference with SortedMap objects is that the key may not be a null value.

Source file   A source file is a plain text file containing your Java code. A source file may only have one public class or interface and an unlimited number of default classes or interfaces defined within it, and the filename must be the same as the public class name. *See also* Java source file.

Stack trace   If you could print out the state of the call stack at any given time, you would produce a stack trace.

Static inner classes   Static inner classes are the simplest form of inner classes. They behave much like top-level classes except that they are defined within the scope of another class, namely the enclosing class. Static inner classes have no implicit references to instances of the enclosing class and can access only static members and methods of the enclosing class. Static inner classes are often used to implement small helper classes such as iterators.

Static methods   The static keyword declares a method that belongs to an entire class (as opposed to belonging to an instance). A class method may be accessed directly from a class, without instantiating the class first.

Static variable   Also called a class variable. A static variable, much like a static method, may be accessed from a class directly, even though the class has not been instantiated. The value of a static variable will be the same in every instance of the class.

String literal   A string literal is a source code representation of a value of a string.

String objects   An object that provides string manipulation capabilities. The String class may not be subclassed.

Superclass   In object technology, a high-level class that passes attributes and methods (data and processing) down the hierarchy to subclasses. A superclass is a class from which one or more other classes are derived.

Switch statement   The expression in the switch statement can only evaluate to an integral primitive type that can be implicitly cast to an int. These types are byte, short, char, and int. Also, the switch can only check for an equality. This means that the other relational operators like the greater than sign are rendered unusable. *See also* Decision statement.

Synchronized methods   The synchronized keyword indicates that a method may be accessed by only one thread at a time.

Temporary focus events   Temporary focus events indicate that the component has lost focus temporarily due to window deactivation or scrolling.

Thread   An independent line of execution. The same method may be used in multiple threads. As a thread executes instructions, any variables that it declares within the method (the so-called automatic variables) are stored in a private area of memory, which other threads cannot access. This allows any other thread to execute the same method on the same object at the same time without having its automatic variables unexpectedly modified.

Time-slicing   A scheme for scheduling thread execution.

Transient variables   The transient keyword indicates which variables are not to have their data written to an ObjectStream. You will not be required to know anything about *transient* for the exam, other than that it is a keyword.

Unchecked exceptions   *See* Runtime exceptions.

Variable access   Variable access refers to the ability of one class to read or alter (if it is not final) a variable in another class.

Visibility   Visibility is the accessibility of methods and instance variables to other classes and packages. When implementing a class, you determine your methods' and instance variables' visibility keywords as *public, protected, package,* or default.

Visual object modeling languages   Visual object modeling languages, such as the Unified Modeling Language (UML), allow designers to design and easily modify classes without having to write code first because object-oriented components are represented graphically. This allows the designer to create a map of the class relationships and helps them recognize errors before coding begins.

Volatile keyword   The volatile keyword indicates that a variable may change unexpectedly.

Weak references   Weak references are similar to soft references in that they allow you to refer to an object without forcing the object to remain in memory. Weak references are different from soft references, however, in that they do not request that the garbage collector attempt to keep the object in memory. Weak references are best used if you are tracking an object that someone else owns. You do not want to keep the object in memory; you just want to know if the object is still in memory.

INDEX

A

abs() method for java.lang.Math class, 317, 323

Abstract classes, 52–53

Abstract methods, 61–62

Abstract modifiers, 8, 21

Access control
and class modifiers, 50–53
two types of, 55

Access modifiers, 8, 20–21

Access to class members, 55

Access.Globalknowledge Web site, 582

Accessor.java example of visibility, 216

acos method for java.lang.Math class, 320

ActionEvent semantic event in
java.awt.event package, 432–433, 440

ActionListener interface, 440–443

Adapter classes in java.awt package, 431
certification summary of, 447
implementing listener interfaces with, 443–445

add and remove methods in Collection interface, 365

add() methods for containers in java.awt package, 402

Addition/positive (+) arithmetic operator, 95–96

addLayoutComponent methods 406–407

AdjustmentEvent low-level event in java.awt package, 439, 440

AdjustmentListener interface, 440, 443

Algorithms in collections, 363

Allows duplicates property of collections, 364

and (&) bitwise operator, 101

Angles, methods for returning arcs, cosines, sines, and tangents for, 319–320

Anonymous inner classes, 264–268, 444

append(object obj) method, using with StringBuffer class, 350

args arguments array, 15

Arguments, methods for, 317–319, 321–322

Arithmetic operators, 95–96

Array class members, 27–28

Array elements, uninitialized and unassigned type of, 25–31

ArrayList class, implementing List interface with, 372

Arrays, 7, 36–39

ASCII set, number of characters in, 32

asin method for java.lang.Math class, 320

Assignment operators, 88–90

atan methods for java.lang.Math class, 320–321

Attributes for collections, 382

Automatic primitives and objects, 28–31

Automatic variables, 18, 65–66, 286

AWT-EventQueue-0 priority for threads, 303

AWT-Windows priority for threads, 303

AWTEvent class, 431–432

AWTEvent event, 440

AWTEventListener interface, 440

B

Background color, setting for components in java.awt package, 395

Base classes, 8

Benchmark Yourself summary screen on CD-ROM, 579

Bitwise operators, 101–104

Blank files, compiling, 3

Blocks of code, performing with else keyword, 127

Boolean equals() method, 109–112

boolean keyword, 21, 23

Boolean literals, 34–35

F

J

K

L

Custom Corporate Network Training

Train on Cutting Edge Technology   We can bring the best in skill-based training to your facility to create a real-world hands-on training experience. Global Knowledge has invested millions of dollars in network hardware and software to train our students on the same equipment they will work with on the job. Our relationships with vendors allow us to incorporate the latest equipment and platforms into your on-site labs.

Maximize Your Training Budget   Global Knowledge provides experienced instructors, comprehensive course materials, and all the networking equipment needed to deliver high quality training. You provide the students; we provide the knowledge.

Avoid Travel Expenses   On-site courses allow you to schedule technical training at your convenience, saving time, expense, and the opportunity cost of travel away from the workplace.

Discuss Confidential Topics   Private on-site training permits the open discussion of sensitive issues such as security, access, and network design. We can work with your existing network's proprietary files while demonstrating the latest technologies.

Customize Course Content   Global Knowledge can tailor your courses to include the technologies and the topics which have the greatest impact on your business. We can complement your internal training efforts or provide a total solution to your training needs.

Corporate Pass   The Corporate Pass Discount Program rewards our best network training customers with preferred pricing on public courses, discounts on multimedia training packages, and an array of career planning services.

Global Knowledge Training Lifecycle   Supporting the Dynamic and Specialized Training Requirements of Information Technology Professionals

- Define Profile
- Assess Skills
- Design Training
- Deliver Training
- Test Knowledge
- Update Profile
- Use New Skills

College Credit Recommendation Program   The American Council on Education's CREDIT program recommends 53 Global Knowledge courses for college credit. Now our network training can help you earn your college degree while you learn the technical skills needed for your job. When you attend an ACE-certified Global Knowledge course and pass the associated exam, you earn college credit recommendations for that course. Global Knowledge can establish a transcript record for you with ACE, which you can use to gain credit at a college or as a written record of your professional training that you can attach to your resume.

Registration Information

COURSE FEE: The fee covers course tuition, refreshments, and all course materials. Any parking expenses that may be incurred are not included. Payment or government training form must be received six business days prior to the course date. We will also accept Visa/MasterCard and American Express. For non-U.S. credit card users, charges will be in U.S. funds and will be converted by your credit card company. Checks drawn on Canadian banks in Canadian funds are acceptable.

COURSE SCHEDULE: Registration is at 8:00 a.m. on the first day. The program begins at 8:30 a.m. and concludes at 4:30 p.m. each day.

CANCELLATION POLICY: Cancellation and full refund will be allowed if written cancellation is received in our office at least six business days prior to the course start date. Registrants who do not attend the course or do not cancel more than six business days in advance are responsible for the full registration fee; you may transfer to a later date provided the course fee has been paid in full. Substitutions may be made at any time. If Global Knowledge must cancel a course for any reason, liability is limited to the registration fee only.

GLOBAL KNOWLEDGE: Global Knowledge programs are developed and presented by industry professionals with "real-world" experience. Designed to help professionals meet today's interconnectivity and interoperability challenges, most of our programs feature hands-on labs that incorporate state-of-the-art communication components and equipment.

ON-SITE TEAM TRAINING: Bring Global Knowledge's powerful training programs to your company. At Global Knowledge, we will custom design courses to meet your specific network requirements. Call 1 (919) 461-8686 for more information.

YOUR GUARANTEE: Global Knowledge believes its courses offer the best possible training in this field. If during the first day you are not satisfied and wish to withdraw from the course, simply notify the instructor, return all course materials, and receive a 100% refund.

In the US:

CALL: 1 (888) 762-4442

FAX: 1 (919) 469-7070

VISIT OUR WEBSITE:

www.globalknowledge.com

MAIL CHECK AND THIS FORM TO:

Global Knowledge

Suite 200

114 Edinburgh South

P.O. Box 1187

Cary, NC 27512

In Canada:

CALL: 1 (800) 465-2226

FAX: 1 (613) 567-3899

VISIT OUR WEBSITE:

www.globalknowledge.com.ca

MAIL CHECK AND THIS FORM TO:

Global Knowledge

Suite 1601

393 University Ave.

Toronto, ON M5G 1E6

REGISTRATION INFORMATION:

Course title _____

Course location _____ Course date _____

Name/title _____ Company _____

Name/title _____ Company _____

Name/title _____ Company _____

Address _____ Telephone _____ Fax _____

City _____ State/Province _____ Zip/Postal Code _____

Credit card _____ Card # _____ Expiration date _____

Signature _____

LICENSE AGREEMENT

THIS PRODUCT (THE "PRODUCT") CONTAINS PROPRIETARY SOFTWARE, DATA AND INFORMATION (INCLUDING DOCUMENTATION) OWNED BY THE McGRAW-HILL COMPANIES, INC. ("McGRAW-HILL") AND ITS LICENSORS. YOUR RIGHT TO USE THE PRODUCT IS GOVERNED BY THE TERMS AND CONDITIONS OF THIS AGREEMENT.

LICENSE: Throughout this License Agreement, "you" shall mean either the individual or the entity whose agent opens this package. You are granted non-exclusive and non-transferable license to use the Product subject to the following terms:

(i) If you have licensed a single user version of the Product, the Product may only be used on a single computer (i.e., a single CPU). If you licensed and paid the fee applicable to a local area network or wide area network version of the Product, you are subject to the terms of the following subparagraph (ii).

(ii) If you have licensed a local area network version, you may use the Product on unlimited workstations located in one single building selected by you that is served by such local area network. If you have licensed a wide area network version, you may use the Product on unlimited workstations located multiple buildings on the same site selected by you that is served by such wide area network; provided, however, that any building will not be considered located in the same site if it is more than five (5) miles away from any building included in such site. In addition, you may only use a local area or wide area network version of the Product on one single server. If you wish to use the Product on more than one server, you must obtain written authorization from McGraw-Hill and pay additional fees.

(iii) You may make one copy of the Product for back-up purposes only and you must maintain an accurate record as to the location of the back-up at all times.

COPYRIGHT; RESTRICTIONS ON USE AND TRANSFER: All rights (including copyright) in and to the Product are owned by McGraw-Hill and its licensors. You are the owner of the enclosed disc on which the Product is recorded. You may not use, copy, decompile, disassemble, reverse engineer, modify, reproduce, create derivative works, transmit, distribute, sublicense, store in a database or retrieval system of any kind, rent or transfer the Product, or any portion thereof, in any form or by any means (including electronically or otherwise) except as expressly provided for in this License Agreement. You must reproduce the copyright notices, trademark notices, legends and logos of McGraw-Hill and its licensors that appear on the Product on the back-up copy of the Product which you are permitted to make hereunder. All rights in the Product not expressly granted herein are reserved by McGraw-Hill and its licensors.

TERM: This License Agreement is effective until terminated. It will terminate if you fail to comply with any term or condition of this License Agreement. Upon termination, you are obligated to return to McGraw-Hill the Product together with all copies thereof and to purge all copies of the Product included in any and all servers and computer facilities.

DISCLAIMER OF WARRANTY: THE PRODUCT AND THE BACK-UP COPY OF THE PRODUCT ARE LICENSED "AS IS." McGRAW-HILL, ITS LICENSORS AND THE AUTHORS MAKE NO WARRANTIES, EXPRESS OR IMPLIED, AS TO RESULTS TO BE OBTAINED BY ANY PERSON OR ENTITY FROM USE OF THE PRODUCT AND/OR ANY INFORMATION OR DATA INCLUDED THEREIN. McGRAW-HILL, ITS LICENSORS, AND THE AUTHORS MAKE NO GUARANTEE THAT YOU WILL PASS ANY CERTIFICATION EXAM BY USING THIS PRODUCT. McGRAW-HILL, ITS LICENSORS AND THE AUTHORS MAKE NO EXPRESS OR IMPLIED WARRANTIES OF MERCHANTABILITY OR FITNESS FOR A PARTICULAR PURPOSE OR USE WITH RESPECT TO THE PRODUCT. NEITHER McGRAW-HILL, ANY OF ITS LICENSORS, NOR THE AUTHORS WARRANT THAT THE FUNCTIONS CONTAINED IN THE PRODUCT WILL MEET YOUR REQUIREMENTS OR THAT THE OPERATION OF THE PRODUCT WILL BE UNINTERRUPTED OR ERROR FREE. YOU ASSUME THE ENTIRE RISK WITH RESPECT TO THE QUALITY AND PERFORMANCE OF THE PRODUCT.

LIMITED WARRANTY FOR DISC: To the original licensee only, McGraw-Hill warrants that the enclosed disc on which the Product is recorded is free from defects in materials and workmanship under normal use and service for a period of ninety (90) days from the date of purchase. In the event of a defect in the disc covered by the foregoing warranty, McGraw-Hill will replace the disc.

LIMITATION OF LIABILITY: NEITHER McGRAW-HILL, ITS LICENSORS NOR THE AUTHORS SHALL BE LIABLE FOR ANY INDIRECT, SPECIAL OR CONSEQUENTIAL DAMAGES, SUCH AS BUT NOT LIMITED TO, LOSS OF ANTICIPATED PROFITS OR BENEFITS, RESULTING FROM THE USE OR INABILITY TO USE THE PRODUCT EVEN IF ANY OF THEM HAS BEEN ADVISED OF THE POSSIBILITY OF SUCH DAMAGES. THIS LIMITATION OF LIABILITY SHALL APPLY TO ANY CLAIM OR CAUSE WHATSOEVER WHETHER SUCH CLAIM OR CAUSE ARISES IN CONTRACT, TORT, OR OTHERWISE. Some states do not allow the exclusion or limitation of indirect, special or consequential damages, so the above limitation may not apply to you.

U.S. GOVERNMENT RESTRICTED RIGHTS: Any software included in the Product is provided with restricted rights subject to subparagraphs (c) (1) and (2) of the Commercial Computer Software-Restricted Rights clause at 48 C.F.R. 52.227-19. The terms of this Agreement applicable to the use the data in the Product are those under which the data are generally made available to the general public by McGraw-Hill. Except as provided herein, no reproduction, use, or disclosure rights are granted with respect to the data included in the Product and no right to modify or create derivative works from any such data is hereby granted.

GENERAL: This License Agreement constitutes the entire agreement between the parties relating to the Product. The terms of any Purchase Order shall have no effect on the terms of this License Agreement. Failure of McGraw-Hill to insist at any time on strict compliance with this License Agreement shall not constitute a waiver of any rights under this License Agreement. This License Agreement shall be construed and governed in accordance with the laws of the State of New York. If any provision of this License Agreement is held to be contrary to law, that provision will be enforced to the maximum extent permissible and the remaining provisions will remain in full force and effect.